# The Ecological Modernization of the Chemical Industry

Hendrik Hermann Eckart Ahrens

# The Ecological Modernization of the Chemical Industry

## Predictors for Adoption of Innovations to Reach Carbon Neutrality in the Chemical Industry

Springer Gabler

Hendrik Hermann Eckart Ahrens
Triagon Academy
Ismaning, Germany

Doctor of Business Administration (DBA) Thesis comment

ISBN 978-3-658-45388-6 ISBN 978-3-658-45389-3 (eBook)
https://doi.org/10.1007/978-3-658-45389-3



This Springer Gabler imprint is published by the registered company Springer Fachmedien Wiesbaden GmbH, part of Springer Nature.
The registered company address is: Abraham-Lincoln-Str. 46, 65189 Wiesbaden, Germany

*The economist Rudi Dornbusch once said that in economics, things take longer to happen than you think they will, and then they happen faster than you thought they could. (Lagarde, 2021)*

# Acknowledgement

Transitions are times of uncertainty and journeys into the unknown. And they are times of change and opportunity. The pathway to sustainability is about exploring, learning, discovering, matching patterns, and adapting. Times of change are a challenge to identify and categorize new contexts for decision making. The chemical industry is particularly complex and change, therefore, presents a particular challenge in identifying strategies and developing an approach to implementing sustainable resources. This dissertation was the right setting to address this exciting issue that will completely change the industry.

I am glad to have found an academic environment at Triagon Academy that inspired and supported me to complete this dissertation and achieve a personal goal. I am very grateful and would like to thank my thesis advisor, Professor Christian Werner, for the opportunity to work on this research topic. The courses and seminars have enhanced my knowledge and methodological skills. This dissertation has increased my interest in scientific work even more and made it a passion. I would also like to thank my interviewees for participating in this research and for their valuable insights into the use of renewable raw materials and their properties. Finally, I would like to thank my family and friends for their support and interest.

# Abstract

Reducing greenhouse gas emissions is undoubtedly one of the greatest social and economic challenges of this century. With the European Green Deal from 2019, the European Union has made climate neutrality, a circular economy and a pollution-free environment its main goal and calls for greenhouse gas emission reduction and more sustainable use of scarce fossil resources. The theory of reasoned action provides the framework for the case study research of this paper. 14 semi-structured expert interviews identified key predictors for the use of renewable raw materials for the European chemical industry with the aim of reducing greenhouse gas emissions. Results from case studies were triangulated with results from document analysis of CEFIC corporate members' annual sustainability reports and other publications and identified five innovation-specific and five organizational predictors for the adoption of renewable raw materials. Proposals for transition management are developed, applying the framework of the multi-level perspective of socio-technical transition and technological innovation systems. Renewable carbon raw materials are biomass, plastic recyclates and CO2 as the starting molecule together with green hydrogen. Biomass and plastics recycling are currently the focus of most business attention, but availability is limited. Carbon capture and utilization aims to fill the carbon demand gap. The discussion attempts to conceptualize a low-carbon reorientation of the European chemical industry and to provide guidance for practitioners in transition management.

# Executive Summary

1. **Background and purpose**

   The European Green Deal announced in 2019 is a political agenda for the entire EU to achieve net carbon neutrality by 2050 together with the mobilization of a circular economy and a toxic-free environment. The decarbonization and modernization of energy-intensive industries put the chemical industry in the focus of the European Green Deal as one of the largest contributors to greenhouse gas emissions. CO2 accounts for 92% to greenhouse gas emissions from combustion of fossil fuels for power and heat generation, or as a by-product of chemical processes. Other greenhouse gases are methane, nitrous oxide and fluorinated gases. About 90% of the carbon demand for chemicals are sourced from fossil raw materials adding additional challenges for escape from the oil dependency. Mitigation strategies are abatement technologies to prevent either the formation or the release of greenhouse gases. Retrofits, more efficient use of energy and raw materials, phasedown of fluorinated gases with highest global warming potential and the use of renewable energies are applied. Reuse and recycling concepts for plastics, the use of biomass feedstocks and carbon capture and utilization are suggested as replacements for fossil raw materials. The purpose of the dissertation is to provide an understand how chemical companies are adapting to the transition to carbon neutrality. Subject for research are eco-innovations to achieve CO2 neutrality and their properties from the point of view of chemical companies and innovators, and the relationship between mitigation technologies and their key predictors for adoption. Finally, the dissertation attempts to conceptualize the transition to carbon neutrality applying the framework of multi-level perspective of socio-technical transition and technological innovation systems.

2. **Method of data collection and sources of the data**
   The testable model for research is built on the theory of reasoned action adapted for innovations to achieve carbon neutrality in chemical companies. Attitude towards the use and behavioral intention to use are mediator variables to predict the actual use of renewable raw materials. The model describes the linking logic between companies' characteristic environments and innovation specific attributes with attitude and behavioral intention towards environmental innovations. A qualitative research approach is chosen in order to explore and identify predictors for adoption and to test the research hypotheses. The main data collection technique uses semi-structured interviews with experts from the European chemical industry. A total of 14 telephone interviews were conducted, two of which were interviews in a pilot study. Saturation was reached after 12 interviews in the main study. Document analysis provides supplemental research data to verify findings and support evidence from case study research. The secondary data sources are companies' latest publications on sustainability and greenhouse gas saving activities from corporate members of CEFIC, the European Chemical Industry Council. Meaning units such as keywords, phrases, topics or statements from interview narratives and company documents are sorted into categories and subcategories and compared for pattern matching. The mixed methods approach with 2 reference points for triangulation increased the accuracy of the research results.
3. **Description of innovation types and attribute**
   Strategies to shift to carbon neutrality employ a mix of instruments to reduce greenhouse gas emissions. Efficiency gains focus on efficient use of energy and heat, upgrading existing operating units with newer devices to best-practice technologies, abatement technologies to avoid formation or release of greenhouse gases and electrification of processes. Second, phasedown is an option for greenhouse gases with high global warning potential, high radiation and ozone depletion properties, such as fluorinated gases. Third, the use of renewable energies for heat and power generation and their use in chemical plants instead of fossil fuels is the main instrument to reduce Scope 1 and Scope 2 greenhouse gas emissions. Fourth, plastic recycling, biomass-based resources to avoid steam cracking and carbon capture and utilization complete the toolkit to achieve carbon neutrality in the European chemical industry and are considered sustainable and renewable carbon sources. Keyword density search in company publications provide further evidence for the strategies that

are relevant to reducing greenhouse gases. Efficiency programs, use or renewable energies for heat and electricity, recycling concepts for plastic waste and use of biobased raw materials are the main focus and receive roughly equal attention in publications across the chemical industry. A small share is related to carbon capture and utilization and the use of CO2 as starting molecule, mainly published by petrochemical and large backward integrated specialty chemical companies.

4. **Innovation-specific predictors**
   Five innovation-specific predictors for adoption of renewable feedstocks were identified in this dissertation: Cost of renewable raw materials, CO2 savings potential, availability of renewable raw materials, compatibility with existing technological paradigms and transparency of supply chains and origin of materials. Barriers to adoption are higher costs compared to existing fossil raw materials, scarce material availability, missing data of greenhouse gas savings potentials or inconsistencies in carbon footprint calculations. The greatest perceived barrier is the higher price of renewable raw materials. Main drivers for adoption are compatibility with customers' expectations and technological paradigms, as well as perceived transparency of certification schemes for mass balanced and segregated supply chains models. Same performance, sufficient availability, production of existing products with the same performance in existing assets and a moderate price increase support the use of renewable raw materials with the aim of reducing greenhouse gas emissions. The requirements are combined with sustainability goals without additional land use, without competition for food and feed and without loss of biodiversity. Other compatibility requirements are same performance and quality of the final materials from renewable raw materials and the manufacture in existing assets. Expectations for transparency and traceability of origin of the materials are analytical methods to identify biogenic carbon content, e. g. by the 14C radiocarbon method. Alternatively, there are certification schemes such as RSPO and ISCC Plus certifications for coprocessing of sustainable and non-sustainable raw materials and verified accounting models to attribute the renewable input share to parts of the finished goods. Finally, consumers expect full transparency of supply chains and origin of materials.

5. **Organizational predictors**
   Five organizational predictors for adoption of renewable feedstocks were identified: Existing use of renewable raw materials, company's sustainability strategy, management advocacy, cooperation skills, implementation of industry standards and expectations of Government regulations. The main driver for the intention to use renewable resources reported in interviews is a positive attitude of the companies and the support of the management. Other strong drivers are cooperation skills with suppliers, customers, universities and research institutes, corporate sustainability strategy and expected Government policies. A weaker driver for behavioral intention to use renewable raw materials are existing industry standards. Participants report inconsistencies in life cycle assessments, lack of CO2 emissions data and conflicting sustainable development goals, such as greenhouse gas emission savings, biodiversity, biodegradability and competition to food and feed, with a need for standardization of renewable raw materials. A pattern of actual use and behavioral intention was not identified. Mission statements in companies' publications and voluntary corporate engagement in industry initiatives confirm a positive attitude. The majority of corporate members of CEFIC refers to the UN sustainability goals, publishes greenhouse gas emissions and savings targets according to GRI standards, and participates in the voluntary Carbon Disclosure Program. More than half of the corporations are recognized for the active management of greenhouse gas emissions and receive high A and B scores in the Carbon Disclosure Program. They jointly intend to reduce Scope 1 and Scope 2 greenhouse gas emissions by 27% by 2030 and by 71% by 2050, based on company publications available in August 2021.
6. **Sector-specific strategies**
   The demand for lower prices, sufficient availability, high CO2 savings potential, compatibility and transparency of renewable raw materials are shared by all chemical companies. Also, renewable electricity is relevant for all sectors to reduce Scope 1 and Scope 2 greenhouse gas emissions from operations. Energy-intensive companies can benefit most from renewable electricity to avoid carbon taxes. Additional sector-specific strategies have been identified by document analysis and are confirmed by case study research. The halogen

sector contributes only 4% of operational greenhouse gas emissions but has the highest average operational product carbon footprint of 1 kg CO2e/EUR sales. Substitution of fluorinated gases with high global warming potential is most relevant for the sector and the use of renewable energy and recycling concepts are paid greater attention than by the average of the companies. The petrochemical sector has the largest share of greenhouse gas emissions in the chemical industry at 74% and the second highest average operational carbon footprint of 0,8 kg CO2e/EUR of sales. The overall greenhouse gas emission reduction targets are −27% by 2030 and −70% by 2050. The sector has the highest burden for transition to carbon neutrality. The use of renewable energies, recycling concepts, the use of bio-based raw materials and carbon capture and utilization are paid greater attention, while efficiency programs receive similar amount of attention compared with the average of chemical companies. The specialty chemicals sector has the second highest absolute greenhouse gas emissions and an average operational carbon footprint of 0,4 kg CO2e / EUR sales. The sector contributes 21% of operational greenhouse gas emissions to the corporate members of the CEFIC group. The overall reduction targets are −26% by 2030 and −75% by 2050. Efficiency programs, recycling concepts and the use of bio-based raw materials receive a similarly high level of attention compared to the average of CEFIC corporate members. The pharmaceutical sector is characterized by a low average operational carbon footprint of 0,09 kg CO2e/EUR turnover. The sector contributes only 1% of operational GHG emissions of the corporate members of the CEFIC group and focuses on efficiency programs and plastic recycling concepts. Mitigation strategies for climate change in general receive less attention in the annual reports compared with the average of the CEFIC corporate members.

7. **Conceptualization of low-carbon transition of the chemical industry**
   The attempt to conceptualize the sustainable transition to carbon neutrality applies the frameworks of multi-level perspective of socio-technical systems and technological innovation systems to the European chemical industry. Three niche innovations are proposed as a substitute for fossil raw materials: Biomass, plastic recycling and CO2 as starting molecule together with green hydrogen. A transformation pathway is likely under the fact that niche innovations for the substitution of fossil raw materials have not yet been developed. Landscape pressure from a combination of policy programs, public discourse and consumer expectations drive the adoption of environmental technologies. The technology mix is initially adopted by climate leaders and fast followers. Emerging technologies are at the stages of experimentation,

piloting and small-scale demonstration plants. Biomass and mechanical plastics recycling are more advanced than other renewable feedstocks. Extended use of these resources is constrained due to limited availability of biomass and losses of functionality of the mechanically recycled materials. Chemical recycling, electricity-based processes and the use of CO2 as a starting molecule supposed to fill the gap of the sustainable carbon demand are at an embryonic stage. Carbon capture and utilization technologies are developed mainly at petrochemical companies and backward integrated specialty chemical companies. This gives the hint, that incumbent firms develop the new niche technology, and prepare for the co-evolution of technologies and response scenarios to climate change. The prices for every type of renewable raw material are high, availability is scarce and there is a lack of data on CO2 emission savings. Analysis of the available data from corporate publications suggests that greenhouse gas emission savings from operations will commence with solar and wind technologies and increased use of biomass, leading to a first S-shaped reduction of the industry's GHG emissions. A second S-shaped greenhouse gas reduction curve is likely after the year 2040 by advancements in chemical plastic recycling and carbon capture and utilization technologies. Last are the difficult to change sectors of the chemical industry. However, government policy is triggering the shift towards sustainability across the chemical industry and is the main force to overcome lockout effects of renewable raw materials.

8. **Recommendations for transition management and further research**
Further research can focus on quantitative methods to explain the magnitude of each predictor variable of renewable feedstock adoption to achieve carbon neutrality. Econometric analyses can survey European chemical companies with structured questionnaires containing company- and innovation specific questions on the proposed predictors. Online surveys are suggested to gather empirical evidence using a validated 5− or 7−point Likert scale from a sufficiently large sample size. Proposed performance indicators for adoption are e. g. raw material use, GHG emissions and emissions reduction, production volume, sales and innovation and investment activities. Another quantitative research on innovation diffusion can use patent data and keyword searches renewable raw materials. Next to the continued research on predictors for adoption of renewable raw materials, further business research needs to gather information on sustainable carbon supply for chemistry in a decarbonized world. Corporate research needs to explore technological advances in chemical plastics recycling, the availability of second and third generation biomass for biochemical processes, chemical plastic recycling and carbon

capture and utilization technologies. Renewable energy sources, green hydrogen and concentrated CO2 play key roles, and market shifts will depend on their availability and costs of renewable alternatives. Corporate research must identify science-based targets for the use of renewable raw materials and how conflicting goals of sustainable development can be reconciled. Carbon neutrality in chemistry can conflict with biodiversity, biodegradability, competition for biomass for food and feed, water use, land use and land use change, and responsible use of other finite resources. Further research is also needed to collect emission data for carbon footprint calculations and accepted practices for life cycle assessments. Finally, corporate research is proposed to closely monitor and follow the political discourse and the elaboration of policies, laws and regulations at national, European and global levels with an impact on carbon pricing and use of renewable raw materials for chemical industry.

# Contents

# Abbreviations

| | |
|---|---|
| B2B | Busines-to-business |
| B2C | Business-to-consumer |
| BTX | Butene, toluene, xylenes |
| CCU | Carbon capture and utilization |
| CDP | Carbon Disclosure Project |
| CH4 | Methane, greenhouse gas |
| CO2 | Carbon dioxide, greenhouse gas |
| CSR | Corporate Sustainability Responsibility |
| DUI | Doing-learning-interacting |
| EC | European Commission |
| ESG | Environmental and social governance |
| GHG | Greenhouse gas |
| GIS | Global innovation system |
| GRI | Global Reporting Initiative |
| HFC | Hydro fluoro carbon, substances of the family of fluorinated gases |
| ICCA | International Council of Chemical Associations |
| IPCC | International Panel for Climate Change |
| ISCC | International Sustainability and Carbon Certification |
| MEK | Methyl ethyl ketone |
| MtO | Methanol-to-olefin |
| N2O | Nitrous oxide, greenhouse gas |
| NACE | Statistical classification of economic activities in the European Community derived from the French title "Nomenclature générale des Activités économiques dans les Communautés Européennes" |

| | |
|---|---|
| NIS | National innovation system |
| OECD | Organization for Economic Co-operation and Development |
| PFC | Perfluorinated carbons, substances of the family of fluorinated gases |
| PLA | Polylactic acid |
| PtL | Power-to-liquid technology |
| R&D | Research & Development |
| RC | Responsible Care |
| RSPO | Roundtable on Sustainable Palm Oil |
| SBTi | Science based targets initiative |
| SC model | Supply chain model |
| SF6 | Sulfur trioxide, fluorinated gas with the highest global warming potential, substance of the family of fluorinated gases |
| SIS | Sectoral innovation system |
| STI | Science-technology-innovation |
| TIS | Technological innovation systems |
| TfS | Together for Sustainability |
| UN SDG | United Nations Sustainable Development Goals |
| VCI | Verband der Chemischen Industrie Deutschlands e. V. |

# List of Figures

# List of Tables

# Introduction

# 1

Greenhouse gas emission reduction and CO2 neutrality have become an integral part of the politics of the European chemical industry. In addition to fossil fuels for energy production, a particular challenge is the resource dependency of crude oil as a raw material for the production and emissions of volatile chemicals with a greenhouse effect. The central topic of this dissertation is the identification of predictors for the adoption of innovative technologies to achieve CO2 neutrality in the European chemical industry. Decarbonization of society and industry, including the chemical industry, requires changes of existing supply chains and operating practices. It is an opportunity for new products and services as well as for process and business model innovations. This dissertation tries to contribute to knowledge in transition management and to give practitioners and researchers insights into the effects and perspectives for the adoption of innovations to reach carbon neutrality.

## 1.1 Carbon Neutrality

Climate change mitigation is part of a larger political agenda and greenhouse gas emissions have been identified as the leading cause of global warming. The legitimation for the agenda comes from climate models and scientific consensus on the connection between the global rise in surface temperature and the concentration of greenhouse gases in the atmosphere. The atmospheric CO2 concentration and its connection with weather and climate was first described in 1957 and

**Supplementary Information** The online version contains supplementary material available at https://doi.org/10.1007/978-3-658-45389-3_1.



H. H. E. Ahrens, *The Ecological Modernization of the Chemical Industry*,
https://doi.org/10.1007/978-3-658-45389-3_1

reached the political arena in the 1970 s and 80 s. With increasing confidence in the cause-effect relationship, the United Nations signed the Framework Convention on Climate Change in 1992 with the aim of stabilizing greenhouse gas concentrations in the atmosphere (Brulle, 2018; Revelle. & Suess, 1957; UN, 1992). The Intergovernmental Panel on Climate Change (IPCC) plays a major role in making recommendations on climate change and climate mitigation programs. The scientific panel was commissioned by the UN in 1988 to collect the evidence and identify the causes of global warming (Meadows, Meadows, Randers & Behrens III, 1972; IPCC, 2021a). The United Nations signed the Kyoto Protocol in 1997 to requested necessary measures to mitigate climate change, and finally recognized the fundamental priority of climate protection and the goal of carbon neutrality in the 2015 Paris Agreement (UN, 1997; UN, 2015b). Climate protection is one of the 17 Sustainable Development Goals (SDGs) of the UN, which were adopted in September 2015 and became part of the framework for sustainable development towards 2030 (UN, 2015a) (Fig. 1.1).

**Fig. 1.1** UN Sustainable Development Goals (UN, 2020)

## 1.2 Climate Discourse

Man-made emissions are the main reason for the increasing concentration of greenhouse gases in the atmosphere. Carbon dioxide levels rose from 260 ppm before industrialization to around 410 ppm in 2020. More than 30% of greenhouse gases come from industry; and within the industrial sector, around 10% of emissions come from the chemical industry. Legitimation for politics and regulation is the consensus on the cause and effect relationships between anthropogenic greenhouse gas emissions and climate change. The majority of climate scientists agree that humans are causing recent global warming and civil society is ready to accept it (Bray & von Storch, 2016; Cook et al., 2016). The Intergovernmental Panel on Climate Change (IPCC) developed a model, which serves as a physical science base, and found that the temperature increase has reached about 1,09° C compared to pre-industrial times. The panel suggests that the transient climate response to anthropogenic effects is likely to be in the range of up to 2,5° C if greenhouse gas emissions continue to increase at the existing rate (IPCC, 2021c; Stocker et al., 2013). Critics of the IPCC model claim the limited prediction, the exaggeration of the greenhouse gas effect, and that solar radiation may have a greater impact on climate change than accounted for (Berhhout, 2020; Shaviv, 2015). Other conservative lobby groups use typical denial arguments such as conspiracy theories, fake expertise, the impossibility of climate predictions and misinterpretation of data to de-legitimize climate protection for economic reasons (Busch & Judick, 2021; Christoff, 2013; Jylhä, 2017; Washington, 2011). The complexity of global climate change and the models are difficult to understand for laypeople. Even if people accept the anthropogenic causes of climate change, in a typical dilemma of public goods they retain the perception that their individual actions have no effect (Dilling & Moser, 2004). Ultimately, leading scientific associations and the majority of climate scientists agree that current global warming is caused by man-made emissions of greenhouse gases that trap heat in the atmosphere (The Royal Society, 2020). Greenhouse gases (GHG) absorb the infrared radiation emitted by the earth's surface and prevent the heat from being released into space. Many of these greenhouse gases occur naturally but have increased due to human activity. In particular, the concentrations of carbon dioxide (CO2), methane, nitrous oxide (N2O) and fluorinated gases have increased and cause global warming and are associated with higher surface temperatures (American Chemical Society, 2019; European Commission, 2021a; NASA, 2021a, 2021c) (Fig. 1.2).

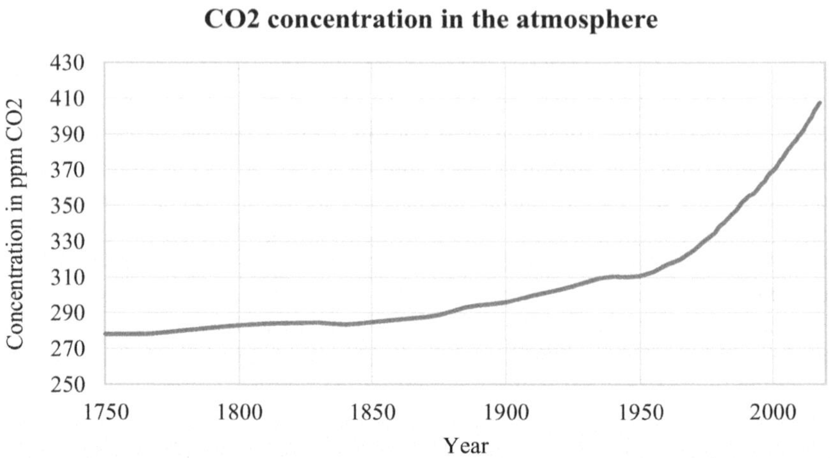


**Fig. 1.2** Trends in atmospheric concentrations of CO2 in ppm. (Source: EEA, 2021)

Further consequences of rising greenhouse gas concentrations are the warming of the oceans and the rise in mean sea levels. The climatic zones have shifted towards the poles, the average rainfall over land has increased since 1950 and extreme weather patterns have become more frequent and violent. Reducing greenhouse gas emissions has become a priority among sustainability issues in the 2015 Paris Agreement (UN, 2015b). Finally, the announcement of the European Green Deal by the European Commission on December 11, 2019 provides a framework for the regulatory authorities to make Europe the first climate-neutral continent by 2050 and to transform the economy and society of the European Union on a sustainable path (European Commission, 2019).

## 1.3 Global Emissions

The main causes of rising greenhouse gas concentrations are the burning of fossil fuels with the emission of carbon dioxide and deforestation. Industrial activity and increased agricultural activity have increased methane and nitrous oxide levels. The release of fluorinated gases with a greenhouse effect that is several times higher than CO2 occurs purely through industry (European Commission, 2021a). CO2 has a concentration of around 410 ppm in the atmosphere. The other gases are methane ($CH_4$), nitrous oxide ($N_2O$) and fluorinated gases with a lower concentration but a global warming potential (GWP) and trap heat in the atmosphere even at low concentrations (NASA, 2021a) (Table 1.1).

**Table 1.1** Global warming potential (GWP) values relative to $CO_2$ (Greenhouse Gas Protocol, 2021)

| Common name | Formula | GWP for a 100-year time horizon |
|---|---|---|
| Carbon dioxide | $CO_2$ | 1 |
| Methane | $CH_4$ | 28 |
| Nitrous oxide | $N_2O$ | 265 |
| Fluorinated gases | HFC, PFC | 4 - 12.400 |
| Sulfur hexafluoride | $SF_6$ | 23.500 |

Fluorinated gases are a family of volatile fluorinated substances and consist of three classes, namely sulfur hexafluoride ($SF_6$), fluorocarbons (HFC) and perfluorocarbons (PFC). The value of the global warming potential takes into account the radiation efficiency relative to $CO_2$ and the average lifespan of the substance in the atmosphere. For better comparability, emission data for GHG are given in $CO_2$ equivalents or $CO_2e$ for short (EPA, 2021a; Greenhouse Gas Protocol, 2013) (Fig. 1.3).

Global GHG emissions of 36,11 Gt $CO_2e$ are reported for 2019 and 33,13 Gt $CO_2e$ for 2020 (Tiseo, 2021). The largest contribution to global warming is made by $CO_2$ with 76%. $CO_2$ emissions arise from the burning of fossil fuels such as coal, crude oil and natural gas for transport, heat and power generation in the private, municipal and industrial sectors. $CH_4$ and $N_2O$ are released from industry and other sources such as agriculture, livestock and as a decomposition product in landfills and wastewater treatment (EPA, 2021a). Industrial activities account for 30% of global $CO_2$ emissions and within the industrial sector, the global chemical industry contributed 1.522 Mt $CO_2$ in 2010, which corresponds to 10% of global industrial emissions (Fischedick et al., 2014; Friedlingstein et al., 2020) (Fig. 1.4).

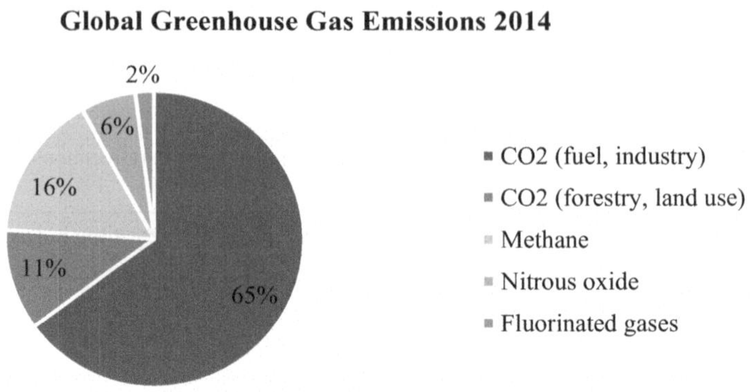


**Fig. 1.3** Global emissions by greenhouse gas 2014. (Source: EPA, 2021a)

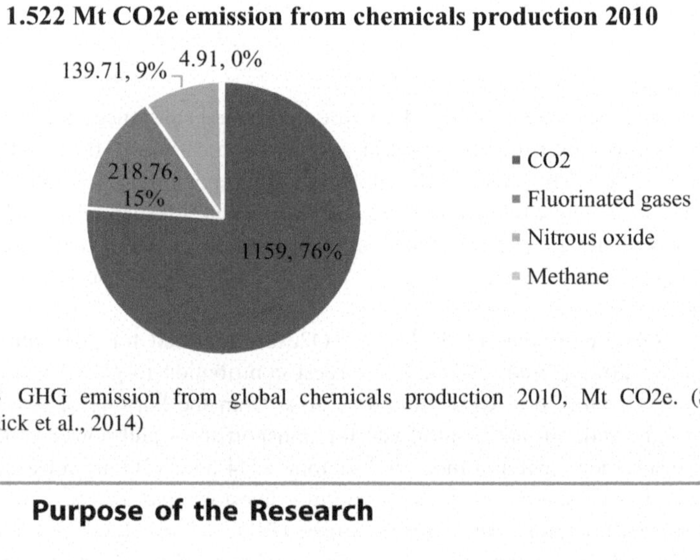


**Fig. 1.4** GHG emission from global chemicals production 2010, Mt CO2e. (Source: Fischedick et al., 2014)

## 1.4 Purpose of the Research

The research aims to identify choices for the innovation strategy as key success factor for future performance of companies (Servatius, 2012). The final purpose of the dissertation is to identify eco-innovation practices with uncertain market potential in the face of regulatory changes. Dealing with expectations from government push / pull programs to compensate for financial inferiority and insufficient competitiveness of environmental innovations plays a key role (Souto &

Rodriquez, 2015). In 2019, the European Green Deal brought clarity for consumers and industry to the European climate agenda after controversial discourses in the media and politics. Climate protection is an opportunity for chemical companies to offer environmental innovations, like other environmental regulations in the past. However, the scale and extent of the change are greater than other environmental protection measures, since 90% of chemicals are affected by the change in carbon flux. At the same time, the industry is facing two challenges: The shift from fossil fuels for power generation to renewable resources and the shift in oil dependency and supply chain for manufacturing toward renewable raw materials. The latter perspective is peculiar to the chemical industry and has the potential for disruptive change. Lock-in effects and technology and market uncertainty are the two biggest obstacles, and research is needed to understand how chemical companies are adapting to the new business environment. The purpose of the research is to identify the potential of eco-innovations to reduce greenhouse gases and best practices for business organizations facing the uncertainties of transition. The subject of research are eco-innovations to achieve CO2 neutrality and their properties from the point of view of chemical companies and innovators. Another issue is the relationship between key determinants of their adoption and the role of standards and regulations. The aim of the research is to identify patterns of environmental innovation introduction activities and best practices for successful transition management. Qualitative case study research with semi-structured expert interviews is used to identify drivers and barriers to transition. Document analysis from company publications is used to triangulate and synthesize results.

## 1.5 Structure of the Dissertation

After the introduction in Chapter 1, Chapter 2 of this dissertation described the European chemical industry including its GHG emissions and strategies for reducing them. The chapter also summarizes technologies that promise to reduce greenhouse gas emissions: The use of renewable resources, including renewable energies, biomass as a raw material, plastics recycling and technologies for carbon capture and utilization.

Chapter 3 follows with a literature review on determinants for adoption of environmental innovations in general and in particular on eco-innovations for the chemical industry to reduce greenhouse gas emissions. The state of research provides existing knowledge on barriers and drivers for adoption of eco-innovations and leads to research gaps in the use of renewable raw materials.

Chapter 4 deals with three perspectives on the theoretical framework. First, the theory cluster deals with determinants for innovation adoption in organizations and innovation processes. Second, ecological modernization theory provides a general overview of types of innovation including open innovation, incremental, evolutionary, radical and disruptive innovation, as well as the multilevel perspective of socio-technical transition and technological innovation systems. The theory cluster also includes the catch-up cycle and the window-of-opportunity perspective of technological change. Third, innovation diffusion studies and agent-based models are presented as framework for research of human decision-making processes in economic contexts.

Chapter 5 derives a testable model based on theory of reasoned action. Research questions and hypotheses for qualitative research on the use of renewable raw materials for chemical production are summarized.

Chapter 6 introduces the research methods. Qualitative research uses case studies with semi-structured interviews to measure attitudes, intentions and actual use of renewable resources in chemical companies. Data collection, interview guidelines and analysis techniques are described. Document analysis serves to triangulate results from case study research and uses content analysis to search for meaning units and their categorization in company publications.

Chapter 7 presents the results of the case study research. Qualitative data from 2 interviews from a pilot study and from a further 12 interviews in the main study. Hypotheses are tested and expert perceptions on the attitude of companies, behavioral intentions in the context of predictors are described. Research provides innovators' perception of eco-innovation attributes and predictors for adoption.

Chapter 8 presents the results from secondary sources. The document analysis is based on 69 sustainability and integrated annual reports from 73 CEFIC company members. Publications on websites and on sustainability initiatives are used and keywords, company activities and predictors related to the use of renewable raw materials are categorized. Results from interviews and document analysis are combined for pattern matching and synthesis.

Chapter 9 discusses the research results, provides conclusions and implications of the study. Additional suggestions for business practices and an outlook for future research are given. The dissertation aims to present the state of the art in the adoption of innovations to achieve carbon neutrality in the European chemical industry and to provide predictor for the adoption of technologies as drivers for transition. The research findings are placed within the larger framework of socio-technical transition research and technological innovation system analysis and seek to complement existing transition management and sustainable innovation theory.

# Business Case Description 2

This chapter describes the boundaries of the business case and scope of research. The European chemical industry is the unit of analysis with chemical companies as embedded business cases. Existing literature publishes sources of GHG emissions and mitigation strategies to reduce them. Around 128 Mt CO2-equivalents of greenhouse gases were released from the European chemical industry into the atmosphere in 2018 (CEFIC, 2021a). "*Within the industrial sector, chemical production together with cement production and metals are the biggest sources of emissions*" says Martin Brudermüller, Chairman of the Board of Executive Directors and Chief Technology Officer at BASF on the World Economic Forum in 2020 (Brudermüller, 2020). Burning fossil fuels for energy and CO2 as a by-product contribute around 92% to greenhouse gas emissions. Other greenhouse gases are methane, nitrous oxide and fluorinated gases. These gases are released from chemical processes, leaks, upstream operations or the downstream use of chemicals. Increases in production efficiency, abatement installations and retrofits have limits for further emission reductions and the carbon flow in the chemical industry, however, requires a technological paradigm shift. To overcome the chemical industry's dependence on oil, renewable technologies such as bio-based raw materials, plastic recycling, and carbon capture and utilization are proposed. Greenhouse gas savings potential, technical feasibility and economic attractiveness are key performance indicators for eco-innovations to achieve CO2 neutrality.

**Supplementary Information** The online version contains supplementary material available at https://doi.org/10.1007/978-3-658-45389-3_2.



H. H. E. Ahrens, *The Ecological Modernization of the Chemical Industry*,
https://doi.org/10.1007/978-3-658-45389-3_2

## 2.1 Industry Sectors

The European chemical industry is a diverse industry producing commodities, intermediates, specialties and consumer goods. Chemical companies have in common the manufacture of chemical products and the use of chemical processes. Chemical products arise from chemical processes that are a complex combination of chemical reactions and physical refining methods such as distillation, separation and drying (National Research Council, 1999). The boundaries of the European chemical sector are set from different perspectives. 16 manufacturing sectors are listed according to the statistical classification of the European Union: Basic chemicals, fertilizers, agrochemicals, coatings and inks, soap and detergents, primary plastics and synthetic rubber, fibers, and manufacture of other chemical products. Adjacent manufacturing areas are the manufacture of coke and refined petroleum products, finished products made of plastic and rubber, and pharmaceutical chemistry (European Communities, 2008). 670 chemical companies and industry bodies associated with the chemical industry have joined CEFIC, the European Chemical Industry Council. CEFIC is the non-profit organization that represents the interests of the chemical industry with European political decision-makers and institutions of the European Union (CEFIC, 2019). The chemical industry is structured by CEFIC in three branches: The specialty chemicals, petrochemicals and chlorine / halogen sector.

| Specialty Chemicals | Petrochemicals | Halogens |
|---|---|---|
| Oleochemicals & surfactants<br>Water & paper chemicals<br>Pigments, fillers, dyes & catalysts<br>Food & feed additives<br>Bio-based chemicals<br>Biocides<br>Fine chemicals<br>Plastics additives<br>Resins | Intermediates, monomers, solvents, polymers and resins | Any producer of chlor-alkali with manufacturing facilities for products comprise:<br>Products from chlor-alkali electrolysis<br>Chlorinated solvents<br>Chlorinated polymers<br>Fluorocarbons |

Categorization of the CEFIC industry sectors (CEFIC, 2021c)

Many of the specialty chemicals sectors are small and medium-sized companies that manufacture a wide variety of chemical products for many industrial and consumer markets. The petrochemical sector represents 70 companies with large plants and produces intermediate products or bulk polymers from petroleum or natural gas (CEFIC, 2021d). Companies in the halogen sector produce fluorinated, chlorinated and other halogenated substances like solvents, intermediates and polymers (CEFIC, 2021d). Petrochemical companies conduct exploration and production activities and use mineral oil to process petrochemicals. Examples are Cepsa, ExxonMobil, MOL Group, OMV / Borealis, Repsol, Socar and Total (CEFIC, 2020; International Association of Oil & Cas Producer, 2021). Downstream users of chemical products are industrial and consumer markets. The main markets are the industrial market segments with a share of 67% of sales in the chemical industry. Some specialty chemical companies also serve consumer markets with detergents, personal care and health care products like Procter and Gamble. Pharmaceutical companies are also CEFIC members and part of the specialty chemicals sector when chemical processes are used, such as Novartis, Merck and Teva (CEFIC, 2021a). The segmentation helps to identify the most important sources of greenhouse gases and necessary reduction strategies. Exploration and refining are processes that release CO2 and methane into the atmosphere and contribute to industrial greenhouse gas emissions. Manufacturers of fluorinated chemicals are sources of the release of fluorinated gases with a high global warming potential, while GHG emissions from pharmaceutical companies come mainly from energy consumption of their own operations.

## 2.2 Economic Review

With 543 billion EUR in 2019, the European Union (EU 27) has the third largest chemical industry after China and the NAFTA region (Fig. 2.1).

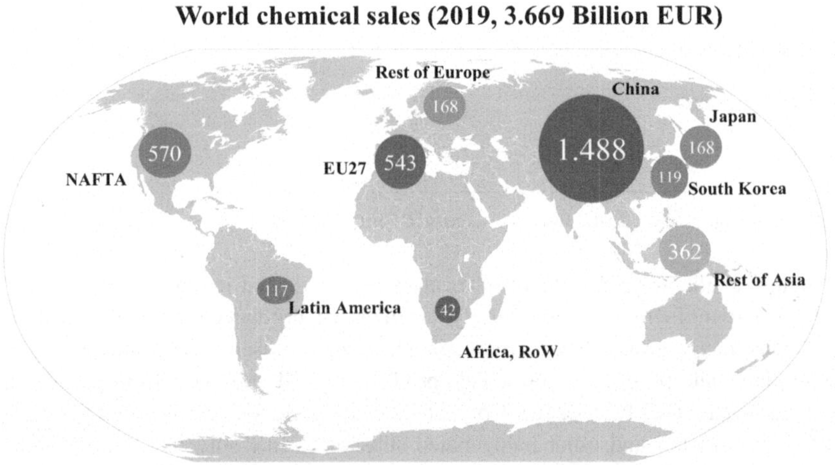


**Fig. 2.1** World chemical sales 3.669 billion EUR in 2019 (CEFIC, 2021a)

China dominates the market with 1.488 billion EUR in 2019 and has grown by 236% since 2009. China's global market share rose from 24% in 2009 to 40% of global chemical sales in 2019. The EU 27 fell from 20% in 2009 in 2009 to 14% in 2019. 67% of the turnover of the European chemical industry are domestic sales and intra-EU27 exports and 33% are destined for export. The European chemical industry has a trade surplus of 45,1 billion EUR with partners. In 2019, chemical products worth 177,5 billion EUR were exported to countries outside the EU-27 and chemical products worth 132,4 billion EUR were imported from countries outside the EU-27. Most of the chemical industry's trade outside the EU-27 went to other European countries, NAFTA and the Asia-Pacific region excluding China and Japan. Countries with increasing market shares in global chemical exports are China, South Korea, Saudi Arabia and India. The share of the EU 27 in the global chemical export market has fallen, which points to a decline in competitiveness of the European chemical industry (CEFIC, 2021a).

## 2.3 Political Environment

Political decision-makers are increasingly using instruments to protect the environment and regulate the chemical industry. This also applies to the reduction of greenhouse gas emissions. The German Renewable Energy Act requires electricity from renewable energies to make the electricity supply more environmentally friendly and to protect the climate (EEG, 2000). European Directive 2009/28/EC promotes and encourages the generation of energy from renewable sources (European Directive 2009/28/EC). The UN Agreement of Paris in 2015 paved the way for a global policy agenda for climate protection and the UN Sustainable Development Goal 13 within the framework of the UN Global Compact calls for combating climate change (UN 2015a; UN 2015b). The EU Commission has transformed the global initiative into the European Green Deal. The regional agenda was announced on December 11, 2019 as an action plan for the entire EU to achieve net zero GHG emissions by 2050. The plan for the EU is a roadmap for decoupling economic growth and resource consumption. Elements of the Green Deal are net carbon neutrality, the mobilization of a circular economy, a toxic-free environment and a shift to sustainable energy supply. The decarbonization and modernization of energy-intensive industries such as steel, chemicals and cement are explicitly mentioned and moves the chemical industry into the focus of the European Green Deal (European Commission, 2019). With the Green Deal, reducing greenhouse gas emissions has become a key issue for the chemical industry.

## 2.4 Greenhouse Gas Emissions

GHG emissions in the EU 27 amount to 4.067 Mt CO2-equivalent (CO2e) in 2019. The industrial sector contributes 20% of the total 775 Mt CO2e (Tiseo, 2021) (Fig. 2.2).

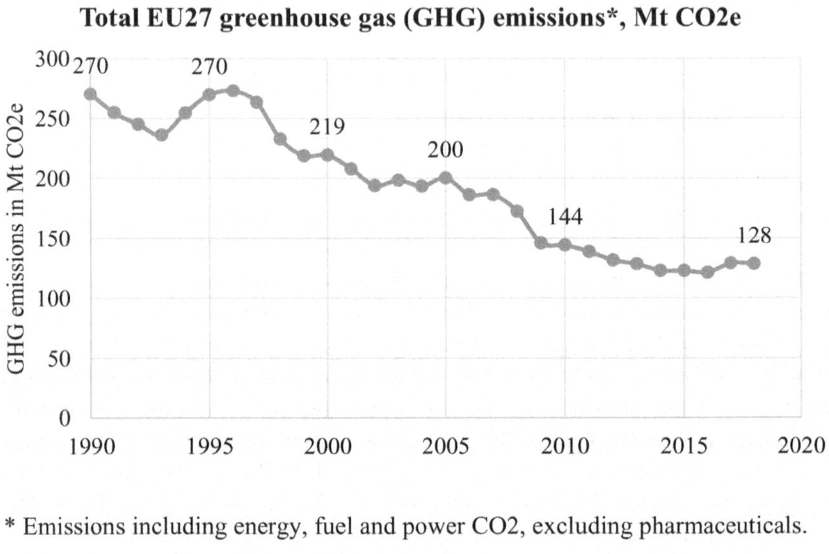


**Fig. 2.2** Total EU27 chemical industry greenhouse gas emissions (CEFIC, 2021a)

The share of the chemical industry is 128 Mt CO2e in 2018, which corresponds to around 3,1% of the total GHG emissions in the EU27. Compared to 1990, more than half of the GHG emissions in the chemical industry have been reduced (Fig. 2.3).

Emissions fell by 52,5% from 290 Mt CO2e in 1990 (CEFIC, 2021a; Garside, 2021). The most important greenhouse gases from the chemical industry are CO2, nitrous oxide and fluorinated gases. Since 1990, CO2 emissions have decreased by 24%, nitrous oxide emissions by 92% and emissions from fluorinated gases by 85% in the period under review (Fig. 2.4).

The reduction in CO2 emissions in the reporting period was due to increased efficiency and lower energy intensity in chemical processes, but further reductions in CO2 emissions have stalled since 2013. CO2 emissions account for 91% of

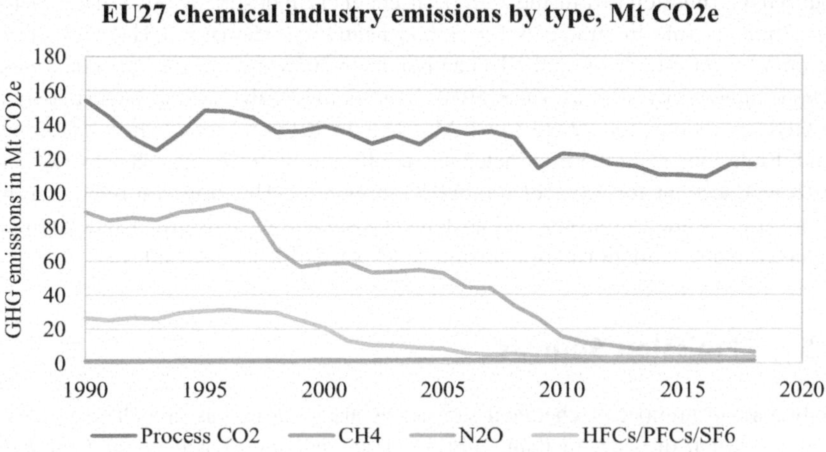


**Fig. 2.3** Total EU27 chemical industry GHG emissions by type (CEFIC, 2021a)

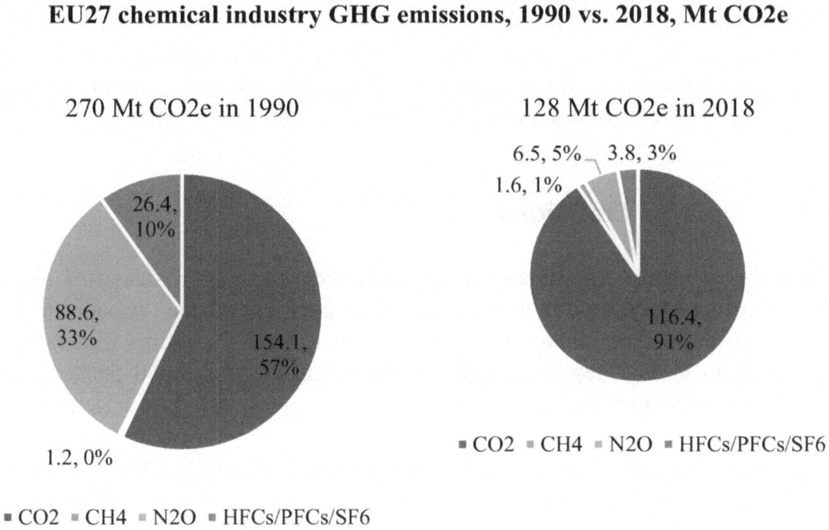


**Fig. 2.4** EU27 GHG emissions of the European chemical industry 1990 vs 2018 (CEFIC, 2021a)

total GHG emissions from the European chemical industry in 2018. They play the dominant role in strategies for carbon neutrality. Methane (CH4) emissions account for only 1.2% of total GHG emissions in 2018 and the absolute emissions have changed only slightly since 1990. Nitrous oxide, the second largest source of GHG emissions, fell 92,6% to 6,5 Mt CO2e in 2018 and makes up 5,1% of the total. Emissions from the fluorinated gas family fell by 97,7% to 3,8 Mt CO2e in 2018 and account for 3,0% of total GHG emissions. The emission reduction of these gases is due to retrofits and abatement installations and further reduction is expected from regulations (Boulamanti & Moya, 2017; CEFIC, 2021a).

## 2.5 Emission Sources

Only a small number of chemical substances are identified as greenhouse gases, namely carbon dioxide, methane, nitrous oxide and fluorinated gases. CO2 has the largest share with 91% of GHG emissions of the European chemical industry and emissions have two sources. CO2 is the exhaust gas formed during combustion of fossil fuels for energy generation in power plants and for the heating of chemical reactors, heat exchangers and crackers. The second source of CO2 is the formation in side-reaction during chemical synthesis. The remainder of about 9% of the greenhouse gases are nitrous oxide from a few processes and the release of fluorinated gases from production of fluorochemicals (VCI, 2019).

### 2.5.1 Process Emissions

Although greenhouse gas emissions have been reduced by more than 50% since 1990, efforts to reduce CO2 have stalled since 2013 due to the oil dependency of the chemical value chain and the use of fossil fuels for energy generation. According to a 2017 report (Boulamanti & Moya, 2017), around 55% of the greenhouse gases in the chemical industry are emissions from power generation (Fig. 2.5).

The remaining 45% are releases from chemical processes. CO2 is emitted as a by-product in the production of ammonia, petrochemicals and carbon black. Ammonia is produced as an intermediate product for fertilizers and its production causes 19% of the greenhouse gas emissions of the chemical industry. CO2 is produced in a side reaction and released into the atmosphere during washing and stripping processes. Other sources of CO2 are the formation of side reactions in

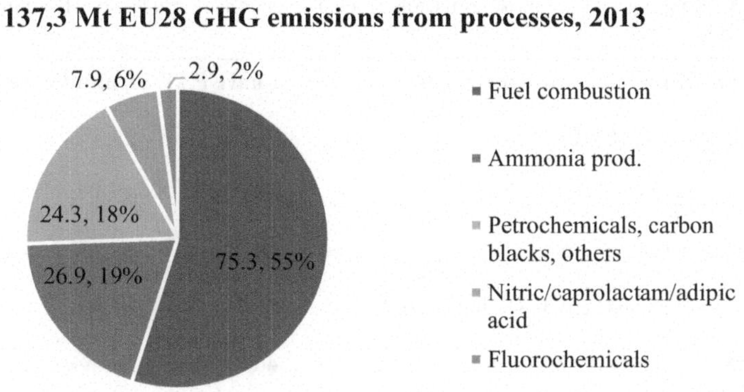


**Fig. 2.5** GHG emissions by production process (Boulamanti & Moya, 2017)

the production of petrochemicals and carbon black. The following table lists the chemical processes with the highest GHG emissions (Table 2.1).

The raw material for petrochemicals is naphtha, a mixture of different hydrocarbons produced by refineries. Emissions from flaring and venting in the refineries are not counted directly as emissions from the chemical industry but are added to the CO2 balance of the raw materials. The attribution of CO2 emissions is passed on to the indirectly held accountable consumer (Boulamanti & Moya, 2017). Nitrous oxide is released as a by-product in the production of nitric acid, caprolactam and adipic acid. These emissions have been reduced by 92,6% since 1990 due to process improvements and higher catalyst efficiency. Fugitive emissions of fluorinated gases can occur in the manufacture of fluorochemicals. Abatement technologies, production adjustments and restrictions on the use of certain fluorinated gases have reduced these emissions by 97,7% since 1990 (European Environment Agency, 2020). GHG emissions are attributed to a few key chemical processes. The main source is steam cracking processes in the petrochemical sector for the production of important building blocks for chemical synthesis. CO2 is released during steam cracking of olefins such as ethylene, propylene, butadiene and butenes, aromatic building blocks and solvents such as benzene, toluene, xylene and styrene. Chlorine / alkali electrolysis in the halogen sector is one of the most energy-intensive processes and is mostly obtained from fossil fuels. Electrolysis produces chlorine and caustic soda, and downstream chemicals are vinyl chloride monomer and PVC. Another energy-intensive chemical process is the synthesis of hydrogen from methane. The connectedness of

**Table 2.1** Ranking of the most emission intensive chemical processes (Boulamanti & Moya, 2017)

| Process with GHG emissions (type) | Share (%) | Cumulative (%) |
|---|---|---|
| Steam cracking (CO2) | 25,5% | 25,5% |
| Ammonia (CO2) | 19,6% | 45,1% |
| Chlorine (CO2) | 10,6% | 55,7% |
| Hydrogen / Syngas (incl. Methanol) (CO2) | 9,2% | 64,9% |
| Aromatics (BTX) (CO2) | 4,8% | 69,7% |
| Nitric acid (N2O) | 3,8% | 73,5% |
| Carbon black (CO2) | 3,4% | 76,9% |
| Ethylbenzene / Styrene (CO2) | 2,9% | 79,8% |
| Ethylene chloride / Vinyl chloride / PVC (CO2) | 2,6% | 82,4% |
| Ethylene oxide / Monoethylene glycol (CO2) | 2,6% | 85,0% |
| Soda ash (CO2) | 1,5% | 86,5% |
| Adipic acid (N2O) | 0,4% | 86,9% |
| Other | 13,2% | 100,1% |

chemical synthesis value chains passes over the carbon footprint to downstream materials (Boulamanti & Moya, 2017).

### 2.5.2 Carbon Dioxide

As the dominant greenhouse gas, CO2 is released when fossil fuels are burned and as a by-product of chemical processes. The use of fossil fuels for power generation is the main source of CO2 emissions into the atmosphere. Energy-intensive processes are steam cracking for the production of olefins and chlor-alkali electrolysis for chlorine synthesis (Fischedick et al., 2014). CO2 is also emitted as a by-product in the chemical synthesis of petrochemicals, carbon black and downstream products of synthesis gas. Examples are ammonia, methanol and urea as byproducts from synthesis gas and olefins, aromatics, vinyl chloride monomers and ethylene oxide derivatives as byproducts of refineries (European Environment Agency, 2020).

### 2.5.3 Methane

Although methane is a powerful greenhouse gas and the second largest contributor to climate change, emissions in the chemical industry are relatively low. Compared to the total emissions of the EU27 of 110.4 million t CO2, the methane emissions of the chemical industry amount to 8.3 kt CO2e, which corresponds to <0.008% of the total amount. Chemical emissions are diffuse leaks in pipelines, in the repair of chemical devices and from the end-of-life phase of plastics. Methane is released from oil and gas exploration and production, from livestock farming and waste treatment. The largest industrial producer of methane emissions is the oil and gas industry (CEFIC, 2021b).

### 2.5.4 Nitrous Oxide

Nitrous oxide is mainly emitted during the production of nitric acid, the production of caprolactam, glyoxal and glyoxylic acid, and the production of adipic acid. Nitric acid production decline and technical measures, new catalysts and process improvements made it possible to reduce N2O emissions from nitric acid plants. N2O is a by-product of caprolactone and adipic acid production. Abatement technologies and the shutdown of production facilities lead to a reduction in N2O emissions from these processes (European Environment Agency, 2020).

### 2.5.5 Fluorinated Gases

Fluorinated gases include sulfur trioxide (SF6), partially fluorinated hydrocarbons (HFC) and perfluorocarbons (PFC). SF6 and HFC have high radiative and ozone depleting properties. Most fluorinated gases have to be classified as substances with a high global warming potential (GWP), which is between 140 and 7.000 for HFCs and between 6.000 and 9.000 for PFCs (Umweltbundesamt, 2011). SF6 is the substance with the highest observed global warming potential of 23.000 compared to CO2. The greenhouse gas is used in electrical gas-insulated high-voltage switchgear due to its low flammability and high dielectric constant. As a substitute for sulfur hexafluoride, alternatives with a lower global warming potential are offered. A significant reduction in emissions is possible through emission reduction technologies and retrofitting in existing systems. Due to their high chemical resistance and flame resistance, HFCs are used as compressor gases in refrigerators and electric heat pumps. HFCs are partially being replaced by fluorinated olefins or ethers with a lower global warming potential. In many applications they have been completely replaced by fluorine-free but flammable alternatives such as propane, butane or dimethyl ether (Gil, Szczepanowska & Rosiek, 2021; Umweltbundesamt, 2011). A smaller share of the emissions of fluorinated gases occurs in chemical plants and a larger share in the downstream residential sector. Fluorinated gases are accidentally released at the end of the electronic device's life due to leakage or mishandling, as well as a lack of recycling and improper disposal (Billen, Maes, Larrain & Braet, 2020; European Commission, 2020).

## 2.6 Mitigation Strategies

The European Green Deal focuses on three targets for European Union: Net carbon neutrality, the mobilization of a circular economy and a toxic-free environment and the chemical industry is ready to contribute. Strategies to shift to sustainable energy supply and to reduce greenhouse gas emissions have been developed (Van Bylen, 2019). Several mitigation technologies are proposed to reduce greenhouse gas emissions in the chemical industry. The focus is on abatement technologies to prevent either the formation or the release through the implementation of closed systems. Another approach is negative emission technologies, which aim to sequester atmospheric carbon dioxide or to separate concentrated CO2 from industrial processes, e.g. in the petrochemical, cement or steel industries (Fawzy, Osman, Doran & Rooney, 2020). Greenhouse gas emissions are reduced by using energy more efficiently and upgrading existing operating units with newer equipment to use proven technologies. Other strategies include increasing energy-saving and material-efficient plastic recycling, the use of renewable energies and alternative biomass-based ways to avoid steam cracking (Fischedick et al., 2014). According to a DECHEMA case study, increasing efficiency and phasing out coal can reduce CO2 emissions in the chemical industry by 27%. The remaining 73% of the emissions to achieve CO2 neutrality could be achieved through the use of new, electricity-based processes, improved mechanical and chemical recycling processes for the reuse of plastics as raw materials for the production of basic chemicals and the use of alternative raw materials (VCI, 2019) (Table 2.2).

**Table 2.2** Technology portfolio for greenhouse gas neutrality pathway (VCI, 2019)

| Electricity-based processes | Alternative raw materials & syntheses | Downstream processes |
|---|---|---|
| Methanol from electrolytic hydrogen and CO2 | Chemical recycling of plastics (pyrolysis, gasification, depolymerization) | Olefins via methanol-to-olefins (MtO) |
| Ammonia and urea from electrolytic H2 and CO2 | Thermo-catalytic biomass conversion into BTX | BTX via methanol-to-aromatics (MtA) |
| Electrically heated cracking | Synthetic naphtha/ methane from biomass | Olefins from synthetic naphtha and cracking |
| Electrically heated steam reforming | Co-firing with biomass | Olefins from synthetic methane + oxidative coupling of methane |
| Synthetic naphtha/ methane from electrolytic H2 and C | Methane pyrolysis | |

## 2.6.1 Efficiency Gains

Steam cracking is the largest emitter of CO2 emissions in the chemical industry and produces important building blocks such as olefins and aromatics for chemical synthesis. The process works at 850°C and is very energy-intensive. Around 40% of the total energy in the entire petrochemical industry is consumed here and more energy efficient operation, heat recovery and efficient design lead to energy savings and reduced CO2 emissions. Efficiency gains require investments in retrofits or the introduction of new production units. New technologies include new furnace designs or new compression and separation sections with higher efficiency. Switching fuels from oil to natural gas offers further CO2 reduction potential. These technologies reduce both energy consumption and greenhouse gas emissions (Bazzanella & Ausfelder, 2017; Boulamanti & Moya, 2017). The same approach applies to the production of basic chemicals like ammonia, methane and hydrogen synthesis and many other chemical processes. Improved heat recovery, more efficient catalysts, new plant design and advanced heat integration are important sources of short-term improvements to reduce energy consumption and greenhouse gas emissions. The phase-out of coal and the shutdown of coal-fired power plants as well as the reduction of oil use in favor of natural gas lead to energy savings and the carbon footprint will continue to improve. However, the potential for further increases in efficiency to reduce GHG emissions by optimizing conventional processes is limited and will soon be exhausted (Bazzanella & Ausfelder, 2017; VCI, 2019). The second largest greenhouse gas, N2O emissions, is also subject to efficiency increases. The strategy for removing N2O from waste gas streams from nitric acid, caprolactam and adipic acid production is catalytic or thermal decomposition to nitrogen and oxygen (CEFIC, 2013; Inger, Moszowski, Ruszak, Rajewski & Wilk, 2020; Winiwarter, Höglund-Isaksson, Klimont, Schöpp & Amann, 2018).

### 2.6.2 Phasedown

Another strategy to reduce emissions is to phase out the production that causes greenhouse gas emissions. The strategy is applied to some of the fluorinated gases with the highest global warming potential that are also ozone-depleting substances, such as fluorocarbons (HCF) and sulfur hexafluoride (SF6). According to the Montreal Protocol on Substances that Deplete the Ozone Layer in 2016, HFCs will be phased out in most economies, and also the EU states have signed the amendment to the Montreal Protocol (UN, 2016). Instead, alternative compressor gases are used for refrigeration and air conditioning. Propane, butane, ammonia, carbon dioxide and selected perfluorinated carbons (PFCs) are compressor gases with less potential for global warming and ozone depletion. The signatory countries agreed to phase out HFCs by 2030, a process that began in 2015 (Australian Government, 2018). The gradual lifting of existing bans, the further installation of emission reduction systems in the remaining plants and a portfolio shift towards less harmful fluorinated gases will reduce greenhouse gas emissions from fluorinated gases from production facilities (European Environment Agency, 2020).

### 2.6.3 Renewable Energy

The next GHG reduction strategy is the use of renewable energies for heat and power generation and their use in chemical plants instead of fossil fuels such as coal, oil and natural gas. Renewable energy comes from sources such as wind, sun, hydropower and geothermal sources. Burning biomass such as wood and wood waste, municipal waste, biogas, bioethanol and biodiesel also provides renewable energy sources (U.S. Energy Information Administration, 2021). 19,7% of energy consumption in the EU27 came from renewable energies in 2019. Increasing the share of renewable energies in the European Union is a cornerstone of the EU's climate targets. Greenhouse gas emissions are to be reduced by at least 55% in 2030 compared to 1990 levels. Increasing electricity generation from sun and wind can improve the competitiveness of sustainable energy sources and offer an opportunity to reduce the carbon footprint of the chemical industry (European Commission, 2021a; De Graaff, 2015). A second category includes the electrification of heat for chemical processes in operation. Today, heat is mainly generated by burning natural gas and, to a lesser extent, heating oil. Retrofitting enables electricity to be used directly to generate heat. Technological change requires investments and the direct use of renewable energy sources in chemical production. New technologies use microwave, photo and electric powered heating and require reactors and processes to be redesigned. Power-to-hydrogen and power-to-chemicals, the use of electricity for electrolysis and direct chemical synthesis from CO2 are discussed together with carbon capture and utilization (Centi, Iaquaniello, & Perathoner, 2019; Van Kranenburg et al., 2016).

### 2.6.4 Reuse and Recycling

The circular economy and the reduction of (plastic) waste are high priorities for the European Union. The aim is to increase the recycling of single-use plastic products such as packaging to 90% by 2030. One possibility is the mechanical recycling of plastic waste. Further options are the development of biodegradable plastics and the use of biomass as a raw material for the production of bioplastics (Directive (EU) 2019/904). Mechanical recycling as the most common process is limited, however, as mixtures with other types of plastic, additives and fillers as well as composite materials cannot be broken down or physically separated (Knappich, Schlummer, Eggert, Wolff & Agulla, 2017). The disadvantage of blends is the incomplete separation of impurities, which has a negative effect on functionality. Chemical recycling is suggested to either recover the monomers or to produce pyrolysis oil and naphtha with properties similar to naphtha from petroleum refining (Ragaert, Delva & van Geem, 2017). The pyrolysis of plastic waste serves two sustainability goals, the reduction of waste and the switch from linear to circular supply chains on the one hand and the reduction of greenhouse gas emissions on the other. Pyrolysis oil is suggested as a drop-in fuel for transportation, as a replacement for diesel, and as an intermediate for cracking and chemical synthesis (Jha & Kannan, 2021; Wang et al., 2021) (Fig. 2.6).

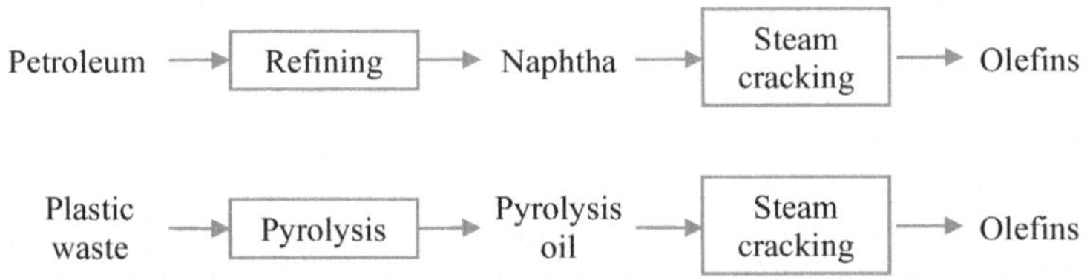


**Fig. 2.6** Petroleum value chain compared with plastic pyrolysis after Carus et al. (2020)

Chemical recycling technologies are future core technologies for recycling plastics and reducing greenhouse gas emissions. Plastic waste is used as a raw material for renewable carbon for pyrolysis oil in chemical recycling and the intermediate product is used as a drop-in for naphtha for the synthesis of chemicals with a reduced carbon footprint (Carus et al., 2020).

### 2.6.5 Biomass Feedstock

Petroleum is used as a raw material for around 80% of chemical products in Germany. The rest is coal, natural gas and a 10% share of biomass. Animal fats, vegetable oils, starch, sugar and cellulose play the largest role. Bio-based raw materials are used for soaps, surfactants, selected paints and adhesives (Keim & Röper, 2010). Some authors consider biomass, along with carbon capture technology, to be negative emission technologies. Biomass biologically captures atmospheric CO2 through photosynthesis and stores carbon. Carbon utilization technologies capture industrial CO2 for chemical synthesis (Fawzy, Osman, Doran & Rooney, 2020) (Fig. 2.7).

The bioeconomy offers new ways of using biomass for different types of bio-based chemicals. Drop-ins and smart drop-ins are chemicals made from biomass and replace existing and established chemicals made from fossil fuels. Smart drop-ins also offer an additional benefit over the conventional variant. Dedicated

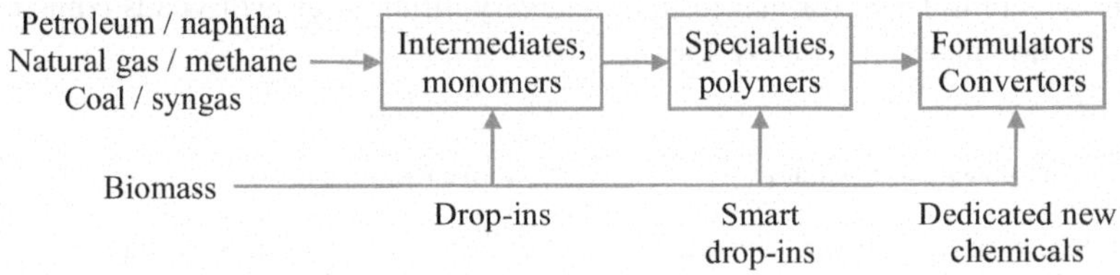


**Fig. 2.7** Bio-based drop-in, smart drop-in and dedicated chemicals (Carus, Dammer, Puente, Raschka & Arendt, 2017)

bio-based chemicals are chemicals with no fossil counterpart and offer unique and superior properties (Carus, Dammer, Puente, Raschka & Arendt, 2017). An example of a bio-based value chain is the hydrotreatment of vegetable oils. The process leads to bio-naphtha, which is used for biofuels and as a raw material for chemical production and can replace oil-based naphtha as a drop-in (Hilbers et al., 2015) (Fig. 2.8).

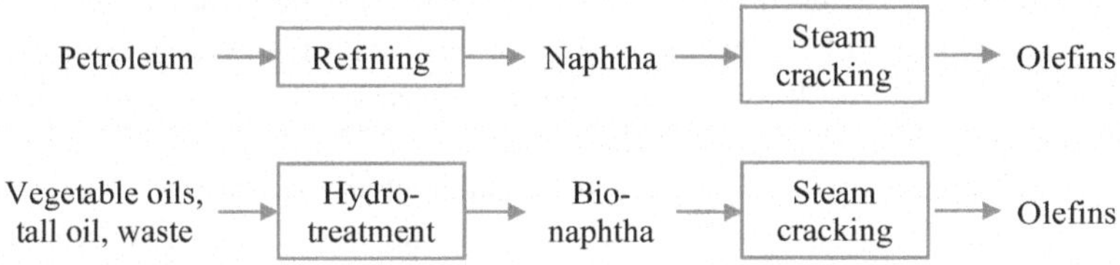


**Fig. 2.8** Bio-naphtha from vegetable oils (Hilbers et al., 2015)

Other processes in biorefineries include the enzymatic fermentation of starch and lignocellulose to bioethanol, the enzymatic synthesis of new polymers, the gasification of biomass and new catalytic synthesis routes for the production of drop-ins and bio-based versions of existing intermediates in use (Blaauw, van Haveren, Scott & Bos 2008; Mood et al., 2013; Shogren, Wood, Orts & Glenn, 2019). These new chemical and biochemical synthesis routes require bio-based raw materials. The platforms for biofuels and biochemicals are diverse, ranging from oil crops, lignocellulose, starch-based plants and cellulose to protein crops. Biofuels and raw materials for chemicals should not be produced in competition with food and feed. Edible plants are therefore classified as 1st generation biomass and distinguished from inedible biomass as 2nd generation biomass (Anastassiadis, 2016; Huber, Iborra & Corma, 2006). A third classification of biomass is introduced for algae due to the very different growth yields compared to other raw materials (Lee & Lavoie, 2013) (Fig. 2.9).

| 1st Generation biomass | 2nd Generation biomass |
|---|---|
| Sugar, starch, glucose, sucrose, other polysaccharides, edible plant oils, fatty acids | Wood and forestry residues, (cellulose, hemicellulose, lignin, tall oil), bagasse, corn stover, biowaste |

**Fig. 2.9** Classification of biomass (Anastassiadis, 2016)

### 2.6.6 Carbon Capture and Utilization

Carbon capture and utilization (CCU) is proposed as the third cornerstone of the chemical industry in a circular economy, alongside plastic recycling and the use of biomass as a raw material. A forecast for 2050 describes three sources for the total global carbon demand of the chemical industry. According to Carus et al. (2021), 55% of the required carbon is expected to come from plastics recycling, 20% from biomass and the remainder of 25% from CCU. The CCU technology captures carbon dioxide from the ambient air or industrial processes as a starting material for the synthesis. Together with the use of green hydrogen from renewable sources, CO2 is converted into chemical substances (Carus, Kähler, Porc & vom Berg, 2021). Processes for converting CO2 into methanol and olefins for the further chemical synthesis of basic and specialty chemicals are reported (Zhao et al., 2018) (Fig. 2.10).

The power-to-liquid (PtL) process uses CO2 from the atmosphere or industrial sources and converts hydrogen and the carbon source into chemicals with methanol as the main intermediate product (Kätelhön, Meys, Deutz, Suh & Bardow, 2019; Zitscher, Neuling, Habersetzer & Kaltschmitt, 2020) (Table 2.3).

The most promising synthetic routes in the demonstration stage are the conversion of methanol to olefins (MtO) and methanol to aromatics (MtBTX) with methanol as an intermediate and the Fischer-Tropsch (FT) synthesis of synthetic fuels with synthesis gas as an intermediate. The technologies use CO2 as a starting molecule and green hydrogen as a reactant. Bioethanol is a commercially available biofuel and is converted into bioethylene (Bazzanella & Ausfelder, 2017).

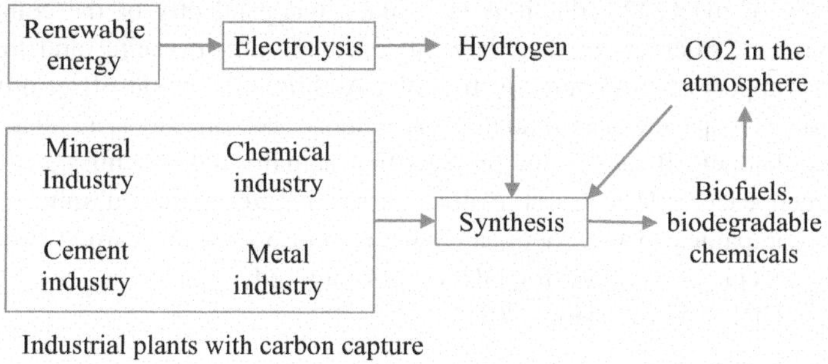


**Fig. 2.10** Use of biogenic and fossil CO2 (Zitscher, Neuling, Habersetzer & Kaltschmitt, 2020)

**Table 2.3** CCU technologies in commercial and demonstration stages (Bazzanella & Ausfelder, 2017)

| Reactants | Intermediate | Acronym | Products |
|---|---|---|---|
| CO2 + H2 | Methanol | MtO | Olefins (ethylene, propylene, others) |
| CO2 + H2 | Methanol | MtBTX | Aromatics (benzene, toluene, xylenes) |
| CO2 + H2 | Syngas | FT | Synthetic fuels |
| Biomass | Bioethanol | | Bio-ethylene |

### 2.6.7 Carbon Offset Programs

Six strategies deal with reducing the greenhouse gas emissions of one's own operations, reduction of raw material carbon footprint and downstream improvements. A seventh strategy deals with offsetting greenhouse gas emissions in voluntary climate protection programs. Carbon offset credits are obtained by funding afforestation and certified carbon capture projects, such as co-financing wind farms in developing countries. (Broekhoff, Gillenwater, Colbert-Sangree & Cage, 2019; Umweltbundesamt, 2021). Climate protection programs appear attractive in view of the difficulties in reducing greenhouse gas emissions from operations or the supply chain. The disconnect between business model and offset program struggles to prove that CO2 savings would not be possible if the system did not exist. Many of the CO2 reductions take place independently of the compensation program. Critics claim that they are used for greenwashing and to make a company appear environmentally friendly. Additionally, credit offset programs are undermining progress in reducing greenhouse gas emissions, as their credit purchases channel off money for projects that actually reduce emissions (Elgin, 2020; Greenpeace, 2021). Carbon offset programs are applied despite the criticism by companies in the chemical industry and accredited carbon disclosure programs accept the strategy for GHG emissions reduction if they are reported separately (GRI 305: Emissions 2016).

## 2.7 Performance Indicators

Greenhouse gas emissions from companies are important performance indicators for strategies to mitigate climate change. Most companies report GHG emissions data in annual, integrated or sustainability reports and follow the guidelines of the Global Reporting Initiative (GRI).

### 2.7.1 GRI Reporting Standard

The GRI reporting standard ensures transparency and comparability of the disclosure of sustainability indicators. GRI Standard 305 requires the indication of greenhouse gas emissions in metric tons of CO2 equivalents, including CO2, CH4, N2O and fluorinated gases. There are three categories Scope 1, 2 and 3 emissions. Scope 1 emissions come from our own operations, such as energy generation, processing and volatile or uncontrolled emissions. Scope 2 emissions come from the generation of purchased energy and Scope 3 emissions come from sources outside the organization (GRI 305: Emissions 2016) (Fig. 2.11).

Scope 1 + 2 emissions from upstream processes become Scope 3 emissions for downstream users of purchased materials. While these emission categories are controlled directly by the company through the choice of energy, heat and power source, the upstream Scope 3 emissions are only indirectly controlled through the choice of input materials. The product carbon footprint of the raw materials is also influenced by downstream use, leakage and disposal outside the control of the manufacturing company. The GRI methodology with the 3 GHG emission categories offers an instrument for monitoring and controlling existing GHG emissions, reduction targets and successes. Collecting primary data along the supply chain is a challenge that requires effort and commitment from suppliers.

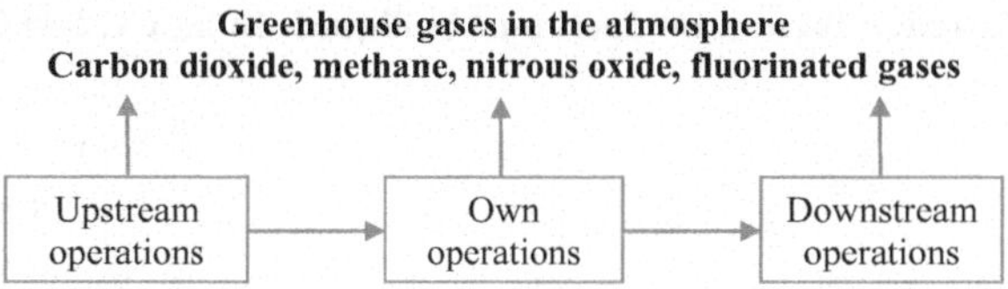


**Upstream categories**

1. Purchases goods and services
2. Capital goods
3. Fuel- and energy-related activities
4. Upstream transportation and distribution
5. Waste generated in operations
6. Business travel
7. Employee commuting
8. Upstream leased assets

Other upstream

**Downstream categories**

9. Downstream transportation and distribution
10. Processing of sold products
11. Use of sold products
12. End-of-life treatment of sold products
13. Downstream leased assets
14. Franchises
15. Investment

Other downstream

**Fig. 2.11** Guidance for Disclosure 305–3 (GRI 305: Emissions 2016)

After all, the product carbon footprint is the performance indicator for mitigation measures and the selection of low-emission suppliers (Erhard, Kubis, Krebs & Liedke, 2019).

## 2.7.2 Default Values

Directive (EU) 2018/2001 promoting the use of energy from renewable sources has listed emission default values for biofuels and liquid biofuels along with databases from the IPCC and elsewhere. Emission factors for fossil fuels, biofuels and bioliquids are compiled from the source in the electronic supplementary material (ESM) Table 1. and calculated according to the calorific value in the denominator. They vary depending on the origin of the material and process. Emission factors are displayed in the following figure (Fig. 2.12).

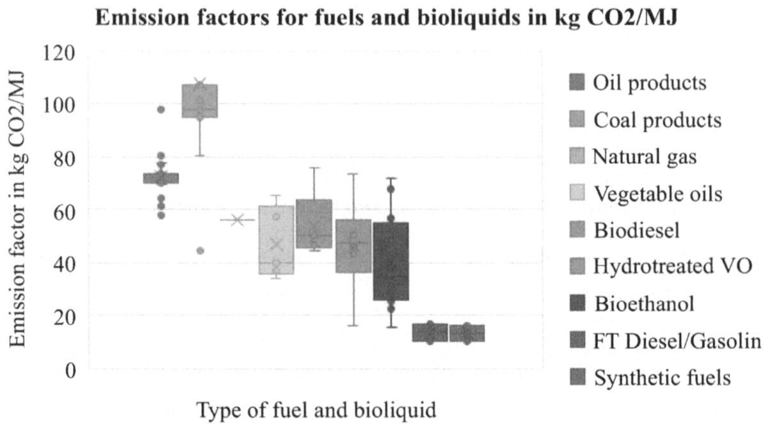


**Fig. 2.12** Emission factors for fuels and bioliquids based on heating values (Directive (EU) 2018/2001; Greenhouse Gas Protocol, 2017)

The methodology counts the greenhouse gas emissions from cultivation, processing, transport and distribution. Effects from indirect land use change and negative emission factors for carbon sequestration during the growth of the biomass are not taken into account. Biodiesel, bioethanol and hydrotreated vegetable oils (HVO) are commercially available, are used for transport including aviation and marine fuels and reduce greenhouse gas emissions by up to 50%. Fischer-Tropsch (FT diesel / gasoline) and synthetic fuels with a reduction potential of up to 80% have the lowest emission factors. FT diesel / petrol and synthetic fuels are not yet on the market in technical grades and the values are estimates (Directive (EU) 2018/2001; Greenhouse Gas Protocol, 2017). Data for pyrolysis oils are completely missing. CCU technology with green hydrogen and CO2 capture from carbon-neutral sources achieves an emission reduction of up to 90% compared to oil products (Rosental, Fröhlich & Liebich, 2020).

## 2.8 Technological Uncertainties

The chemical industry, along with the cement and steel industries, is reported hard-to-decarbonize (Bataille et al., 2018; Gross, 2021). Fossil fuels are the main source of greenhouse gas emissions and the oil-dependency makes it twofold challenging for chemical industry. Firstly, like many other industries, fossil fuels are used to generate energy and, secondly, they are the main raw material for manufacturing of products. The GHG reduction in chemistry must take place on two levels: Through climate-neutral production facilities and through climate-neutral chemical products. The challenge for the chemical industry is to achieve climate neutrality on both levels at the same time without losing international competitiveness (Tillmann & Peter, 2021). Exploration, side reactions, use of end products and disposal at the end of life generate CO2 emissions from the carbon content of the products and contribute significantly to greenhouse gas emissions (VCI, 2019). The use of biomass, the chemical recycling of plastic waste and technologies for carbon capture and utilization are three alternative sources of the carbon needs of the chemical industry and a possible substitute for fossil raw materials. The use of biomass is a technology that is already in use. Biomass is used for biofuels and for bio-based chemicals. Biodiesel, bioethanol and hydrotreated vegetable oils are raw materials for the production of downstream chemicals. Chemical recycling of plastic waste and technologies for carbon capture and utilization are being developed. Uncertainties arise from the time-to-market of these new technologies and adoption by the industry. The availability of renewable carbon supply for the chemical industry in a decarbonized world depends on these technologies. Investors need certainty what renewable carbon supply will be available, what are the timeframes for their development, what volumes of renewable raw materials for chemistry will be available and what is their cost position. Further uncertainties are connected with the GHG saving potential of abatement technologies and evaluation methods for the comparison of reduction efforts. Technologies that contribute to GHG savings are potentially conflicting with other sustainability goals, e. g. biodiversity, biodegradability, land use and land use change, water consumption or social and economic development. The industry needs certainty of what technologies best match these sustainability requirements. In addition, political uncertainty contributes to the opaque environment for businesses and makes knowledge- and data-based decision-making more difficult. To address these technological uncertainties, research is required before transition managers can make investment decisions.

# Review of Determinants for Eco-innovation Adoption

# 3

The following paragraphs provide a general overview of the literature on environmental innovations in the context of innovations to achieve CO2 neutrality in the European chemical industry. The review provides the state-of-the-art research on determinants for adoption of environmental innovations (OECD, 2009). But little specific knowledge is available about determinants for the adoption of renewable raw materials as a contribution to GHG savings and predictors for the chemical industry to achieve carbon neutrality. The research gaps are summarized at the end of the chapter and lead to questions for research of this dissertation and for the identification of patterns and best practices.

## 3.1 Drivers

On a macro-economic level, main barriers for adoption of environmental innovations are cost increases and spill-over effects. Main drivers for adoption are efficiency increases and government regulations. Efficiency gains and cost savings increase profitability and are self-sufficient eco-innovations. Other relevant determinants for adoption are regulatory push / pull effects together with cooperation and external knowledge acquisition which support the successful dissemination and acceptance of eco-innovations in general (Belin, Horbach & Oltra, 2011) (Table 3.1).

---

**Supplementary Information** The online version contains supplementary material available at https://doi.org/10.1007/978-3-658-45389-3_3.



H. H. E. Ahrens, *The Ecological Modernization of the Chemical Industry*,
https://doi.org/10.1007/978-3-658-45389-3_3

**Table 3.1** Major drivers for eco-innovations

| **Major determinants for eco-innovations** |
| --- |
| • Efficiency gains, cost saving and improved competitiveness<br>• Regulatory push/pull effects<br>• Cooperation and external knowledge sourcing |

Several further determinants are described as having a positive effect or as a prerequisite for eco-innovation activities. They are categorized into customer expectations and the specific skills of companies for successful eco-innovation activities, namely R&D skills, CSR strategy, management advocacy and cooperation activities. From an industry perspective, standards accelerate the diffusion of innovation, and finally, government push / pull programs are the main drivers of environmental innovation.

### 3.1.1 Innovation Eonomics

Eco-innovations are driven by technological developments (technology push), demand factors (market pull) and regulatory push / pull policies. Technology push factors are efficiency gains and favorable product attributes such as quality and eco-efficiency (Fig. 3.1).

Market pull factors are customer demand and competitiveness, as well as market characteristics, including demand for environmentally friendly innovations. What is special about eco-innovations is the need for regulatory support (Rennings, 2000). If the technology push and market pull are not strong enough, diffusion of eco-innovations is not self-enforcing and political measures are required to support the introduction or to finance the development (Hoff, 2012; Rennings, 2000). The great importance of regulatory support also extends to the expected future regulations for environmentally relevant product innovations. The model of Horbach, Rammer and Rennings (2012) also adds company-specific factors as a category of determinants, including company-specific characteristics such as business practices, organization and external relations of the company (OECD, 2005; Horbach, Rammer & Rennings 2012).

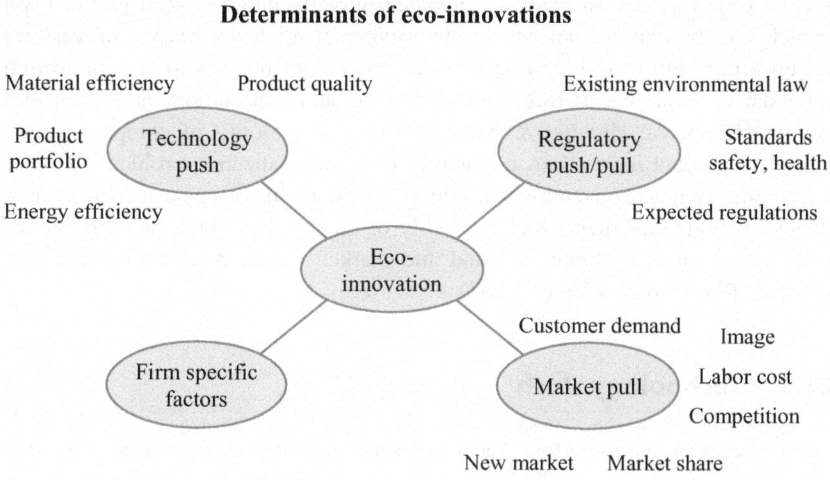


**Fig. 3.1** Determinants of eco-innovations after Rennings (2000) and Horbach, Rammer and Rennings (2012)

### 3.1.2 Market Pull

Demand factors determine the decision of companies to invest in eco-innovation, and market demand for green products triggers the supply of eco-innovations. However, eco-innovations require more complex or greater efforts due to their lower price competitiveness. Conventional technologies usually do not pay for negative externalities and make eco-innovations less attractive financially (Cainellia, d'Amato & Mazzanti, 2020). The demand for eco-innovations is driven by consumers when they bring value and add value. Consumers are willing to pay a premium for environmentally friendly products that offer significant additional benefits. Examples are organic food and clothing with eco-labels, where consumers benefit from higher quality, better health and product safety (Horbach, Rammer & Rennings 2012). Another example is the replacement of chlorofluorocarbon-free refrigerators. Products are sold with a markup and additional features, including the latest in environmentally friendly and energy efficient technology. The environmental standard can help create a competitive advantage in a standardized market (Nishitani & Itoh, 2016). In general, economic aspects, higher prices and lack of financial attractiveness are seen as the main obstacles to the commercial use of environmental products. Market uncertainty and uncertain return on investment are the two main barriers to eco-innovation that must be overcome before customer needs and expectations are taken into account (Karakaya, Hidalgo & Nuur, 2014). The majority of companies with ecological product innovations complain of commercialization problems. Higher prices compared to conventional products are more likely to be perceived as a barrier to acceptance than lower reliability or quality. Regulation is seen as necessary to stimulate customer demand and market attraction for eco-innovations (Rehfeld, Rennings & Ziegler, 2007).

### 3.1.3 Technology Push

Entrepreneurship is important for innovation and depends on new scientific knowledge with new technological and economic opportunities. Substantial new knowledge and guidance enables technological progress. Radical eco-innovations offer considerable benefits and overcome existing path dependencies. The adoption has a discontinuous effect for conventional technologies and can include cultural and social aspects. Technological transition is often confronted with lock-in effects, requires great effort and regulatory support (Geels, 2005b; Kemp, 1995). The creation of protected niche markets is a political tool to promote radical innovation and technological change. Governments can create a temporary niche market to support the development of the new technology through a policy mix of strategic niche management, regulation and subsidies (Rennings, 2000). Examples are the California Zero Emission Vehicle Rule from 1990 and the German Renewable Energy Sources Act from 2000 (Collantes & Sperling, 2008; Renewable Energy Sources Act—EEG, 2000). Ecological modernization has gained momentum thanks to stricter regulations, including the agenda of the European Green Deal. Technologies to reduce greenhouse gas emissions and CO2 neutrality in the chemical industry are in development (BMU, 2018; VCI, 2019) (Table 3.2).

**Table 3.2** Greentech sectors for carbon neutrality (BMU, 2018)

| | |
|---|---|
| **Hazardless materials** | • Avoiding and replacing hazardous materials<br>• Enables recycling of plastics and chemicals |
| **Efficiency gains** | • Energy efficiency programs<br>• Material efficiency programs |
| **Circularity** | • Shared economy<br>• Reuse of manufactured materials<br>• Mechanical, physical, chemical and thermal recycling of plastics<br>• Waste management |
| **Renewable energy** | • Carbon neutral power generation<br>• Sustainable mobility |
| **Renewable resources and carbon cycle** | • Renewable raw materials, e.g. biobased feedstocks, biogas, biowaste<br>• Chemical recycling of plastics<br>• Carbon capture & utilization and electricity-based processes with CO2 as feedstock |

The chemical industry needs carbon as a raw material for the production and replacement of fossil raw materials by more sustainable sources. Three sources for sustainable carbon supply for chemical industry are proposed: Biomass, plastic recycling and carbon capture and utilization technology (Fig. 3.2).

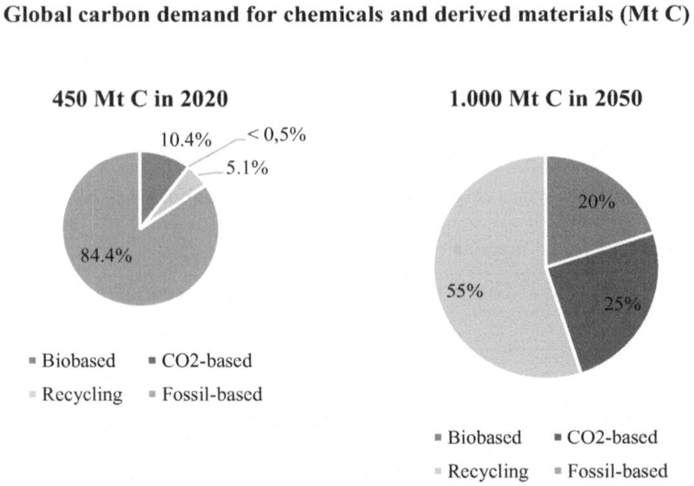


**Fig. 3.2** Global carbon demand for chemicals and derived materials in Mt C after Carus et al. (2021)

Biomass, preferably from biowaste is already used by the chemical industry and its used is projected to grow. Mechanical and chemical recycling technologies are being developed to prepare for a circular economy. As a third source, technologies for carbon capture and utilization (CCU) is proposed to fil the gap of the carbon demand. CCU uses carbon dioxide from industrial exhaust gases or the atmosphere and green hydrogen for synthesis. According to the study by Carus et al. (2021) 20% of the future renewable carbon demand will come from biomass, biogas, bio-waste and inedible corps. 55% of renewable carbon needs will come from chemical recycling methods for plastics. The remaining 25% of the renewable carbon demand is accounted for by technologies for carbon capture and use (Carus et al., 2021; VCI, 2019).

### 3.1.4 Environmental Policies

Environmental policies are critical to environmental innovation for three reasons: Market failure to internalize environmental externalities, consumer unwillingness to pay a premium for public goods, and spill-over effects that create incentives for businesses reduce investing in eco-innovations. These three barriers block voluntary environmental innovations to mitigate climate change. The main determinants of eco-innovations are regulatory push-pull instruments and cost savings through efficiency gains (Horbach, Rammer & Rennings, 2012). Most greenhouse gases are naturally occurring gases and are not directly toxic to humans or the environment. As a result, helping to reduce greenhouse gas emissions is not personally beneficial behavior, and the rewards for mitigating global warming are perceived far distant in the future. The adoption of innovations is slow. "*The rewards to the individual from adopting the preventive innovation are delayed in time, are relatively intangible, and the unwanted consequence may not occur anyway. Thus, preventive innovations are relatively low in relative advantage, compared to non-preventive innovations*" (Rogers, 2002). The unwillingness to pay for public goods requires that environmental policy internalize negative externalities in products and services. Another reason for environmental policy is the spill-over effect for R&D investments. R&D investments are risky and are therefore sometimes avoided by risk-averse managers. Even where companies are innovative, other companies will learn from their experience and skim off part of the return. The spill-over effect for R&D investments creates another barrier to eco-innovation (Hoff, 2012; Rennings, 2000) (Table 3.3).

**Table 3.3** Reasons for environmental policies

| Reasons for environmental policies |
|---|
| • Market failure to internalize environmental externalities |
| • Consumers' unwillingness to pay a premium for a public good |
| • Spill-over effects for R&D investments |

Where the market fails, environmental policies reduce the impact on the environment and reverse the environmental damage. Policy makers use a variety of policy tools to overcome market failures and customer reluctance to pay for public goods, and to combat R&D spill-over effects. Policy instruments support measures to improve resource productivity and require the replacement of devastating technologies (Hemmelkamp, 1996).

#### 3.1.4.1 Types of Policy Instruments

Government interventions are proposed to improve adoption rates (Hoff, 2012; Horbach, Rammer & Rennings, 2012; Vertesy, 2017). The political instruments are divided into non-legislative, economic and regulatory instruments (Table 3.4).

**Table 3.4** Types of policy instruments (Hoff, 2012)

| | |
|---|---|
| **Non-legislative measures** | • Voluntary measures (Green pricing, certification, self-obligations)<br>• Informative / administrative measures (Resource mapping, investor advising, campaigns) |
| **Economic instruments** | • Supply-push measures (Direct subsidies, tax and depreciation incentives, subsidized loans)<br>• Demand-pull measures (Feed-in tariffs, tax exemption, quotas for renewable portfolio standards) |
| **Regulatory instruments** | • Demand-control measures (Forced invest, mandated technologies, forced shutdowns) |

#### 3.1.4.2 Voluntary Initiatives

Non-legislative measures encourage voluntary adoption. Voluntary measures are company pledges and industry commitments. Administrative measures require disclosure of environmental performance parameters and provide information on solutions. Self-commitments are an important instrument and contribute to effective environmental action and awareness among stakeholders (Söllner, 2002).

#### 3.1.4.3 Economic Instruments

Economic instruments can provide demand-pull and supply-push effects and either support the transition to sustainability in general or for a specific technology. They work through price mechanism and offer incentives to adopt low-emission technologies. Economic demand-pull instruments are feed-in tariffs, tax exemption and quotas for renewable portfolio standards. The emissions trading system of the European Union offers a feed-in tariff system for renewable energies at a fixed price. Economic supply-push measures are direct subsidies, tax and depreciation incentives, subsidized loans and bypass financial contains of environmental innovators (Enzensberger, Wietschel & Rentz, 2002; Hoff. 2012). In addition to financial support, fiscal and regulatory instruments are required to increase the acceptance of green technologies (Börner, Bröring. & Laibach, 2019; Brouwer, Dijkstra & van Beukering, 2020).

#### 3.1.4.4 Regulatory Instruments

Regulatory instruments control the activities of companies through standards. They direct the activities of market participants through rules and regulations and guide companies to develop products and processes that meet the requirements. Technological standards prescribe methods, equipment or technology, and performance standards control emission levels or limit emissions per unit of production. These instruments directly support certain technologies or restrict the use of down-phased technologies (Bergek & Berggren, 2014).

#### 3.1.4.5 Effect of Policy Instruments

Push / pull instruments concern the place of support, be it for innovations or customers. Both instruments either directly support an innovation or a transition in different phases of the product life cycle of the technology. Technology-push and demand-pull policies complement each other. Technology push instruments support innovators in the early stages of the product life cycle. Push instruments lower the cost of innovation and encourage innovators to invest in developing green innovations. Economic incentives provide equity substitutes and include government-backed venture capital, grants / allowances, subsidized loans, equity investments and hybrid instruments for innovative companies. Technology-push instruments mainly support innovation activities such as R&D, demonstration plants, niche market creation, network support and standardization. They promote the formation, conception and early growth of the environmental innovation start-up (Bergek & Berggren, 2014; Hoff, 2012, Kemp, 1995). Market-pull instruments support the demand-side and are more effective for later stages of the product life cycle for expansion, growth and stabilization. Demand-pull policy makes it possible to extend, scale and learn market applications in order to reduce component failures (Gallagher et al., 2012; (Hoff, 2012). Policies with market-pull effects are intended to overcome technology lock-in effects (Fig. 3.3).

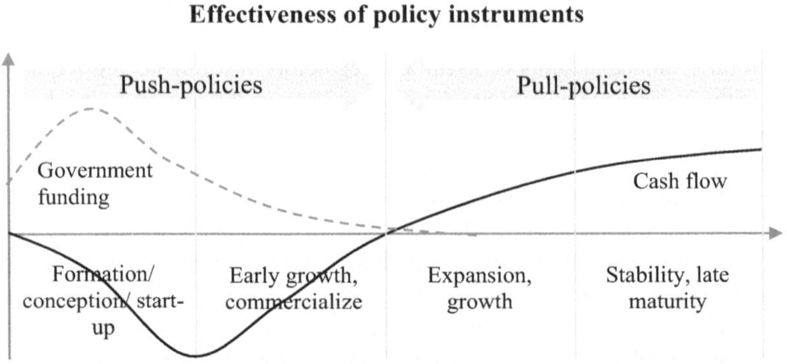


**Fig. 3.3** Effectiveness of technology-push and market-pull instruments (Hoff, 2012)

Market-pull instruments to increase demand are fiscal incentives, taxes on conventional technologies, feed-in tariffs for ecological alternatives, subsidies for consumer purchases and direct government procurement. They create and expand markets and increase the payoff of successful innovations. Examples are tax credits for eco-innovation customers and investors (Leibowicz, 2016) (Table 3.5).

**Table 3.5** Push/pull policy instruments

| Technology-push instruments | Market-pull instruments |
|---|---|
| • Equity substitutes grants/ allowances, subsidized loans, equity participations and hybrid instruments<br>• Public funding of fundamental research | • Fiscal incentives. e.g. taxes and feed-in tariffs<br>• Direct government procurement<br>• Regulatory instruments, e.g. maximum emission levels, restrictions and bans for conventional technologies |

#### 3.1.4.6 Stringency of Policy Instruments

Stringency of the support describes the effect of instruments and ranges from soft instruments such as voluntary commitments, product labeling and public procurement to hard policy instruments with bans and restrictions. Public procurement is one of the soft instruments to improve the acceptance of environmental innovations. The inclusion as a relevant product category in public tenders enhances the eco-innovation and justifies the use for other users (Peuckert & Quitzow, 2016). Voluntary agreements and certifications only stimulate ecological product innovations to a limited extent (Rehfeld, Rennings & Ziegler, 2007). Hard political instruments in the form of bans and restrictions enforce environmental objectives (Hemmelkamp, 1996) (Table 3.6).

**Table 3.6** Hard/soft policy instruments

| Soft policy instruments | Hard policy instruments |
|---|---|
| • Voluntary company pledges and industry commitments<br>• Voluntary eco-labelling<br>• Public procurement | • Fiscal/economic instruments, e.g. taxes, allowances, quotas, emission trading systems to increase cost for standard technologies<br>• Restrictions and bans |

Hard measures are considered necessary for the diffusion of environmental innovations when non-innovative companies are too hesitant to integrate measures to protect the environment (Rennings, 2000).

#### 3.1.4.7 Directives of the European Commission

The European Green Deal was announced on December 11, 2019 as the political framework for upcoming regulatory measures. The goal of the Green Deal is net carbon neutrality for the EU by 2050. The objectives are circularity of material flows, zero pollution for a toxic-free environment, biodiversity, a shift to sustainable energy and mobility and the decarbonization for energy intensive industries like steel, chemistry and cement (European Commission, 2019). The goals of the Green Deal have since been further specified. In September 2020, the Commission adopted its proposal for a European climate law to reduce net greenhouse gas emissions by at least 55% compared to 1990 levels by 2030 (European Commission, 2021b). With more stringent goals of the Green Deal to reach carbon neutrality, upcoming regulations and guidelines for the chemical industry are likely to become stricter.

### 3.1.5 Company-specific Factors

Company-specific characteristics have a significant positive influence on ecological product innovations (Rehfeld, Rennings & Ziegler, 2007). Strategy, business model, size, profitability, skills of employees and many other factors influence eco-innovation activities. Younger companies seem to be more innovative, combined with more dynamic employment (Horbach & Rennings, 2013). A list of common determinants for eco-innovation activities was taken from the literature and compiled in the following table (Hoff, 2012; Horbach, Rammer & Rennings, 2012; Horbach, 2016) (Table 3.7).

Company-specific features are complex and still have a strong influence on eco-innovation activities. Quantitative studies with structured surveys, which are used for econometric analyzes with structural equation models, cannot capture the complexity of determinants that influence innovation decisions in companies (Rennings, 2000). The challenge is to identify the key company-specific determinants given the complexity of the innovation environment and the uncertainty of the market potential.

**Table 3.7** Company-specific characteristics

| Financial characteristics | Business model characteristics |
|---|---|
| • Revenues of the past years, used also as proxy for size<br>• Number of employees<br>• Profitability<br>• Research intensity<br>• Growth potential<br>• Capital endowment | • Year of foundation<br>• Legal entity type<br>• Business model<br>• Vision and mission statements<br>• Company values and leadership<br>• Strategy formulation<br>• Innovation strategy and capabilities |
| **Company-specific capabilities** | **Company-specific activities** |
| • Technological and marketing competences<br>• Product portfolio<br>• Production capacity<br>• International presence | • Investment activities and CAPEX<br>• Product launches<br>• R&D and innovation activities<br>• Collaboration & cooperation<br>• Participation in associations & sustainability programs |

### 3.1.6 Customer Expectations

Environmental protection is a leading driver of public opinion and consumer behavior. Mitigating climate change is one of the greatest concerns. Customers in the chemical industry expect solutions for a circular economy and ecological optimization along the value chain. Transparency and chain-of-custody are core requirements of customer industries for chemicals. In addition, the industry is called upon to avoid hazardous substances and there is cross-industry claim for a "poison-free" living (Santiago Advisors, 2019). Customers are willing to pay more for eco-friendly properties, and eco-innovations offer a price premium and greater competitiveness (Nishitani & Ithoh, 2016). Consumers translate moral preferences and awareness of environmental protection into buying intentions for environmentally friendly products. Female consumers express even more environmental awareness, awareness of environmentally friendly products and responsibility than male consumers (Hojnik, Ruzzier, & Konecnik Ruzzier, 2019). According to a poll of European Parliament voters, climate change was the second top reason to vote in the 2019 European elections (DG Communication, 2019). In order to be successful in the long term, the chemical industry must integrate environmental protection into production. Customers and society expect chemical companies to increase product safety and apply the concept of circular economy. Saving finite resources, more efficient use of resources, increasing product life and closing the supply cycle are among the expectations of customers. These measures support the values of responsible care and the UN Sustainable Development Goals in general, and in particular mitigating climate change and reducing greenhouse gas emissions (Deloitte, 2017).

### 3.1.7 Efficiency Gains

In general, market orientation is the main driver for profitability, but the pull effects of the market for environmental innovations are rather weak. The main drivers for the introduction of eco-innovations are cost savings and regulatory push / pull incentives (Horbach, Rammer & Rennings, 2012; Rennings, 2000). Customer expectations and regulatory pressure are the trigger for environmental innovations. They are self-accelerating when they lead to efficient use of resources and improve business profitability (Chan, Yee, Dai & Lim, 2016). The motives for reducing the consumption of fossil fuels in the chemical industry are cost savings and the reduction in CO2 emissions is a spill-over effect. Eco-innovation activities that lead to cost savings are self-sustaining as they offer a quick return on investment. These efficiency gains have been the main drivers for reducing greenhouse gas emissions in the chemical industry since 1990 (CEFIC 2021a; VCI, 2019). Sources of efficiency gains are material and energy savings in operation. Regulation and cost savings are the main motivators for eco-innovation (Belin, Horbach & Oltra, 2011). Efficiency gains through material and energy savings are directly related to the profitability and competitiveness of the company. A positive correlation between green new product development, cost efficiency and business profitability is reported (Chan, Yee, Dai & Lim, 2016). In addition to cost savings and resource efficiency, the acceptance of eco-innovations is increased if they serve egoistic motives, contribute to risk avoidance and fulfill the values of green development as intrinsic motivational factors (Liao, Xu, Cheng & Dong, 2018).

### 3.1.8 Innovation Capabilities

Another driver for more environmental protection is innovation. However, eco-innovation requires specific skills for successful development and implementation. Challenges for eco-innovation represent the frontier of innovation: Exploration and exploitation of innovations is more difficult because of the high uncertainty for future technological trajectory. Technologies have not yet been introduced on a large scale, technical standards are lacking, and the market has not been developed. The market does not exist, and it is difficult to assess future sales potential. These uncertainties make eco-innovations difficult (Cainellia, d'Amato & Mazzanti, 2020).

#### 3.1.8.1 Innovation Culture

A specific skill is known as research and development ambidexterity. Ambidexterity is the ability to research and use eco-innovations and to handle both aspects of the innovation process. Exploration is the search for and discovery of new knowledge and / or new markets and exploration is the ability to translate the new knowledge into marketable products and to develop the market. R&D spending has a positive and significant impact on eco-innovation activities and the results of the organization (Alos-Simo, Verdu-Jover & Gomez-Gras, 2020). A culture of innovation promotes and rewards innovation values, attitudes and behaviors and generally produces more innovations than a culture of conformity and standardization (Briganti, 2019).

#### 3.1.8.2 External Knowledge Sourcing

Another characteristic of eco-innovation described in the literature is the ability to cooperate, obtain external information and for open innovation. Eco-innovation seems to require more external sources of knowledge and information than innovation in general (Belin, Horbach & Oltra, 2011). The generation of knowledge is an essential driver for eco-innovation activities and depends on R&D expenditure, the availability of qualified workers as well as internal and external information flows The knowledge flows make co-creation, cooperation and open innovation projects essential elements for environmental innovations (Horbach, 2020). Internal barriers are a lack of creative and innovative culture. Exploratory business areas require a more open culture with more unstructured work. Creative cultures enable innovators to test new ideas and give freedom to explore new technologies and skills (Mirow, Hoelzle & Gemünden, 2017). More intensive external relations, formal cooperation with external partners and especially the cooperation with suppliers are described as important in order to obtain environmentally friendly input materials. Internal instruments to support eco-innovations are staff training as a competence-enhancing and motivating factor as well as networking and formal cooperation with external partners (Cainelli, de Marchi & Grandinetti, 2015). One source for external knowledge flows are collaborations with universities. It is not the size and number of universities that are important, but the type and quality of the faculty and the knowledge spillover (Slavtchev & Fritsch, 2005).

#### 3.1.8.3 Innovation Strategy

Another aspect is the innovation strategy. Misleading research strategies can reduce the competitiveness of companies. Innovations aimed at reducing external production effects such as air, water, noise pollution and pollutants increase costs, reduce profitability and the competitiveness of companies. Moving forward too quickly can jeopardize long-term value creation, reduce market share and lead to financial constrains and even bankruptcy. A preferred strategy for combining economic and ecological goals is an innovation strategy to enable increases in efficiency and cost savings. The strategy of incremental innovations enables economic growth to be sustained and environmental performance to be reconciled (Ghisetti & Rennings, 2014). Design-driven radical innovations are considered riskier. New innovative niches have limits. When users are too far removed from existing practices, innovation can fail and innovators are advised to make radical innovations appear more incremental (Sovacool, Noela & Orsato, 2017).

#### 3.1.8.4 Internal R&D Capabilities

Internal R&D seems to be important for material and energy savings. These projects focus on the incremental improvement of the production process (Horbach, 2016). Organization and culture influence innovation activities in companies. Centralization efforts have a negative impact on exploratory innovations. Formalization has a positive influence on exploitative innovation and connectedness within the company and with other organizations are important factors for both exploratory and exploitative innovation (Jansen, Van Den Bosch & Volberda, 2006).

### 3.1.9 CSR Strategy

Aside from the main drivers of eco-innovation, cost savings and regulatory push / pull incentives, eco-organizational innovations are reported to have the highest positive effects on business performance. Business model innovations have a greater impact on profitability than eco-product and eco-process innovations. Eco-organizational innovations are strategic orientations of the business model towards ecological issues. This includes a strategy for sustainable corporate responsibility, training courses, programs for eco-product design programs and work teams for dealing with sustainability. The administrative effort activates the resources for eco-product and eco-process innovations and contributes to a positive corporate image in public communication (Cheng, Yang & Sheu, 2014). An eco-innovation-friendly culture is mentioned as a driving force for sustainable transitions and includes the strategic orientation and the development of skills for the development of eco-innovations. The eco-innovation-friendly culture is an important management tool for sustainable change (Kiefer, Del Río González & Carrillo-Hermosilla, 2018). Only the voluntary adoption of corporate social responsibility guidelines and strategies offers opportunities for profit. CSR strategies offer ethical codes for fair dealings with stakeholders and guide management in decision-making processes in order to take into account the responsibility of the stakeholders and to avoid short-term profit thinking with the increased risk of irresponsible decisions. Corporate social responsibility, corporate reputation, and financial performance are closely related, and the market rewards good environmental management (Armstrong & Green, 2012; Lee & Hu, 2018).

### 3.1.10 Management Advocacy

In addition to the CSR strategy, management advocacy is another management tool used in corporate management. Supporting and financing projects, activating employee engagement and removing organizational barriers are all aspects of positive management advocacy. Management's interest in innovation and its support for CSR strategy has a strong business and performance impact (Mumford & Hunter, 2005). Leadership behavior is important for the type and level of environmental and sustainability performance. Sustainability leaders are characterized by a strong commitment to sustainable development and use instruments for the proactive implementation of corporate sustainability (Hahn & Scheermesser, 2006).

### 3.1.11 Cooperation

Knowledge generation is the source of new ideas, product developments and requires information flows within the organization and with other organizations. Due to the high complexity of eco-innovations in connection with limited resources, open innovation, the ability to cooperate and network capacity are important factors in increasing the stock of knowledge (Horbach, 2020). Green innovators need and acquire information and expertise through inter-organizational relationships (Cainelli, de Marchi & Grandinetti, 2015). An example for the positive effect of cooperation is the transfer of competencies and R&D information between Western and Eastern European countries of the European Union (Horbach, 2016). Knowledge spillovers occur between companies when customers and suppliers work closely together. Manufacturers can draw on the knowledge of the producers, integrate it into their products and sell it to other customers (Hoppmann, 2018). Design-driven innovations result from close cooperation between users and producers and facilitate new product features that allow recycling and reversed supply chains (Krikke, Blanc & van de Velde, 2004). Other cooperation networks aim at environmental education programs, the acquisition of environmental knowledge and the establishment of links to business associations, research institutes and universities (Leonidou, Christodoulides, Kyrgidou & Palihawadana, 2017). The collaboration extends to internal and external sources of knowledge transfer in the field of sustainability. External cooperation for sustainability ranges from customer and supplier cooperation to knowledge transfer with science, industry associations and regulators (Fobbe, 2020) (Table 3.8).

### 3.1.12 Standardization

Standardization provides common norms for technologies and ensures that processes, products and services are usable, interchangeable and compatible. Standards describe specified product properties and include norms, certification schemes, specifications and labeling characteristics. They ensure transparency, accountability and harmonization of products within a market and create better communication between partners. A lack of harmonization of regulations is a technical barrier, and harmonization of standards increases the efficiency of trade (Mujica, 2019). In general, standards for industry are voluntary and non-binding, but they offer advantages. They promote rationalization, quality assurance and improve the comparability of products, services and / or processes and their performance characteristics.

**Table 3.8** Cooperation with external partners

| Customers | Suppliers |
|---|---|
| • Cooperation with customers, joint developments<br>• Participation in trade shows, and conferences | • Acquisition of new input materials<br>• Supplier cooperation<br>• Cooperation with start-ups |
| **Scientific information flows** | **Regulatory information flows** |
| • Cooperation with trade research institutes and universities<br>• Patent watch and activities | • Participation in trade associations Regulatory watch<br>• Preparation for policy changes |

#### 3.1.12.1 Types of Standards

Certain standards are binding if they are mentioned in contracts, laws or ordinances and can become legally binding with national or international validity (DIN, 2020). Standards are set either by government agencies, private or non-profit organizations. Industry standards are issued by bodies such as DIN, CEN, ASTM or ISO. Specific environmental standards such as the German Blue Angel from the RAL Institute or the Nordic Swan from the Nordic Council are issued by government authorities or councils. Voluntary industry initiatives, private and non-profit organizations develop specifications with different environmental effectiveness and transparency that go beyond existing legal requirements. The lack of clear minimum requirements for standards, certificates or eco-labels creates problems. Despite these limitations, standards are found to improve the flow of information and to raise awareness of new technical and management practices (Paton, 2000).

#### 3.1.12.2 Eco-labels

Environmental labels, or eco-labels for short, give consumers and producers orientation, which products contribute to environmental protection and reduce hazards for people. The international standard ISO 14020 series supports companies in communicating their efforts with three types of environmental labels to minimize the environmental impact (Metthew, 2010) (Table 3.9).

**Table 3.9** Three types of environmental labels (International Organization for Standardization, 2019)

| | |
|---|---|
| **Eco-labels** | |
| ISO 14024, Environmental labels and declarations - Type I environmental labelling – Principles and procedures | • Procedures to operate eco-logo program<br>• Third-party certification process to verify product compliance with a set of criteria<br>• Provides guidance on developing criteria |
| **Self-declarations** | |
| ISO 14021, Environmental labels and declarations – Self-declared environmental claims (Type II environmental labelling) | • ISO 14021 clarifies commonly used terms used in claims, advertising or reports<br>• Evaluation methods for each term in order to help ensure validity |
| **Sustainability declarations** | |
| ISO 14025, Environmental labels Type III environmental declarations – Principles and procedures | • Specifies format for reporting quantifiable life cycle data<br>• B2B declarations require independent verification<br>• B2C declarations require third-party certification |

Eco-labels that match the type I eco-label help consumers to identify environmentally friendly products. Examples of environmental labeling type I are the Nordic Svan, the European eco-flower and the German Blue Angel. Type I environmental labeling focuses on the effect of the product on people and the environment during the use phase (Jørgensen & Moen, 2015).

#### 3.1.12.3 Supply Chain Certifications

Sustainability declarations cover the origin of the material and life cycle analyzes. They fall into the category of type 3 eco-labels and exemplary certification systems are ISCC Plus and REDcert2. These optional sustainability standards and declarations require suppliers, processors and customers along the supply chain to meet sustainability metrics, including human rights, health and safety issues and the environmental impact of business practices (Bissinger et al., 2020) (Fig. 3.4).

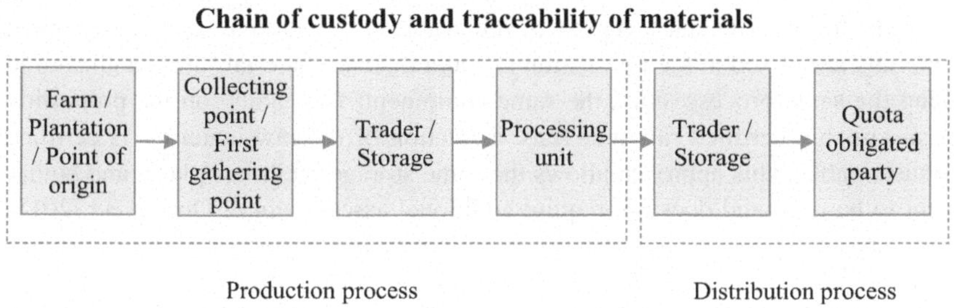


**Fig. 3.4** Sustainability certification schemes (ISCC, 2018)

The ISCC Plus and REDcert2 certification systems certify sustainable supply chains. The certification initiatives enable the traceability of the origin of the raw materials and guarantee the sustainability of the products. Type III environmental standards focus on the origin of the product and how workers and the environment are treated during production processes and along the chain of custody (Mol & Oosterveer, 2015; ISCC, 2018). Two supply chain models are standardized and proposed by certification bodies in order to increase transparency and traceability for sustainable materials. In the segregation model, only sustainably certified material is used for the production of finished goods. There is no mixing or cross-contamination with conventional material. The approach requires separate processing of materials and, in many cases, separate assets such as storage facilities, plants and equipment (ISCC, 2018) (Fig. 3.5).

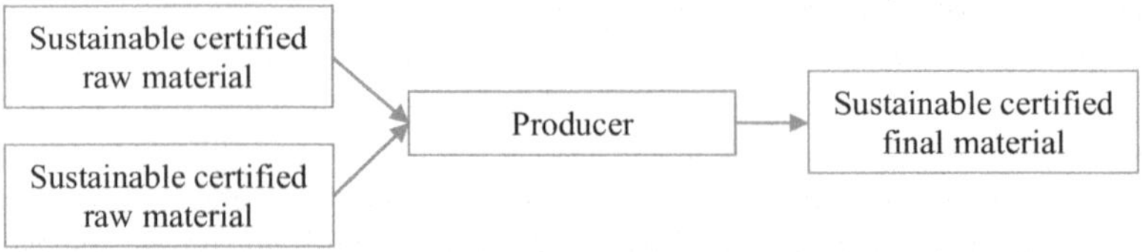


**Fig. 3.5** Segregation model

With the mass balance approach, renewable raw materials and conventional materials are mixed at the production site and the end materials are manufactured using the same processes and the same equipment. Depending on the proportion of sustainably certified raw materials, a fraction of the raw materials is certified as sustainable. This approach allows the same storage facilities, plants and equipment to be used and does not require additional assets (Mol & Oosterveer, 2015) (Fig. 3.6).

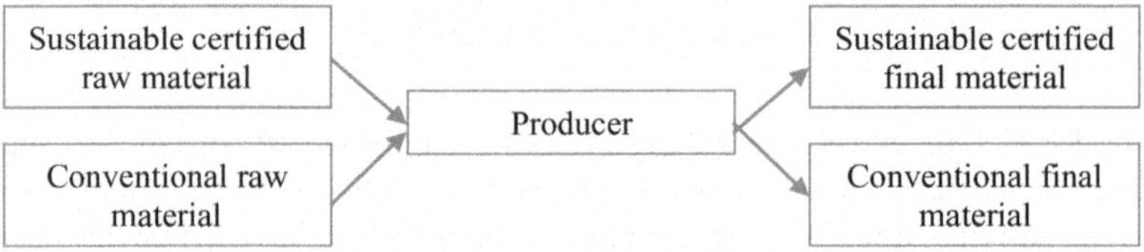


**Fig. 3.6** Mass balance model

Eco-labels can create added value in consumer markets and eco-labeled products deserve a premium in certain segments of the consumer market. Larger retailers can achieve higher margins for the additional product features. Eco-labels and country of origin declarations are considered extra features and can generate additional revenues (Zhang, Sogn-Grundvåg, Asche & Young, 2018). Depending on the choice of the eco-label, market acceptance for green products is increased. It is recommended to use simple and clear messages and select eco-label organizations with good credibility and multiple partners. Eco-labels create transparency, avoid conflicts of interest, and improve recognition and credibility for consumers. The higher credibility increases the demand for labeled products and additional added value is created (Delmas, M. A., Nairn-Birch, N. & Balzarova, M., 2013; Horbach, Rammer, & Rennings 2012).

#### 3.1.12.4 Industry Initiatives

Measures to encourage voluntary adoption of environmental technologies are also promoted by non-governmental organizations and industrial associations. Sustainability initiatives help companies to reduce environmental and social risks in accordance with the 17 UN sustainability goals. Voluntary initiatives set standards for reporting, target setting and traceability of sustainability criteria (Sustainable Development Goals, 2015). They often prepare standards before they become legally binding (Depoers, Jeanjean & Jérôme, 2016). Reporting initiatives improve the consistency of the data and information disclosed. Examples of reporting initiatives are the Dow Jones Sustainability Index, GRI and CDP. Robeco Sam tracks economic, ecological and social criteria in the Dow Jones Sustainability Indices (Robeco Sam, 2017). The GRI Global Reporting Initiative sets standards for the disclosure of performance indicators in annual reports and the CDP Carbon Disclosure Program provides guidelines for reporting on greenhouse gas emissions (CDP, 2021) (Fig. 3.7).

Roundtable of Sustainable Palm Oil

Carbon Disclosure Project

Responsible Care

Together for Sustainability

Dow Jones Sustainability Index

UN Global Compact

**Fig. 3.7** Voluntary sustainability initiatives

Target setting sustainability initiatives are Responsible Care, Together for Sustainability and the UN Global Compact. They deal with issues of environmental protection and of taking precautionary measures for health and safety (Peukert, & Sahr, 2010; Together for Sustainability, 2021). Traceability initiatives create transparency for the chain of custody and quality guidelines for the origin of sustainable materials. Examples are the RSPO's certification systems for sustainable palm oil and ISCC's certification for renewable biomass. The Roundtable of Sustainable Palm Oil (RSPO) is a certification system for supply chains for producers and customers of sustainable palm oil and palm kernel oil (RSPO, 2017). The International Sustainability and Carbon Certification (ISCC) agency certifies the traceability and chain of custody of biofuels and biochemicals from renewable raw materials (ISCC, 2018).

### 3.1.13 Chemical Regulations

The main drivers for the introduction of eco-innovations are regulatory push / pull instruments and directives that drive the change towards environmental innovations. Regulations and directives are effective instruments for protecting the environment in the chemical industry. Examples are Council Directive 73/404/ EEC on detergents, after fish in rivers died in the 1960 s and 70 s due to non-biodegradable detergents, or the ban on DDT and other persistent pesticides by Directive 79/117/EEC. The use of specific dangerous substances of very high concern and persistent organic pollutants is restricted. Less dangerous substances have replaced the pollutants (Council Directive 73/404/EEC; Council Directive 79/117/EEC). Greenhouse gas emissions from the chemical industry are CO2, methane, nitrous oxide and fluorinated gases and are considered pollutants for the atmosphere. Fluorinated gases are already regulated by EC directives. Regulation (EC) 1005/2009 is published in response to the Montreal Protocol on the Depletion of the Ozone Layer. Regulation (EU) 517/2014 further restricts the use of the substances as a reaction to the Kyoto Protocol on climate change and prepares the phase-out of fluorinated gases with the highest global warming potential (Regulation (EC) No 1005/2009; Regulation ( EU) No 517/2014). The main sources of nitrous oxide and methane are nitrogen fertilizers and livestock. The revision of the Fertilizer Ordinance is an essential instrument for reducing N2O emissions. The chemical industry has reported that it will continue to reduce emissions. The most efficient way to reduce methane emissions is to change human nutritional practices (Umweltbundesamt, 2019). Methane and CO2 emissions from the chemical industry are related to the chemical industry's oil-dependency. The existing literature suggests that the chemical industry's dependence on oil is a socio-technical barrier with a lock-in effect and requires a paradigm shift. It is likely that push / pull regulatory tools will be required. Recycling, biomass and carbon capture and utilization technologies are suggested as a replacement for fossil raw materials as future carbon sources. The challenge of the technological paradigm shift is the sufficient supply of green electricity at a competitive price for the increased demand of the European chemical industry and the supply of renewable raw materials as feedstock for chemical synthesis (Appunn, 2021; Carus et al. 2021; Rothermel, 2020).

## 3.2 Barriers

While the main drivers for the introduction of eco-innovations are regulatory push / pull instruments by governments and cost savings from efficiency gains, main barriers to eco-innovation are higher prices and lock-in effects, (Horbach, Rammer & Rennings 2012) (Table 3.10).

**Table 3.10** Major barriers for eco-innovations

| Major barriers for eco-innovations |
|---|
| • Higher costs and reduced competitiveness<br>• Lock-in effects of existing technology paradigms |

### 3.2.1 Price Concerns

Price concerns are the biggest barrier to market uptake for eco-products. It is not enough to offer a green product and additional incentives are needed for the customer to increase willingness to pay a premium. It is therefore recommended to offer extra benefits to offset the inferior price competitiveness of eco-products (Biswas, 2016). Although costs decrease over time and product differentiation partially compensates for competition, green consumerism will only modestly absorb higher prices. Premiums are only accepted by consumers who voluntarily fully internalize externalities in an unregulated market. The introduction of green products that compete with financially more attractive but environmentally harmful versions is delayed and there is a need for regulations and taxes (Erikson, 2004). Consumers are aware of the lack of competitiveness and higher prices are seen as the main barrier to purchase, while all other factors are less important. Lower financial attractiveness is the inhibitor to green consumption (Gleim, Smith, Andrews & Cronin, 2017).

### 3.2.2 Cost Barriers

Higher prices of environmentally friendly products are due to higher production costs and reluctance to pay more is the main barrier to their adoption (Madrid-Guijarro, Garcia & Van Auken, 2009). With no performance benefits, consumers avert switching to the more environmentally friendly products. It requires regulatory instruments to reduce the competitiveness of conventional technologies and to support the market acceptance of environmental alternatives such as in the B2C case of unleaded petrol (Battisti & Stoneman, 1998). A similar picture emerges at the B2B level. Companies that develop processes with improved environmental performance generally fail to internalize the benefits of their eco-innovations. One example are labor-intensive recycling concepts with the aim of increasing resource efficiency and reducing greenhouse gas emissions. Society benefits from progress in the circular economy. Additional costs for resources and waste management cannot be passed on to customers and remain within the framework of the company organization (Cainelli, D'Amato & Mazzantic, 2020).

### 3.2.3 Financial Constrains

Companies that invest in green product and process development are more likely to suffer from financial constraints than other companies. Green start-ups are heavily reliant on state-funded risk capital. There is a lack of early-stage private equity and the proportion of companies that receive government support is high. Mature companies are also supported by the government (Hoff, 2012). Small and medium-sized companies in the greentech industry are more susceptible to financial constraints when their business model is about converting processes to cleaner or more energy-efficient production. Process innovations related to green technologies are more vulnerable than product innovations. Companies bringing new products or services to the market for end users are also constrained, but to a lesser extent. As a consequence, the financing gap delays the realization of projects (Jensen, Schäfer & Stephan, 2019). After all, financial constrains at start-ups with environmentally friendly product portfolios can lead to bankruptcies. Examples are start-ups in the emerging biofuel market such as Energiepark Süptitz GmbH. The company's profitability fell due to high and volatile raw material prices and temporary supply bottlenecks. Margins eroded in 2012 despite a 40% increase in sales (Bundesanzeiger, 2014). The company filed for bankruptcy and was liquidated in 2013 (Bundesanzeiger, 2019). Another example is Bioamber. a Montreal-based startup funded with $ 140 MUSD government funding.

The company opened the first large-scale plant for bio-based succinic acid in Canada and offered the biomaterial as a replacement for conventional succinic acid made from fossil fuels. Bio-based succinic acid had the same properties and was used as a building block for plastics through to cosmetics. Despite a positive life cycle analysis for its product range and zero net carbon dioxide emissions, Bioamber Inc filed for voluntary bankruptcy on May 4, 2018 (Bioplastics News, 2018; Form 8-K, 2018). These two cases are examples of environmental innovation business models that went bankrupt due to high raw material costs and financial constraints.

### 3.2.4 Socio-technical Barriers

Aside from economic barriers, the diffusion and adoption of eco-innovations also suffer from socio-technical barriers that hinder the diffusion process. Complexity of the innovative system, uncertainty about the quality, lack of experience as well as trust and risk aversion are socio-technical barriers. Other barriers are the uncertainty of the market potential and future profitability of eco-innovations (Karakaya, Hidalgo & Nuur, 2014) (Table 3.11).

**Table 3.11** Socio-technical barriers for environmental niche-innovations

| **Causes for lock-out effects** | |
|---|---|
| • Existing infrastructure | • Technological paradigms |
| • Large physical assets | • Societal expectations and beliefs |
| • Long depreciation times | • High transaction costs |

The lock-in effect of an existing technology is the most important socio-technical barrier and rules out new options. Lock-in effects exist due to technological paradigms that have been built and consist of physical assets and existing infrastructure. The built environment takes decades to depreciate and slows down innovation and diffusion processes. Technological paradigms have advantages in terms of transaction costs, learning curves and economies of scale. The superior cost-benefit ratio and the good fit with existing lifestyles are barriers to change. Oil-based chemistry is an example (Rennings, 2000).

Other socio-technical barriers to environmental innovations are existing standards and methods, product requirements and technological path dependencies for sustainable transitions (Kiefer, Del Río González & Carrillo - Hermosilla, 2018). Environmental innovations tend to be more expensive than existing technologies, do not meet market expectations and are perceived as strange and unreliable, which reduces cultural legitimacy, social acceptance and access to financial resources (Geels, 2019).

### 3.2.5 Resource Availability

New tangible and intangible resources are required for eco-innovation activities and the introduction of environmentally friendly technologies. The transition from oil-based chemistry to the use of renewable resources requires new knowledge, technologies and resources. The availability of knowledge and the forecast demand for renewable energies and renewable raw materials are of crucial importance for the transition to carbon neutrality. The availability and generation of knowledge is the key to eco-innovation activities. Environmentally innovative companies perceive knowledge barriers as more intense and more numerous than in other innovation activities (Pinget, Bocquet & Mothe, 2015). The generation of knowledge is an important driver for eco-innovation activities and depends on R&D expenditure, the availability of skilled workers and internal and external information flows (Horbach, 2020). An important driver for the introduction of eco-innovations is the availability of sufficient renewable energy and raw materials to replace fossil fuels. The chemical industry is an energy-intensive industry. 26% of the energy demand of the German chemical industry is covered by electricity, the rest is covered by various fuels, mainly natural gas for heating and operating chemical processes. If fossil fuels are replaced by renewable energy sources such as wind and sun, the electricity demand increases from approx. 206 TWh (740 PJ) to approx. 600 TWh of green electricity per year. That is more than Germany's total electricity consumption of around 500 TWh in 2018 according to the roadmap of the German chemical industry 2050. The development of hydrogen, CO2 capture and renewable energy infrastructure with a competitive electricity price of 4 cents / kWh is required (Appunn, 2021; Rothermel, 2020). Plastic recycling, biomass and CO2 capture are future sources of carbon flux. The use of CO2 capture needs further development and depends on the availability of green electricity, carbon capture utility programs, and hydrogen infrastructure (Carus et al., 2021) (Table 3.12).

**Table 3.12** Bio-based feedstocks (Energias Market Research, 2019)

| Bio-based feedstock by type | Bio-based feedstock by source |
|---|---|
| • Starch | • Lignocellulosic biomass |
| • Vegetable oils | • Forestry biomass |
| • Cellulose and lignin | • Agro-based biomass |
| • Proteins | • Industrial and municipal waste |

The market for bio-based raw materials is already seeing a growing demand for bio-based chemicals. The availability of biomass for chemical synthesis is also subject to ethical considerations. Increased use of biomass can have an impact on biodiversity, land use and land use changes as well as on competition with food and feed value chains. The forestry segment has the largest share of the biomass market. Agricultural residues and waste from agri-food value chains have further potential and open up opportunities for supplier industries (Energias Market Research, 2019).

## 3.3 Research Gaps

The transition to carbon neutrality poses a number of challenges and there is a gap in empirical research on environmental innovations and their determinants (Hoff, 2012). The transition of the chemical industry to leave the technological trajectory of oil-based chemistry, and the literature suggests three alternative technology categories of renewable raw materials for chemical synthesis as a substitute for fossil resources.

### 3.3.1 Technological Option

Transition of the oil-depending chemical industry requires new feedstocks for carbon supply. Biomass is already used for 10% of the chemicals and is available for expansion to new applications. Mechanical and chemical plastics recycling and carbon capture and utilization are novel technologies, but they are still under development. The renewable feedstocks have the potential for the transition to carbon neutrality, but there is a lack of knowledge about their resources, availability, capabilities, competitiveness and market potential. The complexity of the innovation system makes decision making difficult and the purpose of the research is to identify the state of transition in the industry and best practices for transition management in business organizations (Karakaya, Hidalgo & Nuur, 2014; Sovacool, Noela & Orsato, 2017). Insights into the economic value of the suitable substitutes for fossil raw materials are only partially given by the existing literature. It is uncertain how the chemical industry will deal with lock-in effects and oil dependency with strong paradigms, and which eco-innovations will be adapted for the transition to carbon neutrality with complex supply chains and several intermediate products (Bröring, Golembiewski & Sick, 2015). The chemical industry has high capital requirements and the burden of investing to reduce greenhouse gas emissions comes at the expense of industry, while society and the environment benefit from change. It is the uncertainty of how, when and whether regulators will share the burden of moving towards carbon neutrality that is beneficial to society but places financial constraints on business actors. Governments must play an active role in the transition to renewable raw materials and need to provide financial and regulatory support for renewable technologies. The European Green Deal announced regulations and taxes for the use of fossil fuels. However, it is unclear what support companies can expect and how they have to prepare their business model with regard to the necessary ecological modernization towards CO2 neutrality (Loorbach & Wijsman, 2013, Vertesy, 2017). There is a lack of knowledge about the eco-innovation types and their properties that are propose for replacement of fossil feedstocks. In addition, there is a lack of knowledge about company-specific determinants for innovation acceptance amid the complexity of the innovation environment. Greenhouse gas emission savings, financial attractiveness, and technical benefits are viewed as major attributes for adoption (Hoff, 2012). The situation in the chemical industry is diffuse and companies have special needs in the transition to carbon neutrality. There is a lack of knowledge about customers' willingness to pay for environmentally friendly product innovations. Research needs to find out whether renewability is seen as a key customer benefit (Garcia, Wigger & Hermann, 2019). Biomass in particular, with an existing market share of 10% in the chemical supply, could have an advantage and there is a need for research on the attitude of chemical companies towards the use of bio-based raw materials as a substitute for fossil raw materials (Bröring, Golembiewski & Sick, 2015).

### 3.3.2 Company-specific Determinants

The challenge is to capture the most important company-specific determinants for the adoption of innovations: There is a lack of knowledge about the most important predictors for the adoption of eco-innovations in order to achieve carbon neutrality. Company-specific characteristics are complex, but the literature describes CSR strategy, leadership behavior and collaborative skills with suppliers, customers and other stakeholders as key factors for the adoption of innovations (Rennings, 2000). It needs research whether these determinants adequately describe the relationship between attitudes, intentions to use and actual use of eco-innovation and which patterns support the adoption of renewable raw materials (Loorbach & Wijsman, 2013, Vertesy, 2017). The results of the research will provide insights into best practices and suitable innovation strategies in order to achieve carbon neutrality from the perspective of the practitioner (Rehfeld, Rennings & Ziegler, 2007).

### 3.3.3 Standards and Regulations

The main driving forces behind environmental innovations are regulatory push / pull instruments and cost savings while the main barriers to eco-innovations are higher prices, higher costs for goods and input materials and other technological disadvantages for the adoption of eco-innovations, mainly lock-in effects. In the literature, industry standards are described as a further driver for the introduction of innovations. There is a lack of knowledge of the role of industry standards and expected government support in overcoming major barriers. Research is needed to confirm the barriers and drivers for use of biomass and other renewable resources to reach carbon neutrality (Horbach, Rammer, & Rennings 2012). Research is needed to identify the need for regulation and standardization for market acceptance of eco-innovations. The research will provide insights into the connection between political announcements and the implementation of guidelines on the one hand and innovation activities in companies to achieve carbon neutrality on the other.

### 3.3.4 Research Method

Actor-based patterns are suggested to provide evidence for transition theory, and research using agent-based models is a suitable methodology (Geels, 2005b). Previous studies applied agent-based models for environmental innovation (Arpan, Chen & Xu 2017; Jansson, Westin, Nordlund & Nielsson, 2020). But agent-based models have not been applied to the introduction of renewable raw materials for the chemical industry, and the attitudes and intentions to use renewable resources to reduce greenhouse gas emissions are unknown. The model promises to provide a predictive tool for the adoption and actual use of renewable raw materials by the chemical industry based on the agents' perception of innovation (Ajzen, 1991; Davis, 1985). The replacement of fossil feedstocks and adoption of renewable raw materials for chemical synthesis is unique for chemical industry. There is a lack of knowledge about attitude and intention to adopt renewable raw materials and to identify patterns and strategies for decarbonization of production in chemistry. Econometric models neglect the complexity of determinants that influence innovation decisions in companies, and there is a lack of actor-related patterns that provide evidence for the existing transformation theory (Geels, 2005b; Rennings, 2000). Case study research provides the tools to analyze eco-innovation in complex and unsafe environments and the interrelationship between technology and company-specific characteristics (McDermott & O'Connor, 2002). The application of the methodology promises to identify factors for the acceptance of renewable raw materials and to collect data from actors about their preferences.

# Theoretical Framework

# 4

The theoretical framework comprises two theory clusters, innovation research and environmental science studies. Innovation research examines predictors, processes and the impacts of innovations. Environmental sciences examine the ecological preservation and the multilevel perspective for socio-technical transitions. A combination of innovation research and behavioral sciences contributes agent-based models for innovation diffusion and sets the decision makers in the focus for study. These theory clusters provide the background for studies of environmental innovations and their adoption in general and are also applicable for study of transition to carbon neutrality of the chemical industry. The theoretical framework begins with an overview of innovation research at various levels in organizations and describes categories and types of innovation. Ecological modernization theory outlines elements for industry to contribute to sustainable development and explains the need for transition to carbon neutrality. Multilevel perspective for socio-technical transitions forms the framework for transition management and ecological modernization (Geels, 2001). The theory cluster also includes technological innovation systems studies, the catch-up cycle and the window-of-opportunity perspective of technological change. Both multilevel perspective for socio-technical transitions and technological innovation systems are frameworks frequently applied to environmental innovations and allow to explain and conceptualize the research findings. Innovation diffusion studies focus on models for innovation adoption from the user's point of view and agent-based models

---

**Supplementary Information** The online version contains supplementary material available at https://doi.org/10.1007/978-3-658-45389-3_4.



H. H. E. Ahrens, *The Ecological Modernization of the Chemical Industry*,
https://doi.org/10.1007/978-3-658-45389-3_4

are based on reasoned action, planned behavior and the technological acceptance model. The reasoned action approach is the basis for the testable model for research of adoption predictors of this dissertation.

## 4.1 Innovation Types

Innovations are categorized according to scope and degree of continuity. According to Freeman, "*an invention is an idea, sketch or model for a new or improved device, product, process or system*". The innovation differs from the invention in that, in addition to novelty, it offers added value to the user. In innovation economy, an invention becomes an innovation with the first commercial transaction (Freeman & Soete, 1994). Ecological innovations create value for the environment, reduce pollution or contribute to sustainability goals. Eco-innovations range from new ideas, products and processes to changes in lifestyle and consumer behavior (Rennings, 2000; Kemp 2008). Innovations to reach carbon neutrality fall under the categories for eco-innovations and the Oslo Manual provides a list for various types (OECD, 2005) (Table 4.1).

**Table 4.1** Eco-innovation types (Kemp, 2008; OECD, 2005)

| **Eco-innovation types** | |
|---|---|
| Product innovation | New materials with improved environmental profile |
| Service innovation | New services with positive impact on the environment, sometimes part of product innovation |
| Marketing innovation | New methods to market and sell products |
| Process innovation | New manufacturing procedures to reduce or prevent adverse effects on the environment |
| Business model innovation | New organizational methods in business practices or external relations |

### 4.1.1 Product Innovation

New product innovations include new and environmentally improved goods and final materials (OECD, 2005). Examples in the chemical industry are products with a lower CO2 footprint or substitutes for greenhouse gases with a lower global warming potential. Chemicals with a lower carbon footprint are made from new raw materials with lower or even negative emission factors if the raw materials are derived from biomass or carbon sequestration technologies (Kemp, 2008). Product innovation includes the replacement of existing materials. The use of bio-based raw materials for the development of drop-ins and smart drop-ins or dedicated new chemicals are examples of product-type eco-innovations in chemistry (Carus et al., 2020). The term also includes design-driven innovations. The application of the 12 green chemistry rules can lead to design-driven eco-product innovations (Anastas & Kirchhoff, 2002).

### 4.1.2 Service Innovation

Service is immaterial and is sometimes grouped with product innovations. They are activities that offer a benefit. Innovations in the field of environmental protection enable the longer use and reuse of materials such as plastics. They require product-service concepts such as the collection of used goods and offer potential for greenhouse gas savings (Edwards-Schachter, 2018; (Kotler, Wong, Saunders & Armstrong, 2005).

### 4.1.3 Marketing Innovation

Another innovation category are new marketing concepts. These innovations are intended to change the behavior of the actors and give the product more value through marketing instruments (OECD, 2005). One example is the use of new sales channels and digital technologies, and digitization has the potential for reducing global GHG emissions with new marketing concepts (Eckholm & Rockström, 2019).

### 4.1.4 Process Innovation

Process innovations include improved methods, equipment, and / or skills for manufacturing the product. This includes the optimization for lower use of resources or the substitution of processes by improved production methods with less harmful side reactions (OECD, 2005). Less waste, higher yields and the use of materials with a lower global warming potential lead to savings in greenhouse gas emissions through process innovations. The emission of fluorinated gases and nitrous oxide has been reduced through process innovations and technological improvements. Nitrous oxide is catalytically or thermally broken down into nitrogen and oxygen. Another example is avoiding the flaring of methane in refineries and using it for energy generation Fischedick et al., 2014).

### 4.1.5 Organizational Innovation

Business model and organizational innovations are used synonymously and describe new methods in business practices or external relations. New utilities and quality management systems are new organizational methods. A new organizational method is the implementation of recycling concepts and co-processing of fossil and biogenic materials to reduce greenhouse gas emissions. Another example is certified supply chains for tracing sustainable raw materials and manufacturing methods through environmental certification systems that require collaboration with customers, suppliers and stakeholders (ISCC, 2018; OECD, 2005). The typology of eco-innovation makes it possible to classify the new technologies and business models. When it comes to innovation decisions in companies, the question arises as to the contribution of eco-innovations and the determinants for their introduction under complex circumstances (Rennings, 2000).

## 4.2 Innovation in Organizations

Transition to carbon neutrality is requiring new feedstocks, new processes and even new business models for chemical industry and innovation sciences analyze predictors for their adoption in business organizations. Innovation itself is seen as a process of creating something new and as the result of this process (Barringer & Ireland, 2010). Most innovations are carried out in organizations where innovators collaborate and work together to innovate. First, innovations are necessary in order to remain competitive, and the ability to innovate is a key determinant for economic performance in business organizations. It promotes economic growth and the competitive advantage of companies. Second, several factors at the personal, group and organizational level of the companies and the environment of the organization influence the rate of innovation in organizations (Woodman, Sawyer & Griffin, 1993). At each level, from the individual, group, organizational to environmental level, the requirements for innovation are different and the determinants that drive innovation efficiency are presented in the following sections (Mumford & Hunter, 2005).

### 4.2.1 Individual Level

At the individual level, certain personality traits have a positive effect on the innovation rate. Knowledge and skills, their cognitive activities, disposition and motivation describe the skills and ways of thinking of creative and strategically thinking people. Required mindset for innovative personalities is openness, flexibility and autonomy. Innovation is a social process and requires communication skills. Individuals interact in the organization in a complex setting (Mumford & Hunter, 2005). The production of new and useful knowledge for innovation involves creativity. Creativity seeds require values and beliefs in creativity and openness as well as the cognitive ability for strategic, systems and transformational thinking (Dundon, 2002). Organizations can encourage creativity through exercises, workshops, and training (West, 1999). In addition to creativity, knowledge building processes, work culture and innovation-supporting leadership styles are determinants of effective innovation (Mumford, 2000).

### 4.2.2 Group Level

Organizational structure and management attitude have a great influence on the innovation activities of companies at group level. Specialization and functional differentiation in groups and departments support the effectiveness of the innovation process. The innovation performance is positively influenced by a supportive attitude of the management and the availability of technical knowledge resources. Factors with a negative influence on innovation performance are formalization and centralization (Damanpour, 1991). Leadership and management advocacy play a central role for the climate and culture of the group and for the orientation towards successful innovations. Leaders in successful innovation teams must have seasoned skills and mindsets to enable the innovation process. Knowledge of techniques and activities, of human behavior and interpersonal processes; and analytical ability to solve problems and identify opportunities are cognitive skills of innovation managers. Management advocacy is an instrument for leading employees and managers translate the strategy and allocate resources accordingly (Yukl, 2010). Managers also shape the team culture, which is based on the values, beliefs and experiences of group members and the leadership. Managers have a role model function through teaching and coaching and shape the culture through allocating rewards and status (Schein, 2004). Group culture, values and a positive climate, and leadership that supports innovation and enables work processes have a positive effect on innovation output at the group level. Ad hoc teams and small work groups are effective for incremental innovations. Core design teams, a larger structure, and larger group size are better suited to complex design-driven development tasks. (Mumford & Hunter, 2005).

### 4.2.3 Organizational Level

Formalization and centralization are the determinants of successful eco-product innovation at the organizational level. The internal formalization of innovation processes correlates positively with eco- innovativeness and connectedness within the organization. On the other hand, centralization has a negative effect on exploratory innovation (Jansen, Van Den Bosch & Volberda 2006). Control elements of management, resource allocation and management support influence creativity and innovation within workgroups. The top management controls the activities according to project selection, performance goals and corporate culture. Funding resources and active engagement signal management support for innovation and motivate employees to be more engaged (Mumford & Hunter, 2005). The attitude of top managers to innovation and people plays an essential role in attitude and behavior in companies. The attitude of managers towards entrepreneurship has a positive effect on the creation of innovations and innovation adoption (Damanpour, & Schneider, 2006). Further determinants for the organizational innovativeness are system openness and the degree of connection with external innovation networks. Centralization and formalization trend have a negative impact on the ability to innovate in general. To some extend, formulization of processes increases the success rate of innovation activities. Centralization improves the efficiency of design-driven innovations. The ability to innovate correlates with size, the ability to absorb failures, the complexity of the structure and the internal and external connectedness of companies (Rogers, 2003).

### 4.2.4 Environmental Level

Determinants for successful eco-product innovations at the environmental level are the ability to cooperate and the flow of information. Technology transfer is an important factor in the diffusion of eco-innovations. Complementary companies and external R&D partners, e.g. consultants, universities and research institutes are external sources of knowledge. An example of spill-over effects is the technology transfer from lead markets in Western Europe as an important source for companies in Eastern Europe (Horbach, 2016). Cooperative practices can include upstream exchanges with suppliers or downstream exchanges with customers. This includes knowledge sharing with universities and the academic community (Vachon, & Klassen, 2008). Open innovation, co-creation and cooperation with companies for joint innovation projects as well as the interaction of key stakeholder engagement are named as drivers for eco-innovations (Kiefer, González, & Carrillo-Hermosilla, 2019).

### 4.2.5 Innovation Processes

Research teams are more effective than individual researchers alone and produce more new ideas, patents or innovations. Innovation teams perform different tasks than other teams in organizations and are dependent on different resources. They don't perform routines and have the explicit goal of creating something new. Structured innovation processes are suggested to increase the success rate and guide innovators through the sometimes lengthy and resourceful innovation process. The tailored innovation processes guide the individual through the development and implementation of innovations and improve cooperation within the teams and the organization (Thayer, Petruzzelli & McClurg, 2018). The learning processes are enforced by the orientation and cooperation of the individuals. Temporary project teams made up of different specialist departments are best suited for innovation and solving complex problems (Lam, 2006). A structured and linear approach to innovation is the stage-gate process. The approach divides the process into 4–5 phases of preliminary assessment, business case preparation, development, testing and market introduction (Cooper, 1990) (Fig. 4.1).

**Fig. 4.1** Stage-gate-process, modelled after Cooper (1990)

Another structured approach is the parallel prototyping strategy, where product development is unguided by developing a number of alternative solutions and customers choosing the most appropriate for their needs. Another approach is the incremental improvement of previously introduced products (Terwiesch, 2009) (Fig. 4.2).

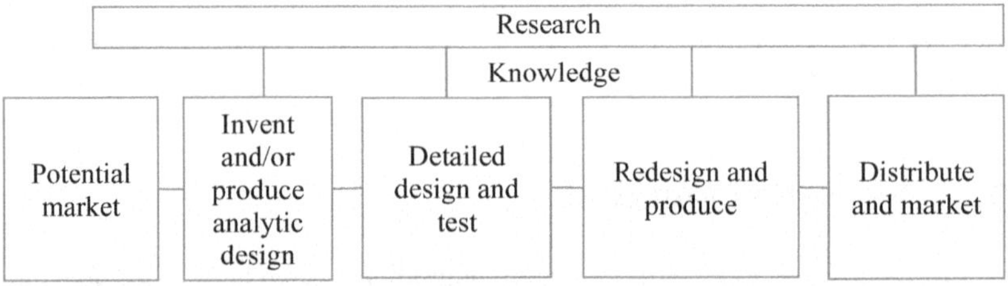


**Fig. 4.2** Elements of the chain-linked-model (Kline & Rosenberg, 1986)

The chain-linked model completes the linear innovation process with learning and feedback loops at every level. Each innovation level is linked to a knowledge pool and innovation network outside the organization. The innovation network outside the organization provides the desired knowledge, market needs and information on new technologies. The chain-linked model can be understood as a problem-solving process that is supported by cooperation with external partners, search loops, feedback and sources from outside the organization (Kline & Rosenberg, 1986).

## 4.3 Innovation Scope

The creation of a novelty and a change is seen as the consequence of innovation. Although all innovations represent novelties, they differ in the degree of efforts and consequences. The following paragraph present different kinds of innovations from a larger perspective which apply also to innovations with the aim to reach carbon neutrality and fall under the categories are social, environmental and preventive innovations. Open versus closed, radical and disruptive innovations are categories with specific efforts and consequences for the innovators and are also discussed in this paragraph.

### 4.3.1 Social, Environmental and Preventive Innovations

According to Schumpeter (quoted in Frank, 1998), entrepreneurial innovation leads to economic change. From the consumer's point of view, the novelty of an innovation is the change in behavior or the need to learn if the innovation is implemented. This definition also includes social changes as innovations (Hirsch, Peters, & Shepherd, 2010). Environmental innovations, or eco-innovations for short, are classified from the perspective of the environment and reduce harmful effects such as environmental degradation and pollution or increase resource efficiency (Kemp, 2008; OECD, 2009). Preventive innovations are novelties that reduce the likelihood of an adverse event for adopters. Examples are seat belts, soil conservation and contraceptives as well as, on a larger scale, substitution technologies for coal-fired systems to mitigate climate change. Peculiar for preventive innovations is the slow adoption rate. The reason is the delayed reward to the adopting an innovation that prevents an event, that is perceived as uncertain, distant in time and difficult to demonstrate (Rogers, 2002; 2003).

### 4.3.2 Open Innovation

Open innovation as an antonym for closed innovation practices that emphasize cooperation, alliances and the co-creation of innovations in cooperation with business partners. The open innovation paradigm combines internal and external innovation skills and uses tactics such as reviewing, licensing or acquiring external technologies, funding and collaborating with universities, research institutes, corporations and start-ups (Chesbrough, 2003). The innovation process is shifted away from internal research and development and incorporates the knowledge and innovation skills of surrounding companies (Chesbrough, Salter, Vanhaverbeke & Westa, 2014). Tactical activities of resource allocation and procurement are complemented by regulatory monitoring activities, the evaluation of ongoing political changes as well as innovation and market observation activities (Loorbach, 2010). Further sources of information are customer and supplier contacts, market research, observation of competitors and international contacts in industry associations and consulting firms (Mumford & Hunter, 2005). Innovation flows are inbound, which use the inflow of knowledge to develop internal skills, and outbound, in order to expand the market potential for innovation (Huizingh, 2011). Cooperation and external knowledge acquisition have been identified as relevant determinants for the successful dissemination and adoption of eco-innovations in general (Belin, Horbach & Oltra, 2011).

### 4.3.3 Radical Innovation

Radical innovation is an antonym to incremental innovation. Both types are new on the market but differ in the degree of technical change and market uncertainty (Freeman, 1982 in Rennings, 2000). Incremental innovations are characterized as continuous improvements to existing technological systems. Minor modifications are part of continuous changes and relate to progress along a technological path that is defined by a technological paradigm (Dosi, 1982) (Fig. 4.3).

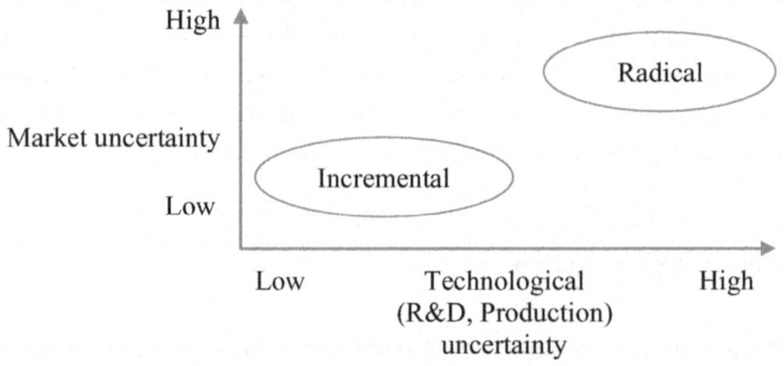


**Fig. 4.3** Risk in radical innovation according to McDermott & O'Connor (2002)

Radical innovations are significantly new technologies and require a dramatic change in behavior. They change the technological trajectory and paradigms and are associated with the highest level of market uncertainty and risk of failure (McDermott, & O'Connor, 2002). Level of uncertainty, risk of failure, learning requirements and need for change are described as a classifier for radical versus incremental innovation on a continuous scale. There is no consensus on the definition of radical innovation and terms or radical, groundbreaking, disruptive, discontinuous, significant or pioneering are used interchangeably. The need to learn before adopting the innovation is another determinate for radicalness.

The higher the learning requirements, the more radical the innovation. (Amara, Landry, Becheikh & Ouimet, 2004).

### 4.3.4 Disruptive Innovation

Disruptive and radical innovation both have a high degree of uncertainty, the risk of failure, learning requirements and the need for change in common. The term disruptive adds the implication of the radicalness to the industry landscape. Disruptive innovations change the industry, value chains or business models and are an opportunity for newcomers to replace both traditional technology and incumbent companies. Disruptive technologies have a number of different product attributes, such as: Easier, cheaper, more reliable or more convenient, but inferior to the main attributes of the sustaining technology (Christensen, 1997). Disruptive innovations have the potential to change the demands and needs of a mainstream market. Their emergence starts in niche and low-end markets and is rated as inferior by mainstream customers. After the creation of new niche markets, they expand into the mainstream market and offer new market entrants with superseding technologies the opportunity to replace existing products and business models (Thomond & Lettice, 2002). The question is when will a radical new technology approach and take over the market. Incumbent companies on existent technological trajectories must adopt the new technologies, and timing is key to switching the S-curves (Fig. 4.4).

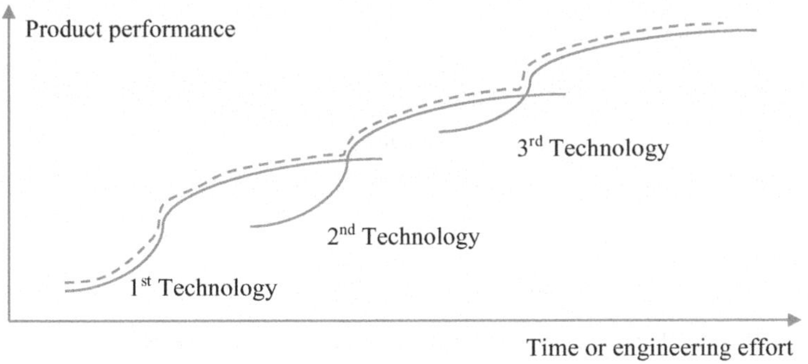


**Fig. 4.4** Prescriptive S-curve strategy by Christensen (1992)

Christensen (1992) suggests following the prescriptive S-curve strategy on the dashed line as a hypothetical trajectory for successful transition management. Attackers are typically not rewarded to exploit the new technology as a first mover. There is no first mover benefit. Large incumbents are advised to switch to S-curves of new technologies late, when the market has been prepared by the early adopters (Christensen, 1992). If incumbents fail to allocate the resources and to develop the new technology, they offer opportunities for new entrants and are threatened with replacement (Govindarajan & Kopalle, 2006).

## 4.4 Ecological Modernization

The second large theory cluster gathers around environmental science studies. Ecological modernization is the legitimation and motivation for changes with the goal of climate neutrality. The ecological modernization theory analyzes imbalances between human activity and the environment, their causes and the policies for sustainability. The theory usually has three perspectives: It aims to promote economic development, ensure ecological sustainability that does not exceed the capacities of the earth, and welfare and justice (Mol & Spaargaren, 2000). The mission of every ecological modernization policy is the balance between economic development, ecological sustainability and social justice and welfare (Huber, 2000) (Fig. 4.5).

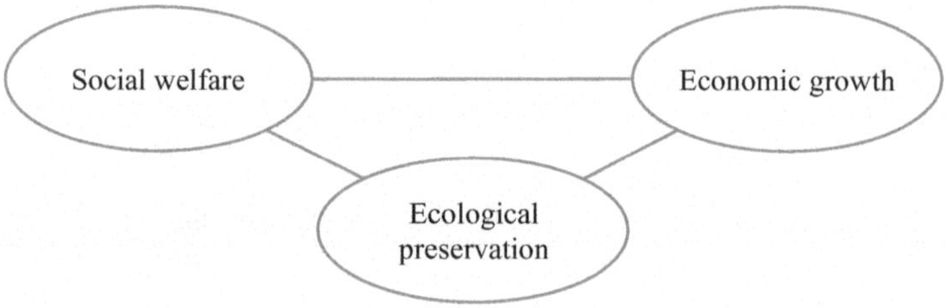


**Fig. 4.5** Ecological modernization model (Huber, 2000)

The concept of ecological modernization calls for measures to overcome the existing imbalances between industrial production and resource consumption and aims at the reconciliation of human activity and the environment. Ecological modernization theory considers several goals for a sustainable development strategy, including the use of natural resources and economic growth, and modernization results from a process of political, economic and social change (Eisenstadt, 1966; Gibbs, 1988). The concept provides the basis for political reforms and a framework for social, economic, political and ecological changes. The theory of ecological modernization is based on the description and explanation of environmental degradation and its causes. It goes beyond repairing and compensating for ecological damage and calls for a mind change and a shift of production and consumption to a sustainable, ecological economy. It requires producers and consumers to change their attitudes and behavior (Gibbs, 1988; Mol, Spaargaren & Sonnenfeld, 2009). The interaction between society and the economy requires political activities to steer this process. The institutional reforms within society are regulated by political actors. Political instruments are used to initiate and control the ecological modernization process (Mol & Spaargaren, 1992; Mol, 2002). Such instruments are regulatory push and pull incentives, which are crucial for the introduction of ecological innovations. Political instruments are reporting tools, auditing, eco-label branding, eco-taxes, allowances and much more are described in the literature review. The theory also describes economic growth that is triggered by ecological modernization itself (Rennings, 2000; Spaargaren, 2003).

### 4.4.1 Corporate Social Responsibility

Corporate Social Responsibility (CSR) is often used for corporate environmental and sustainability issues. CSR is an instrument for voluntary action for ecological modernization and an agenda for companies that creates value not only for owners and shareholders, but also for society. The holistic approach is based on the idea of the triple bottom lines of the 3Ps: People, Planet and Profit (Slaper & Hall, 2011) (Fig. 4.6).

**CSR Terminology**

- Triple- bottom line
- People-planet-performance
- Integrated reporting
- Corporate social responsibility (CSR)
- Sustainability

**Fig. 4.6** CSR terminology

The idea of the triple bottom line was originally born as a voluntary initiative for companies to achieve better sustainability performance. The main element of the concept is a balance of interests. Companies want a positive image and avoid negative public confrontations. The idea of the triple-bottom-line encourages businesses to track economic, social, and environmental performance into the annual report of organizations. Sustainability is viewed as an opportunity to gain long-term competitiveness. Stakeholders also profit from CSR and NGOs and public actors can achieve their goals through these voluntary sustainability initiatives (Elkington, 1998). CSR practice beyond the legal requirements contributes to the financial performance of companies and is rewarded with a positive effect on market value (Yoon, Lee & Byun, 2018). The interaction between customers and suppliers creates a further impetus for voluntary environmental innovations and ecological modernization. Market needs and customer expectations lead to a demand for environmentally friendly goods and technologies and are drivers for ecological innovations in companies (García-Granero, Piedra-Munoz. & Galdeano-Gomez, 2018; Boons & Lüdeke-Freund, 2013).

### 4.4.2 Environmental Regulations

Environmental regulations shift the motivation from customer orientation to compelling technological changes where markets are not effective enough for ecological modernization. Ecological innovation is mandatory through policies and environmental regulations. Compliance with environmental regulations is seen as an opportunity for companies to upgrade existing technologies and bring new products to market to generate revenue (Nidumolu, Prahalad & Rangaswami, 2009). Regulation can have a positive effect on economic growth. They drive environmental innovations and signal the need for technological improvements. Regulations create clarity and inform about negative properties of existing technologies, reduce uncertainty about future market requirements and encourage investments in alternatives with an improved environmental profile. Finally, regulations create pressure for progress and levels the playing field for transition (Porter & van der Linde, 1995). Policies and regulations can guide incremental improvements towards environmental progress and are the tools to facilitate the escape from technological lock-out situations (Frantzeskaki & Loorbach, 2010).

### 4.4.3 Lock-out Effects

Lock-out effects occur when the switching costs are higher than the economic benefit. The innovative technology is locked out and society is locked-in in a traditional technological regime. In some markets with a dominant design of an existing technology, ecological modernizations and environmental innovations are excluded from the adoption. Reasons for lock-out effects are individual technology architectures resulting from standardization, economies of scale and benefits of learning cures (Schiller, 1998). Other reasons for lock-out effects are high investment costs for innovations and for new infrastructure. In addition, opportunity costs strengthen the continued use of traditional technology. Additional economic barriers to environmental innovation arise from unpriced costs, as in a typical tragedy of the commons effect, and from many ecological externalities (Palley, 2017). Another reason for lock-out effects for environmental innovations are mental factors. New sustainable technologies have different characteristics that are considered inferior and associated with uncertainties. They do not correspond to the shared experiences and expectations of customers. The situation supports the interest in sticking to the existing technological paradigm and hinders the transformation to a sustainable economy (Perkin, 2003). After all, technological regime changes are often radical technologies and have long lead times. They require special skills, infrastructure and institutional changes for their operation (Kemp, 2003). The multi-level perspective of socio-technical transition management has developed strategies for overcoming regime paradigms and lock-out effects. The main elements of transition management are innovation activities in niches and institutions that support economic change (Nelson & Winter, 1982). In the following sections, elements of the technological regimes and changes are discussed in more detail.

## 4.5 Multi-level Perspective of Transition

Multi-level perspective of socio-technical transitions forms the framework for transition management and ecological modernization and is a theory to explain driving forces for adoption of innovations with the goal of environmental modernization. The research branch is rooted in two theoretical clusters, innovation research and environmental science studies and has been applied to low-carbon system transformation (Geels, 2018; Geels, Sovacool, Schwanen & Sorrell, 2017; Loorbach, Frantzeskaki & Avelino, 2017). Technical progress is usually driven by economic forces and influenced by institutional and social factors on the market demand side. On the supply side, problem-solving activities provide science-technology production and operate along technological trajectories. Advances in the technological trajectory are sustained by complementarity technologies with shared patterns of knowledge, experience and skill that make it difficult to change trajectories (Dosi, 1982). The transition to a sustainable regime requires a change in the technological trajectory but is blocked by factors known as the lock-out effect. For a regime change, the question arises of how the opportunities for innovation can be improved, which R&D strategy is required and what are the environmental factors for the breakout from the old regime to a new regime (Nelson & Winter, 1982). Transition research is concerned with the answers to how technological regime changes can take place and initially focused on the analysis of historical cases of economic and technological transitions. Three approaches to transition research are presented: Socio-technical, socio-institutional and socio-ecological transition models. The three models have in common path dependency, regimes, niches and governance. They provide guidelines for transition strategies and policy instruments (Loorbach, Frantzeskaki & Avelino, 2017).

### 4.5.1 Socio-technical Transitions

The multi-level perspective of socio-technical systems provides a framework for the dynamics of socio-technical transition and regime change. The analysis of the technological system has three perspectives: The description of the three levels of the socio-technical system, landscape, regime and niches, then the connecting social and technical perspective and a governance for transition management (Geels, 2011; Grin, Rotmans & Schot, 2010). Technologies are seen in the social context of practices and are mutually dependent. Technological regimes are sets of rules in a complex of engineering practices and technologies that are embedded in institutions and infrastructures. Regimes are intermediaries between specific innovations and overall socio-technical landscapes. The sets of rules are the result of previous changes that have emerged as novelties within existing regimes and socio-technical landscapes. Novelties start at the micro-level of local practices, spread over time, and eventually change the socio-technical landscape (Rip & Kemp, 1998). A dynamic multi-level perspective on technological systems was developed by Geels (2002), with a focus on micro-, meso- and macro-levels of economic sectors. Socio-technical regimes are viewed as a patchwork of technology, user practices, application domains (markets), cultural expectations and social practices, infrastructure, industrial structure, politics and scientific knowledge. Changes at the landscape level put the regime under pressure and create windows of opportunities for new technologies. Changes at the landscape level are cultural changes, demographic trends, broad policy changes, and are generally slow (Fig. 4.7).

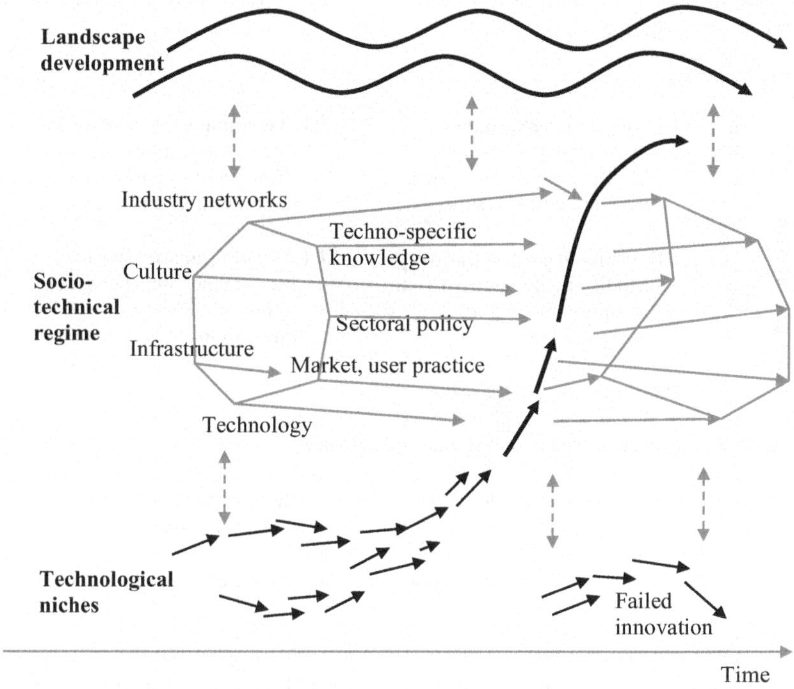


**Fig. 4.7** The dynamic multi-level perspective on technological systems (Geels, 2002)

Thick long arrows represent the slowly developing landscape developments in the multi-level model. Niches at the micro-level of the socio-technical system account for the generation and development of radical innovations. Novelties emerge in the niches in the context of the existing regimes and landscapes with its specific environmental conditions. Many may seem promising at the beginning, but there is no guarantee of success. Narrow arrows represent the emergence of radical innovations. As the radical innovations stabilize, they gradually become a dominant design and the stabilizing radical innovations are represented in the multilevel model with arrows that become longer and thicker (Geels, 2002). Geels and Schot (2007) propose a transition typology depending on the extent of the landscape pressure and the readiness for market introduction of the innovation. Without landscape pressure, the reproduction process (P0) follows the technological trajectory with individual small improvements of the technologies. If the landscape pressure is low, either a transformation pathway (P1) without niche innovations or, if radical niche innovations have been developed, a reconfiguration pathway (P4) emerges (Fig. 4.8).

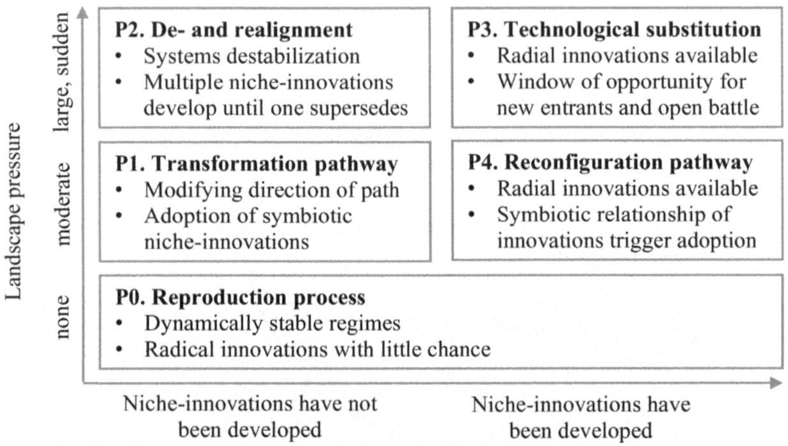


**Fig. 4.8** Typology of sociotechnical transition pathways after Geels & Schot (2007)

Incumbent firms generally grow in transformation paths with the new regime, while reconfiguration paths include new alliances between incumbents and new entrants and a takeover occurs for economic reasons. When the landscape pressure is great, sudden or shock-like, the socio-technical regime is destabilized. Several niche innovations develop and coexist until a dominant design is displaced in the de- and realignment (P2). If the radical innovation has already been developed, the avalanche effect offers a window of opportunity for technological substitution (P3) (Geels & Schot, 2007). Selective pressure on a socio-technical regime can be addressed through governance with the aim of promoting more sustainable solutions. Governance can change the pace and direction of the transformation process and select the instruments. It can either support "endogenous renewal" through the creation of new knowledge, new markets and new resources, or instead promote "purposeful transition" with pressure on regime membership, resource allocation and legal conditions (Smith, Stirling & Berkhout, 2004). Transition studies are not only paying attention to the emergence and growth of innovations into a new technological paradigm, but also to the destabilization and decline of maturing technologies. Socio-technical transitions are understood as iterative processes of building and dismantling socio-technical regimes and changes follow path-dependent principles (Fig. 4.9).

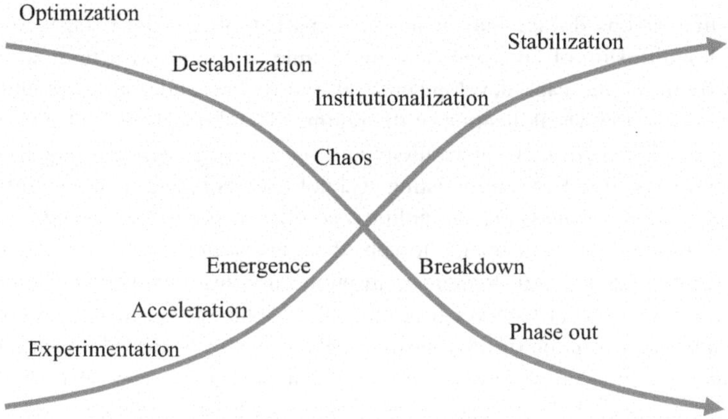


**Fig. 4.9** Dynamics of societal transitions after Loorbach, Frantzeskaki & Avelino (2017)

Technological regimes in decline go through phases of optimization, destabilization, chaos, collapse and phasing out. Emerging technologies go through optimization phases of experimentation, acceleration, emergence, institutionalization and stabilization over time. The actual transition is chaotic and disruptive as combinations of emerging alternatives grow into the new regime (Loorbach, Frantzeskaki & Avelino, 2017). Socio-technical transitions can take several decades and are divided into four phases of core activities (Fig. 4.10).

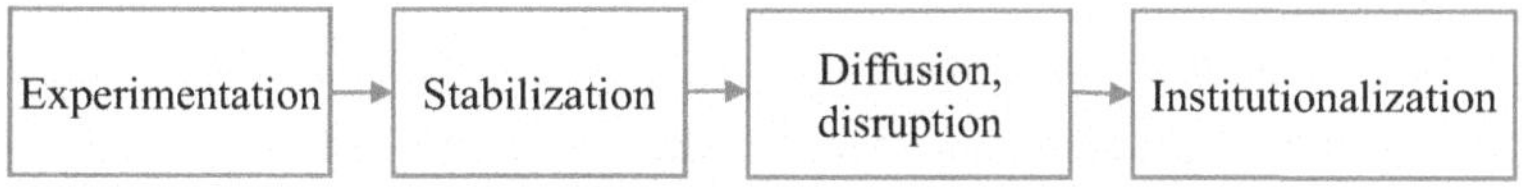


**Fig. 4.10** Phases of socio-technical transition after Geels (2019)

The first phase is characterized by experimentation and trial-and-error learning. There is a lot of uncertainty, competing claims and promises, and high failure rates. In the second stage, innovations stabilize into a dominant design. The second stage is characterized by activities that aggregate around standardization, prototyping, articulation of best practices, product specifications, and design guidelines. Innovators cooperate in engineering communities, standardization committees or industry associations to form alliances for open sourcing. The socio-cognitive activities help to stabilize the innovation trajectories. Then, radical innovations diffuse into mainstream markets in the third stage. Specific drivers for diffusion of environmental niche-innovations are structural windows of opportunity. Landscape developments put the regime under pressure and lead to tensions and the destabilization of the regime. The third phase is characterized by struggles between niche innovations and the existing regime along conflicting lines in society. New and existing technologies compete, new entrants and incumbents fight for market share, political conflict lines run over agenda setting, problem framing and adjustments to subsidies, taxes and regulations and social groups contest for cultural dominance in public debates. Attention is also given to phase out of existent technologies, built of societal and business support, and to alleviate the disruption of the transition. Blueprints of historical transitions are formulated for low-carbon innovation policy that should focus on R&D, financial incentives and stakeholder engagement. In the fourth phase, the new innovation is institutionalized and anchored as a new standard in the socio-technical regime (Geels, Sovacool, Schwanen & Sorrell, 2017; Geels, 2019). Driving forces that support the diffusion during stage 3 of the model are summarized (Table 4.2).

**Table 4.2** Drivers for diffusion of environmental niche-innovations (Geels, 2019)

| Drivers for diffusion of environmental niche-innovations |
|---|
| • Price/performance improvements<br>• Economies of scale<br>• Development of complementary technologies<br>• Support from powerful actors<br>• Structural windows of opportunity created by landscape developments<br>• Taking advantages from regime pressure, tensions and regime destabilization |

### 4.5.2 Transitions in Retrospect

Historical cases of socio-technical transitions were examined as examples of the generalizability of the multilevel perspective and the analysis of the respective niches played a decisive role in the course of the transition. In historical cases, traditional technologies and social practices dissolve over time and new social practices realign themselves with the newly built large technical systems. Transitions are complex processes that cannot be overlooked or controlled from one point of view. The de-alignment and re-alignment processes are emergent results of interactions between social groups. Social groups try to cope with the transition, to find their way through searching and learning, interact in power struggles, controversies and debates (Geels, 2005b) (Table 4.3).

**Table 4.3** Case studies of historic and present socio-technical transitions

- Transition in water supply and personal hygiene in the Netherlands 1850–1930 (Geels, 2005a)
- Transition pathway from horse-drawn carriages to automobiles 1860–1930 (Geels, 2005b)
- Transformation of aviation systems and the shift from propeller to turbojet 1930–1970 (Geels, 2006)
- Substitution pathway of the German and transformation pathway of the British renewable electricity transitions (Geels et al., 2016)

A leaning from historic cases is the social shaping of regime change and patters are transferred to the current case for sustainable transition. At the beginning, the change is prepared through social narratives and a change in values and beliefs. Niche innovations are developed as a solution and the niche actors de-legitimize the regime by classifying industrial practices as negative. Opponents of niche innovations defend existing regimes and point out possible disadvantages of niche innovations. Eventually activists and social movements develop discourses until political actors respond to the pressure. Sustainability transitions are different because technological change is prepared by the social context and not by the common market-driven need for innovations (Geels, 2010).

### 4.5.3 Socio-institutional Transition

The socio-institutional perspectives on sustainability transitions emphasize political and institutional changes in order to avoid chaos and manage smooth transitions. The aim of governance is to navigate from an equilibrium to a new stable one by reorganizing a socio-technical system. The institutional dimension of change is normative and relates to the protection of niche innovations (Loorbach, Frantzeskaki & Avelino, 2017). Environmental innovations require regulatory push / pull policies and protected niche spaces to support against a lack of competitiveness and lock-out effects. Public laws create these shielded spaces with less competitive pressure for the development of niche innovations. Innovators with alternative cultural values can experiment with the new technologies that have inferior performance at the beginning. In these niches, new norms, routines and competitiveness establish themselves for widespread diffusion as path-breaking innovations (Geels, 2014; Smith & Raven, 2012). Experimental niche innovations require technology-push support to strengthen market competitiveness, and regulations to undermine established regimes and to create market pull support (Raven & Smith, 2012) (Table 4.4).

**Table 4.4** Signs for policy change and social tipping points

| Signs for policy change and social tipping points | |
|---|---|
| • Experimental niche innovations receive push/pull support<br>• Public funding for universities, institutes and private coalitions<br>• Regulations and laws in preparation to restrict use of incumbent technologies | • Destabilization through landscape developments, accidents, crises and megatrend events<br>• Advocates of alternative technologies form coalitions<br>• Social tipping point is close if supporters' share reaches 17–20% |

Landscape factors that trigger regime change are university niche strategies, research institutes / science-society-strategies and coalitions of institutions and individual actors. National niche-strategies and coalitions are helpful in promoting sustainability and developing the potential of regional capabilities

(Schneidewind & Augenstein, 2012). Political change is explained by the framework of advocacy coalitions that frame the political discourse. In phases of destabilization (adaptive cycle model) and landscape developments (multi-level perspective), new political issues, accidents, crises, megatrends or technological advances in other sectors put pressure on the existing systems. Proponents of alternative technologies will engage in political discourse and strengthen their position in the public media and their links with political parties. Following the discourse, changes in advocacy coalitions and in basic beliefs are the beginning of a tipping point in political change (Markard, Suter & Ingold, 2016). The participation in social movements increases the pressure on the established actors in the political discourse. The pressure to change rises and manifests itself in processes of expansion in the social network until a social tipping dynamic occurs. It is reported that a market or population share of 17–20% is enough to pass the tipping point and become the dominant pattern. The time it takes to trigger the tipping should not exceed 15 years (Otto et al., 2020).

### 4.5.4 Socio-ecological Transition

The socio-ecological approach to transition is based on adaptive cycle models and the resilience theory in ecosystems. This approach to transition provides an understanding of the dynamics of the ecosystem during the transition from one stable equilibrium to another and patterns for the progression of resistance through regime change. The socio-ecological approach emphasizes the study of thresholds and resilience of ecosystems (Loorbach, Frantzeskaki & Avelino, 2017) (Fig. 4.11).

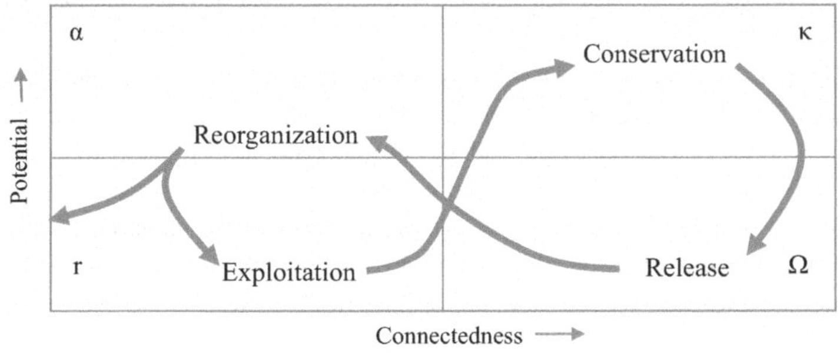


**Fig. 4.11** The adaptive cycle with four ecosystem functions (Holling & Gunderson, 2002)

The adaptive cycle model is a schematic representation of the transition phases of an ecosystem. The succession of ecosystems is seen as controlled by exploitation with rapid growth in an arena of scramble competition. The phase of full symmetrical competition refers to a situation in which all competitors have access to the resources. The growth phase (r), which corresponds to an entrepreneurial market, is followed by a conservation phase (κ), in which slow accumulation and competitive competition optimize resource efficiency. Two additional functions are needed to describe the decay and restructuring of the ecosystem. The closely interconnected ecosystem becomes increasingly fragile in the conservation phase until it is suddenly released from the stage due to external factors. The sudden release phase (Ω) is followed by a reorganization phase (α) (Fig. 4.12).

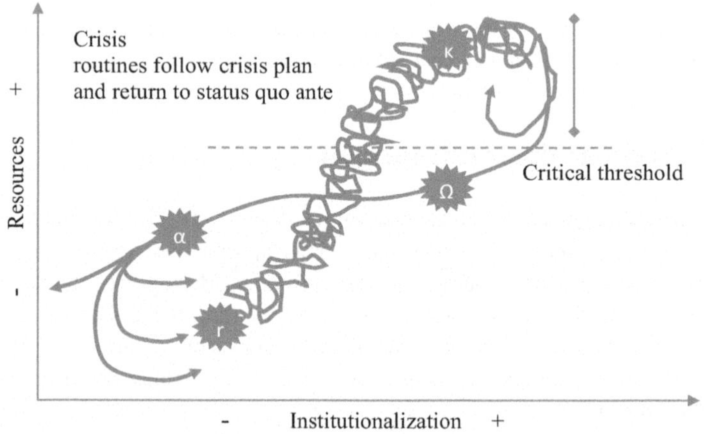


**Fig. 4.12** Adaptive cycle applied to social systems (Fath, Dean & Katzmaier, 2015)

A stylized representation of the four ecosystem phases and event sequences is combined in the adaptive cycle model. In this model, the accumulated resources represent the potential and the connectedness represent the degree of mutual dependence of elements in the ecosystem. High networking means less redundancies and higher efficiency. The progression in the adaptive cycle (α, r, κ and Ω) proceeds from the exploration in the growth phase, denoted by r, to slow changes and long-term, stable conditions in the conversation phase, denoted by κ. Rapid release phases, denoted by Ω, are triggered by external factors such as disasters and other disruptive events and put the ecosystem back into a rapid reorganization phase known as the α phase. Reorganization is equivalent to innovation and restructuring in an industry at times of economic recession or social transformation. The progression from r to κ represents long periods of predictable behavior and short periods of chaotic behavior during which the boundaries of the ecosystem are tested (Holling & Gunderson, 2002). Another version applies the adaptive cycle model to social systems. The model adds the critical threshold to the maintenance κ phase and the systems collapse when resources fall below the threshold. Resilient ecosystems successfully navigate through all phases of growth r, development and conservation κ, release Ω and reorientation α of the adaptive cycle. Resilient ecosystems have resources to grow during the r phase and to maintain structure and complexity during the maturity of the κ phase. Contingency plans prevent collapse in the event of shocks and enable a return to the status quo ante. Success factors for a reorganization in the α phase require capacities, resources, skills and cultures to realign the organization. The resilience of the system is a synonym for sustainability and shows the stability over time and the maintenance of the system functions. Resilient ecosystems withstand disturbances with little deformation and recover in the reorganization α phase from the release Ω phase (Fath, Dean & Katzmaier, 2015). The table contains guidelines and traps for successful transition management (Table 4.5).

When ecosystems collapse, windows of opportunity arise. These opportunities are rare, and breakdown usually requires combinations of different developments (Holling, Gunderson & Peterson, 2002). Incumbent agents can get confused in the release phase Ω and fast exploration of niche-innovations, testing and prototyping in the reorganization phase α deliver opportunities for new entrants. The rapid orientation in the transition of the ecosystem prepares growth in the new normal. Phasedown of the old requires a smooth and structured dismantling. Sustainability transitions offer many opportunities, but there is a risk that companies, workers and parts of the communities will be decoupled from progress and posted. Attention to politics is needed to avoid victimization of parts of society in low-carbon transitions (Sovacool, 2021).

**Table 4.5** Resilience strategies of adaptive phases (Fath, Dean & Katzmaier, 2015)

| Trap | Risks | Guideline |
|---|---|---|
| **Poverty trap during r-phase** | • Lack of positive feedback loops<br>• Growth is not driven internally | • Sufficient resources for activation<br>• Network connections<br>• Autocatalysis and self-sustained expansion |
| **Rigidity trap during κ-phase** | • High concentration of influence<br>• Vulnerability to disturbance due to reduced diversity | • Crisis plans respond to disturbance<br>• Reserves to reestablish the equilibrium |
| **Dissolution trap during Ω-phase** | • Confusion during crisis and collapse<br>• Dissolution of social systems | • Large resource stocks<br>• Maintain vital functions<br>• Learning skills and reorientation needed |
| **Vagabond trap during α-phase** | • Inability to reorientate<br>• Loss of systems memory<br>• Circling without moving into r-phase | • Awareness of irreversibility of disturbance<br>• Systemic development during r and κ-phase |

## 4.6 Technological Innovation Systems

Technological innovation systems research is another framework for transition management and ecological modernization and adds the actors, spatial and temporal perspectives to the innovation studies. An industry sector is viewed as a technological innovation system and the framework provides understanding for the dynamics of technological change, including ecological modernization. Technological innovation systems framework has been applied to identify actors, strategies and resources for sustainability transitions, e. g. UN sustainable development goals and the Paris climate agreement (Farla, Markard, Raven & Coenen, 2012; Markard, Geels & Raven, 2020). Originally, the idea of innovation systems was described as an important innovation driver in national and regional innovation systems and relationship networks. New discoveries, inventions, insights, and improvements have been generated within the boundaries of nation-states before they form intellectual capital (Freeman, 1995). Indicators to assess national innovation systems (NIS) are R&D efforts, patent applications, quality of education systems, cooperation between universities and industry and the availability of venture capital. Finally, technological innovation systems (TIS) are broken into smaller sectoral innovation systems and extend to global technological networks of relationships.

### 4.6.1 Sectoral Innovation Systems

Technological innovation systems overlap with the geographical dimensions of national innovation systems. They are combinations of interconnected sectors and companies, institutions and regulators across borders and they are embedded networks within technological regimes and niche innovators. Technology diffusion takes place as a social process between individuals and collectives of the variable network of the technological innovation system. TIS indicators are a range of actors, networks, relevant institutions, R&D and regulatory activities such as patent publications, guidelines, laws and standards, and monitoring of these indicators is necessary to understand the dynamics of technological change (Hekkert, Suurs, Negro, Kuhlmann & Smits, 2007). The indicators are categorized into structural and functional elements. Main structural elements are actors, including companies, institutions legal and regulatory power and networks of agents for learning and political discourse. Knowledge development, entrepreneurial experimentation and resource formation are examples for functional elements of technology innovation systems. The formation of a supportive system enables entrepreneurial activity and the formation and evolution of technology innovation systems. Identifying systems drivers supports regulators for governance of protected spaces and nursing market and it supports entrepreneurs for knowledge development and direction search (Bergek, Hekkert & Jakobson, 2008) (Fig. 4.13).

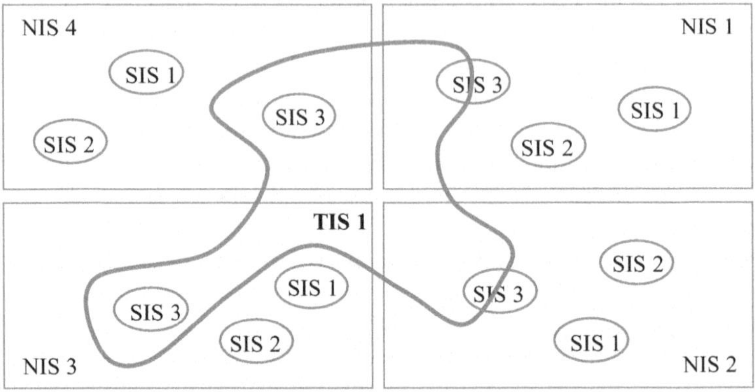


**Fig. 4.13** Boundaries between National (NIS), sectoral (SIS) and technology specific innovation system (TIS) after Hekkert, Suurs, Negro, Kuhlmann & Smits (2007)

Next to competence building factors, complementary technologies have a crucial role in socio-technical transitions as they accelerate technology development. Complementary technologies within industry sectors have a positive interaction and are competence enhancing. The combinations yield synergies and create value for each other but also lead to an interdependency with the risk of bottlenecks in case of supply shortages. The graphical presentation of technological innovation systems provides a useful tool for analysis (Markard & Hoffmann, 2016) (Table 4.6).

**Table 4.6** Strengths and weaknesses of regional technological innovation systems (Hellsmark et al., 2016)

| Possible strengths of regional innovation systems | Possible weaknesses of regional innovation systems |
|---|---|
| • Policy instruments in support of environmental innovations<br>• Knowledge development and diffusion<br>• Strong networks between academia and industry<br>• Experiences from the industry<br>• Long-term research efforts | • Market risk and absence of niche markets for products<br>• Lack of basic funding for research<br>• Difficulty in retaining key competences<br>• Lack of confidence in government<br>• Lack of participation from key parts of industry |

Regional areas of the technology innovation systems are places that enable local cooperation, niche innovations and competence building. Regional innovation systems are characterized by strengths and limitations due to their narrow expansion (Hellsmark, Mossberg, Söderholm & Frishammar, 2016). Two modes of innovation with an impact on the resilience of industrial ecosystems are observed in technology innovation systems (Table 4.7).

**Table 4.7** Innovation activities in technological innovation systems

| Science-technology-innovation (STI) | Doing-using-interacting (DUI) |
|---|---|
| • Promotion of R&D<br>• Utilization and creation of codified explicit knowledge<br>• Vertical coupling of value chains | • Engagement in organizational learning and cooperation<br>• Learning of implicit knowledge<br>• Coupling in local networks |

The Science-Technology-Innovation Mode (STI) emphasizes the promotion of R&D and the use and creation of codified, explicit knowledge. The other innovation strategy deals with organizational learning and interaction and is called Doing-Using-Interacting-Modus (DUI). The DUI mode uses tacit, experience-based knowledge and promotes interactive learning. Innovation activities in both modes can lead to new knowledge as a resource for the competitiveness of industry in national, sectoral and regional innovation systems. Determinants for innovation systems are the local proximity of actors and regional regulatory push / pull policies for niche innovations that support the creation of diversity and the selection of superior companies, products and processes (Lundvall, 2005). Both Science-Technology-Innovation (STI) and Doing-Using-Interaction (DUI) modes can achieve a competitive advantage. Formal R&D activities in companies and universities characterize science-technology innovation modes (Freeman & Soete, 2009). User-driven innovation, lead-user cooperation and open innovation approaches strengthen the doing-using-innovation modes (Chesbrough, 2003; von Hippel, 1986).

### 4.6.2 Global Innovation Systems

Vertical links between companies along the value chain can arise at different locations and around the world and are labeled global innovation systems. Interactions with domestic customers and suppliers are more common in developing groundbreaking and radical innovations, and companies that combine local niche innovations with global pipelines do better when they are not solely dependent on local markets (Lundvall, 2015). The distinction between separate national innovation systems is becoming increasingly blurred with globalization, in which actors are involved in global supply chains (Fig. 4.14).

The innovation-valuation framework provides a model for the resilience of industry within a global innovation system (GIS). The two dimensions of GIS are the mobility of knowledge resources and the degree of product standardization. Product standardization enables branding and delivery without major adjustments. Sectors with individual assessments have to tailor products to the needs of specialized user groups. Standardization makes the manufacture of products footloose, unless the production is embedded in grown territorial contexts with implicit, experience-based knowledge. Markets for tailor-made products either have a regional demand for certain products or require dense user-producer intimacy.

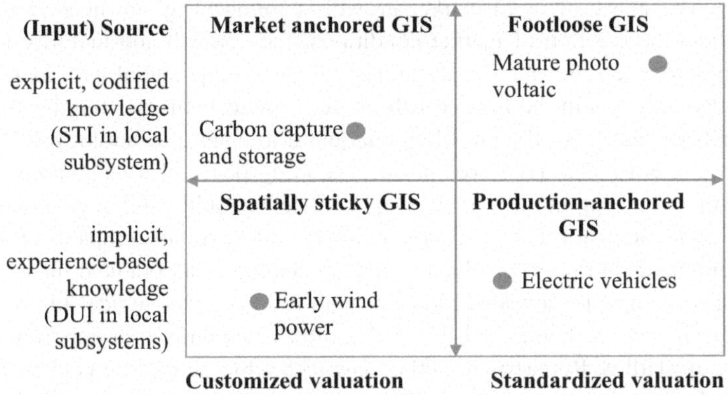


**Fig. 4.14** Innovation-valuation framework and industry positioning (Binz & Truffer, 2017)

These markets are described as market-anchored and spatially sticky (Binz & Truffer, 2017). The knowledge resource and the degree of product standardization affect how global innovation systems respond to demand-pull policies. Footloose innovation systems tend to be mobile as demand increases, while customized product value chains and DUI-based industries are more resilient to global competition. Governmental transition management needs to consider the effect of demand-pull policies on footloose global innovation systems and regulatory changes influence companies' survival in regional innovation systems (Binz & Hipp, 2020). On the other hand, politics can create favorable conditions in order to benefit from international developments. Global innovation systems help developing countries catch up. China, for example, has not only achieved the catch-up process due to top-down government instructions, but rather due to technology-specific policy mixes and the mobilization of technological capacity upgrading (Binz, Gosens, Hansen & Hansen, 2017).

### 4.6.3 Life Cycle of Technology

The life cycle of a technology adds the temporal component to technology diffusion and innovation. Improvements and incremental innovations follow the natural, technological trajectory. In an idealized model, the output of successive incremental innovations follows the familiar S-shaped path from introduction to maturity. The phase of rapid market growth is followed by an increase in production and the creation of market conditions. Late growth and maturity phases are no time for newcomers. The technological catch-up potential with its technological dynamism is in the first growth phase. New technologies require training in specialized areas, but the knowledge required to enter a technology system in its early stages is often publicly known. The early phase of a technology offers new entrants the opportunity to develop knowledge, skills and experience with the new technological life cycle (Perez & Soete, 1988). Small companies founded by entrepreneurs are often involved in new technologies and radical innovations. Established companies are also pioneers with radical technological innovations. However, the new technological life cycles offer new entrants an opportunity for catching up (Hill & Rothaermel, 2003). The technology life cycle is also applied to technological innovation systems framework and the four key stages of development, formation, growth, maturity and decline are also found here (Markard, 2020) (Fig. 4.15).

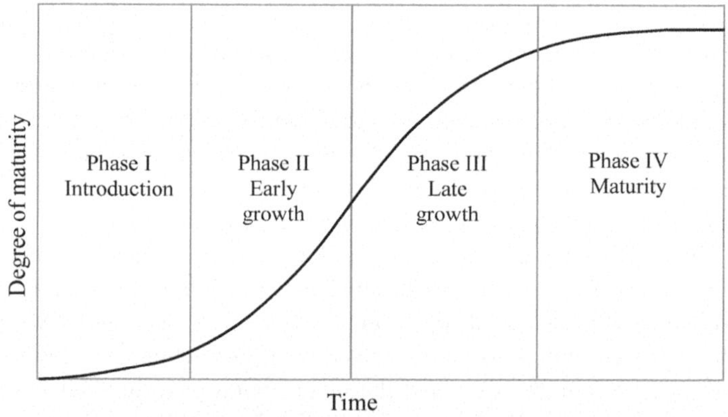


**Fig. 4.15** Technological life cycle (Perez & Soete, 1988)

### 4.6.4 Windows of Opportunities

New technological trajectories create windows with opportunities to catch up. Preconditions are new market segments with short cycle time of technology and to quickly manufacture with high levels of engineering excellence. Leapfrogging as a fast catching-up process requires the ability to choose the right technologies and standards, create initial markets, and be first on the market with the best integrative designs. Windows of opportunity for leapfrogging are prepared in stages of technological catch-up. Capabilities are built by duplicating imitation and path-following catch-up. The second stage is the creative imitation and stage-skipping catching-up and the final stage advances to real innovation and path-creating or leading catching-up (Lee, 2005). Path creation strategies require that industrial development include strong technological innovations. The breakaway of the original technological path leads to the disappearance of traditional production schemes and the new technology and market knowledge to be supported by various technical assets (Xu, Xiong & Li, 2018) (Table 4.8).

**Table 4.8** Preconditions for leapfrogging and rapid catching-up

| Preconditions for leapfrogging and rapid catching-up |
|---|
| • Preparedness for rapid catching-up cycles<br>• Selection of right technology and standards<br>• Creation of initial markets<br>• Supply of best integrative designs |

The phenomenon of successive changes in industrial leadership and its superiority in technology, production or marketing in global markets is known as the catch-up cycle. In catch-up cycles, latecomers and countries emerge as international frontrunners, while established companies lose their previous positions. Sectoral changes related to changes in knowledge and technology, changes in demand, and changes in institutions and public order create windows of opportunity. The main windows of opportunity are based on these changes in a sectoral system. New technologies and innovations, demand from users and consumers and institutions / public policies can initiate changes in a sectoral system, create a window of opportunity and take a new path (Lee & Malerba, 2017) (Table 4.9).

**Table 4.9** Windows of opportunities (Lee & Malerba, 2017)

| **Windows of opportunities** |
|---|
| • New technologies and innovations (tech-push)<br>• Demand changes of users and consumers (market-pull)<br>• Institutions/public policy (regulatory push/pull agendas) |

Technological innovation systems are characterized by structural components. Elements of the system are actors and networks that have an impact on the institutional structure with functional patterns for knowledge generation, market formation and legitimation (Bergek, Jacobsson, Carlsson, Lindmark & Rickne, 2008). A guide to the search for the novel technological trajectory advises monitoring the strategies of these actors and the narratives of the selection environment, which are shaped by actors who influence the requirements of a new technology (Table 4.10).

**Table 4.10** Actors in technological innovation systems

| **Actors in technological innovation systems** |
|---|
| • Public discourse/society<br>• Governments<br>• Alliances/industry networks<br>• Companies<br>• Customer/markets |

Search guidelines include the formulation of visions and expectations, standards, regulations and policies that ultimately affect the growth and shape of technological developments. The skills of the companies require an adaptation to the selection criteria for the selection of the technical variants and the product design through standards and regulations (Yap & Truffer, 2019) (Fig. 4.16).

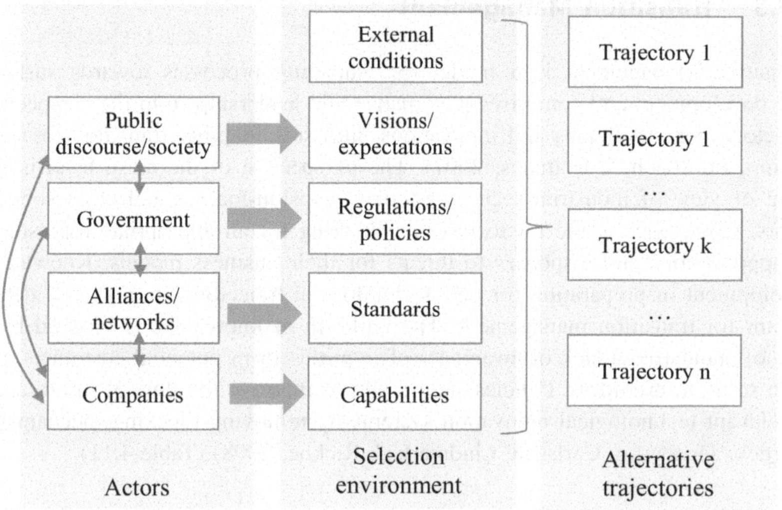


**Fig. 4.16** Guidance for search of novel trajectories (Truffer & Yap, 2019)

Capabilities building focuses on creating knowledge along the technological value chain, adjacent and emerging technologies that complement, compete and interact with one another. The scope of technology monitoring is defined by the focus on TIS and its suppliers and actors with an influence on knowledge development (Bergek et al., 2015). Progressive, self-evolving technology strategy is suggested as the best strategy for latecomers in catch-up cycles of high-tech industries. In-house development is preferred to co-development or open innovation strategies (Zhang, Shi, Liu & Wu, 2021). Organizational learning skills are essential for established companies in order to avoid mistakes in the catch-up process. Traps for incumbents during transition are lack of technological and financial capabilities, wrong timing, sunk costs, and inadequate responses to changing trajectory. Determinants of successful preparation strategies are skill building, proper assessment of future needs, and quick responses when windows of opportunity open. After all, a successful transition can require sheer luck (Vertesy, 2017).

### 4.6.5 Transition Management

Transition Management is a model for managing processes towards sustainable development and comprises governance and leadership from the perspective of actors, e.g. politicians and innovations, into sustainability transition research (Kemp, Loorbach & Rotmans, 2007). The perspective of the meso level is the point of view of industrial sectors, political decision-makers and other societal actors. Companies at the micro level are looking for an appropriate assessment of opportunities and responses to threats for their business models. Knowledge development in preparation for new technological trajectories is a crucial determinant for transition management. The build-up of knowledge is blocked by a lack of standards, a lack of awareness of inquiries from potential customers and from solution providers. Policies should aim to improve the flow of information in relevant technological innovation systems by removing blocking mechanisms (Bergek, Jacobsson, Carlsson, Lindmark & Rickne, 2008) (Table 4.11).

**Table 4.11** Determinants of transition management

| Drivers for transition management | Barriers for transition management |
|---|---|
| • Tech and regulatory research<br>• Evaluation of future demand<br>• Response scenario development for emerging window of opportunity<br>• Capability building<br>• Preparing for catching-up | • Lack of knowledge development<br>• Lack of transition management<br>• Absence of standards<br>• Poor fit with company's values & processes<br>• Technological inferiority |

Co-evolution of technologies and macro-level landscape changes open up windows of opportunities. The co-evolution of technologies is understood as developments in industries, policies and institutions that influence and support one another over time. An example is the development of software, hardware and related technological knowledge, skills and abilities in connection with technological changes (Nelson, 1995; Niederman, Ferratt & Trauth, 2016). Another example for an inducement mechanism is the change of consumers' pro-environmental attitude and the evolution of environmental technologies (Zeng, Dong, Shi, Wang & Li, 2020). The transition management must prepare for the co-evolution of innovation and institutions and take multi-level perspectives of the technological system into account. Technical and regulatory monitoring prepare for the response scenarios (Hoogstraaten, Frenken & Boon, 2020). Financial difficulties due to technological inferiority or immaturity are reported as a barrier to sustainable transition and widespread commercial deployment (Sovacool, Noel & Orsato, 2017) (Fig. 4.17).

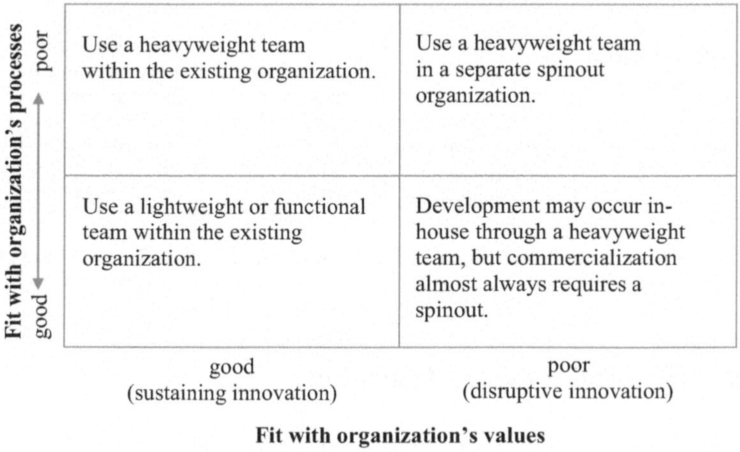


**Fig. 4.17** Responses to disruptive innovations after Christensen & Overdorf (2000)

Technological change can lead to a market shakeout if the resulting innovation is disruptive and competence-destroying. Established companies have to cope with this disruptive turbulence while facing triple challenges. They need to refine existing technologies, develop new ones, and incorporate the new knowledge into superior next-generation products and solutions (Bergek, Berggren, Magnusson & Hobday, 2013). Organizations need to provide the resources, processes and values to adapt to new types of discontinuous technologies. Appropriate reactions to disruptive innovations depend on the business fit and the type of change. Within the existing organization, it is proposed to build skills for sustaining or incremental innovations. In the case of poor fits to existing business models and disruptive innovations, the development of skills in spinouts can be better (Christensen & Overdorf, 2000). The core of transition management is the practical implementation of transition measures in a structured learning process. Agenda setting and transition experiments are followed by monitoring and evaluation of the results

(Loorbach & Rotmans, 2010). The process is embedded in the environment of the organization and the transition management is influenced by the market forces of the economic context, the public landscape and regulatory push / pull policies (Wirth, Markard, Truffer & Rohracher, 2013) (Fig. 4.18).

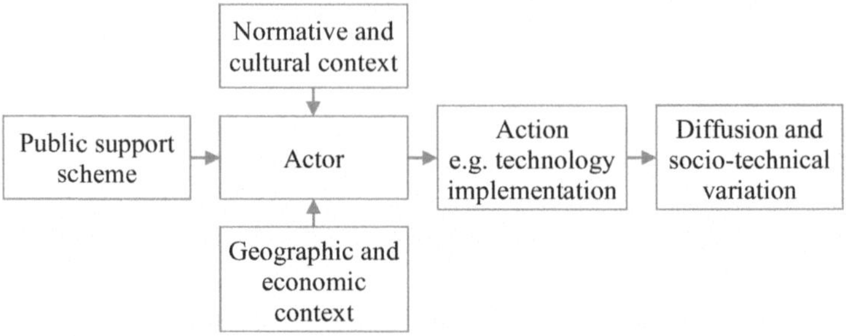


**Fig. 4.18** Market forces for transition management (Wirth, Markard, Truffer & Rohracher, 2013)

### 4.6.6 Chemical Industry Transition

Transition management was examined for the chemical industry. The chemical industry operates under an extremely stable, global socio-technical regime based on petroleum and natural gas as the main carbon source. Global regimes in the chemical industry are locally embedded in regional markets. Intermediate supply is focused on clusters of steam crackers that use naphtha, ethane and other fossil fuels as platform chemicals to produce chemical synthesis intermediates such as ethylene and propylene. Regional sustainability initiatives contradict global institutional regimes and are forced to follow energy efficiency and economic regimes in other specialized sectors. The contradiction leads to tensions between regional sustainability initiatives towards bio-based and circular economy with global socio-technical configurations (Bauer & Fuenfschilling, 2019). Strategic niche management is suggested to expand into technological niches such as carbon dioxide capture and use (CCU), biotechnological processes, circular supply chain models and application of the 12 green principles targeting processes. The standardization efforts for renewable raw materials are being pursued by the industry initiatives Science Based Targets and Together for Sustainability (TfS). Orientation towards global sustainability challenges, policy support, cooperation of industry with research institutes in projects and capability building are further drivers for inducement of transition to low carbon emission technologies (Karakaya & Nevzorova, 2020). The development of innovative technologies depends on the destabilization of the regime and carbon trading, drastic changes in institutional rules and tailored policies in support of sustainable chemistry are proposed (Falcone & Hiete, 2019). Barriers to transition include the limited availability of biomass, controversies over land use change and uncertainties about the ecological footprint of liquid biofuels. Even a substitution of 15–25% of fossil raw materials by biomass is likely to have a significant impact on production, demand and infrastructure and to be associated with great uncertainty about future scenarios (Wydra et al., 2021). Policy measures are recommended to increase the pressure for socio-technical regime change, e.g. promoting specific R&D investment for key enabling innovations and bio-based technologies (Börner, Bröring & Laibach, 2019).

## 4.7 Innovation Diffusion Studies

Innovation diffusion studies move the actor as a decision-making agent into the focus of innovation research. The agent-based models provide a theoretical framework for the research strategy of this dissertation. Innovation diffusion studies analyze the decision-making process and structure the adoption in a chronological and sequential order. This research attempts to identify determinants for the adoption of innovations to reach carbon neutrality and applies the view at innovation diffusion as a social process with the customer as the agent at the center. Innovation diffusionists examine innovation adoption and analyze the relative advantages of innovation over traditional technologies, the adoption process, and the environment (Rogers, 2003). Agent-based models are presented in this paragraph that contribute to variations in the adopter-centered view and examine the motivation, attitude and behavior of individuals and organizations that accept and implement innovations (Ajzen 1991; Davis, 1985). The models provide an understanding of the decision-making process and a tool for predicting the introduction of environmental innovations in the context of competitive markets (Schwarz & Ernst, 2009).

### 4.7.1 Elements of the Diffusion

The central core of the innovation diffusion study are the decision-making process and the perceived attributes of the innovation. Innovation diffusionists have a customer-centric view. For Everett M. Rogers (2003), diffusion has four elements and "*is the process through which (1) an innovation (2) is communicated through certain channels (3) over time (4) among the members of a social system*" (Table 4.12).

**Table 4.12** Elements of the innovation diffusion process according to Rogers (2003)

| Four elements of the innovation diffusion process | |
|---|---|
| 1. Innovation | with 5 characteristics |
| 2. Communication channels | mass media and word-of-mouth |
| 3. Timely diffusion process | with 5 mental stages |
| 4. Members of a social system | with 5 adopter categories |

The first element is innovation. Innovativeness is not assigned by the innovator, but by the customer and is assigned by potential adopters based on their perception as either favorable or less favorable (Table 4.13).

**Table 4.13** The five characteristics for an innovation according to Rogers (2003)

| The five characteristics for innovations and their effects | | | |
|---|---|---|---|
| Relative advantage | + | Trialability | + |
| Complexity | – | Observability | + |
| Compatibility with existing technology | + | | |

The subjective perception of the innovation determines the rate of adoption. Five characteristics for an innovation are distinguished by Rogers: Relative advantage, complexity, compatibility, trialability and observability of the innovation. The greater the relative advantage of the innovation of existent technologies, the greater the compatibility, trialability and observability, the higher is the rate of adoption and the faster the diffusion process. Complexity of the innovation has an adverse effect. Perceived attributes of innovation are more important than objective benefits from the 5 characteristics of innovation. The second element of the diffusion process is the communication channel. Mass media channels and interpersonal channels are two different channels that change attitudes towards innovation. The mass media incubates adoption, but most people imitate adoption based on pear-like reviews. Innovation diffusion is seen as a social process in which individuals go through an innovation decision-making process with 5 consecutive cognitive stages (Fig. 4.19).

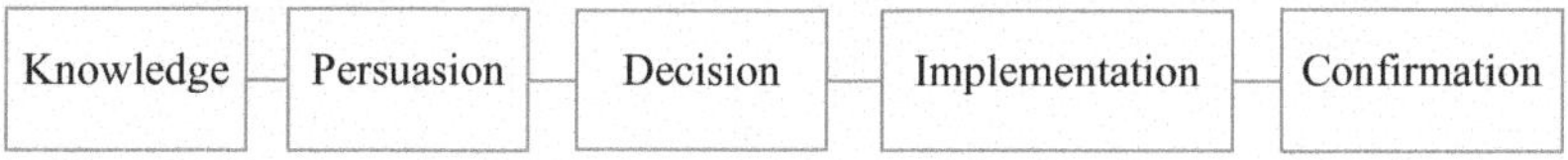


**Fig. 4.19** Innovation-decision process (Rogers, 2003)

The timely process is the third element of Rogers innovation diffusion model and considers different mental stages. In the first stage, individuals learn and seek information about the innovation. They form an attitude in a second stage and take a decision in a third stage. The innovation is then implemented in a fourth stage and reconsidered in a final confirmation stage. The fourth element of the model are the members of the social system in the context of the diffusion process. Adopters are divided into five categories according to their innovativeness. Innovators are the first group and have the highest innovativeness. They are followed by early adopters who are considered opinion leaders, are highly respected by their peer group and represent the critical mass for the adoption of a new idea or innovation. This point in the diffusion process is often referred to as the time-to-take-off. As soon as the critical mass of acceptance is reached, the diffusion process becomes self-sustaining. The next groups are the early majority, the late majority, and finally the laggards. The determinant of group participation is the socio-economic background of the adopters. Laggards are the least wealthy, educated, and cosmopolitan. The same critical mass scheme applies to d discontinuance of a defected technology. As soon as a critical mass of rejecting users of an old technology is reached, the drop-out rate increases and stipulates further drop-outs. This underscores the importance of the group of early adopters and marketing campaigns specifically aimed at this group of opinion leaders (Rogers, 2002, 2003) (Fig. 4.20).

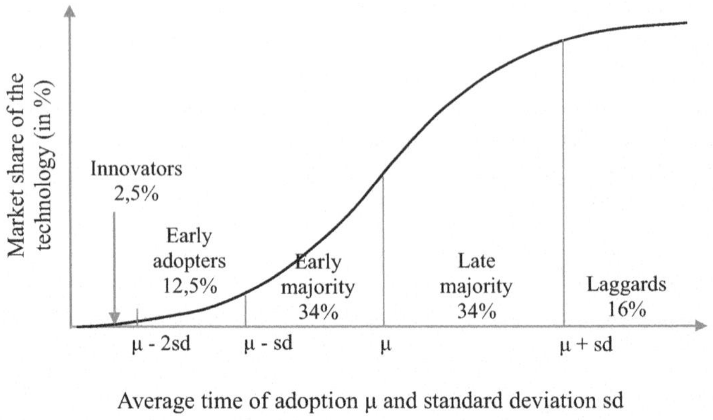


**Fig. 4.20** Adopter categorization based on innovativeness (Rogers, 2003)

The S-curve of the innovation adoption is correlated by regression analysis in the Bass model. The model assumes that potential users of an innovation are influenced by two means of communication: Mass media and word of mouth. The probability corresponds to the term P (T) = p + (q/m) Y (T), where p and q/m are constants and Y (T) is the number of previous buyers at time T, p is the probability of first-time buyers, q/m is the pressure to imitate the buyer and m is the total number of buyers who bought during the period. S (T) is the purchase probability at time T. The model offers terms for innovative (p) and imitative (q) behavior (Bass, 1969).

$$S(T) = pm + (q - p)\,Y(T) - q/m\,[Y(T)]^2$$

Exhibit 1. Probability equation for Bass' innovation diffusion model (Bass, 1969)

The model provides a mathematical description of diffusion processes in retrospect. The idealized innovation diffusion of the Bass model was used in connection with sales forecasts, but the results are only working hypotheses and are only partially predictable for actual sales (Mahajan, Muller & Bass, 1990).

### 4.7.2 Agent-based Models

Agent-based models apply behavioral theory to the innovation decision-making process and center around the subjective view of the consumer as a decision maker about innovation as an attitude object. Agent-based models use statistical methods and measure attitudes, behavior, and factors that correlate with both.

#### 4.7.2.1 Predictor Variables

The central core of agent-based models is the decision-making unit and perception of the characteristics of the innovations and not the objective value of the innovation. While Rogers identifies 5 characteristics as predictors of adoption, other scientists suggest different numbers as predictors. Tornatzky and Klein propose a series of 10 characteristics as predictors for the adoption of innovations. In addition to Rogers' five characteristics, it adds cost, portability, divisibility, profitability, and social recognition (Tornatzky, & Klein, 1982). Moore and Benbasat developed a tool to measure the perception of adopting innovations in information technology and identified 8 predictors (Moore & Benbasat, 1991). Behavioral researchers have expanded the decision-making logic to include attitude and behavioral intent as additional mediator variables. These models measure attitudes and behavioral intent and factor the mediators with predictor variables as stimuli and actual usage as response variable. Most prominent examples of these agent-based models are Fishbein's and Ajzen's theory of reasoned action (1975), Ajzen's theory of planned behavior (1985), and Davis' technological acceptance model (1985).

#### 4.7.2.2 Attitude

In these models, attitude is a mediator variable for behavioral intention in the beliefs—attitude—behavior relationship (Ajzen & Fishbein, 2005; Schwartz, 1994). In Roger's model, the attitude towards and innovation is formed during a decision-making process. The process includes cognitive components and is supported by observations and trials. The process goes through stages from the first interest with the gathering of knowledge about an innovation, the formation of an attitude towards the innovation, over the decision to accept or reject, up to the implementation of the new idea and the confirmation of this decision. First knowledge arises when the person is exposed to the existence of the innovation and gains an understanding of how it works. Persuasion occurs when the person develops a positive attitude towards innovation (Rogers, 2003). Attitude comprises three different aspects, cognition, affect and conation. Cognition is the acquisition of knowledge and understanding through thoughts, including underlying beliefs, perceptions, and concepts. Affection reflects a person's feelings and inclinations towards an element. Conation is the will to perform an action and includes perceived consequences of the behavioral intention or actual behavior in relation to the subject of the attitude. Attitude in a narrower definition is limited to the affective element formed by salient beliefs (McClelland, 2001) (Table 4.14).

**Table 4.14** Attitude aspects

| **Aspects of attitude** | |
|---|---|
| • Cognition | Underlying beliefs, perceptions and conceptualizations |
| • Affection | Feelings, provoked by peripheral cues and impulses |
| • Conation | Perceived consequences of the behavioral intent or actual behavior, result of a conscientious process |

Attitude in the broader definition refers to the degree to which a person assesses the perceived consequences of its implementation positively or negatively (Ajzen, 1991, 2011, 2012; McClelland, 2001). Attitude is interpreted as affection and as a state of positive, positive opinion. In this study, attitude is the result of a cognitive process and evolves from gathering information, sharing with experts, exploring capabilities, and assessing advantages and disadvantages (Bond Jr., Krosnick, Ostrom & Sedikides, 1994; Rylan, Ryley & Thring, 2018). The activities correspond to the persuasion state of Roger's innovation decision-making process (Rogers, 2003). The attitude is a product of this evaluation process in a certain context. Building a stable attitude requires motivation and cognitive resources (Fischer, 2017). Peripheral cues become more important as the motivation and ability to process arguments decrease. In this context, cues and impulses can cause quick attitude shifts and attitude stability is low (Cacioppo & Petty, 1886). After a conscientious elaboration process, the persuasion process leads to a more stable attitude and desire (Fischer, 2017; Kruglanski, Baldner, Chernikova, Destro & Pierro, 2018). Attitude in this state tends to be stable over time and is reconstructed based on recombination of associations with the attitude object (Fischer, 2017).

#### 4.7.2.3 Behavioral Intention

Behavioral intention is separate from attitude in agent-based models known as reasoned action and planned behavior. A goal must become sufficiently dominant to induce behavior that it is not overridden by other, more pressing concerns (Kruglanski, Baldner, Chernikova, Destro & Pierro, 2018). Behavioral intention is described as willingness to perform the behavior and it is believed that people's behavioral intention follows their beliefs about performing the behavior in a reasonable, consistent, and often automatic manner (Fishbein & Ajzen, 2010). Behavioral intention occurs in activities that result in a choice to adopt the innovation. This state corresponds to the decision stage of Roger's innovation decision process (Rogers, 2003). It is difficult to make a clear distinction between attitude and behavioral intention. Both are interdependent, attitude is time and context dependent, and differentiation is an interpretive act.

#### 4.7.2.4 Attitude Measurements

Attitude measurement attempts to convert a person's behavior towards an object into an index that represents the preference and direction of the attitude. Attitude is measured in self-reporting scale tests using structured questionnaires (Antonak & Livneh, 1995). Measurement techniques in structured interviews use self-reporting methods such as Likert's summated rating scheme. The Likert scales offer five- to seven-point approval scales or the binary approval-disapproval scale (Krosnick, Judd & Wittenbrink, 2005). In an unstructured interview, the researcher is free to examine the answers in ways that are believed to add insight into the question under study (Antonak & Livneh, 1995). Narratives from semi-structured interviews are analyzed by content analysis. The literal content of the narrative is converted into codes, sub-categories, categories and topics. Then semantic orientations of adjectives and terms are identified, and the latent meanings are translated into agreement-rejection scales (Erlingsson & Brysiewicz, 2017). The sentiment of attitudes is measured through language use in content analysis. Adjectives and adverbs are used in language to distinguish the semantic orientation of nouns (Rocklage & Fazio, 2015) (Table 4.15).

**Table 4.15** Semantic orientations of meaning units

| Positive semantic orientation | Negative semantic orientation |
|---|---|
| • Adjectives indicating praise or promotion<br>• Participle clauses indicating activities, goals and desires | • Adjectives indicating criticism or resistance<br>• Participle clauses indicating passiveness, rejection and disappointment |

A positive semantic orientation indicates praise or promotion and a negative semantic orientation indicates criticism or resistance (Littman & Turney, 2003). In addition to adjectives, the semantic orientation of attitudes and behavioral intention are assessed from participle clauses indicating activities, goals and desires to adopt innovations (Taboada, Anthony & Voll, 2006). Researchers need to consider that identifying sentiment orientation is an interpretive act during content analysis of interview transcripts. Therefore, a structured approach is used to improve the consistency of the study. An additional interpretation is required to separate attitude from intention. Participles which describe a mental state, are associated with attitude and participles, which describe the active promotion and implementation of innovation are associated with behavioral intentions. Examples of codes that describe a positive attitude are seeking information, scouting, talking to suppliers, asking customers, having expectations and being convinced. Examples of codes that describe behavioral intentions are prototyping, sampling, try, launch, available, planning, and developing (Table 4.16).

**Table 4.16** Differentiation of attitude and behavioral intent

| Attitude | Behavioral intention |
|---|---|
| Participles describing a mental state are associated with attitude | Participles describing active promotion and implementation |

### 4.7.3 Theory of Reasoned Action

The central construct of theory of reasoned action is intention as the closest determinant of behavior. In this theory, intention reflects the extent to which a person is likely to plan to pursue and to make efforts to pursue a particular behavior (Hagger, 2019) (Fig. 4.21).

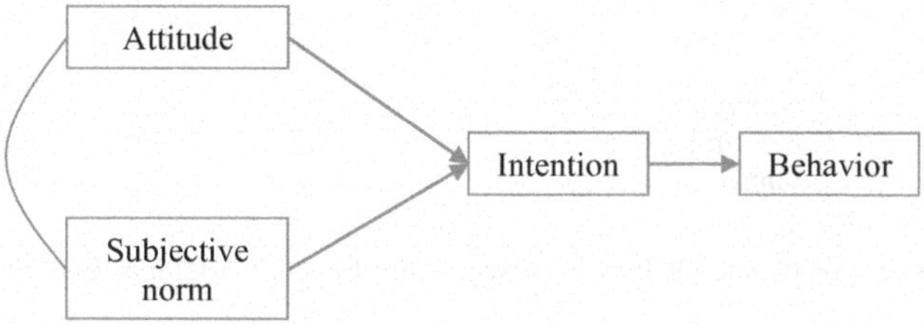


**Fig. 4.21** M. Fishbein's and I. Ajzen's theory of reasoned action (Leone, Perugini & Ercolania, 1999)

The main goal of the reasoned action model is to understand the causes of planned behavior and intention as a direct predictor of the behavior (Ajzen & Fishbein, 1980). The original theory by Martin Fishbein and Icek Ajzen from 1975 applies only to behaviors under volitional control where there is no external or internal barrier to prevent behavior once there is an intention to do so (Leone, Perugini & Ercolania, 1999). Attitude towards behavior and subjective norms are the two predictor variables of behavioral intention in this original model. Since the assumption of total volitional control is difficult and very rare, the model is expanded to include incomplete volitional control to explain past behavior. The additional variable is the perceived behavioral control and describes the perception of how difficult a behavior is to perform.

### 4.7.4 Theory of Planned Behavior

The theory of planned behavior differs from the theory of reasoned action in that it adds perceived behavior control (Ajzen, 1991). Perceived behavioral control is assumed as the third direct predictor for intention and behavior according to the theory of planed behavior. The greater the perceived behavioral control, the more positive the behavioral intention and the more likely the behavior to be carried out (Ajzen, 1985; Leone, Perugini & Ercolania, 1999). Attitude towards a behavior is the evaluation of the perceived consequences of its implementation (Ajzen, 1991, 2011, 2012; McClelland, 2001) (Fig. 4.22).

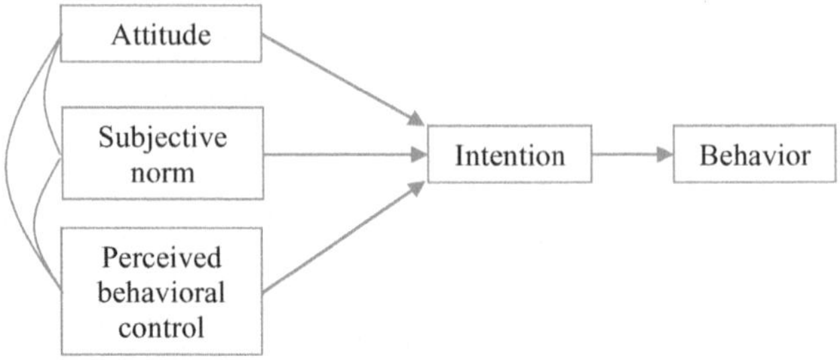


**Fig. 4.22** Theory of planned behavior (Ajzen, 1985; Leone, Perugini & Ercolania, 1999)

The attitude is factored out of cognition, affection and conation. Cognition is the conscious retrieval of underlying beliefs, perceptions, and concepts. Affection summarizes feelings provoked by peripheral cues and impulses and conation attempts to anticipate the consequences of the actual behavior (Ajzen & Fishbein, 2010; Cacioppo & Petty, 1886; McClelland, 2001). The term subjective norm refers to the perceived social pressure to perform or not to perform the behavior. Normative beliefs are the underlying determinants of subjective norms and deal with the likelihood that individuals or groups will approve or disapprove of behavior (Ajzen, 1991). Subjective norms relate to perceived social pressures to perform or not to perform a behavior and to self-expectations and feelings about an obligation to do moral behavior. The value–belief–norm theory by Stern et al. specifically examines the influence of normative beliefs and social norms on pro-environmental behavioral (Fang, Ng, Wang & Hsu, 2017; Stern, 2000) (Table 4.17).

The perceived control over one's own behavior are internal factors and external factors. Internal factors of perceived behavior control are belief in personal control or lack of control, availability of information, or negative emotions about behavioral performance. External factors of perceived behavioral control are resources and dependence on other people. Behavioral intention is predicted by circumstantial factors such as time and available opportunities (Ajzen, 1985). In

**Table 4.17** Predictor variables of the planed behavior model

| Attitude | Subjective social norms | Perceived behavioral control |
|---|---|---|
| • Opinion, perceptions and concepts<br>• Evaluation of the behavioral performance<br>• Affection, feelings<br>• Perception of consequences of the actual behavior | • Perceived social pressure / peer pressure<br>• self-expectations and feelings about obligations<br>• Moral preferences | • Beliefs in personal control<br>• Availability of information<br>• Negative emotions<br>• Absence of resources (time, opportunities)<br>• Dependency on other persons |

another extension of the theory of reasoned action, planned behavior is a behavioral achievement that is jointly dependent on intention and behavioral control. People's behavior is influenced by the confidence in their ability of behavioral performance and the dashed line in the model expresses the relationship (Ajzen, 1991) (Fig. 4.23).

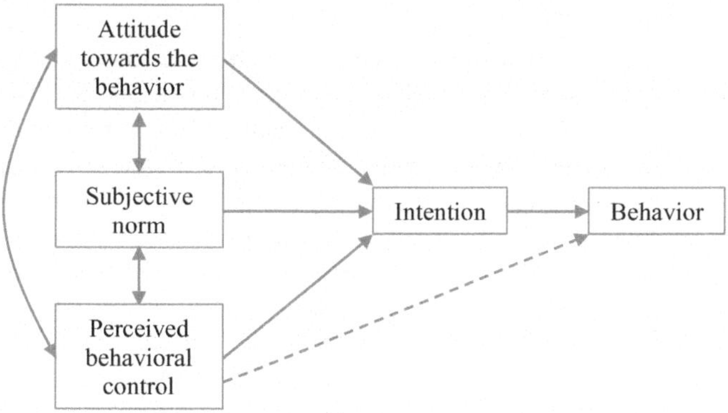


**Fig. 4.23** Theory of planned behavior (Ajzen, 1991)

### 4.7.5 Technology Acceptance Model

The technology acceptance model uses a stimulus-response model with two mediator variables, perceived usefulness and perceived ease of use. The model was developed by Fred D. Davis based on theory of reasoned action of Fishbein & Ajzen (1975) and uses the motivational linkages between external stimuli and resulting behavior of that theory. The theory of reasoned action provides the criteria for developing operational measures to observe motivational phenomena before behavioral performance. External variables include all variables that are not explicitly represented in the original model (Davis, 1989) (Fig. 4.24).

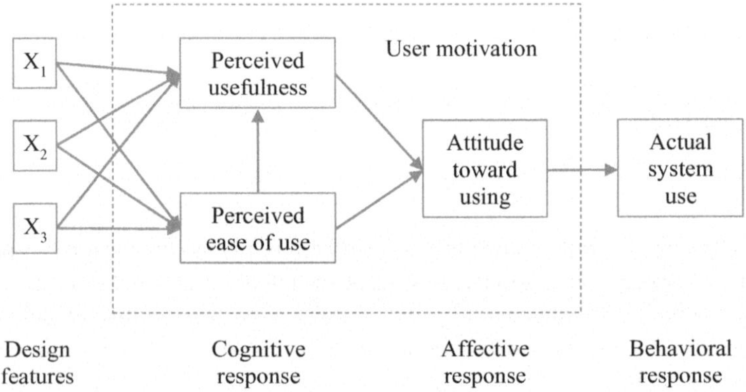


**Fig. 4.24** Technology acceptance model (Davis, 1985)

According to the technological acceptance model, the overall attitude of a potential user to the use of a technology determines the actual use. The attitude towards use, in turn, is a function of two important beliefs: Perceived usefulness and perceived ease of use. Two cognitive responses to design features are separated and prioritized as predictors of attitudes towards using the technology. The technology acceptance model is proposed to determine the relationship between user perception and design of computer-based information systems. In this model, perceived usefulness and perceived ease of use have been identified as two dominant innovation characteristics for adoption of novel information systems and chosen as the determining predictors for acceptance. The two predictor variables help to understand the attitude of potential adopters of information technologies and to predict intention to use as a function of perceived usefulness and perceived ease of use. For Davis (1989), *"perceived usefulness is defined as the degree to which an individual believes that using a particular system would enhance his or her job performance"* and *"perceived ease of use is defined as the degree to which an individual believes that using a particular system would be free of physical and mental effort."* The advantage of the technology acceptance model lies in the emphasis on external effect variables that are technology-specific and support designers and innovators in the development and implementation of this technology. The model is a tool to understand users' needs for technological acceptance, like required system characteristics and training programs (Davis, 1989; Venkatesh & Davis, 2000). The model is derived from the theory of reasoned action and optimized to focus on external effect variables and specific design features of information technology. Usefulness has been shown to be critical to the introduction of information technology, and the ease of use of the system has a strong impact on users' perception of usefulness. Attitude formation based on usefulness and ease of use ultimately leads to a robust prediction of the actual use of the innovation (Liu, & Ma, 2004).

### 4.7.6 Later Reasoned Action Framework

A universal approach to theory of reasoned action is further elaborated and expanded in a later version through mediator variables and background factors in order to predict and understand intended behavior. The expanded version focuses on individuals' beliefs about the future performance of a particular behavior. In this version, intention is conceptualized as a function of attitudes, subjective norms, and perceived behavioral control. The reasoned action theory encompasses the belief system of adopters and assumes that human behavior follows reasonably and often spontaneously from the information or beliefs that humans have about the observed behavior. Beliefs can come from personal experience, knowledge, information from the media and other sources, depending on culture, background and education. The model distinguishes three types of beliefs, behavioral beliefs, normative beliefs, and control beliefs. Behavioral beliefs are assumed to determine people's attitude towards the personal execution of the behavior. Normative beliefs represent the perceived social pressures to engage or disregard the behavior, and beliefs about personal and environmental factors aggregate as control beliefs. Once attitudes, perceived norms and behavioral controls have been formed, they are directly accessible and available to guide intentions and behavior (Fishbein & Ajzen, 2010) (Fig. 4.25).

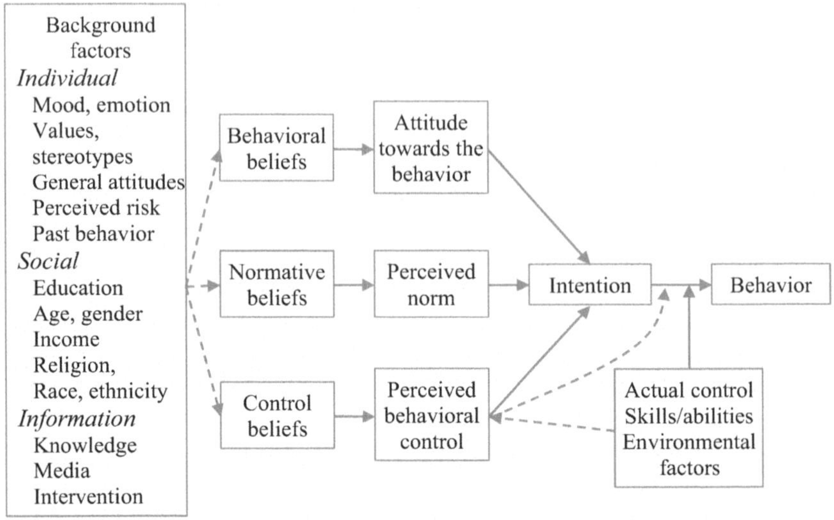


**Fig. 4.25** Schematic presentation of the reasoned action model (Fishbein & Ajzen, 2010)

Moral preferences for environmental innovations were examined using models of reasoned action and planned behavior. The intention to introduce battery electric vehicles is examined in terms of attitudes towards electric cars and subjective norms, perceived familiarity and ease of use. The results show the need to examine the impact of policies on innovation diffusion. The analysis of specific characteristics as external impact variables of environmental innovations is suggested (Hamilton, & Terblanche-Smit, 2018; Kaplan, Gruber, Reinthaler, & Klauenberg, 2016).

### 4.7.7 Reasoned Action Framework for Study

To prepare a testable model for research, the concept of the reasoned action model is adapted to the minimal required variables for adoption of environmental innovations in a business environment. The aim is to prepare for a testable model that can be applied to the available time and resources in semi-structured interviews (Fig. 4.26).

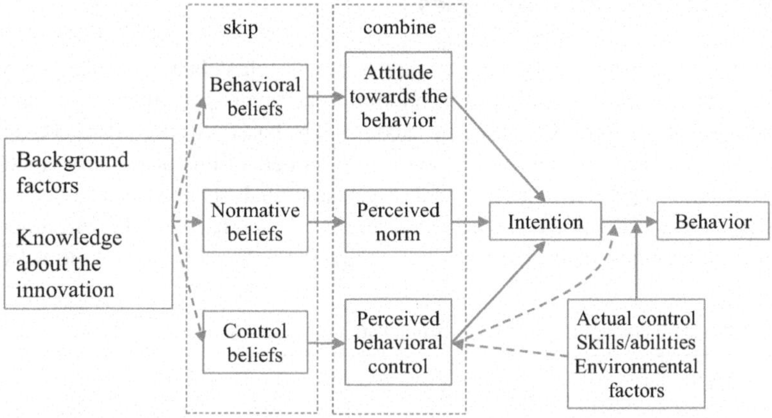


**Fig. 4.26** Adaptation of the reasoned action model to environmental innovations

Mediator variables of behavioral, normative and control beliefs are skipped. Attitude towards behavior and perceived norms are combined as attitude, driven by sustainability characteristics of the innovation. Background factors are reduced to individual, company- and technology-specific factors (Fig. 4.27).

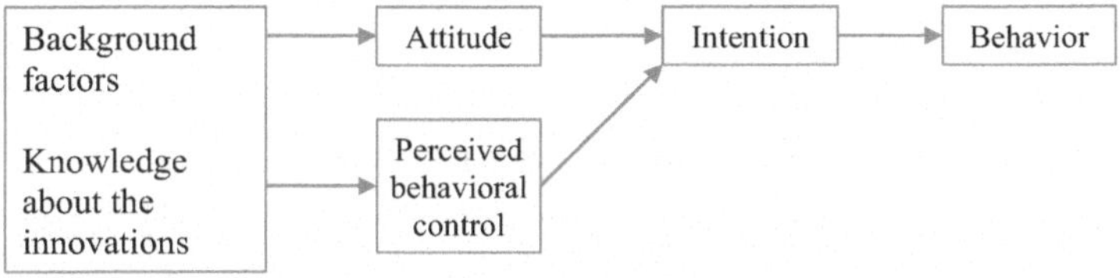


**Fig. 4.27** Adapted reasoned action model for environmental innovations

It is assumed that the decision making-process in the business environment is purely data-driven and behaviors are under volitional control. Perceived behavioral control is influenced by external effect variables such as company characteristics, industry specific standards, Government regulations, market and customer needs and attributes of the environmental innovation. The adapted model is the basis for study of environmental innovations to reach carbon neutrality in the chemical industry and is used as a, adapted reasoned action framework for study.

### 4.7.8 Econometric Analyses

Econometric analyzes apply static stimulus-response models to statistical analysis methods and set lists of variables in relation to company performance or innovation output parameters. Econometric analyzes are based on large data sets from surveys in industries or market segments. Researchers of this quantitative method use structured equation modeling with regression analysis and correlate a set of predictor variables with a response variable. Drivers and barriers of environmental innovation adoption identified from these studies are listed below (Table 4.18).

**Table 4.18** Drivers and barriers for eco-innovations from econometric analyzes

**Drivers**

- Market pull factors, competitive pressure and customer demand, consumer needs for eco-innovations, egoistic motivations
- Organizational factors, business strategy and instruments, CSR
- Regulatory push/pull instruments
- Efficiency gains and cost savings from reduced energy or materials use, cost saving programs
- Cooperation and spill-over effects, external R&D sources

**Barriers**

- Cost increases from externalities reduction measures

Market pull factors such as competitive pressure and customer demand, organizational factors such as business strategy and instruments, and government regulatory instruments are the driving forces for adoption of process eco-innovations in Slovenian companies. Increased effectiveness is steering process eco-innovation more that expected future benefits from such eco-innovations (Hojnik & Ruzzier, 2016). Innovations that reduce the use of energy or materials correlate positively with competitiveness. Eco-innovations to reduce externalities, e.g. hazards for humans and the environment, reduce the competitiveness of the implementing companies. Eco-innovations that aim to reduce externalities reduce the profitability in the short term. Their implementation may increase profitable in the long term if regulators make the innovation mandatory (Ghisetti & Rennings, 2014). Eco-innovations are classified as eco-organization, eco-process, and eco-product innovation, and statistical analysis among Taiwanese companies shows that all three types of eco-innovations improve business performance. Organizational eco-innovations have the strongest relationship with corporate performance. Organizational eco-innovation can be the basis for eco-innovation developments in a company and offers all employees an awareness and orientation for eco-innovations. Eco-process innovations have a greater impact on business performance than eco-product innovations (Cheng, Yang & Sheu, 2014) (Fig. 4.28).

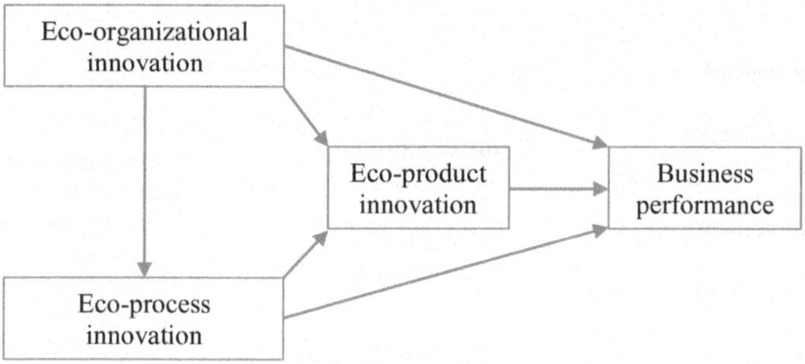


**Fig. 4.28** Eco-innovation performance model of Cheng, Yang and Sheu (2014)

Innovation diffusion models and econometric analyzes have identified several key drivers and barriers for eco-innovations. Cost increases and spill-over effects are key barriers and efficiency gains, government regulations and cooperation among companies are important drivers for environmental innovations. Efficiency gains and cost savings increase profitability and are self-sustaining eco-innovations. Relevant determinants for the successful dissemination and introduction of eco-innovations are regulatory push / pull effects together with cooperation and external knowledge acquisition (Belin, Horbach, & Oltra, 2011). According to an econometric analysis of 2952 responses to a questionnaire survey among German industrial companies, regulations, cost-saving programs and consumer needs are identified as the most important for eco-innovation companies. Government regulations urge companies to develop eco-innovations to reduce air, water and environmental pollution, avoid hazardous substances and establish recycling concepts. Cost savings are the drivers for eco-innovations that enable more efficient use of materials and energy or avoid penal taxation, e.g. carbon dioxide taxes. A third motivator are customer requirements (Horbach, Rammer & Rennings, 2012). An econometric analysis with data from a survey by the European Commission in 19 countries and 121.395 observations confirms regulations and subsidies as important modulators for eco-innovations. Other factors for eco-innovations are spill-over effects from cooperation and information flows. Technology is transferred from west to east in cooperation with external R&D as a source of information (Horbach, 2016). According to a study of 120 Shanghai A-share companies in China, eco-innovations are triggered by environmental policies, including environmental regulation and taxation, customer and market needs, and egoistic motivations (Liao, Xu, Cheng & Dong, 2018) (Fig. 4.29).

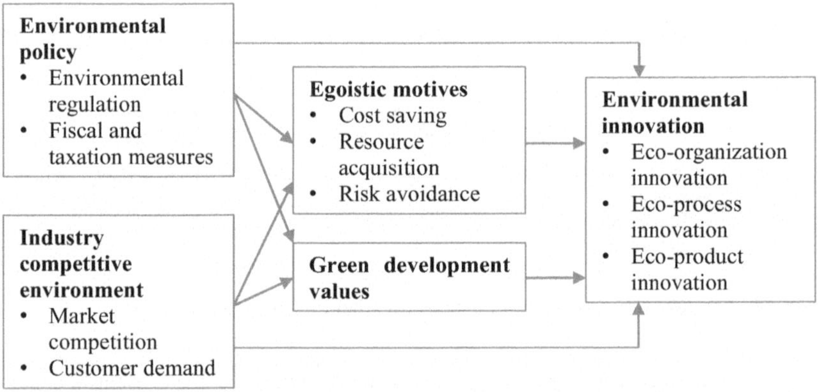


**Fig. 4.29** Model for eco-innovations on a company level of Liao, Xu, Cheng & Dong (2018)

# Testable Model 5

The testable model for research builds on the decision-making logic of agent-based models. The reasoned action framework for the study makes it possible to examine the effects of external factors, which are defined by the characteristics of the company, industry-specific standards, market and customer needs on attitudes and behavioral intentions towards environmental innovations. The reasoned action framework for the study is adapted for innovations to achieve carbon neutrality in chemical companies and uses the attitude towards the use and behavior intention as mediator variables to predict the actual use of renewable raw materials (Fig. 5.1).

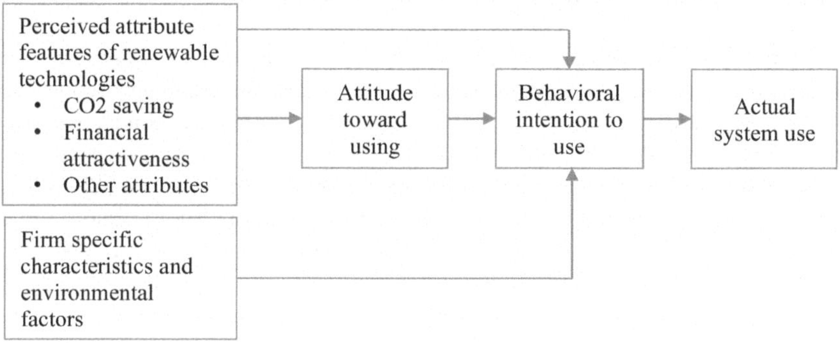


**Fig. 5.1** Reasoned action model for innovation adoption to reach carbon neutrality

---

**Supplementary Information** The online version contains supplementary material available at https://doi.org/10.1007/978-3-658-45389-3_5.



H. H. E. Ahrens, *The Ecological Modernization of the Chemical Industry*,
https://doi.org/10.1007/978-3-658-45389-3_5

The attitude and behavioral intention to use renewable raw materials are based on the perceived properties of renewable raw materials, company-specific characteristics and environmental factors. Literature review and theory on ecological innovation suggest important predictor variables and uncover a lack of knowledge for research. Research questions are derived from research gaps and hypotheses build on existing knowledge from innovation and ecological modernization theory.

## 5.1 Predictor Variables

Predictor variables for the adoption of environmental innovations have been suggested in the earlier literature. Major predictor for the use of environmental innovations are the costs in relation to standard technology. The same relationship is assumed for renewable raw materials. Since renewable raw materials are supposed to replace fossil raw materials, the GHG saving potential is another predictor variable that influences attitudes and behavioral intentions. Predictor variable V1 for the actual use of renewable raw materials is the attitude towards use. The predictor variable V2 for the actual use of renewable raw materials is a behavioral intention as shown schematically in the reasoned action model for the adoption of innovations to achieve carbon neutrality. Variable V3 is a group variable for innovation attributes and types of renewable raw materials (Table 5.1).

Company-specific predictor variables that are described in the literature are the company's actual use of renewable raw materials, the company's corporate sustainability strategy, company's management advocacy and the company's ability to cooperate (Rogers, 2003; Chan, Dai, Lim & Yee, 2016). Actual use of renewable raw materials is predictor variable V4, the predictor variable V5 is the corporate sustainability strategy of the company, the predictor variable V6 is the company's management support for the support of renewable raw materials and the predictor variable V7 is the company's ability to cooperate. Cooperation is the ability and activity to work with suppliers, customers, industry associations, universities and research institutes, NGOs and political bodies in order to achieve one's own goals in a common endeavor. Cooperation involves the exchange of information and the more cosmopolitan the company, the more advanced the innovator category and the greater the openness to adopting innovations (Rogers, 2003). Further drivers for innovation are the company's response to standards and Governmental regulations. Standards are found to improved information flows and promotes awareness of new technical and management practices

**Table 5.1** Variables of the testable model

| Symbol | Variable |
|---|---|
| V1 | Attitude towards the use of renewable raw materials (A) |
| V2 | Behavioral intention to use renewable raw materials (BI) |
| V3 | Innovation attribute feature and type of renewable raw materials |
| V4 | Company's actual use of renewable raw materials |
| V5 | Company's corporate sustainability strategy |
| V6 | Company's management advocacy |
| V7 | Company's cooperation skills |
| V8 | Company's implementation of industry standards for renewable raw materials |
| V9 | Company's expectations of Governmental regulations for renewable raw materials |

(Paton, 2000). Predictor variable V8 is the company's implementation practice of industry standards and encompasses knowledge, introduction, participation in development of standards and the awareness of needs for standardization. Governmental regulations include all actions to support the use of renewable raw materials, particularly taxation of the use of fossil feedstocks and support for renewable technologies. The predictor variable V9 is the company expectation of Governmental regulations. Policy instruments range from soft regulations, such as voluntary labels, tax benefits, feed-in allowances, grants, loans to hard regulations like restrictions, authorization regimes and taxation of traditional technologies. Governmental policies are the legal and fiscal framework of the market (Hoff, 2012).

## 5.2 Research Questions and Hypotheses

The first research question Q1 deals with the attitude of the chemical company to eco-innovations with greenhouse gas savings potential and reduction of carbon dioxide emissions to mitigate climate change. Based on literature review, companies are expected to have a positive attitude towards eco-innovations, which is reflected in the first hypothesis H1 (Cheng, Dong, Liao & Xu, 2018). The second research question Q2 deals with the behavioral intention to use environmental innovations with greenhouse gas savings potential. According to Davis (1985), attitudes are positively correlated with the intention to use a technology and the proposition is used for research question Q2 and hypothesis H2 (Davis, 1985). The higher the CO2 savings, the more likely it is that there will be a positive attitude towards renewable raw materials. However, certain features of the innovation attributes can have a negative effect on the intention to use, namely the lack of financial attractiveness (Hoff, 2012). Higher costs for use of renewable raw materials has a negative impact on the behavioral intention and lead to research question Q3 and hypothesis H3 (Table 5.2).

**Table 5.2** Research questions and hypotheses about attitude and intention

| Symbol | Research question and hypothesis |
|---|---|
| Q1 | What is the attitude of chemical companies towards the use of renewable raw materials? |
| H1 | Chemical companies have a positive attitude towards the use of renewable raw materials. |
| Q2 | What is the intention to use renewable raw materials? |
| H2 | The intention to use renewable raw materials is positively correlated with attitude toward the use of renewable raw materials. |
| Q3 | Is the use of renewable raw material stalled due to the higher prices? |
| H3 | The intention to use renewable raw materials is stalled due to the lower financial attractiveness as compared to petrochemically based products. |

Existing literature and research describe several company-specific predictors. Renewable raw materials are already being used by lead users, early adopters or pioneers, and the expansion of the existing use of renewable raw materials can take place faster than starting from scratch. The relationship between the actual use and intended use of renewable raw materials is described by question Q4 and hypothesis H4 (Sonnack, Thomke & von Hippel, 1999; Rogers, 2003; Vertesy, 2017). Company-specific factors influence the adoption of innovations in organizations based on innovation theory. The implementation of environmental innovations is to be promoted by corporate sustainability strategy (Cheng, Yang & Sheu, 2014; Zhang, Loh & Wu, 2020). Senior management advocacy is reported to improve research team performance and alignment with business strategy (Damanpour, 1991; Mumford & Hunter, 2005). Research questions Q5 and Q6 are formulated accordingly and hypotheses H5 and H6 form the basis for testing in the case study. External cooperation with customers and suppliers, industry associations and external research increases knowledge transfer and leads to higher innovation activities (Fobbe, 2020). Research question Q7 and hypothesis H7 are formulated based on the relationship between the company's ability to cooperate and environmental innovation activities (Table 5.3).

The harmonization of standards, methods, specifications and product assessments increases the efficiency of trade and the comparability of technical innovations. They ensure transparency and compatibility and promote the adoption of new technologies (Mujica, 2019). The company's knowledge of existing and required standards for renewable raw materials supports the introduction of renewable raw materials. Research question G8 asks about the company's knowledge of standards as a predictor for the intended use of renewable raw materials and leads to hypotheses H8. A success factor for use of renewable raw materials are beneficial preconditions of the political system, such as Government funding, push/pull programs and regulations supports the use or renewable raw materials (Binz, Gosens, Hansen, Hansen, 2017). The company's expectations of Government regulations are another predictor for intention to use renewable raw materials. Research question Q9 asks about the company's expectations of government regulations. Hypothesis H9 predicts a positive correlation between expected government regulations and the intention to use renewable raw materials (Horbach, Rammer & Rennings 2012) (Table 5.4).

**Table 5.3** Research questions and hypotheses about company's characteristics

| Symbol | Research question and hypothesis |
|---|---|
| Q4 | What is the actual use of renewable raw materials of chemical companies? |
| H4 | Companies that already use renewable raw materials have a higher intention to use and extend the use of renewable raw materials. |
| Q5 | What is the impact of company's CSR strategy on the intention to use renewable raw materials? |
| H5 | Companies with sustainability values and corporate social responsibility mission have the intention to use renewable raw materials. |
| Q6 | What is the impact of company's management advocacy on the intention to use renewable raw materials? |
| H6 | Companies with a supportive management towards the use of renewable raw materials have the intention to use renewable feedstocks. |
| Q7 | What are the company's cooperation and joined development activities, either with customers, suppliers, associations or external research for use of renewable raw materials? |
| H7 | Companies with cooperation and joined development activities, either with customers, suppliers, associations or external research have the intention to use renewable feedstocks. |

The complexity of the innovation ecosystem and the multitude of possible predictor variables with significance suggest a qualitative research strategy. The exploratory approach will allow further significant variables to be identified and

**Table 5.4** Research questions and hypotheses about environmental factors

| Symbol | Research question and hypothesis |
|---|---|
| Q8 | What is the company's knowledge about existing and needed standards for renewable raw materials? |
| H8 | Chemical companies with a knowledge about existing and needed standards about renewable raw materials have the intention for use. |
| Q9 | What is the company's expectation on Government regulations to support the use of renewable raw materials? |
| H9 | Companies that expect Governmental regulations to foster renewable raw materials have the intention for use. |

respondents are asked to share their views, concerns, contributing factors and success cases for the use of renewable raw materials. Many other company-specific characteristics are also important factors such as company size and innovation intensity. Larger companies generally have greater financial capacity and companies with higher R&D spending for revenue are said to be more innovative. Further employee numbers in the company's R&D department, innovation strategies, number of patents, projects or new products could have an impact (Rogers, 2003; Chan, Dai, Lim & Yee, 2016).

## 5.3 Linking Logic

The link logic is based on agent-based modeling, with the innovator being the focus of research. The perceived attributes of renewable raw materials as substitutes for fossil feedstocks form the attitude and behavioral intention for use of those acting as decision makers. Specific characteristics of the companies are the control elements for behavioral intention to use as well as disadvantageous attributes of renewable raw materials. The main barrier to environmental innovations is high costs, and research is carried out to determine the relationship between costs and behavioral intention when using renewable raw materials in the chemical industry. The CO2 saving potential of the renewable raw materials is assumed to be the main driver for the adoption. The object of research is to test the hypotheses of existing theories and paradigms, which are collected from the literature and the theoretical framework. The subject of the research is also the investigation of further attributes of renewable raw materials for the substitution of fossil raw materials and the investigation of further company-specific characteristics for which no significant effects on the adoption of renewable raw materials in the chemical industry with the aim to reduce GHG emissions and to reach carbon neutrality have been identified. The linkage logic for the use of renewable raw materials in chemical companies is based on the adapted reasoned action model (Fig. 5.2).

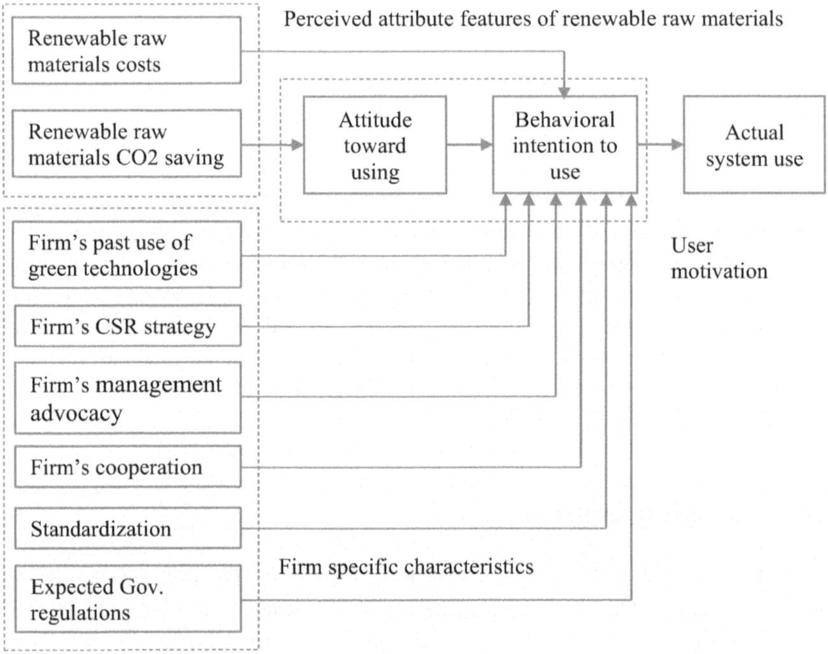


**Fig. 5.2** Linking logic for adoption of renewable raw materials in chemical companies

Background factors are individual's tasks in the company and knowledge about environmental innovation. Actual control, skills/abilities and environmental factors are external effect variables defined by the characteristics of the company, industry specific standards, market and customer needs and the environmental innovation. Perceived attribute features of renewable raw materials are predicting both attitude and behavioral intention. Company specific characteristics, industry standards, market needs and expected Government cooperation are external effect variables and predictors for behavioral intention and actual use of renewable raw materials to reach carbon neutrality in the chemical industry. The qualitative research design allows direct interaction with innovators and provides opportunities to explore additional predictor variables for further research. The linking logic is the theoretical framework for hypothesis testing. Deductive pattern matching attempts to verify the hypotheses (Fig. 5.3).

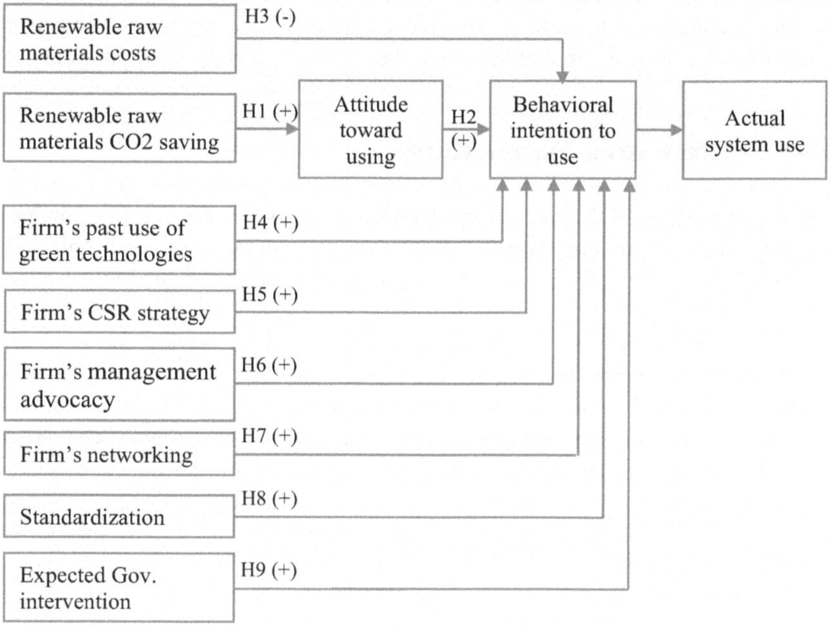


**Fig. 5.3** Testable model for use of renewable raw materials to reduce greenhouse gas emission in the chemical industry

Renewable raw materials with the potential to reduce GHG emissions of the companies should create a positive attitude towards use according to hypothesis H1. The behavioral intention to use renewable raw materials correlates with the attitude towards the use according to hypothesis H2. Higher costs for the use of renewable raw materials creates a barrier for use or its rejection until a more favorable financial attractiveness is given according to hypothesis H3. Past experiences and successful adoption of eco-innovations are positively related to the intention to use according to hypothesis H4. According to hypothesis H5, company's corporate social responsibility strategy supports the intention to use of renewable raw materials. According to hypothesis H6, company's management advocacy supports the intention to use of renewable raw materials and according to hypothesis H7, company's cooperation skills comprising cooperation with suppliers, customers, industry associations, external research and NGOs support the intention to use of renewable raw materials. The knowledge of standards on renewable raw materials and the further need for standardization in the industry also support the intention to use renewable raw materials according to hypothesis H8 and according to hypothesis H9, the intention to use raises with expected Government regulations including market pull and technology push programs.

## 5.4 Alternative Explanations

The unit of analysis of the study is the chemical company, represented by employees who know about the status of the innovation adoption of renewable raw materials. These are research and development managers, sustainability leaders and marketing experts. The agents perceive the attributes of the renewable raw materials either as drivers or as barriers for adoption. GHG saving and costs are the main drivers, as described in the literature. Qualitative research aims to find additional attributes of renewable raw materials that have an impact on adoption. In the literature, six characteristics of companies, the company's previous use of renewable raw materials, CSR strategy, management advocacy, cooperation skills, application of industry standards and expected government regulations are suggested and referred to as predictor variables V4—V9. The qualitative research aims to find additional company-specific predictors that have an impact on the behavioral intention to use renewable raw materials. Standards ensure transparency, accountability and harmonization for products within a market and create better communication between partners (Mujica, 2019). The aim of qualitative research is to find existing industrial standards that have an impact on the use of renewable raw materials and the decision-making process of chemical companies. Government regulations are instruments that prescribe the use of certain materials and support, regulate, or restrict the manufacture and marketing of chemicals. Policy instruments are either described as hard or soft instruments and range from public procurement directives, eco-labeling regulations, tax incentives, public loans and funding to hard intervention tools like taxation of traditional technologies, feed-in tariffs, restrictions, allowances and quotas (Hoff, 2012).

# 6 Research Methodology

A qualitative research approach was chosen for the dissertation in order to examine the predictors for adoption of environmental innovations to reach carbon neutrality in the European chemical industry. The aim of the study is to identify barriers and drivers for innovation adoption and to lay the foundation for conceptualization of transition process for industry and subsectors. Semi-structured interviews with industry experts for data analysis were chosen as the most important research strategy (Fig. 6.1).

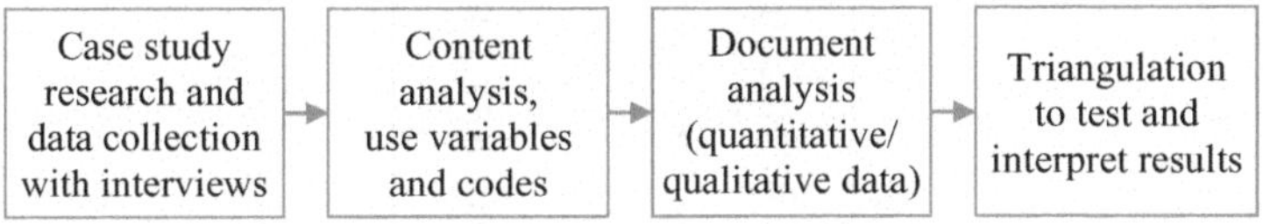


**Fig. 6.1** Exploratory sequential design of the case study research

Mixed methods research is recommended to increase rigor of the study, and industry companies' document analysis serves as a second source. Interviews offer flexibility, the opportunity to ask open-ended and in-depth questions, and explore the latest barriers to innovation. Documentary research is readily available and accesses official company statements. The two sources are reference points for triangulation of data and research results. Data from both sources are analyzed separately and sequentially (Creswell, 2015; Saunders, Lewis & Thornhill, 2012).

**Supplementary Information** The online version contains supplementary material available at https://doi.org/10.1007/978-3-658-45389-3_6.



H. H. E. Ahrens, *The Ecological Modernization of the Chemical Industry*,
https://doi.org/10.1007/978-3-658-45389-3_6

**Table 6.1** Research subjects of the method toolset

| |
|---|
| 1. Attitude and behavioral intention of the industry to reach carbon neutrality |
| 2. Company-specific predictors for adoption |
| 3. Innovation types |
| 4. Innovation-specific predictors for their adoption |

Proposals for predictors for the adoption of renewable raw materials to reduce greenhouse gas emissions are collected from literature studies. The theoretical framework provides the testable model and research questions and hypotheses are formulated. Textual data from the two sources of the study are analyzed to describe topics and interpret the meaning of the text data (Table 6.1).

The mixed methods are the tools to identify meaning units concerning attitude and behavioral intention of the industry to achieve carbon neutrality, company-specific predictors for adoption, innovation types and technology-specific predictors for their adoption. Furthermore, the findings will be used to conceptualize the industry's transition pathway to carbon neutrality applying the frameworks of multi-level perspective of socio-technical systems and technological innovation systems to the European chemical industry.

## 6.1 Case Study Design

The qualitative research method has a case study design with a semi-structured interview technique. Interview guidelines are prepared with main interview questions and additional in-depth questions to collect data for testing the 9 research hypotheses. The cases are selected from an expert database. 14 interviews are completed with data recording, including 2 pilot case studies that have been conducted prior to the main study to test the research process and interview technique. Data processing includes transcription of interviews, translation into English and content analysis. Meaning units of the interview narratives are codified and categorized, and attitudes are measured using the semantic orientation of term and adjectives. The interview technique and the data analysis are developed in preparation for the pilot study. The relevant data to answer the research questions is collected in narratives from semi-structured expert interviews. Existing theories are tested, and the method makes it possible to find new predictors for the use of renewable raw materials. The consistency is increased by interview guidelines for the data collection process. A mixed methods approach is chosen to triangulate the results and documentary analyzes of corporate literature are used as a second data source. The validity of the results of the empirical research study is increased by statistical methods of pattern comparison and keyword density analysis (Grenier, 2018; Yin 2003; 2018). The pilot leads to experience and proves the concept of the research strategy. The effectiveness of the interview process is tested and enables to optimize interview guidelines with the structured questions. In the pilot study, two predictors that have not been tested initially are identified, the company's ability to cooperate and the company's knowledge of industry standards (Alajamy, Al-Mamari, Martins, Nunes & Zhou, 2010; Weichhold, 2019). Document analysis of company publications is chosen as the second method for triangulating the results from field research. Sources of information are sustainability reports, integrated and CSR reports from the 73 corporate members of CEFIC, the European association of the chemical industry, and the documents are examined for the company's intention to use and the actual use of renewable raw materials. The pattern matching technique is used for triangulation and to relate results from documentary analyzes and interview analyzes.

## 6.2 Data Collection

The main data collection technique for case study research uses semi-structured interviews with experts in the chemical industry. The selection criteria for interviews are the business model and company size. Interview partners are selected from among research managers, sustainability managers and marketing experts with an insight into the company's innovation activities. Decision-makers for innovation processes in companies must be available for an interview. The contact person, company and location are coded using identifiers. Potential candidates are collected in an expert database and 2 companies are randomly selected for pilot case studies and 12 companies are randomly selected for the main study from 64 companies with 120 contacts (Table 6.2).

**Table 6.2** Selection criteria for business case studies

| Selection criteria for business cases |
|---|
| • Business model for manufacturing of chemical materials within the EU<br>• Minimum turnover of 10 Mio EUR p.a.<br>• Interview partners from the group of research managers, sustainability leaders and marketing experts |

### 6.2.1 Expert Interviews

Interview guidelines are prepared in order to maintain focus and reduce the susceptibility to influence in semi-structured interviews. The structured approach improves the consistency, validity and reliability of the results. A copy of the guidelines is attached to the electronic supplementary material (ESM) Table 2. They serve as the storyline and minutes for a limited time available during interviews. Most of the questions are open-ended to provide an opportunity for exploratory research (Huffcutt & Culbertson, 2011; Liebold & Trinczek 2009). An attempt is made not to mix the role as researcher with the role as salesperson, teacher or consultant. The interviewer follows active listening and gives the respondents enough time to express themselves (Bolderston, 2012). Respondents need time and freedom to process the answers from understanding the question in context, to access knowledge, to judge the correct answer and to respond. Open-ended questions in expert interviews offer respondents space for accessing in-depth knowledge and background information (Larsen, 2002; Tourangeau, Rips & Rasinski, 2000). A total of 14 telephone interviews were conducted, two of which were interviews in a pilot study (Ahrens, 2021). Saturation is reached after 12 interviews in the main study. The advantage of telephone interviews over face-to-face interviews is the greater flexibility and less effort. Interview technique requires specific knowledge and interpersonal skills for interviewers and informed experts to arrive at the best evaluation of the case (Holt, 2010; Mezirow, 1990) (Table 6.3).

**Table 6.3** Four major compounds of answering a question (Tourangeau, Rips & Rasinski, 2000)

| **Four major compounds of answering a question** |
|---|
| 1. Comprehension of the question |
| 2. Retrieval of information |
| 3. Judgement on the right answer |
| 4. Response |

The sample size of 12 cases is reported to be sufficient for non-probability tests and credibility of the study increases with expertise of the participants (Saunders, Lewis & Thornhill, 2012). Interviews are recorded to provide evidence for the source of information and to increase accuracy of data collection (Davidson & Halcomb, 2006). All informants are asked to agree to the voice recording on the condition that the identifiers of the participants are destroyed, and the data records are anonymized after the transcription. The approach provides the necessary confidentiality of the business information exchanged, otherwise some interviewees may not want a record. The interview partner is given a declaration of consent to confirm that the data set will not be passed on to third parties and that the research results will be used for the dissertation only. A copy of the declaration of consent is attached in the electronic supplementary material (ESM) Table 3. The privacy of the informants is protected under these conditions and the data record on the object of investigation in audio recordings is available for transcription and further analysis (Arrasvuori, Liang & Kuusisto, 2014; Seeley et. al., 2020). All interviews are recorded using the recording function of a smartphone. The strongest evidence of validity comes from the recording of the semi-structured interviews. The approach prevents human factors that memories fade and ability to distinguish between experience and parts added through inference and imagination gets lost (Tourangeau, 2000).

## 6.2.2 Data Processing

Interview recordings are transcribed into a Word document and translated into English if the original language was German. Transcription and translation are both interpretive acts and involve judgments of details and meanings. Linguistic, factual and functional similarity of target and source text are quality criteria and require careful transcription of the verbal records (Vandepitte, 2017). Quality is supported by knowledge of context information and understanding of the subject (Bailey, 2008, Lucas, 2003). Verbatim transcription of the audio data into written text tries to avoid loss and uses word-for-word transcription with filter words, conjunctions and unnecessary repetitions. A new paragraph begins with each lap of the speaker. Interruption inserts are placed in square bracket unless a new subject or paragraph is started (Rincon, 2018; Thomas, 2017). The Microsoft Word Dictate tool is tried out for automated transcription. The automated speech recognition software promises to save time but is rejected. Much information is lost during machine transcription due to poor recording quality and background noise. Unclear pronunciation and misinterpretation of the machine tool lead to errors. Additional editing is required to meet transcription rules. Finally, all recordings are translated manually and the transcription results in text versions of the recorded interviews in the original language (Bokhove &

Downey, 2018). Interviews conducted in German are translated into English and to provide evidences in a base language. The main purpose of translation is to preserve the meaning of the text across two languages, and interpersonal and situational components are taken into account to avoid cultural filters and ensure equivalence of semantic, lexical and textual meaning (Williams, 2009). Machine translation saves time and Google Translate serves as online translation software with translations of the entire files (https://translate.google.com/). The computer tool provides accurate translations between English and German and preserves the contextual meanings of the text (Aiken, 2019; Cieślak, 2011). The limitations of the online translation service are loss of meaning and non-equivalence in scientific texts and technical content (Bunsom, Keyuravong & Vidhayasai 2015). Incorrect translations of idiomatic expressions and syntax errors require adaptation and translations are subject to editing and proofreading as a test procedure in separate activities. Proofreading initially focuses on the meaning of the text and, in the second step, proofreading to correct mistakes, grammar and punctuation errors. Editing also improves flow, quality and focuses on terminology. Proofreading enables grammar and spelling errors to be checked (Flatworld Solutions Pvt. Ltd., 2020; Global Voices Ltd, 2020).

### 6.2.3 Secondary Source

Document analysis provides complementary research data to verify results and support evidence from case study research and semi-structured expert interviews. The mixed methods approach is used to increase the rigor of the research study and to provide a more comprehensive understanding of the transition to carbon neutrality. The use of 2 reference points is the basis for triangulation and analysis of the convergence of the data (Creswell, 2015) (Table 6.4).

The secondary data sources are company's most recent publications on sustainability and greenhouse gas savings activities. The group of corporate members of CEFIC, the European council of the chemical industry with 670 participating organizations and 73 salient corporate members, is the focus group for document analysis. Corporate members are chemical companies with an annual turnover of more than EUR 1 billion and publish annual integrated sustainability or CSR reports on websites and in the mass media. Further documents are CDP climate change responses with published goals and successes for greenhouse gas savings and reports according to the Global Reporting Initiative (GRI). The GRI 305 standard on emissions serves as standardized guideline to report GHG emissions values.

**Table 6.4** Secondary data source

| **Secondary data source** |
|---|
| • Annual reports, Form 10-K issues<br>• Integrated, sustainability, CSR or ESG reports<br>• CDP climate change responses<br>• GRI-reports<br>• Supplementary documents |

## 6.3 Data Analysis

The interview analysis requires data processing. Converting textual data into an organized summary of key findings is the goal of content analysis. In doing so, the obvious and literal content is extracted, and latent content is converted into codes, sub-categories, categories and themes (Erlingsson & Brysiewicz, 2017). Categories are obtained from two sources. They are either identified from the collected data or derived from existing theory and literature (Saunders, Lewis & Thornhill, 2012). The data processing transfers the translated transcripts to an Excel spreadsheet and each lapse of the interviews is assigned a row for data processing. Meaning units are identified through skimming and in-depth reading and the data analysis is subject to organization, sorting, extracting and pattern matching of the meaning units (Grenier, 2018).

### 6.3.1 Codification

Companies with potential interview candidates are collected and assigned to a code F with an ascending number. Contact person, country and location are codified with P, C and L and the number behind them. Meaning units from interview narratives are categorized into five code levels. Keywords, phrases, themes or statements are meaning units with the same central meaning of interest for study. Each meaning unit represents a code and all codes are sorted into categories and sub-categories (Graneheim & Lundman, 2004) (Table 6.5).

**Table 6.5** Code level 1 categories

| Symbol | Code level 1 categories |
|---|---|
| V1 | Attitude towards the use of renewable raw materials |
| V2 | Behavioral intention to use renewable raw materials |
| V3 | Innovation attribute feature and type of renewable raw materials |
| V4 | Company's actual use of renewable raw materials |
| V5 | Company's corporate sustainability strategy |
| V6 | Company's management advocacy |
| V7 | Company's cooperation skills |
| V8 | Company's implementation of industry standards |
| V9 | Company's expectations of Governmental regulations |

The highest code level 1 represents categories matching with company- and innovation specific determinants that have been suggested in previous literature or have been identified in the pilot case studies. All texts that represent a given category are marked in the first text review. These marked passages are coded by one of the predetermined predictor categories. The approach leaves room to identify new categories for meaning units that do not match with a given category and 2 new categories have been identified in the pretest for the main study: Company's cooperation skills and implementation of industry standards. Code level 2 is a sub-category of code level 1. Sub-categories of attitude (V1) are knowledge, belief and affection. Sub-categories of behavioral intention (V2) are planning, implementation and commitment. Sub-categories for innovation (V3) are renewable raw materials, biobased products, segregated material, mass balance materials, oleochemicals, biobased acetic acid, biogas, bio-ethylene, biomass, forestry waste, native oils, plastic waste and others renewable raw materials and innovation types. Uncategorized text is given a new code and the text review is repeated several times until all major terms, nouns and attributes are categorized (Hsieh & Shannon, 2005) (Table 6.6).

**Table 6.6** Hierarchy of codes and categories

| Hierarchy of codes and categories | |
|---|---|
| Categories and predictor variables of the model V1 – V9 | Code level 1 |
| Sub-categories, e.g. innovation types, cooperation types | Code level 2 |
| Attribute features, linked to the category | Code level 3 |
| Attribute value, adjective or participle with semantic orientation | Code level 4 |
| Semantic orientation of the attribute, positive of negative, as driver or barrier for adoption | Code level 5 |

Further categories are company's actual use of renewable raw materials (V4), company's corporate sustainability strategy (V5), company's management advocacy (V6), company's cooperation skills (V7), company's implementation of industry standards for renewable raw materials (V8) and company's expectation for Governmental regulations for renewable raw materials (V9) (Table 6.7).

Coding processes the narrative in a reflective and interpretative way and repeated reading, comparing and seeking of variations is required. Some interview lapses contain meaning units that fit in more than one initial category and are assigned to more than one category or subcategory (Bengtsson, 2016). Categories are usually opinion words or nouns with an adjective or a participle. Adjectives convey a large part of the subjective content in a text and the semantic orientation of the adjectives gives the words a meaning for the person. Either the noun already has an orientation or is given by the adjective or participle. The semantic orientation is a measure of the subjectivity and records the positive or negative evaluation factor of the words (Taboada, Brooke, Tofiloski, Voll & Stede, 2011; Taboada, Anthony & Voll, 2006). Code level 3 is the attribute feature of the predictor variable and the noun of the meaning unit. Code level 4 is the adjective or participle as an attribute value of the predictor variable that carries the semantic orientation. Refinement from the context of the interview or literature that conveys an intended meaning is necessary in some cases to conceptually develop the value (Coast 2012). Finally, code level 5 is the interpretation of the semantic orientation of the adjective or participle and is derived in an interpretive process

**Table 6.7** Code level 2 sub-categories of meaning units

| | | |
|---|---|---|
| **Attitude** | **Behavioral intention** | **Innovation type** |
| Belief, commitment, seeking knowledge, opinion | Conditional behavior, planning, implementing | Availability, $CO_2$ saving, complexity, impact, mass balance scheme, niche products, no feed-food competition, norms, origin, quality, price, supply chain, transparency, type |
| **Actual use** | **Strategy** | **Advocacy** |
| Type | no further subcategory | no further subcategory |
| **Cooperation** | **Standardization** | **Expected Government regulations** |
| Customers, norm committees, suppliers, universities | 14C method, mass-balancing, $CO_2$ emission, life cycle assessments | $CO_2$ tax, levy import tariff, intervention, incentives, restriction, support |

from the meaning of the code in the context. The process interprets the meaning unit either as a driver or a barrier for innovation adoption. Identification of the semantic orientations of units of meaning prepares a bottom-up sorting scheme for the data and for pattern matching (Graneheim & Lundman, 2004).

### 6.3.2 Codification Example

The procedure of the content analysis is further demonstrated by the following example. Respondent P15 gives the following answer to the questioner's question "*What is your and your company's attitude towards renewable raw materials?*" in lapse 2: "*What attitude? So, in the end, it is our endeavor to use or draw on new raw materials in such a way that, ideally, we can offer our existing product portfolio 1:1 in bio-based or sustainable form without sacrificing performance at a similar price. The price doesn't necessarily have to be 1:1, which will probably be difficult anyway—at least at the beginning now—but we say it can cost a maximum of 20% more in terms of raw materials than what it will cost so far. That is roughly the*

**Table 6.8** Example for codification

| Code level 1 category | Code level 2 subcategory | Code level 3 attribute feature | Code level 4 attribute value | Code level 5 effect |
|---|---|---|---|---|
| Attitude | Commitment | - | high | Driver |
| Behavioral intention | Conditional behavior | Certainty | uncertain | Barrier |
| Innovation attribute | Price | - | high | Barrier |
| Innovation attribute | Availability | - | low | Barrier |
| Innovation attribute | Compatibility | - | high | Barrier |
| Corporate sustainability strategy | Product strategy | Availability | available | Driver |

*framework that we have set ourselves"* (Interview partner P15, personal communication, Sep 15, 2020). The phrase *"it is our endeavor to use or draw on new raw materials in such a way that, ideally, we can offer our existing product portfolio 1:1 in bio-based or sustainable form without sacrificing performance at a similar price*" is identified as condensed meaning unit and expresses statements on attitude (V1), behavioral intention (V2), innovation attributes (V3) and corporate sustainability strategy (V5). sorting procedure and codification. Keywords and phrases are sorted in 6 categories and sub-categories and provide meanings with semantic orientation. Commitment as an attitude is interpreted as high. Behavioral intention is not confirmed and depends on price and performance of the renewable materials Three innovation attributes are mentioned in the response: Price, availability and compatibility with customers expectation. A sixth meaning unit in the response is the existing product strategy of the company (Table 6.8).

### 6.3.3 Data Synthesis and Content Analysis

Interviews are merged and reorganized into a single spreadsheet template. Questions, introductory and closing sentences are deleted. The remaining answers of the respondents are sorted according to categories, either predictor variables or mediator variables and other codes, e.g. according to innovation type or according to the orientation of the codes. The template prepares the recognition of patterns (Liebold & Trinczek, 2009). Pattern matching involves combining and comparing a predicted theoretical pattern with an observed empirical pattern. The basic pattern matching specifies and conceptualizes a theoretical pattern and matches the expected pattern with the observed data pattern (Trochim, 1989; Sinkovics, 2018). A pattern is understood as an arrangement of occurrences or outcomes that are evident in the raw data. The pattern matching technique identifies the patterns through familiarity (Almutairi, Gardner & McCarthy, 2014). To strengthen internal validity results and data from more cases are combined. A series of iterations lead to a further revision of the explanations and undergo the hermeneutic cycle until saturation (Yin, 2018). Content analysis of interviews follows the categorization and codification of the interview narratives. In the first step, the synthesized narratives involve skimming as a kind of superficial read-across, thorough reading and interpretation in an iterative process that combines elements of content analysis including the pattern matching technique. Codes related to the nine predictor variables are grouped into categories similar to the content analysis of interview narrations. These category codes are compared between interview transcripts and data from documents. Findings obtained from the interview narratives complement the knowledge base and provide the data base for case study results (Bowen, 2009) (Table 6.9).

**Table 6.9** Content analysis of interview narratives

| Content analysis of interview narratives |
|---|
| • Interview analysis of renewable raw materials (innovation types) |
| • Interview analysis of organizational predictors for adoption |
| • Hypothesis testing of proposed organizational predictor variables |
| • Identification of new predictor variables |
| • Pattern matching of innovation types and relevant attributes from interviews |
| • Pattern matching of company- and innovation-specific predictors |

In a second step, the obtained data are processed for content analysis and the findings are presented in the chapter with case study results. The presentation begins with a description of business cases and statistical results. Predictor variables and attitude and behavioral intention to use renewable raw materials are set in relationship for pattern matching. Hypotheses are tested in the explanatory part of the data analysis with the pattern matching technique. The closer the correlation, the more adjacent and similar are the results of the different cases. The study uses the hermeneutic cycle and saturation is reached after 12 semi-structured interviews (Trochim, 1989). Predictor variables from the testable model relate the informants' perceptions to renewable raw materials and provide the explanatory part of the research. The descriptive display of informants perception of feedstock origin, supply chain model, traceability of the origin of materials, availability, price, compatibility with existent materials, customer needs, CO2 saving and sustainability provide insight in the relevant attributes of renewable technologies to reach carbon neutrality. The specification requirements for an optimal renewable technology are derived from the insights of the informants and correlated with the activities published in the publications of the CEFIC corporate members. Pattern matching of meaning units from the interview analysis and from the document analysis is correlated as a method for triangulation (Almutairi, 2013).

### 6.3.4 Document Analysis

A mixed method approach is chosen to increase the rigor of the study and a document analysis serves as a secondary research method to review results from

**Table 6.10** Variables for document analysis

| Predictor variable | Indicator in document analysis |
|---|---|
| Attitude | • CDP score<br>• Keyword frequency in documents<br>• Vision and mission statements |
| Behavioral intention | • GHG saving targets<br>• Targeted year of carbon neutrality |
| Company-specific predictors | • Company's existing use of renewable raw materials<br>• Company's CSR strategy<br>• Company's advocacy, e.g. projects, investments<br>• Company's cooperation skills<br>• Company's implementation of industry standards<br>• Company's expectation of Government regulations |
| Innovation types | • Efficiency programs<br>• Renewable energy use<br>• Recycling concepts and materials<br>• Biobased raw materials<br>• Carbon capture and utilization technologies |

case study research. Triangulation includes statistical and thematic data analysis techniques of corporate documents. The results of the analysis are combined and compared with the results from expert interviews and supplement or discard the findings. The mixed methods approach combines the strengths and neutralizes the weaknesses of the two methods and offers a more comprehensive understanding of the industry's transition to carbon neutrality (Creswell, 2015; Teddlie & Tashakkori, 2009). The case study design is sequential. The first part is exploratory and examines predictor variables and codes from interview analysis. Predictors are used and tested in document analysis and are listed below. Document analysis uses qualitative and quantitative content analysis techniques. Company CDP scores, GHG reduction targets and keyword density analyses in company publications provide the quantitative data for the content analysis. Mission statements, strategy and activity reports serve as qualitative data for the content analysis. Findings from the document and interview research are triangulated for each predictor using the following linking logic. A comparison with literature serves as a third angle for evaluation and triangulation. Reflection on the findings shall reduce the impact of personal beliefs on interpretation. Finally, a discussion of the research and conclusion suggests limitations of the research, implications for practitioners and future research (Creswell, 2015) (Table 6.10).

### 6.3.5 Validity of the Research

Validity of qualitative research has three aspects, consistency, credibility and transferability of the results. Credibility is one aspect of the validity of research results and equivalent to construct validity in quantitative research. It is concerned with the quality of coverage between categories and data. Each code is chosen to describe one meaning unit, either a single word or a single phase, in order to avoid losing meaning of the text during the condensation. Codes are given until all topics are covered and and two additional predictors have been found by the approach in the pilot study (Graneheim & Lundheim, 2004). Words have specific meanings for a particular speech community and their meanings are not fixed but in fact undergo change. Coding meaning units and identifying semantic orientation are therefore highly interpretative acts (Cook & Stevenson 2010). The pilot study is used as opportunity to identify new relationships and to revise the research approach. The credibility of the study design is tested during the pilot and two additional predictor variables are added to the research, the company's collaborative skills, and the company's implementation of industry standards (Ahrens, 2021; Kezar, 2000). Consistency of data corresponds to internal validity in quantitative research. The consistency of the respondents' information depends on the stability of their perceptions. Attitude is built on cues and affects apart of a conscientious cognitive process. Attitudes to innovation and behavioral intentions can change over time as a result of new information, observations, and experiences. Attitude measures are therefore limited, time-dependent and context-dependent (Cacioppo & Petty, 1986; Ostrom, Krosnick & Sedikides, 1994). To increase consistency and validity of the study, the data collection and analysis are both standardized in the previously described way. The risk of inconsistencies in data collection is reduced through a structured approach with preset interview questions based on research hypotheses and the theoretical framework. Pattern matching requires a clear understanding of the respondents' thoughts and an understanding of the context. Understanding of themes and context of the interviews are improved by good preparation, information on the company's business models and analysis of the results of the previous interviews as part of the hermeneutic cycle of research. Four interpretative acts are involved in data collection and analysis. Understanding what the informant said during the interview is the first interpretative act. The questioner's expertise and judgment, as well as the informant's ability to provide valuable information, have a major influence on the quality of the interview. The advantage of expert interviews over surveys is that the respondents are viewed as informants and partners in order to gain information from deeper, unconscious layers of knowledge of the respondents (Kvale, 1996). Then the data processing including transcription and preparation of the verbal recordings in written text documents and translation is the second act of interpretation. Structuring interviews with interview guidelines and machine translation support standardization and improves its validity and consistency (Sinkovics, 2018). The third interpretative act is the transfer of meaning units into codes and categories in the content analysis. Identifying attribute features and values is a cognitive process and understanding of the sentiment of adjectives and participles is an interpretative act to capture semantic orientation. The fourth interpretative act is the matching and evaluation of patterns. The structured approach of content analysis increases the consistency and credibility of the study (Tourangeau, 2000). Finally, transferability is another aspect of the research quality and corresponds to external validity in quantitative research. It is important to clearly describe the context, participant selection, data collection, and analysis process to facilitate transferability. In general, qualitative research has limited transferability or external validity and the results are limited to the case studied. It is up to the reader whether the results can be transferred to another context (Graneheim & Lundheim, 2004).

# Case Study Results 7

The presentation of the research results includes outcomes content analysis of expert interviews. The presentation of the interview results consists of three parts, a descriptive part with the results from the interviews, a hypothesis testing and an explorative part with the barriers and drivers for renewable raw materials in the chemical industry. Results from the case study research are presented and prepared for triangulated with results from document analysis of companies' publications.

## 7.1 Company's Specific Predictors

128 contacts from 63 companies were collected using the snowball method. Experts from 11 companies declined a telephone interview due to lack of time or interest or postponed the interview indefinitely. The actual reasons remain unknown. 14 experts agreed to be interviewed on condition of confidentiality, 2 interviews are conducted as pretest and 12 interviews are part of the main study. 2 respondents are from SME companies with a turnover of 10—100 million EUR in 2019, 5 respondents are from MNCs with sales of 100—1.000 million EUR and 7 from MNCs with sales of > 1.000 million EUR in 2019. All companies have chemical production sites and sales activities in the European Union. 3 companies are headquartered in Germany, 3 in Switzerland, 6 in other EU countries, one MNC is headquartered in the USA and one in Japan. All respondents

**Supplementary Information** The online version contains supplementary material available at https://doi.org/10.1007/978-3-658-45389-3_7.



H. H. E. Ahrens, *The Ecological Modernization of the Chemical Industry*,
https://doi.org/10.1007/978-3-658-45389-3_7

are active in research and development, sustainability and management positions (Fig. 7.1).

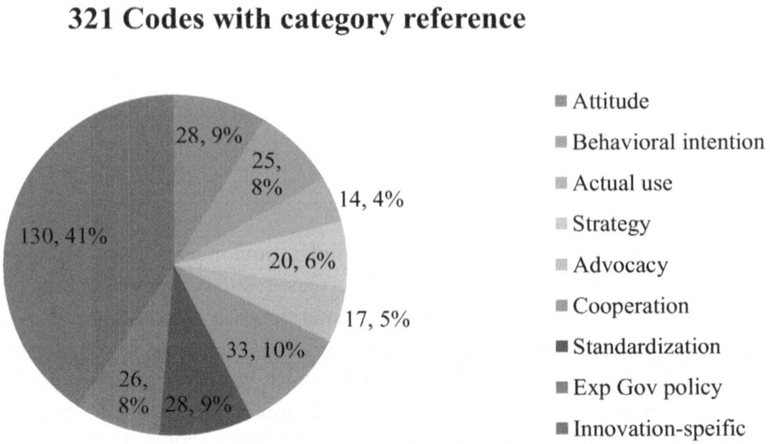


**Fig. 7.1** Number of meaning units from interview narratives

Personal and organizational statements in the interviews are not considered and the interview questions and answers with a total duration of 298 minutes are transcribed for the analysis. 321 meaning units are coded and assigned to the 9 predictor variables. The interview statistics are attached to the electronic supplementary material (ESM) Table 2.3.

### 7.1.1 Attitude

All 14 experts articulated a positive perception and report a positive attitude of companies towards the use of renewable raw materials in the chemical industry. Companies are focusing their innovation efforts on using new raw materials and reducing greenhouse gas emissions, and have set themselves on the path to carbon neutrality. The attitude towards the use of renewable raw materials is "*basically a positive one, it is strategically positioned for renewable raw materials...*" (Interview partner P10, personal communication, Apr 14, 2021). Interview partner P18 admits that this "*is an important issue and we are working on the development of products based on renewable raw materials*" (Interview partner P18, personal communication, May 17, 2021). Interview partner P12 reports, that the attitude towards renewable raw materials *"is hung high"* (Interview partner P12, personal communication, Mar 01, 2021) and companies *"endeavor to use or draw on new raw materials ...to offer existing product portfolio 1:1 in bio-based or sustainable form without sacrificing performance at a similar price"* (Interview partner P15, personal communication, Sep 15, 2020). Researchers are personally convinced, find the new technology exiting and are personally committed. The conversion *"of plastic waste back into a product to replace crude oil feedstock"* is found exciting (Interview partner P12, personal communication, Mar 01, 2021) and straightforwardness leads to the conclusion *"that's why I'm personally, and that's my very personal opinion now, a big fan for this mass balancing"* (Interview partner P8, personal communication, Oct 02, 2020). Market competition, customer needs and opportunities from own operational capabilities are driving forces and motivators for a positive attitude. Companies *"do see opportunities"* (Interview partner P12, personal communication, Mar 01, 2021) and already have *"opportunities and potential"* (Interview partner P8, personal communication, Oct 02, 2020) based on company-specific capabilities and product portfolios. Repeatedly mentioned as motivator for attitude are market forces. Customers create a new demand for products made from renewable raw materials and suppliers *"are directly affected and want to support customers"* with renewable products (Interview partner P51, personal communication, Mar 23, 2021). Renewable product launches receive interest from the market and the competition. *"And so, for example, F36 has some products on the market, that are identical to the fossil-based chemicals. They have made analog products, that are prepared from biobased raw materials"* (Interview partner P50, personal communication, Mar 03, 2021). Company F12 launched a green product and interview partner P12 describes the competitive situation as follows: *"I imagine that customer A has a green product and customer B has an even greener product, the greenest, she can write that on the flag. That's the trend"* (Interview partner P12, personal communication, Mar 01, 2021). Competition and strategic positioning are reported as drivers for adoption of renewable raw materials. "*You have some companies who are pushing it a little bit,*" and interview partner P1 adds: *"You have some bulls pushing it a little bit. But it is more marketing than real sales"* (Interview partner P1, personal communication, Feb 26, 2021) (Table 7.1).

**Table 7.1** Individual background factors and indicators for attitude

**Perceptions for use of renewable raw materials**

- Approval
- Commitment
- Personal convictions

**Motivators for use of renewable raw materials**

- Market competition
- Customer needs
- Opportunities from own operational capabilities
- Strategically positioning
- Reputation and corporate identity
- Environmental and social responsibility towards resource scarcity

**Activities indicating a positive attitude**

- Seeking information
- Seeing opportunities
- Experimenting

Another example is given by interview partner P10. Attitude is "*basically, a positive one*" and company F10 "*is strategically positioned for renewable raw materials*" (Interview partner P10, personal communication, Apr 14, 2021). Finally, environmental and social responsibility is reported as motivator for a positive attitude to "*conserve fossil raw materials, or to no longer use them and to switch to renewable ones*" (Interview partner P8, personal communication, Oct 02, 2020). Respondent P38 explains, "*the added value is also reputation and to be present in the bio-based market. The target is clear. It is necessary to be in this market and to be engaged. The company is gaining reputation using biobased raw materials*" (Interview partner P38, personal communication, Mar 12, 2021). Indicators for attitude towards the use are information seeking, search for opportunities and experimenting with renewables. Company F50 reports, *"at this moment, we are looking for biobased materials for different topics"* (Interview partner P50, personal communication, Mar 03, 2021). Respondent P59 says, that the company is *"looking to use renewable and biobased raw material. But it is very difficult to find out what is the right product. The product quality, performance and the chain of custody are additional issue."* (Interview partner P59, personal communication, May 19, 2021) and company F1 is *"trying to introduce them in new developments"* (Interview partner P1, personal communication, Feb 26, 2021). These activities signal a positive orientation towards the use of renewable raw materials.

### 7.1.2 Behavioral Intention

All 14 interview partners report that companies attempt to use renewable raw materials. Behavioral intention follows attitude building in the decision-making process (Rogers, 2003). Company F1 plans to use renewable raw materials. *"Yes. we plan to use it. We propose it for new products. We try to incorporate it,"* says respondent P1 (Interview partner P1, personal communication, Feb 26, 2021) and company F19 *"is planning to use also partly biobased raw materials, where one part of the material is biobased and the other part is fossil based"* (Interview partner P19, personal communication, Mar 19, 2021). Companies are reporting innovation activities and projects to launch new products based on renewable raw materials. Interview partner P10 reports that *"there are concrete projects ... through joint ventures and development projects"* (Interview partner P10, personal communication, Apr 14, 2021) and company F19 *"had for almost three years a project, where we have looking at biobased materials"* (Interview partner P19, personal communication, Mar 19, 2021). Other companies report that first *"attempts have already run"* (Interview partner P15, personal communication, Sep 15, 2020) and respondent P8 says, *"...we have a finished product, which is C14, that is available for sampling, but it is not yet commercialized"* (Interview partner P8, personal communication, Oct 02, 2020). Company F59 "h*as approaches to use recycled plastic in packaging"* (Interview partner P59, personal communication, Apr 26, 2021) (Table 7.2).

**Table 7.2** Indicators for behavioral intention

| Indicators for behavioral intention | Constraints for behavioral intention |
|---|---|
| • Positive attitude | • Raw material availability |
| • Planning | • Lack of information |
| • Prototyping | • High prices |
| • Innovation activities | • Performance inferiority |

Companies also report constrains and conditional behavioral intent. The main barriers for use are reported to be higher prices, raw material scarcity and lack of information on carbon footprint and other innovation attributes. Product launches depend on a *"maximum price increase of 20% more in terms of raw materials than what it costs so far"* (Interview partner P15, personal communication, Sep 15, 2020). Company F38 reports that it "needs a sustainable source. It needs the carbon footprint and to know the amount of CO2 that is released for production of the raw materials" (Interview partner P38, personal communication, Mar 12, 2021) and decided to wait with the development until information and raw materials are available. Company F1 reports that the CO2 emissions are *"not really the main focus, or not yet"* and biobased raw materials are different, because they *"have more impurities"* (Interview partner P1, personal communication, Feb 26, 2021). Company F51 *"advocates the use of renewable raw materials, provided that the prices are reasonable compared to the petrochemical raw materials"* (Interview partner P51, personal communication, Mar 23, 2021). Another stumbling block is the availability of the sustainability standards. "There are no standards for distinguishing biomass that competes and does not compete with the food chain" says respondent P46 (Interview partner P46, personal communication, May 19, 2021). Without these barriers, all companies agree to use renewable raw materials as replacement for petroleum-based chemicals.

### 7.1.3 Cost Position of Renewables

Inferior cost position and lack of competitiveness of environmental innovations are reported in the literatures as stumbling block for adoption (Hoff, 2012; Horbach, Rammer, & Rennings 2012). Accordingly, hypothesis of the case study is the proposition that intention to use renewable raw materials is stalled due to the lower financial attractiveness and research questions are posed during the expert interviews about the price situation of renewable raw materials. Asked about barriers for adoption, expert P51 responds, that *"the price (is the barrier) too. The raw materials must also be available. If we get more expensive, downstream customers must be willing to pay the higher price"* (Interview partner P51, personal communication, Mar 23, 2021). The same concern from all interview partners, including expert P50, who already buys biobased intermediates and responds *"yes, it is the price,... the price is too high"* (Interview partner P50, personal communication, Mar 03, 2021). The same concern applies to recycled plastics and PLA, polylactic acid, a polymer made from renewable resources. Expert P1 comments, that *"virgin is cheaper, and you have the recycled and then you have PLA, which is the high end, and which is a lot, a lot more expensive"* (Interview partner P1, personal communication, Feb 26, 2021). Market pull and customer demands are reported too weak and regulatory pressure is needed to increase the demand for renewable raw materials. Expert P50 adds to sell *"a little, yes, but not much. If customers are not forced by the Government, then products don't have an advantage"* (Interview partner P50, personal communication, Mar 03, 2021).

### 7.1.4 Actual Use

6 Interview partners report that companies already use renewable raw materials. Company F60 is *"already using some bio-based raw materials in Europe"* (Interview partner P60, personal communication, Apr 28, 2021) (Table 7.3).

**Table 7.3** Reported renewable raw materials by the business cases

| **Reported renewable raw materials** | |
|---|---|
| • Native oils, oleochemicals | • Cellulose |
| • Biobased plasticizer | • Plastic recycling |
| • Biobased ethylene glycol | • Polylactic acid biopolymer |

Company F1 uses native oils and respondent P1 says, that "there is a lot coco nut, palm, rape seed and sunflower oils. That are the most major raw materials" (Interview partner P1, personal communication, Feb 26, 2021). Company F51 uses "cellulose as a raw material as well as starch and starch derivatives" (Interview partner P51, personal communication, Mar 23, 2021). Next to biobased raw materials, also intermediates are used and respondent P50 says, that "the only molecule, which we buy, even though it is more expensive, is diethylene glycol" (Interview partner P50, personal communication, Mar 03, 2021). The consumption of renewable raw materials is estimated by respondent P15 "*spontaneously around 5%*" (Interview partner P15, personal communication, Sep 15, 2020). The highest share of renewable raw materials is reported by company F1 and respondent P1 estimates it to be "*something like between 20 and 30%*" (Interview partner P1, personal communication, Feb 26, 2021). Not every company uses renewable raw materials and respondent P8 says, it is "*not the case with us. However, we have a finished product, which is C14, that is available for sampling, but is not yet commercialized*" (Interview partner P8, personal communication, Oct 2, 2020). Companies also report barriers to actual use of renewable raw materials. Respondent P51 mentions to use already biobased raw materials, but "the other raw materials are based on mineral oil... We have not yet looked at whether these raw materials can also be produced bio-based and who could supply them" (Interview partner P51, personal communication, Mar 23, 2021). Respondent P60 confirms lack of availability as barrier and says, "the problem is where to get the renewable feedstock we need" (Interview partner P60, personal communication, Apr 28, 2021). Existing use of renewable raw materials can be incompatible for replacement of fossil feedstocks and requires new technology development. Unavailability of biobased equivalents to fossil raw materials is reported as a barrier for intention to use renewable based.

### 7.1.5 Sustainability Strategy

Companies with a sustainability strategy are more capable to handle conflicting targets of economic and environmental interests and have greater commitment to drive eco-innovations (Cheng, Yang & Sheu, 2014; Zhang, Loh & Wu, 2020). Interview partners are asked about the impact of company's CSR strategy on the intention to use renewable raw materials (Q4) and only two interview partners associate the question with general goals of sustainability, social responsibility and governance. 7 Interview partners respond with reference to customer needs, market orientation and innovation and product strategies (Table 7.4).

**Table 7.4** Companies' sustainability strategies

| **Companies' sustainability strategies to use renewable raw materials** |
|---|
| • Contribution to UN Sustainable Development Goals<br>• Customer needs and market orientation<br>• Resource efficiencies<br>• Use of renewable raw materials without negative impact on price and performance |

Interview partner P10 refers to the company's *"clear commitment when it comes to sustainability, then we are listed in the index on the stock exchange: Dow Jones Sustainability Index. We also have other topics, for example RSPO palm oil. The company says that's the way to go"* (Interview partner P10, personal communication, Apr 14, 2021). Interview partner P12 responds that *"companies that serve the consumer are on the front lines, ...committing to SDGs and breaking it down on the suppliers. ...The company has committed itself to the UN Global Compact"* (Interview partner P51, personal communication, Mar 23, 2021). UN Sustainable Development Goals and Dow Jones Sustainability Index are reported drivers for sustainability. Other respondents are not aware of the company's sustainability strategy and directly refer to marketing and innovation strategies as driver for sustainability. Activities concerning operational excellence and product portfolio strategies are reported, including efficiency programs, use of recycling material and biobased raw materials. Interview partner P12 says that *"the focus is on the customer..., that you can also create value for the customer"* (Interview partner P12, personal communication, Mar 01, 2021). Customer needs and regional market orientation is also expressed for company F59 that has *"different strategies, depending on the region and the market segment"* (Interview partner P59, personal communication, May 19, 2021). Respondent P1 reports resource efficiency goals of the company and goals "t*o use less energy, to produce less wastewater, to produce less waste and to minimize cargo in total"* (Interview partner P1, personal communication, Feb 26, 2021). Company F15 plans to *"offer the existing product portfolio 1:1 in bio-based or sustainable form without sacrificing performance at a similar price*" and costs are expected to be *"a maximum of 20% more in terms of raw materials. That is roughly the framework that we have set* *ourselves*" (Interview partner P15, personal communication, Sep 15, 2020). Marketing and product development strategies for use of renewable raw materials are drivers for intention to use whereas lack of information is a barrier to intention to use renewable raw materials.

### 7.1.6 Management Advocacy

Company's management allocates resources and is responsible for planning, funding and leading the execution of business strategies. Interview partners are asked how the management supports the use of renewable raw materials and P50 responds to receive *"a big support. The management, the CEO is really pushing it. It is becoming very important"* (Interview partner P50, personal communication, Mar 03, 2021). Respondent P51 reports that *"one management topic is the establishment of a sustainability management system for 2021"* (Interview partner P51, personal communication, Mar 23, 2021) and respondent P18 reports that the use of renewable raw materials *"is an issue in the company. ...we are carrying out a number of projects. The initiative comes from management*" (Interview partner P18, personal communication, May 17, 2021). 6 companies report hiring of new personnel to support the sustainability strategy. Respondent P19 says that the company has invested *"three years in a project, where we have looking at biobased materials for polymerization"* (Interview partner P19, personal communication, Mar 19, 2021). Respondent P51 states to have "research projects," and company F12 supports "recycling projects," according to respondent P12 (Interview partner P12, personal communication, Mar 01, 2021; Interview partner P51, personal communication, Mar 23, 2021) (Table 7.5).

**Table 7.5** Companies' management advocacy of sustainability

| Companies' management advocacy to use renewable raw materials |
|---|
| • Encouragement of the use of renewable raw materials |
| • Funding of new positions, e.g. sustainability managers |
| • Support for development projects |
| • Investments in sustainable product portfolios |

Companies' management encourages the use of renewable raw materials and funds new positions, e.g. sustainability managers. Projects are funded to develop sustainable product portfolios. Interview partner P10 lists a number of management support activities, such as "*investing in companies that produce with renewable raw materials, …investment in development capacities to create these sustainable products, …all of which costs money and it only works if the management is behind it.*" (Interview partner P10, personal communication, Apr 14, 2021). Leadership focus, publication of companies' strategies, employment of sustainability managers, project support, investments in assets and acquisitions are drivers for behavioral intention and all respondents reported support from leadership for adoption of renewable raw materials.

### 7.1.7 Cooperation Activities

Interview partners are asked for their companies' cooperation and joined development activities, either with customers, suppliers, associations or external research for use of renewable raw materials. Cooperation is reported with customers, suppliers, norm committees, research institutes and universities (Table 7.6).

**Table 7.6** Companies' cooperation activities

| Companies' cooperation to use renewable raw materials |
|---|
| • Customers<br>• Suppliers<br>• Research institutes, universities<br>• Regulatory and technology watch, including norm committees |

A market pull effect is observed and developments to use renewable raw materials are "*…due to customer requests*" (Interview partner P8, personal communication, Oct 02, 2020). Company F1 has "*some projects, for example in 100% recyclable materials*" with customers (Interview partner P1, personal communication, Feb 26, 2021). "*Customers ask about the global warming potential and about the CO2 emissions per kg of weight*" (Interview partner P59, personal communication, Apr 26, 2021) and in turn, converters and chemical manufacturers pose the question to their suppliers of raw materials. The use of renewable raw materials requires close cooperation with upstream the supply chain and *"this is where we work most closely with our suppliers,"* says interview partner P51 (Interview partner P51, personal communication, Mar 23, 2021). Respondent P50 reports to cooperate *"more (with) suppliers. At this moment. For biobased and biodegradable materials, yes. There are also projects with universities"* (Interview partner P50, personal communication, Mar 03, 2021). Finally, companies observe regulatory changes and the release of new norms. Expert P15 *"practically always looks in and sees if there is anything new. If there are already CE standards, then of course we take a look"* (Interview partner P15, personal communication, Sep 15, 2020). Respondent P12 reports to cooperate *"closest with research institutes"* (Interview partner P12, personal communication, Mar 01, 2021). Cooperation is a driver for innovation diffusion and the findings of the study are confirmed in the literature (Chesbrough, Gassmann & Enkel, 2010; Huizingh, 2011). Cooperation activities enhance the information flow and tap into the knowledge of different partners to generate new knowledge for product development. Open innovation projects are efficient ways to combine and create new knowledge (Chesbrough, Salter, Vanhaverbeke & Westa, 2014). Also, in this study, cooperation with customers, suppliers, universities and research institutes is reported as a driver for intention to use renewable raw materials. Barriers for use are low customer demand, lack of information from suppliers and high complexity of raw material choices, the innovation landscape, environmental impact factors and supply chains.

### 7.1.8 Standardization

Standards and norms provide transparency to consumers and increase market efficiency (Mujica, 2019). Interview partner P46 responds that *"the customers want to be sure that the materials are biobased and that the source of the carbon is traced by chemical analysis"* (Interview partner P46, personal communication, May 19, 2021). Respondent P15 confirms that customers *"want the C14 method to trace the biobased content, many want to know the biodegradability and compostability"* (Interview partner P15, personal communication, Sep 15, 2020). 14 C radiocarbon method is an analytical procedure to identify the carbon source, either from fossil or biogenic origin. Only material that is made from segregated biobased raw materials is proven sustainable by the method. Coprocessing of biogenic and fossil raw materials leads to a final material with only a portion of tracible bio-content. Instead of analytical methods, certification schemes are available as proof of origin. *"Raw material that has already been certified and is available, especially in energy production—in biogas plants for electricity generation... could be used for the chemical industry's value chain"* (Interview partner P8, personal communication, Oct 02, 2020) (Table 7.7).

**Table 7.7** Standards about renewable raw materials

| Standards about renewable raw materials |
| --- |
| • Certified mass balancing standards |
| • 14C radiocarbon method as analytical procedure for biogenic carbon content |
| • Need for increased information on available standards |
| • Need for addition standards, e.g. biodiversity, carbon footprint calculations and other life cycle assessment criteria |

Lack of knowledge about standards or missing standardization are reported by experts. Respondent P60 says that it is *"important to properly inform the sales people that they are not making false claims"* (Interview partner P60, personal communication, Apr 28, 2021) and respondent P59 states, that *"there are no standards for differentiation of biomass competing with the food chain and that are not competing"* (Interview partner P59, personal communication, May 19, 2021). Marketing claims need standardization to avoid misinterpretation and respondent P18 reports to *"address various claims to customers and they have to be standardized. ...this needs transparency and standardization so that customers can see what is on offer and what they can choose"* (Interview partner P18, personal communication, May 17, 2021). Transparency of supply chains and availability of standards are reported as drivers for intention to use renewable raw materials. Complexity of sustainability goals, e.g. origin of material, competition with food and feed, impact on biodiversity and biodegradability are barriers to the intention to use.

### 7.1.9 Expected Government Policy

Environmental regulations include taxes for traditional technologies and support programs for environmental innovations like Governmental loans, funds, allowances and feed-in tariffs (Hoff, 2012). The German Renewable Energy Act supports renewable energy from wind turbines, photo voltaic panels, hydro and geothermal energy by feed-in tariffs and allowances and the EU Renewable Energy Directive supports the use or renewable raw materials for transportation fuels (Directive (EU) 2015/1513; Erneuerbare-Energien-Gesetz—EEG, 2000). Experts are asked about their expectations for Government policies and respondent P51 says that *"we would appreciate it if there were tax breaks or subsidies for the use of renewable raw materials"* (Interview partner P51, personal communication, Mar 23, 2021). Expert P8 raises the concern that *"everyone agrees that a global solution would of course be best, but that's very difficult in this environment"* (Interview partner P8, personal communication, Oct 02, 2020). Respondent P1 is skeptical and says, *"that would be nice but I don't expect that they will do that"* (Interview partner P1, personal communication, Feb 26, 2021). *"Appropriate funding would be needed to apply for. Appropriate studies could be supported with universities"* (Interview partner P12, personal communication, Mar 01, 2021). The probability of regulatory measures in support of renewable raw materials is rated with a mixed likelihood (Table 7.8).

**Table 7.8** Expectations for CO2 taxes on use of fossil raw materials

| Expectation of CO2 tax | Number of respondents |
|---|---|
| Taxation in between 0 - 5 years | 2 |
| Taxation in between 5 - 10 years | 3 |
| Taxation at later point | 1 |
| No expectation | 8 |

6 Respondents expect CO2 taxes, levy of import tariffs and regulatory support for renewable raw materials, which are drivers for adoption. Two respondents expect CO2 taxation on fossil raw materials in between 0—5 years, 3 respondents between 5—10 years and one respondent does not expect CO2 taxes before 2030 (Interview partner P10, personal communication, Apr 14, 2021). The other 8 respondents are rather skeptical about CO2 taxes and Governmental support for renewable raw materials, sharing their uncertainty about future regulations. At the time of the interviews between October 2020 and April 2021, the difficulty to imagine that CO2 taxes will be levied in favor of renewable raw materials.

### 7.1.10 Summary of Company-specific Predictors

Five company-specific predictors—existing use of renewable raw materials, company's sustainability strategy, management advocacy, cooperation skills, implementation of industry standards and expectations of Government regulations—are determinants for use of renewable raw materials. The meaning units identified in the interviews regarding the company-specific predictors are compiled in the electronic supplementary material (ESM) Table 3.1. In this study, all respondents report a positive attitude and intention to use renewable raw materials for chemical manufacturing. The main driver for the intention to use renewable resources is a positive attitude of the companies and the support of the management towards the use (Table 7.9).

**Table 7.9** Company-specific predictors and semantic orientation of the meaning units

| **Company-specific predictors and semantic orientations of the meaning units** | | | |
|---|---|---|---|
| **Variable** | **Barrier** | **Driver** | **Count** |
| Attitude | 0 | 28 | 28 |
| Behavioral intention | 5 | 20 | 25 |
| Actual use | 8 | 6 | 14 |
| Strategy | 7 | 13 | 20 |
| Advocacy | 0 | 17 | 17 |
| Cooperation | 4 | 29 | 33 |
| Standardization | 17 | 11 | 28 |
| Exp Gov policy | 10 | 16 | 26 |
| Innovation-specific | 71 | 59 | 130 |
| **Total** | **122** | **199** | **321** |

All the meaning units on attitude have positive semantic orientation. The meaning units on behavioral intention mainly have a positive semantic orientation and use is mainly slowed down by higher prices for renewable raw materials. Only 6 out of 14 respondents report that their companies already use renewable raw materials. Innovation-specific predictors as perceived by industry experts are discussed in a separate section. Meaning units from the categories of sustainability strategy, advocacy tools, cooperation activities, and expectations of government support have predominantly a positive semantic orientation, while perceptions of existing standards and innovation-specific predictors have predominantly a negative semantic orientation. After all, positive attitudes and a supportive management are reported to be the main driver for intentions to use renewable raw materials while higher prices for raw materials are the biggest barrier (Fig. 7.2).

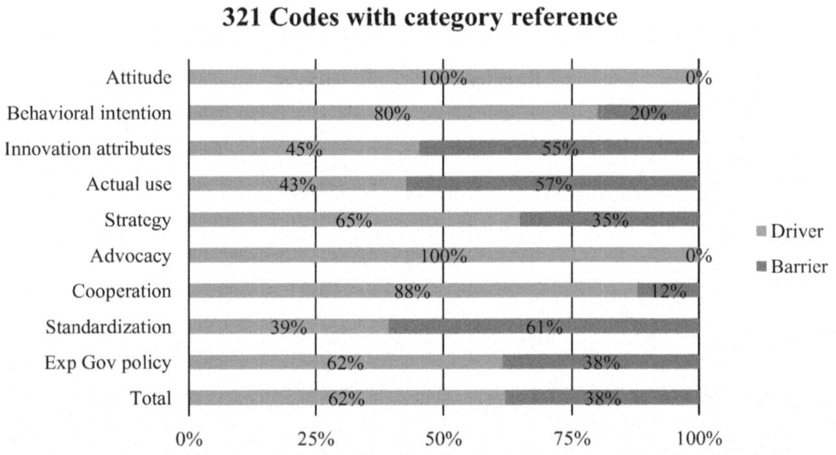


**Fig. 7.2** Staked bar-chart of companies-specific predictors

The staked bar-chart presents positive attitude, advocacy and cooperation skills as the strongest drivers for behavioral intention. Most likely also because respondents with a positive attitude are more willing to accept interviews about sustainability and carbon neutrality. They all share the support of their management, which encourages innovation in the use of renewable energy and allows interviews on this topic. Strong drivers are cooperation skills, CSR strategy and expected Government policies. Weaker drivers for behavioral intention are actual use of renewables and standardization of renewable raw materials. A pattern of actual use and behavioral intention was not identified. Companies are open for standardization of renewable raw materials, but a common understanding of sustainability characteristics is still missing (Table 7.10).

**Table 7.10** Visualization of organizational predictors from case studies

| Environment - Management | Weak driver | Strong driver | Very strong driver |
|---|---|---|---|
| | | CSR strategy | Advocacy |
| | Actual use of renewables | Cooperation skills | Attitude |
| | Standardization of novel technologies | Expected Government policies | |

## 7.2 Hypotheses Testing

Hypotheses derived from the existing literature are critically examined in the following sections. The pattern matching technique is applied as an explanatory part of the data analysis and attempts to find the existing logical relationships among the determinants. The expected patterns are matched with the observed data patterns that emerge from the respondents' answers to the interview questions. Conclusions are drawn by logical deduction and compared with each other and with other relevant statements (Popper, 2002).

### 7.2.1 Hypothesis Testing of the Attitude

The first hypothesis H1 refers to the attitude of chemical companies towards the use of renewable raw materials as predictor variable V1 for behavioral intentions. All 14 industry experts from research and development departments or with management positions report a positive attitude of chemical companies towards the use of renewable raw materials with the aim of reducing greenhouse gas emissions and achieving carbon neutrality. Respondents report personal conviction and support from customer demand. Other motivators for a positive attitude towards the use of renewable raw materials are economic interests and environmental and social responsibility. "*It is right to go in that direction*" says respondent P15 (Interview partner P15, personal communication, Sep 15, 2020) and respond P5 says, "at the end, it is the customers" (Interview partner P5, personal communication, Mar 17, 2021). Respondent P1 says, "*we always try to use them (renewable raw materials) in new development*" (Interview partner P1, personal communication, Feb 26, 2021), and attitude "*is hung high*" for respondent P12 (Interview partner P12, personal communication, Mar 01, 2021). Seeking information and having expectations are signs of intrinsic motivation and respondent P5 reports, that "*at this moment, we are looking for biobased materials for different topics*" (Interview partner P5, personal communication, Mar 17, 2021). Respondent P59 reports, that "*expectations and demands are high*" (Interview partner P59, personal communication, May 26, 2021). Attitude is reflected by participation in sustainability initiative like the one reported by respondent P51: "*We are involved in the program of the VCI Chemie Hoch 3*" (Interview partner P51, personal communication, Mar 23, 2021). Respondents mention market competition, customer needs and demands, opportunities from own operational capabilities, strategically positioning, reputation and corporate identity and environmental and social responsibility towards resource scarcity. Activities indicating a positive attitude are information seeking and commitment. Chemical companies have a positive attitude towards the use of renewable raw materials and hypothesis H1 is confirmed.

### 7.2.2 Hypothesis Testing of the Behavioral Intention

The second hypothesis H2 refers to the intention to use renewable raw materials as predictor variable V2 for actual use. All companies support the use of renewable raw materials for chemical synthesis, and interview partners report planning activities, testing of renewable raw materials, and prototyping of final products. The intention to use renewable raw materials is expressed by the group of interview partners, and none of the respondents reject or deny the intention to use renewable raw materials (Table 7.11).

**Table 7.11** Evidence for behavioral intent from expert interviews

| Citation | Source |
|---|---|
| *"Absolutely, yes."* | (Interview partner P15, personal communication, Sep 15, 2020) |
| *"…we have a finished product, …that is available for sampling, but is not yet commercialized."* | (Interview partner P8, personal communication, Oct 02, 2020) |
| *"Yes. we plan to use."* | (Interview partner P1, personal communication, Feb 26, 2021) |
| *"We support recycling projects"* | (Interview partner P12, personal communication, Mar 01, 2021) |
| *"We are ready to test all samples and new products that are offered to us."* | (Interview partner P38, personal communication, Mar 12, 2021) |
| *"For us it is the main thing that biomass and bio-raw materials are used."* | (Interview partner P5, personal communication, Mar 17, 2021) |
| *"… next we launch our first biobased version for paints. So, we are present and prepare for new technology."* | (Interview partner P19, personal communication, Mar 19, 2021) |

(continued)

**Table 7.11** (continued)

| Citation | Source |
|---|---|
| *"We advocate the use of renewable raw materials, provided that the prices are reasonable compared to the petrochemical raw materials."* | (Interview partner P51, personal communication, Mar 23, 2021) |
| *"Yes. One can see the intention. For example, by seeing the investment that has been made..."* | (Interview partner P10, personal communication, Apr 14, 2021) |
| *"We have approaches to use recycled plastic in packaging."* | (Interview partner P59, personal communication, Apr 26, 2021) |
| *"We are looking to use renewable and biobased raw material."* | (Interview partner P46, personal communication, May 19, 2021) |
| *"We are looking for suppliers for ISCC certified material, direction HVO."* | (Interview partner P60, personal communication, Apr 28, 2021) |
| *"We are working on the development of products based on renewable raw materials."* | (Interview partner P18, personal communication, May 17, 2021) |

Both attitude and behavioral intention are reported positive and hypothesis H2 is confirmed. The intention to use renewable raw materials is positively correlated with attitude toward the use of renewable raw materials and hypothesis H2 is confirmed.

### 7.2.3 Hypothesis Testing of the Price Effect

The third hypothesis H3 is about the price impact on behavioral intention to use of renewable raw materials. Higher costs for environmental innovations are reported to be main barrier for adoption (Hoff, 2012). Financial unattractiveness is proposed as predictor V3 for behavioral intention and interview analysis provides 18 meaning units with respect to high prices for renewable raw materials for chemical synthesis apart from other barriers for their adoption (Table 7.12).

**Table 7.12** Evidence for financial unattractiveness of renewable raw materials

| Citation | Source |
|---|---|
| *"...it is still difficult to really step on the gas with the still relatively high raw material prices in contrast to petroleum-based ones."* | (Interview partner P15, personal communication, Sep 15, 2020) |
| *"... most of the time it's more expensive than the standard products."* | (Interview partner P1, personal communication, Feb 26, 2021) |
| *"...these products are still too expensive."* | (Interview partner P50, personal communication, Mar 03, 2021) |
| *"The suppliers had high costs and the customers did not want to pay a premium over the standard product."* | (Interview partner P59, personal communication, May 26, 2021) |
| *"It is not enough just to be sustainable. It is not enough."* | (Interview partner P10, personal communication, Apr 14, 2021) |
| *"We are not using the biobased additives ...because of the extra costs"* | (Interview partner P19, personal communication, Mar 19, 2021) |

Companies are aware to be in the dilemma to meet market needs on one side and to reduce GHG emissions and to reach carbon neutrality without loosing competitiveness on the other side. *"At the end, it is the customers. ... It is rather us and we need to work this out, where we want to go."* (Interview partner P5, personal communication, Mar 17, 2021). All respondents indicated that higher prices are a barrier to adoption. Adoption of renewable raw materials is impeded by the higher prices and hypothesis H3 is confirmed.

### 7.2.4 Hypotheses Testing of the Actual Use

Hypothesis H4 states that companies that already use renewable raw materials have a higher intention to use and expand the use of renewable raw materials. The actual use of renewable raw materials is proposed as predictor V4. 6 respondents report the use of biobased raw materials. One respondent reports using partially bio-based raw materials, one respondent reports offering a bio-based prototype, and the other 6 respondents do not use any materials based on renewable raw materials (Table 7.13).

**Table 7.13** Evidence for actual use of renewable raw materials

| Citation | Source |
|---|---|
| *"Yes. Just like native oils, for example."* | (Interview partner P15, personal communication, Sep 15, 2020) |
| *"For example, we have a plasticizer, that has 33% biobased content."* | (Interview partner P1, personal communication, Feb 26, 2021) |
| *We already use bio-based raw materials and that is already the main part."* | (Interview partner P51, personal communication, Mar 23, 2021) |
| *"The only molecule, which we buy, ... is ethylene glycol. So, ethylene glycol, biobased is the only raw material ...., that is 100% biobased, with the same chemistry as fossil-based chemicals."* | (Interview partner P50, personal communication, Mar 03, 2021) |
| *"For example, products made from corn, sugar."* | (Interview partner P10, personal communication, Apr 14, 2021) |
| *"We already do since many years, also before the question of climate change."* | (Interview partner P46, personal communication, May 19, 2021) |

6 companies already use renewable raw materials, but all 14 companies have plans and activities signaling behavioral intention. Actual use is not identified as predictor for behavioral intention in the interviews, but companies that already use renewable raw materials for replacement of fossil intermediates may be advanced and may have higher aspirations to extend the use of renewable raw materials. Additional research is needed to confirm hypothesis H4 and document analysis is planned for triangulation.

### 7.2.5 Hypothesis Testing of the Sustainability Strategy

Hypothesis H5 states that the company's sustainability strategy is a predictor V5 of behavioral intention. Only 3 respondents refer to their companies' sustainability goals (Table 7.14).

**Table 7.14** Evidence for companies' sustainability strategy

| Citation | Source |
|---|---|
| *"Environmental, social and governance, ... is a strategy from our corporate headquarters... to design sustainably."* | (Interview partner P8, personal communication, Oct 02, 2020) |
| *"(We are) committing to SDGs and breaking it down on the suppliers. ... the company has committed itself to the UN Global Compact."* | (Interview partner P51, personal communication, Mar 23, 2021) |
| *"There is a clear commitment when it comes to sustainability, then we are listed in the Dow Jones Sustainability Index"* | (Interview partner P10, personal communication, Apr 14, 2021) |

A second group of 8 respondents translates companies' strategy into product, marketing and innovation strategy. Respondent P15 answers to *"offer our existing product portfolio 1:1 in bio-based or sustainable form"* (Interview partner P15, personal communication, Sep 15, 2020) and respondent P12 replies that *"... the goal is to have a green portfolio"* (Interview partner P12, personal communication, Mar 01, 2021). When asked for strategy, interview partner P4 answers *"the focus is on the customer"* (Interview partner P12, personal communication, Mar 01, 2021) and interview partner P46 answers to have *"different strategies, depending on the region and the market segment"* (Interview partner P46, personal communication, May 19, 2021). Respondents are familiar with CSR objectives and consider sustainability in their innovation strategy with regard to market needs and customer requirements. A total of 11 respondents report strategies to promote renewable raw materials. A third group of 3 interviewees report having no sustainability goals. Interview partner P1, who is managing director responds, *"No, no we don't have any goals"* and estimates the share of renewable raw materials on a high level of *"something like between 20 and 30%"* (Interview partner P1, personal communication, Feb 26, 2021). Respondent P59 says *"I haven't seen them"* (Interview partner P59, personal communication, May 26, 2021) and respondent P18 refers to GHG savings and says, that *"for us it will probably take until 2050, as is the goal of politics"* (Interview partner P18, personal communication, May 17, 2021). The majority of the interviewees have sustainability, marketing or innovation strategies related to renewable resources. In summary, hypothesis H5 and sustainability strategy can be confirmed as predictors of behavioral intentions from the interview case study. However, document analysis is required for triangulation and further evidence.

### 7.2.6 Hypothesis Testing of the Management Advocacy

Hypothesis H6 proposes that a supportive management is a predictor for behavioral intention to use renewable raw materials. Meaning units from 10 interviews support the hypothesis that companies' leadership actively advocates the intention to use renewable raw materials. Other interview partners do not comment on it. Management support, employments, investments and project funding are reported providing evidence that leadership plays a role in behavioral intention. Innovators are encouraged to seek information on novel renewable feedstocks and newly employed sustainability managers are mandated with data collection. It is not reported that leadership impedes the use of renewable raw materials. Hypothesis H6 and management advocacy is confirmed as predictor (Table 7.15).

**Table 7.15** Evidence for companies' management advocacy

| Citation | Source |
|---|---|
| *"They are pretty much pushing it."* | (Interview partner P15, personal communication, Sep 15, 2020) |
| *"a position has also been created"* | (Interview partner P8, personal communication, Oct 02, 2020) |
| *"Off course."* | (Interview partner P1, personal communication, Feb 26, 2021) |
| *"Yes. We support recycling projects."* | (Interview partner P12, personal communication, Mar 01, 2021) |
| *"They hired a new person. ... they set up social, environmental and sustainability targets in the company"* | (Interview partner P50, personal communication, Mar 03, 2021) |
| *"A new colleague and chemist who is starting in this department."* | (Interview partner P38, personal communication, Mar 12, 2021) |
| *"We had for almost three years a project, where we have looking at biobased materials."* | (Interview partner P19, personal communication, Mar 19, 2021) |
| *"A chemist was hired in research. ...there are also research projects."* | (Interview partner P51, personal communication, Mar 23, 2021) |
| *"We are carrying out a number of projects."* | (Interview partner P18, personal communication, May 17, 2021) |
| *"... investments are being made."* | (Interview partner P10, personal communication, Apr 14, 2021) |

### 7.2.7 Hypothesis Testing of Cooperation Activities

Hypothesis H7 proposes that company's cooperation skills are predictors for behavioral intention to use renewable raw materials. All 14 interview partners report cooperation activities with customers, suppliers, universities and research institutes, and norm committees (Table 7.16).

**Table 7.16** Evidence for companies' cooperation activities

| Citation | Source |
|---|---|
| *"We interview our suppliers."* | (Interview partner P15, personal communication, Sep 15, 2020) |
| *"We need to follow the need of the customers."* | (Interview partner P1, personal communication, Feb 26, 2021) |
| *"I think my company sees, ... due to customer requests probably triggered first - already a potential ...."* | (Interview partner P8, personal communication, Oct 02, 2020) |
| *"They are institutes. We are working on pilot systems."* | (Interview partner P12, personal communication, Mar 01, 2021) |
| *"There are also projects with universities, sponsored projects by the Government."* | (Interview partner P50, personal communication, Mar 03, 2021) |
| *"There are research projects to use CO2 from steel mills."* | (Interview partner P38, personal communication, Mar 12, 2021) |
| *"At the end, it is the customers... The customers' demand in the market is a big difference that what is possible..."* | (Interview partner P5, personal communication, Mar 17, 2021) |
| *"It is a R&D project at the Government owned research institute."* | (Interview partner P19, personal communication, Mar 19, 2021) |
| *"This is where we work most closely with our suppliers."* | (Interview partner P51, personal communication, Mar 23, 2021) |

(continued)

**Table 7.16** (continued)

| Citation | Source |
|---|---|
| *"We work with customers."* | (Interview partner P10, personal communication, Apr 14, 2021) |
| *"Customers ask about the lobal warming potential and about the CO2 emissions per kg of weight."* | (Interview partner P59, personal communication, May 26, 2021) |
| *"It needs the chain of custody from five different places."* | (Interview partner P46, personal communication, May 19, 2021) |
| *"We have the raw material side and the customer side. We are looking for suppliers for ISCC certified material."* | (Interview partner P60, personal communication, Apr 28, 2021) |
| *"The cooperation now mainly takes place with suppliers."* | (Interview partner P18, personal communication, May 17, 2021) |

Hypothesis H7 is confirmed by all 14 respondents who report companies' cooperation with suppliers, customers and research from outside the companies. Cooperation activity correlates with behavioral intention to use renewable raw materials.

### 7.2.8 Hypothesis Testing of the Industry Standards

Hypothesis H8 states that the company's implementation of existing standards for renewable raw materials correlates with behavioral intention. All 14 interviewees are aware of the need for supply chain transparency and the need to standardize the environmental impact of renewable raw materials. Biodegradability, competition with food and feed, and social aspects of the raw material are addressed in addition to the origin and emission factors of the raw materials and signal need for further standardization. Also, the need for harmonization of life cycle assessments is reported (Table 7.17).

**Table 7.17** Evidence for companies' knowledge about standards

| Citation | Source |
|---|---|
| *"It needs standards. There are no clear goals as to where to go."* | (Interview partner P18, personal communication, May 17, 2021) |
| *"It is important to properly inform the salespeople that they are not making false claims."* | (Interview partner P60, personal communication, Apr 28, 2021) |
| *"We need full transparency. The chain of custody is important for industrial partners of the brands."* | (Interview partner P46, personal communication, May 19, 2021) |
| *"There are no standards for differentiation of biomass competing with the food chain."* | (Interview partner P46, personal communication, May 19, 2021) |
| *"It is therefore desirable if standards are published that unify the assessment procedures."* | (Interview partner P51, personal communication, Mar 23, 2021) |
| *"Customers ask about the global warming potential and about the CO2 emissions per kg of weight."* | (Interview partner P59, personal communication, May 26, 2021) |
| "If you have an additive, such as 1 to 2 or 3% in the application, then the general opinion in Germany is that you then take 100% bio-based. 100% Renewable and not Mass Balance." | (Interview partner P10, personal communication, Apr 14, 2021) |

(continued)

**Table 7.17** (continued)

| Citation | Source |
|---|---|
| *"The monomers are the major part of the products and you have the mass balance approach... They are loading a part of biobased raw materials in the process. So today they have maybe 25% and tomorrow 50%, and so on."* | (Interview partner P19, personal communication, Mar 19, 2021) |
| *"These are two different approaches. Both are interesting. For certain applications, the segregated material if it is available... Or the mass balance approach... For us it is the main thing that biomass and bio-raw materials are used."* | (Interview partner P5, personal communication, Mar 17, 2021) |
| *"It needs guidance to standardize. There is still not a clear view on how we can make the calculations and estimations and it needs standardization of the methods."* | (Interview partner P38, personal communication, Mar 12, 2021) |
| *"At this moment, we are looking for biobased materials for different topics. But they are now looking more to biodegradable materials than really biobased chemicals with the same chemistry."* | (Interview partner P50, personal communication, Mar 03, 2021) |

(continued)

**Table 7.17** (continued)

| Citation | Source |
|---|---|
| *"We have certified the process according to REDcert and the plastics industry can live with this certificate. Other industries are now increasingly asking about ISCC."* | (Interview partner P60, personal communication, Apr 28, 2021) |
| *"This is a raw material that has already been certified."* | (Interview partner P8, personal communication, Oct 02, 2020) |
| *"I am just talking about the demand with these analytical and measurement methods, what should be measured, what is bio-based and what is not... There is still a lack of standards."* | (Interview partner P15, personal communication, Sep 15, 2020) |

Respondents are aware of the two categories of the supply chains for renewable raw materials, the segregated and mass balanced supply chains and there is knowledge about the existing analytical method to trace biogenic carbon. Respondents also express the needs for further standardization and transparency. Unified life cycle assessments, calculation methods of GHG emissions and balancing conflicts between land use and land use change, use of biobased raw materials, GHG emission reduction, and biodegradability are mentioned. Hypothesis H8 is confirmed. All 14 respondents report interest and knowledge or seek information for standards. Knowledge and use of existing industry standards and awareness of needs where standards are missing correlates with behavioral intention to use renewable raw materials.

### 7.2.9 Hypothesis Texting of Expected Government Regulations

Hypothesis H9 proposes that company's expectation of Government regulations correlates with behavior intention to use renewable raw materials. 6 Respondents expect Government regulations in support of renewable raw materials to take place, 8 don't expect Government regulations or don't respond (Table 7.18).

**Table 7.18** Evidence for expected Government regulations

| **Citations with positive expectation** | **Source** |
|---|---|
| *"Yeah, sure. In the medium to long term, I think it could happen,"* ... *"5 – 10, I would have said."* | (Interview partner P15, personal communication, Sep 15, 2020) |
| *"I like to believe that something will come in 5 years."* | (Interview partner P8, personal communication, Oct 02, 2020) |
| *"No, I think... I hope, between 5 years, coming in this... or more in the direction of 10 years."* | (Interview partner P1, personal communication, Feb 26, 2021) |
| *"It can happen quickly, depending on how good the lobbyists are. I trust them that they will come up with something like that in the next 5 years. That would suit the EU. I expect that."* | (Interview partner P12, personal communication, Mar 01, 2021) |
| *"Over the next 5 to 10 years."* | (Interview partner P51, personal communication, Mar 23, 2021) |
| *"I would like politicians to support the chemical industry as well."* | (Interview partner P60, personal communication, Apr 28, 2021) |
| **Citations with negative expectation** | **Source** |
| *"No. Not yet. It could come. Not yet."* | (Interview partner P50, personal communication, Mar 03, 2021) |
| *"I think that is unlikely. If a state does that, it is in competition with other states. And if it does, not until 2030."* | (Interview partner P10, personal communication, Apr 14, 2021) |

(continued)

**Table 7.18** (continued)

| Citations with negative expectation | Source |
|---|---|
| *"I have the feeling. We are slower."* | (Interview partner P38, personal communication, Mar 12, 2021) |
| *"I can not judge over this. Probably little since most of the CO2 emissions are caused by the manufacturing steps."* | (Interview partner P59, personal communication, May 26, 2021) |

The result of the case study research is mixed. Respondents are aware of the impact of Government regulations and the policies and regulations are important predictors for innovation adoption. A part of respondents expects CO2 taxes to take place in the foreseeable future, while the other part reports uncertainties. EU climate regulations and CO2 taxes are seen as driver for intention to use renewable raw materials whereas uncertainties about timeframe and policy instruments are perceived as barriers. Respondent P60 says: "I would like politicians to support the chemical industry as well. But I can't say more about it" (Interview partner P60, personal communication, Apr 28, 2021), and respondent says: "I'm not up to date. I could also play back the question" (Interview partner P8, personal communication, Oct 02, 2020). Other respondents don't have expectations or express their wishes for regulations, taxes and laws in support of renewable raw materials. Hypothesis H9 that companies that expect Governmental regulations to foster renewable raw materials have the intention for use, is not confirmed and the proposition cannot be generalized. The intention to use is not correlating with expected Government regulations and document analysis is required to find further evidence for relationship and triangulation.

### 7.2.10 Summary of the Hypothesis Testing

Hypotheses H1 to H3 are concerned about the relationship of attitude and behavioral intention. Further the main barrier for adoption of environmental innovation is tested and the results are summarized below (Table 7.19).

**Table 7.19** Hypothesis test results for attitude and behavioral intention

| Hypothesis | | Confirmation |
|---|---|---|
| H1 | Chemical companies have a positive attitude towards the use of renewable raw materials. | Confirmed |
| H2 | The intention to use renewable raw materials is positively correlated with attitude toward the use of renewable raw materials. | Confirmed |
| H3 | The intention to use renewable raw materials is stalled due to the lower financial attractiveness as compared to petrochemically based products. | Confirmed |

Hypotheses H4 to H7 are concerned about companies' characteristics. The relationship between companies' behavioral intention to use and proposed predictors existing use of renewable raw materials, sustainability strategy, management advocacy and cooperation practices is tested (Table 7.20).

Finally, hypotheses H8 and H9 concern about the relationship between intention to use and the predictor variables industry standards and expected Government policy. Behavioral intention correlates with knowledge about existing industry standards but there is no evidence for a correlation between behavioral intention and expectations for Government regulations. An explanation for mismatch may be, that behavioral intention is not correlating with expectations but with implemented and existing Governmental regulations (Table 7.21).

**Table 7.20** Hypothesis test results for companies' characteristics

| Hypothesis | | Confirmation |
|---|---|---|
| H4 | Companies that already use renewable raw materials have a higher intention to use and extend the use of renewable raw materials. | Not confirmed |
| H5 | Companies with sustainability values and corporate social responsibility mission have the intention to use renewable raw materials. | Confirmed |
| H6 | Companies with a supportive management towards the use of renewable raw materials have the intention to use renewable feedstocks. | Confirmed |
| H7 | Companies with cooperation and joined development activities, either with customers, suppliers, associations or external research have the intention to use renewable feedstocks. | Confirmed |

**Table 7.21** Hypothesis test results for environmental factors

| Hypothesis | | Confirmation |
|---|---|---|
| H8 | Chemical companies with a knowledge about existing and needed standards about renewable raw materials have the intention for use. | Confirmed |
| H9 | Companies that expect Governmental regulations to foster renewable raw materials have the intention for use. | Not confirmed in case study research |

## 7.3 Innovation-specific Predictors

Through content analysis of interview reports, categorization and clustering of innovation characteristics, the key innovation predictor variables for the adoption of renewable raw materials with the aim of greenhouse gas savings and contribution to carbon neutrality are identified (Table 7.22).

**Table 7.22** Main innovation-specific predictors for adoption

| Main innovation-specific predictors for adoption |
|---|
| • Availability of materials |
| • CO2 savings incl. availability of CO2 savings data |
| • Price |
| • Compatibility with existing technological regimes |
| • Transparency of the supply chain |

When asked for main barriers for adoption, respondent P38 says "*the availability and the price. Without that, I can not do anything*" (Interview partner P38, personal communication, Mar 12, 2021). And respondent P1 from his perspective says, "*the first question is quality. That's always the first question. The second is price. And thirdly, if they can choose sustainability or biobased, that's what they pick and choose, for time being*" (Interview partner P1, personal communication, Feb 26, 2021). Other respondents indicate that the short supply of renewable raw materials, lack of information on CO2 savings, high complexity of supply chain models and the origin of renewable aw materials, mismatch between customer expectations and supply chain transparency, and low contribution to CO2 savings are barriers to adoption of renewable raw materials. After categorizing the innovation-specific meaning units, the characteristics are clustered around the most important innovation-specific predictor variables.

### 7.3.1 Reported Origin or Renewable Raw Materials

GHG reduction towards carbon neutrality requires the use of renewable raw materials and the origin of the raw material is thematized by respondents with terms like biobased products, oleochemicals, native oils, biogas, biomass, forestry waste, plastic waste, plastic recycling and carbon capture technology. Origin of renewable raw materials is from biobased raw materials, plastic recycling and carbon capture technologies. Respondent handle the complexity of various sources and renewable technologies and search for best fit for their needs. Biobased raw materials *"can be directly based on natural oils* that do not intervene in the food chain," says respondent P15 and adds "there are those who then claim that it is made from some, I shall say, agricultural residues that are not being used in the food industry" (Interview partner P15, personal communication, Sep 15, 2020). Respondent P8 explains, that *"the starting point would be the syngas process... Methane gas is already available in reasonable quantities as a bio-based raw material with corresponding certificates from biogas plants. This could also be used in existing systems"* (Interview partner P8, personal communication, Oct 02, 2020). And respondent P1 reports that *"there is a lot coco nut, palm, rape seed and sunflower oils"* already used for chemical synthesis (Interview partner P1, personal communication, Feb 26, 2021). Respondent P10 reports: *"There are different approaches. For example, products made from corn, sugar. This is an approach given by nature. Then we have an approach that comes from renewable products. The plan is to take waste and recycle it. You don't want to appear as a competitor for the food industry"* (Interview partner P10, personal communication, Apr 14, 2021). Respondent P19, who is not yet using biobased raw materials, reports to *"have two different scopes today: The use of biobased materials and the use of recycled materials"* (Interview partner P19, personal communication, Mar 19, 2021). Recycling technologies are a new source for carbon flow of the chemical industry and also respondent P50 reports new process innovations for company *"with respect to renewable materials and plastic substrates, we are in front. ... All solvent is recycled, recovered and reused"* (Interview partner P50, personal communication, Mar 03, 2021) (Table 7.23).

**Table 7.23** Reported origin of renewable raw materials

| Origin of material | Example |
|---|---|
| Biobased raw material | • Biomass, biogas, forestry waste, agricultural residues<br>• Oleochemicals, native oils, coco, palm, rape seed and sunflower oils<br>• Cellulose, corn starch, molasse, polysaccharides<br>• Polylactic acid, bio-based ethylene glycol |
| Recycling technologies | • Physical and chemical recycling of plastic waste<br>• Solvent recycling, solvent recovery |
| Green hydrogen technologies | • Use of green electricity for green hydrogen, caustic soda, green chlorine |
| Carbon capture technologies | • Use of CO2 rich sources for chemical synthesis and enzymic reactions |

Respondent P1 reports two new sources for substituting products for traditional fossil-based polymers. Polymers are made from recycled plastic and novel biobased polymers. Respondent P1 says that *"virgin is cheaper, and you have the recycled and then you have PLA, which is the high end, and which is a lot, a lot more expensive"* (Interview partner P1, personal communication, Feb 26, 2021). PLA stands for polylactic acid that is a novel biobased polymer produced from renewable resources such as wheat, straw, corn, and sorghum, and it is completely biodegradable (Li et al., 2020). Green electricity and carbon capture and utilization is only reported by one respondent. *"F12 launched green caustic soda this week and it is now available on the market. This is produced by buying green electricity accordingly,"* says respondent P12 and adds, *"chlorine is also produced in electrolysis"* (Interview partner P12, personal communication, Mar 01, 2021). Green electricity is used for electrolysis and makes green hydrogen and halogen elements available potentially without GHG emissions (Ostadi, Paso, Rodriguez-Fabia, Øi, Manenti & Hillestad, 2020). Another novel approach is carbon capture and utilization from human activity. Participant P38 reports "*research projects to use CO2 from steel mills... But the conversion is very low and slow. The carbon source should be enough to supply all European chemical industry*" (Interview partner P38, personal communication, Mar 12, 2021). The respondent cooperates in "*a project to capture CO2 underground but the true value should be to make chemical molecules from it... There are enzymes in the reactor and they are fed with the CO2 but they need too much time*" (Interview partner P38, personal communication, Mar 12, 2021). The technology uses enzymes to consume CO2 from exhausts for upgraded chemical molecules (Fradette, Lefebvre & Carley, 2017; Hannula, Kaisalo & Simell, 2020). The case studies provide evidence for various sources and for complexity of the novelties for innovators. Renewable energy is reported for synthesis of green chlorine and caustic soda. Biomass as origin is most often mentioned by respondents together with plastic recycling concepts. Respondents also report activities from carbon capture and utilization (CCU) and cover the future sources for carbon flow of the chemical industry (Carus et al., 2021; Keim, & Röper, 2010).

### 7.3.2 Perceived CO2 Savings

The major goals of the European Green Deal are climate action to reach carbon neutrality for European continent, along with the substitution of hazardous chemicals and the promotion of a circular economy. When asked for CO2 savings of renewable raw materials, 13 out of the 14 respondents have no quantitative data of the key performance indicator. Respondent P18 comments, that "*it doesn't exist yet. The savings will depend on the carbon footprint of the raw materials*" (Interview partner P18, personal communication, May 17, 2021) and respondent P51 says: "*It (the carbon footprint) is not known*" (Interview partner P51, personal communication, Mar 23, 2021). Respondent P12 adds: "*We have not yet arrived at a viable value. We work on it*" (Interview partner P12, personal communication, Mar 01, 2021). Respondent P12 explains, that in order to achieve a significant CO2 savings, "*the raw material must have a large share in the product*" (Interview partner P12, personal communication, Mar 01, 2021). Whereas additives have a small impact on CO2 savings, "*major part are the monomers and they have the greatest impact,*" says respondent P19 (Interview partner P19, personal communication, Mar 19, 2021). "The raw material must have a large share in the product. Ethylene, for us, of course," explains respondent P12 (Interview partner

P12, personal communication, Mar 01, 2021). Niche products, additives and process aids are less considered for CO2 saving, because *"additives don't make much difference"* (Interview partner P12, personal communication, Mar 01, 2021) and respondent P51 comments: *"Our main raw material is already bio-based. It's the last 2 or 5% that is exhausting"* (Interview partner P51, personal communication, Mar 23, 2021). Respondent P59 explains, why the impact from raw materials is low compared to the operational emissions in the fine chemicals sector. "*This is not surprising because the value chain is deeper and there are processes that are very energy-intensive. This is how it is with fine chemicals.*" And adds, "*the raw materials only make a small contribution to the CO2 balance and the main part of the emissions comes from the refining processes via the heat and energy used*" (Interview partner P59, personal communication, May 26, 2021) (Table 7.24).

**Table 7.24** Reported availability of CO2 savings

| Driver | Barrier |
|---|---|
| • Data collecting in progress<br>• Major raw materials have great impact on CO2 emissions for polymers and specialty chemicals | • Emission factors are not available<br>• Niche products and additives with a small impact on GHG savings<br>• Emissions from operations have greater impact for fine chemicals |

### 7.3.3 Perceived Availability

First prototypes of intermediates from renewable raw materials are reported to be available, like C2 and C3 monomers. *"C2 and C3 intermediates and they are made via co-processing"* says respondent P60 (Interview partner P60, personal communication, Apr 28, 2021). Also respondent P51 reports dependency on intermediates producers and says, *"bio-based ethylene and propylene actually have to be carried out by our suppliers"* (Interview partner P51, personal communication, Mar 23, 2021) and respondent P51 says that *"there is no raw material available on the market"* (Interview partner P51, personal communication, Mar 23, 2021). Intermediates and monomers for polymerization are not yet available for every process. *"These monomers are not available on the market"* yet, says respondent P19 (Interview partner P19, personal communication, Mar 19, 2021), and companies are searching for either drop-in substitutes of existing fossil-based chemicals or for biobased alternatives. Respondent P50 reports to *"look at other biobased polymers as well, e.g. polylactic acid. You have a lot of new biobased materials"* (Interview partner P50, personal communication, Mar 03, 2021) (Table 7.25).

**Table 7.25** Reported availability of renewable raw materials

| Drivers | Barriers |
|---|---|
| • Prototypes of C2 and C3 intermediates and prototypes are available<br>• New biobased substitutes are offered | • Little capacity<br>• Scarcity of biobased feedstocks<br>• Quality of biobased alternatives<br>• Downstream chemicals, monomers and fine chemicals not available |

Although prototypes of intermediates, drop-ins and smart drop-ins are reported to be available, the industry lacks capacity and short supply of raw materials is the dominant barrier for adoption of renewable raw materials. Respondent P38 brings it to the point and says, *"we need both, renewable raw materials with a negative carbon footprint and without competition with the food chain. There is not much available, e.g. used cooking oils, residues form forestry and agriculture"* (Interview partner P38, personal communication, Mar 12, 2021). Respondent P10 completes, that *"the disadvantage of the products is due to the scaling effects. In the beginning there is little capacity and they are expensive to produce."* Respondent P10 adds: *"Availability and price is an issue and disadvantage"* (Interview partner P10, personal communication, Apr 14, 2021). When asked about the key barriers for renewable raw materials, respondent P38 answers: *"The availability and the price. Without that, I can not do anything"* (Interview partner P38, personal communication, Mar 12, 2021)

### 7.3.4 Perceived Price

Interview partners are asked for the cost position of renewable raw materials compared to fossil feedstocks. Respondent P1 says, that *"most of the time it's more expensive than the standard product,"* and completes: *"The first question is quality. That's always the first question. The second is price. And thirdly, if they can choose sustainability or biobased, that's what they pick and choose, for time being"*(Interview partner P1, personal communication, Feb 26, 2021) (Table 7.26).

**Table 7.26** Predictors for acceptance of higher prices for renewable raw materials

| Drivers | Barriers |
|---|---|
| • Consumers expectation of social and environmental governance and sustainable products | • Government regulations to offset customers' unwillingness to pay a premium for ecological products |

Respondent P8 comments about the price as barrier and says, *"we don't see any performance losses occurring anywhere, but it's actually mainly about pricing,"* (Interview partner P8, personal communication, Oct 02, 2020) and respondent P50 says, that *"... these products are still too expensive"* for a widespread adoption (Interview partner P50, personal communication, Mar 03, 2021). Although consumers expect social and environmental governance and sustainable products, willingness to pay for GHG saving is low. When asked, respondent P10 answers: *"It is not enough just to be sustainable"* (Interview partner P10, personal communication, Apr 14, 2021). Respondent P59 explains the situation: *"The suppliers have high costs and the customers do not want to pay a premium over the standard product, even though they would liked to buy bio-based products"* (Interview partner P59, personal communication, May 26, 2021). Respondent P50 comments, that the adoption is slow *"... because these products are still too expensive,"* and adds with reference to customers, that *"if they are not forced by the Government, then they (renewable raw materials) don't have an advantage"* (Interview partner P50, personal communication, Mar 03, 2021). And respondent P15 sets the frame for price increase and says: *"The price doesn't necessarily have to be 1: 1, which will probably be difficult anyway, but we say, it can cost a maximum of 20% more in terms of raw materials than what it costs so far"* (Interview partner P15, personal communication, Sep 15, 2020).

### 7.3.5 Perceived Transparency

Another predictor variable is transparency of the supply chain. Traceability of materials is necessary to proof the origin and to avoid greenwashing. Two supply chain models are proposed to supply renewable raw materials: The mass balanced approach and the segregated approach (Mol & Oosterveer, 2015; Törnqvist, Rosenheim, Hu & Fernandez 2015). Certification schemes are offered for standardization of these management practices which increase market efficiency and information flow on sustainability criteria (Mujica, 2019; Paton, 2000). Both supply chain models have benefits and challenges and are thematized by respondents. The mass balance approach is applied to co-processing of sustainable and fossil raw materials in the same reactors and procedures. *"Raw materials can be exchanged one-to-one, existing products could be kept. Then, of course, that has advantages for the customer because he does not have to qualify new products, but also because, above all, existing assets can be used"* (Interview partner P8, personal communication, Oct 02, 2020). Co-processing is suitable for *"plastic waste. You can do that from biomass too,"* says respondent P12 (Interview partner P12, personal communication, Mar 01, 2021) and respondent P15 plans to *"offer our existing product portfolio 1:1 in bio-based or sustainable form without sacrificing performance"* (Interview partner P15, personal communication, Sep 15, 2020) (Table 7.27).

**Table 7.27** Perceived strengths and weakness of mass balanced supply chain models

| **Perception of the mass balanced supply chain models** | |
|---|---|
| **Strengths** | **Weaknesses** |
| • High compatibility with existing products and qualities | • Complex chain of custody |
| • Rapid implementation in same assets | • Lack of analytical proof |
| • 1:1 Raw material replacement | • Need for a trustful certification scheme |
| | • Risk of greenwashing |

Renewable products made by co-processing and the mass balanced supply chain model are perceived as compatible with existing products and implementation is viewed as rapid compared to segregated supply chain models. Efforts are "*the clarification of how the masses can be balanced and how the proportion of renewable raw materials can be allocated to the products and the customers. What is needed are solutions that are permitted by the IT systems*" (Interview partner P18, personal communication, May 17, 2021). For mass balance approach, "one challenge is the chain of custody. If the biobased raw material comes from, let me say, five different places, it needs the chain of custody from five different places" (Interview partner P46, personal communication, May 19, 2021). Customers doubt traceability of the renewable raw materials in the mass balanced supply chains and "*some people still associate it with greenwashing, because..., if you now have a mixed product, you can also offer your product 100% green or biobased after a mass balance*" (Interview partner P8, personal communication, Oct 02, 2020). "*Customers want to be sure that the materials are biobased and that the source of the carbon is traced by chemical analysis,*" says respondent P46 (Interview partner P46, personal communication, May 19, 2021). The advantage of the segregated supply chain is the detectability of the biogenic carbon content with less room for fraud. "*Products put into the C14 measurement methodology and it can be seen how much is really bio-based,*" says respondent P8 (Interview partner P8, personal communication, Oct 02, 2020). The 14 C radiocarbon method can be used to analyze the biobased carbon content; however, it does not distinguish between carbon from fossil sources and recycled plastic. Performance and quality of products from biobased resources are perceived to be weaker than existing products (Table 7.28).

**Table 7.28** Perceived strengths and weakness of segregated supply chain models

| Perception of segregated supply chain models | |
|---|---|
| **Strengths** | **Weaknesses** |
| • Traceability by analysis | • Slower implementation |
| • Customers' preference | • Different technical performance |

Respondent P1 reports that *"...for very high end, we cannot use the biobased raw materials, because you have more impurities, or we think they have more impurities"* (Interview partner P1, personal communication, Feb 26, 2021). Another barrier for segregation models is the time-to-market. Respondent P18 states, that *"we are also working on new synthesis routes for segregated, bio-based products"* (Interview partner P18, personal communication, May 17, 2021) and respondent P50 points at the long development times of such projects, saying that *"the problem is, that research projects often take 5 years. Before you have it on the market, it takes at least 5 years"* (Interview partner P50, personal communication, Mar 03, 2021).

### 7.3.6 Perceived Compatibility

Compatibility of renewable raw materials substitution is another important predictor for adoption. Compatibility includes as predictors customer expectations, technological adaptation to existing systems, and sustainability requirements with respect to the UN Sustainable Development Goals. Customers expect the same quality and prefer to gradually replace existing materials without sacrificing performance. The co-processing of biomass with fossil raw materials is seen as compatible with existing technological regimes and respondent P15 requests *"existing product portfolio 1:1 in bio-based or sustainable form"* (Interview partner P15, personal communication, Sep 15, 2020). Respondent P8 comments, that *"we don't see any performance losses occurring anywhere"* for mass balanced supply chain model (Interview partner P8, personal communication, Oct 02, 2020). Further requirements are sustainability criteria and availability. Respondent P38 explains: "*We need both: Renewable raw materials with a negative carbon footprint and without competition with the food chain. There is not much available, e.g. used cooking oils, residues form forestry and agriculture. There are research projects to use CO2 from steel mills... But the conversion is very low and slow. The carbon source should be enough to supply all European chemical industry*" (Interview partner P38, personal communication, Mar 12, 2021) (Table 7.29).

**Table 7.29** Perceived compatibility of renewable raw materials

| Origin | Benefit | Weaknesses |
|---|---|---|
| Biobased raw materials | • Renewable raw materials with carbon sequestration<br>• Positive image | • Limited availability<br>• Competes with food/feed<br>• Loss of biodiversity<br>• Complexity |
| Plastic waste | • Reuse of plastic waste | • Negative image |
| Carbon capture | • Clean and w/t conflicts | • Low yield |

Additionally to non-food-and-feed competition, respondent P50 says, *"we do buy biobased materials, but only we look to chemistry, which is biodegradable"* (Interview partner P50, personal communication, Mar 03, 2021) and respondent P1 observes *"a lot of big differences. For very high end, we cannot use the biobased raw materials, because you have more impurities, or we think they have more impurities. But for 90% of the production, no problem"* (Interview partner P1, personal communication, Feb 26, 2021). The use of plastic waste has a negative image and when asked for requirements, respondent P38 says: *"We will exclude plastic waste because at the moment, the materials are not renewable and the final materials from plastic waste have a positive carbon footprint and can't contribute to greenhouse gas saving. We prefer natural waste or pure bio-source without competition to food and feed"* (Interview partner P38, personal communication, Mar 12, 2021). A negative image and the absence of negative emission factors are mentioned as perceived disadvantages for renewable raw materials made from plastic waste, but respondent P38 also mentions conflict potential for biobased raw materials: *"We need to avoid the conflict with the food and feed supply chain and need to source materials that is not used for food"* (Interview partner P38, personal communication, Mar 12, 2021). Compatibility of renewable raw materials is an important predictor variable and includes customer expectations, sustainability criteria, and existing performance standards compared to existing technologies. Converting renewable feedstocks in the same plant for the same end products with the same properties and specifications is preferred and avoids lengthy approval processes.

Renewable raw materials must be compatible with various sustainability criteria and should be non-hazardous and biodegradable. Their use should be free from conflicts with food and feed chains, land use change, or biodiversity loss. The versatility of sources and the increasing complexity of raw material selection are seen as barriers to adoption.

### 7.3.7 Summary of Innovation-specific Predictors

Five innovation-specific predictor variables are categorized from 130 meaning units. Innovation-specific predictors for adoption have predominantly a negative semantic orientation and oppose to the adoption of renewable raw materials. The meaning units about company-specific predictors identified in interview narratives have been collected in the electronic supplementary material (ESM) Table 3.2 (Table 7.30).

**Table 7.30** Visualization of innovation-specific predictors from case studies

| Drivers | Barriers |
|---|---|
| • High greenhouse gas saving potential<br>• Compatibility of the renewable raw materials with existing technological regimes, customer expectations and sustainable development goals<br>• Transparency of the supply chain and origin of material. | • Higher price<br>• Limited availability of material<br>• Missing information on CO2 savings<br>• Small perceived impact of the CO2 savings from the use or renewable raw materials |

Higher price, limited availability of material, missing information on CO2 savings or small perceived impact of the CO2 savings from the use or renewable raw materials have been mentioned as barrier by industry experts. Additional innovation-specific predictors identified in the case study research are compatibility of the renewable raw materials with existing technological regimes, customer expectations and sustainable development goals as well es transparency of the supply chain and origin of material. Meaning units from the availability category with a positive orientation are concerning new product offerings from suppliers or available prototype technologies (Table 7.31).

**Table 7.31** Semantic orientations of attributes of renewable raw materials

| **Semantic orientations of the attributes of renewable raw materials** | | | |
|---|---|---|---|
| **Variable** | **Barriers** | **Drivers** | **Sum** |
| Availability of material | 12 | 16 | 28 |
| CO2 savings data / impact | 16 | 2 | 18 |
| Compatibility | 11 | 24 | 35 |
| Price | 23 | 0 | 23 |
| Transparency | 9 | 17 | 26 |
| **Total** | **71** | **59** | **130** |

Short supply of any kind of renewable raw materials is mentioned and missing data on CO2 savings are reported as barriers to use. The greatest perceived barrier is the higher price of renewable raw materials (Fig. 7.3).

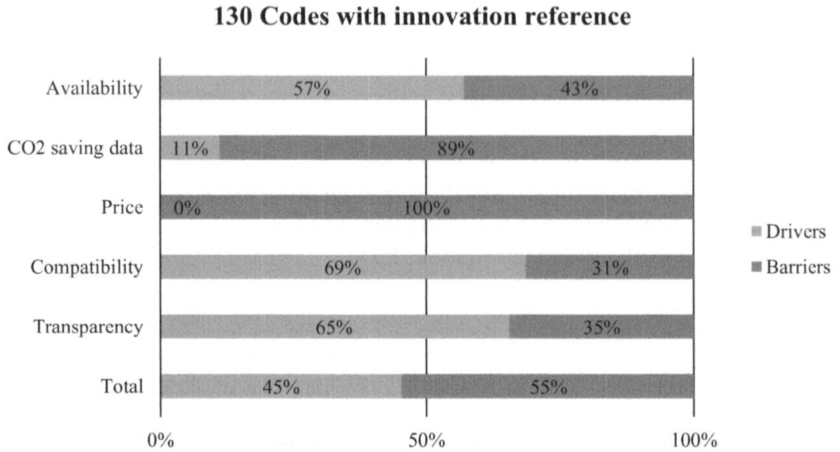


**Fig. 7.3** Perceived drivers and barriers for adoption of renewable raw materials

Meaning units concerning compatibility of renewable raw materials as well as transparency of supply chains from certification schemes and analytical test methods have predominantly a positive semantic orientation and are perceived as drivers for adoption.

## 7.4 Requirement Engineering

Five company-specific predictors—existing use of renewable raw materials, corporate sustainability strategy of the company, management advocacy, cooperation skills, implementation of industrial standards and knowledge of Government regulations—are determinants for the use of environmental innovations and five innovation-specific predictors were identified in this study: Feedstock availability, price, CO2 savings of environmental innovation and their availability, supply chain transparency and compatibility with customer expectations, existing technologies and sustainable development goals (Table 7.32).

**Table 7.32** Visualization of predictors for innovations to reach carbon neutrality

| Company-specific predictors | Innovation-specific predictors |
|---|---|
| • Corporate sustainability strategy<br>• Management advocacy<br>• Cooperation skills<br>• Implementation of industry standards<br>• Expectations of Government regulations | • Feedstock availability<br>• Price<br>• CO2 savings & availability of CO2 savings data<br>• Compatibility with technological regimes<br>• Transparency of the supply chain |

### 7.4.1 Availability Requirements

*"Availability and the price. Without that, I can not do anything"* says respondent P38 (Interview partner P38, personal communication, Mar 12, 2021). *"There is no raw material available on the market,"* says interviewee P51, and adds, that *"the other raw materials are based on ethylene and propylene and the transformation to bio-based ethylene and propylene actually has to be carried out by our suppliers"* (Interview partner P51, personal communication, Mar 23, 2021). Respondent P19 also notes that alternatives to existing products made from renewable feedstocks are not available and says, *"these monomers are not available on the market"* (Interview partner P19, personal communication, Mar 19, 2021). While monomers and intermediate products are not yet available, renewable raw materials such as biogas should be available in abundance and respondent P8 says: "*Renewable natural gas, as it is called, i.e. what is produced from biomass, that's available in reasonable quantities, is already certified and could almost be used*" (Interview partner P8, personal communication, Oct 02, 2020). The availability of building blocks, monomers and intermediate products is mainly perceived as a barrier to the use of renewable raw materials.

### 7.4.2 Price Acceptance

The second barrier to adoption is price. Respondent P10 comments that "the *disadvantage of the products lies in the scaling effects. At the beginning there is little capacity and they are expensive to produce*" (Interview partner P10, personal communication, Apr 14, 2021). Currently, the cost position of renewable raw materials is perceived as unattractive for use "*... because these products are still too expensive,*" and when asked about the main barrier, respondent P50 adds, "*yes, it is the price.*" (Interview partner P50, personal communication, Mar 03, 2021). "*The price doesn't necessarily have to be 1:1, ...but we say it can cost a maximum of 20% more in terms of raw materials than what it costs so far,*" respondent P15 comments on the price target (Interview partner P15, personal communication, Sep 15, 2020).

### 7.4.3 CO2 Saving Requirements

Another requirement for adoption is the CO2 saving. To calculate the CO2 savings, emission factors from renewable raw materials are required, but it is not easy "*easy to get concrete statements from suppliers*" (Interview partner P15, personal communication, Sep 15, 2020) or companies "*have not yet arrived at a viable value*" (Interview partner P12, personal communication, Mar 01, 2021). Information on the CO2 emissions of renewable alternatives is still missing. Companies need renewable alternatives with low emission factors and a high proportion of the end product composition. "*The major part are the monomers and they have the greatest impact on the biobased content, but they are not available today,*" says respondent P19 (Interview partner P19, personal communication, Mar 19, 2021). Components with a low proportion have a low impact and respondent P12 comments: "*Additives don't make much difference*" (Interview partner P12, personal communication, Mar 01, 2021). Respondent P51 comments: "*It's the last 2 or 5% that is exhausting*" (Interview partner P51, personal communication, Mar 23, 2021). Another case with a lower CO2 savings potential through the use of renewable raw materials are fine chemicals with a deep value chain and very energy-intensive processes. "*The raw materials only make a small contribution to the CO2 balance and the main part of the emissions comes from the refining processes via the heat and energy used,*" says respondent P59 (Interview partner P59, personal communication, May 26, 2021). All respondents report missing data on CO2 savings which is inhibiting adoption and industry initiatives and regulators need to develop guidelines for calculation of emission factors and life cycle assessments (Koh et al., 2013; Verones et al., 2017).

### 7.4.4 Compatibility Requirements

The compatibility of renewable technologies with customers' expectations, existing technological regimes and sustainability requirements promotes their acceptance and is driver for the diffusion of innovations (Rogers, 2003). One perspective is the compatibility of environmental innovations with market demand and customer needs. Respondent P12 says, that *"the focus is on the customer"* (Interview partner P12, personal communication, Mar 01, 2021). Interviewee P1 notes that *"we need to follow the need of the customers"* (Interview partner P1, personal communication, Feb 26, 2021). Customer-oriented companies ask for cooperation respondent P50 describes the market demand as follows: *"The customer side, too, a little bit. It is the time. Our people from the Marketing department look at the requirements of the current customers whether there is a need for re-useable, recyclable (materials) and we are setting up ... to re-use and to recycle them"* (Interview partner P50, personal communication, Mar 03, 2021). Customers prefer biogenic carbon content that is traceable through the 14 C radiocarbon method, and respondent P15 reports that customers *"want the C14 method to trace the biobased content, many want to know the biodegradability and compostability"* (Interview partner P15, personal communication, Sep 15, 2020). Customers articulate their needs and define the market attraction for products with improved sustainability performance. Another perspective of compatibility is the fit with existing technological regimes. Respondent P15 summarizes the perspective and pinpoints her company's needs to *"offer our existing product portfolio 1:1 in bio-based or sustainable form without sacrificing performance at a similar price"* (Interview partner P15, personal communication, Sep 15, 2020). *"You want to make it as easy as possible,"* comments respondent P12 (Interview partner P12, personal communication, Mar 01, 2021) and for respondent P1, *"the first question is quality. That's always the first question. The second is price. And thirdly, if they can choose sustainability or biobased, that's what they pick and choose, for time being"* (Interview partner P1, personal communication, Feb 26, 2021). Respondent P12 describes the coprocessing of renewable raw materials like biowaste and recycled plastic in existing assets: *"They do that through a second feedstock in the cracker, where you put biomass in and you've gotten to the point where you can reuse waste plastic"* (Interview partner P12, personal communication, Mar 01, 2021). Respondent P18 adds, that *"the process is in place and it is an elegant method, because you do not need huge investments.*" Respondent P18 reports also activities for segregated synthesis routes: "*We are also working on new synthesis routes for segregated, bio-based products, where we use raw materials from biomass and produce them in a process that is separate from the conventional process. The carbon is then also demonstrably bio-based*" (Interview partner P18, personal communication, May 17, 2021). Respondent P50 comments on the long development time for new product developments: "*The problem is that research projects often take 5 years. Before you have it on the market, it takes at least 5 years. So, we think, what could be important for future*" (Interview partner P50, personal communication, Mar 03, 2021). A third perspective is a set of sustainability requirements for renewable raw materials. For respondent P12, the overarching "*goal is to have a green portfolio*" (Interview partner P12, personal communication, Mar 01, 2021). Respondent P50 explains to be "*looking more for biodegradable materials than really biobased chemicals with the same chemistry*" (Interview partner P50, personal communication, Mar 03, 2021). Respondent P46 explains, that "*the customers like to poove (the biogenic carbon) by C14 measurement, that the raw materials come from biomass,*" and adds, "*it is important to know, whether the products are biodegradable, yes or know*" (Interview partner P46, personal communication, May 19, 2021). Respondent P60 describes additional requirements: "*Products must be free of animal products, GMO-free, do not contain palm oil and are not in competition with the food and feed chain*" (Interview partner P60, personal communication, Apr 28, 2021). Respondent P51 reports, that the company is "*committing to SDGs and breaking it down on the suppliers… The company has committed itself to the UN Global Compact*" (Interview partner P51, personal communication, Mar 23, 2021). Respondent P15 prefers "*agricultural residues that are not being used in the food industry*" (Interview partner P15, personal communication, Sep 15, 2020). Respondent P12 says: "*We support recycling projects,*" and looks for "*crude oil-like material and crude oil-like intermediates,*" produced from plastic waste (Interview partner P12, personal communication, Mar 01, 2021). Respondent P19 is open for the use of plastic waste and biobased feedstocks: "*We have two different scopes today: The use of biobased materials and the use of recycled materials*" (Interview partner P19, personal communication, Mar 19, 2021). Renewable raw materials are required to meet various sustainability criteria as well as customer expectations and technological regimes for rapid implementation. The respondents show a mixed assessment of the different sustainability criteria and there is no common understanding of what is sustainable and green and how to reconcile the various criteria with the goal of carbon neutrality.

### 7.4.5 Transparency Requirements

Another prerequisite for decision-making and the use of renewable raw materials is the transparency of the supply chain and the traceability of the raw material origin. Customers prefer segregated supply chain models, which leads to end products with traceable biogenic carbon content. Respondent P15 says: *"what you hear from customers is more in the direction of a 100% organic approach and not mass balance"* (Interview partner P15, personal communication, Sep 15, 2020). Respondent P60 explains that biobased, renewable raw material *"can be based on natural oils that do not intervene in the food chain. This is such a point that practically you want to see that they are sustainable, preferably certified—keyword RSPO"* (Interview partner P60, personal communication, Apr 28, 2021). RSPO is a certification system for sustainable palm oil and palm kernel oil developed for supply chain transparency and traceability of the origin of materials. Both mass balanced and segregated supply chains are certified for other renewable raw materials, and only a limited portfolio of intermediates made from segregated renewable raw materials and bio-waste is available (Bhartia, 2020; Schill, 2015). Mass-balanced supply chains and co-processing of materials enable the use of plastics and bio-waste along with petroleum and certification schemes prove the origin and the chain of custody. Respondent P46 says: *"It should be certified by REDcert or another standard to make sure, that it is not destroying biodiversity and causing environmental degradation"* (Interview partner P51, personal communication, Mar 23, 2021). Respondent P8 shares the feedback on supply chain certification from the market and says, that *"some people still associate it with greenwashing"* (Interview partner P8, personal communication, Oct 02, 2020). Certification schemes are not fully accepted by customers. Although they improve traceability of the material origin and reduce the complexity of raw material selection, customers have concerns about trustworthiness and transparency.

### 7.4.6 Value Proposition Design

Value proposition design typically includes the steps of eliciting, documenting, validating, consolidating and managing requirements with the main goal of proposing customers a convincing offer of innovation (Oehmig, 2015). Value propositions are developed by balancing customer needs for gain creation and pain relief and products that create value for the customer. A fit is achieved when the offered products address the most important problems and advantages from the customer profile (B2B International, 2021; Osterwalder, Pigneur, Bernarda,

Smith & Papadakos, 2014). The synthesis of innovation-specific predictors and content analysis of the examined business cases results in a proposal for general user requirements for renewable raw materials (Table 7.33).

**Table 7.33** Requirements engineering for renewable raw materials

| Innovation specific predictor | User requirements |
|---|---|
| Availability | • Abundant supply of renewable raw materials<br>• Availability of intermediates and monomers |
| CO2 saving | • Availability of emission data<br>• Low emission factors for feedstocks<br>• Large share in the final product<br>• Low depth of value chain |
| Compatibility | • Customer preference for biogenic sources<br>• Final products with same performance<br>• Manufacture in existing assets<br>• No competition to food & feed<br>• No reduction of biodiversity<br>• Non-hazardous, biodegradable products |
| Price | • Moderate price increase<br>• Maximum acceptable surcharge of 20% |
| Transparency | • Analytical traceability of the renewable carbon content<br>• Certification scheme in place (e.g. RSPO, ISCC Plus certification)<br>• Complete transparency of supply chain |

Same performance, sufficient availability, production of existing products with the same performance in existing assets and a moderate price increase with a maximum acceptable surcharge of 20% support the use of renewable raw materials with the aim of reducing greenhouse gas emissions. The requirements are combined with sustainability goals without additional land use, without competition for food and feed and without loss of biodiversity. The adoption is limited by low proportions of the renewable raw material in the end product or a high energy intensity in deep value chains.

### 7.4.7 Business Fit

Pattern matching of the business strategy with the offered renewable raw materials round off the analysis of the compatibility of renewable technologies. The respondents describe their needs and their existing product portfolio, and evaluate the business, technical and financial feasibility of an implementation (Cadle, Paul & Turner, 2014). While the respondents share the demand for lower prices, sufficient availability, high CO2 savings potential, compatibility and transparency, the strategic fit of the origin of renewable raw materials and supply chain approaches are business model-specific (Table 7.34).

**Table 7.34** Business fit for adoption of renewable raw materials

| Criteria | Eco-innovation requirement |
|---|---|
| Strategic fit | Sector-specific requirements decide on abatement technology selection |
| Price | Similar or 20% maximum price increase |
| Availability | Ample availability |
| CO2 savings | High CO2 savings |
| Compatibility | Compatible with customer expectations, existing technologies and a set of sustainability criteria |
| Transparency | Traceable, either by 14C radiocarbon method or traceable by certification schemes |

Three product categories have been identified in the case study research: Halogens, plastics & polymers from petrochemical sector and specialty chemicals including additives, pigments and fine chemicals. Renewable electricity is available to all sectors to reduce greenhouse gas emissions from operations. Energy-intensive products from the halogen sector can benefit most from renewable electricity to avoid carbon taxes and the case study confirms the successful effect of the governance tool. Respondent P12 reports that *"green caustic soda is now available on the market. This is produced by buying green electricity accordingly"* (Interview partner P12, personal communication, Mar 01, 2021). Plastics, fibers and film manufacturers *"have approaches to use recycled plastic in packaging,"* says respondent P59 (Interview partner P59, personal communication, May 26, 2021). Respondent P12 adds, that chemical recycling converts *"plastic back into a product that you put in the crude oil feedstock... Old plastic is heated up and pyrolyzed without oxygen. Then everything comes out in the back, diesel oils, light petrol, hydrogen"* (Interview partner P12, personal communication, Mar 01, 2021). Respondent P18 says: *"We are currently dealing with mass-balanced issues... We want to use mass-balanced approaches with our plastics"* (Interview partner P18, personal communication, May 17, 2021). Petrochemical companies are open to circular concepts of plastics and include organic solvents in the recycling application. Respondent P50 mentions that *"all solvent MEK is recycled"* (Interview partner P50, personal communication, Mar 03, 2021). Respondent P12 reports the co-processing of plastic waste and biowaste for making of monomers: *"They do that through a second feedstock in the cracker, where you put biomass in and you've got it to the point where you can reuse waste plastic"* (Interview partner P12, personal communication, Mar 01, 2021). Another option is the search for new biopolymers made from segregated building blocks. Respondent P50 reports to *"look at other biobased polymers as well, e.g. polylactic acid. You have a lot of new biobased materials"*(Interview partner P50, personal communication, Mar 03, 2021). And respondent P1 adds the financial attractiveness of the three types of polymers: *"Virgin is cheaper, and you have the recycled and then you have PLA, which is the high end, and which is a lot, a lot more expensive"(*Interview partner P1, personal communication, Feb 26, 2021). Specialty chemicals manufacturers are more orientated toward the use of biobased feedstocks, like biomass and biowaste, mainly due to customer preferences. "*We will exclude plastic waste. We prefer natural waste or pure bio-source without competition to food and feed. ... There is not much available, e.g. used cooking oils, residues form forestry and agriculture"* says respondent P38 (Interview partner P38, personal communication, Mar 12, 2021). Other specialty chemicals manufacturers *"have two different scopes today: The use of biobased materials and the use of recycled materials,"* says respondent P19 and adds, that the co-processing of renewable raw materials with fossil feedstocks enables an incremental shift towards GHG savings: "*so today they have maybe 25% and tomorrow 50%, and so on*" (Interview partner P19, personal communication, Mar 19, 2021) (Table 7.35).

**Table 7.35** Perceived sector specific preferences of origin and supply chains

| **Product category** | **Supply chain model** | **Origin of materials** |
|---|---|---|
| Halogen | Cap-and-trade electricity | Renewable electricity |
| Petrochemicals, incl. plastics & polymers, solvents | Mass balanced | Plastic waste, biomass |
| Specialty chemicals, e. g. additives, polymers | Mass balanced, segregated supply preferred | Biomass preferred |
| Specialty chemicals, e. g. fine chemicals | Cap-and-trade electricity | Low contribution from raw materials |

Additives are a category of specialty chemicals with less potential for GHG saving from switching to renewable raw materials. They are used in small fractions on the end material and have little influence on the CO2 saving potential. Respondent P1 says, that "*our market is not big enough to have an important influence in the total. Our part is only between 0,2 and 1% of the total product. The most are the real polymers*" (Interview partner P1, personal communication, Feb 26, 2021) and respondent P10 reports, that "*if you have an additive, such as 1 to 2 or 3% in the application, then the general opinion in Germany is that you then take 100% bio-based. 100% renewable and not mass balance.*" (Interview partner P10, personal communication, Apr 14, 2021). Consumer markets prefer traceable biobased carbon contents in consumer chemicals and only segregated supply chains offer traceable biogenic carbon containing materials. The segregated supply chain model is preferred over mass balanced supply chains and biobased raw materials are preferred over plastic recycling when it comes to additives and specialty chemicals in this subsector. A special case of specialty chemicals are fine chemicals. *"The raw materials only make a small contribution to the CO2 balance and the main part of the emissions comes from the processes via the heat and energy use,"* says respondent P59 and explains, *"this is not surprising because the value chain is deeper and there are processes that are very energy-intensive"* (Interview partner P59, personal communication, May 26, 2021). It is concluded that *"renewable raw materials are not a major issue. For fine chemicals, the use of renewable energies has a bigger lever"* (Interview partner P59, personal communication, May 26, 2021). The greatest lever for GHG savings is the use of renewable energies for the operation of fine chemicals instead of the use of renewable raw materials.

# 8 Results from Document Analysis

Document analysis is chosen as a secondary research method to review results from case study research. Secondary sources for the triangulation are current annual sustainability reports and company communications on climate protection from the focus group of CEFIC corporate members. The purpose of the study is to analyze predictors for the use of renewable raw materials to reach carbon neutrality from available publications by corporate members of the CEFIC group. CEFIC is the European chemical industry council and 73 companies with an annual turnover of more than EUR 1 billion are nominated as corporate members. The list of companies is found in the electronic supplementary material (ESM) table 7 (CEFIC, 2021e). Of the 73 corporate members, 2 companies have the same principal (Chevron) and 3 companies have no annual reports or disclosures. 69 companies publish official documents as annual reports, issue 10-K forms, integrated sustainability, CSR and ESG reports and provide supplementary data in change responses and GRI reports. The attitude and intention of companies to use renewable raw materials will be examined in the following sections and later linked to innovation- and company-specific predictors.

## 8.1 Corporates' Carbon Footprints

Indications for attitude are the involvement of companies in industry initiatives, numerical targets to reduce Scope 1 and Scope 2 greenhouse gas emissions as well as mission statements for greenhouse gas emissions reducing. Indications for

**Supplementary Information** The online version contains supplementary material available at https://doi.org/10.1007/978-3-658-45389-3_8.



H. H. E. Ahrens, *The Ecological Modernization of the Chemical Industry*, https://doi.org/10.1007/978-3-658-45389-3_8

the intention to use renewable raw materials are commitments, numerical targets to reduce Scope 3 greenhouse gas emissions as well as publications on projects, investments and cooperation for the use of renewable raw materials.

### 8.1.1 Corporates' Initiatives

The disclosure of GHG emissions and reduction targets is not yet mandatory and participation in voluntary industry initiatives with sustainability targets signals commitment towards climate protection. Companies' involvement in industry initiatives serve as indicators for attitude. 61 companies refer to the UN Sustainable Development Goals in their mission statements and strategy declarations. 60 companies publish GHG saving achievements and targets following the GRI standard. 53 companies take part in the voluntary Carbon Disclosure Program and the commitment correlates with GHG reduction targets listed in the electronic supplementary material (ESM) table 8 (Table 8.1).

**Table 8.1** CDP Scores by industry sector

| **CDP Scores by industry sector** | | | | | |
|---|---|---|---|---|---|
| **CDP score** | **A, A-** | **B, B-** | **C, D, E, F** | **n. a.** | **Sum** |
| Halogen | 0 | 3 | 2 | 1 | 6 |
| Petrochemicals | 6 | 3 | 5 | 3 | 17 |
| Pharmaceuticals | 3 | 1 | 0 | 0 | 4 |
| Specialty chem. | 11 | 12 | 7 | 15 | 45 |
| Total | 20 | 19 | 14 | 19 | 72 |
| Share | 28% | 26% | 20% | 26% | 100% |

20 companies reach leadership level with CDP scores A and A−, 19 companies reach management level with CDP scores B and B−. The 39 Companies or 54% out of 72 CEFIC Corporate members are actively managing GHG emissions and receive high scores by the Carbon Disclosure Program. 6 companies have awareness level and 8 companies have not submitted sufficient data (Table 8.2).

**Table 8.2** Participation in industry initiatives by adopter category

| Participation in industry initiative by adopter category | | | | | |
|---|---|---|---|---|---|
| **Category** | **Count** | **SDG** | **GRI standard** | **CDP participants** | **2050 Target** |
| 100% by 2030 | 4 | 4 | 4 | 2 | 100% |
| 45 - 100% by 2030 | 16 | 16 | 8 | 16 | 92% |
| Below 45% | 40 | 34 | 22 | 30 | 67% |
| Non disclosers | 12 | 7 | 19 | 5 | 24% |
| **Total** | **72** | **61** | **61** | **53** | **71%** |

The 14 companies represent 19% of CEFIC corporate members who are dedicated to data collecting and strategy building. 19 companies or 26% of CEFIC corporate members do not participate in the program (CDP, 2019). CEFIC has three sector groups, halogen, petrochemical and specialty chemicals, including pharmaceutical companies. Only 2 out of 6 companies from the halogen industry receive management B or B scores. All pharmaceutical companies get A or B scores. 9 out of 17 petrochemical companies and 23 out of 45 specialty chemicals companies achieve an A or B level, which corresponds to around 50% in both industrial sectors. 18 companies of the 20 CEFIC corporate members with operational GHG emission reduction targets between 45–100% and 30 of 40 companies with reduction targets below 45% participate in CDP disclosures. Results from document analyzes on the participation of industry in sustainability initiatives confirm the positive attitude of leading companies towards reducing greenhouse gas emissions.

### 8.1.2 Corporates' Emission Data

The collection and disclosure of climate data is voluntary and not all company members publish emissions data, goals and successes. Available GHG emissions data are collected from company reports published prior to August 2021. GHG emission data and targets are obtained from company publications. 69 company members publish Scope 1 and Scope 2 emission data from own operations or from purchased energy (Fig. 8.1).

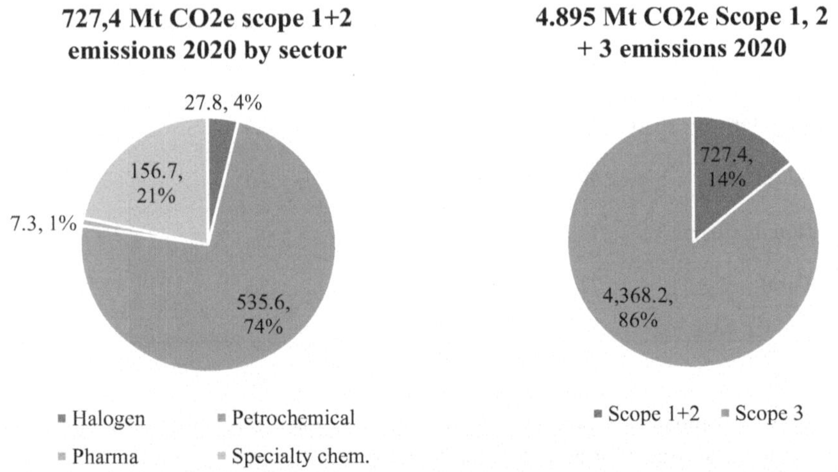


**Fig. 8.1** GHG emissions of CEFIC corporate members

Scope 1 + 2 emissions add up to 727,4 Mt CO2e for 2020 according to the GRI 305 standard. Petrochemical companies make the highest contributions to Scope 1 and Scope 2 emissions in the industry. Of the 72 companies that are members of the CEFIC group, 17 are grouped in the petrochemical sector and contribute 74% of operational GHG emissions. 45 companies are grouped together in the specialty chemicals sector and contribute 21% of operational GHG emissions. 6 companies have halogen-related business models and contribute 4% to corporate GHG emissions and 4 pharmaceutical companies contribute less than 1% of corporate GHG emissions. Scope 3 emissions reduction is most influenced by the use of renewable raw materials instead of fossil raw materials. Scope 3 emissions are only available from 37 company members and amount to 4.895 Mt CO2e Scope 1, 2 + 3 emissions in 2020. 35 companies have no data available and some firms with data only have parts of the Scope 3 emissions categories available. Several companies state that they are in the process of collecting Scope 3 data and therefore the statistics are incomplete and represent the status as of August 2021. 10 companies with the highest Scope 1 + 2 emissions account for

501,7 Mt CO2e emissions or 71% of the group's total GHG emissions of 727,4 Mt CO2e emissions (Table 8.3).

**Table 8.3** Scope 1 and Scope 2 GHG emissions of top 10 emitters

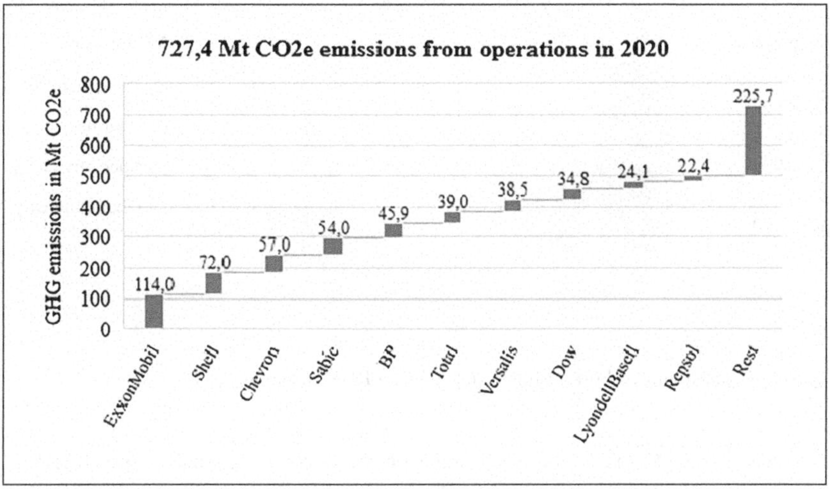


The carbon footprint is the amount of carbon dioxide released into the atmosphere as a result of the manufacture and use of a product. The CO2 footprint from Scope 1 + 2 emissions for each company is calculated from available data listed in the electronic supplementary material (ESM) table 8, and represents an average emission factor per EUR turnover of the company. With 1 kg CO2e / EUR sales, the halogen sector has the highest average company carbon footprint. With 0,8 kg CO2e / EUR sales, the petrochemical sector has the second highest average corporate carbon footprint. The pharmaceutical sector has the lowest average company carbon footprint of 0,09 kg CO2e / EUR sales and the specialty chemicals sector has the second lowest average company carbon footprint of 0,4 kg CO2e / EUR sales (Fig. 8.2).

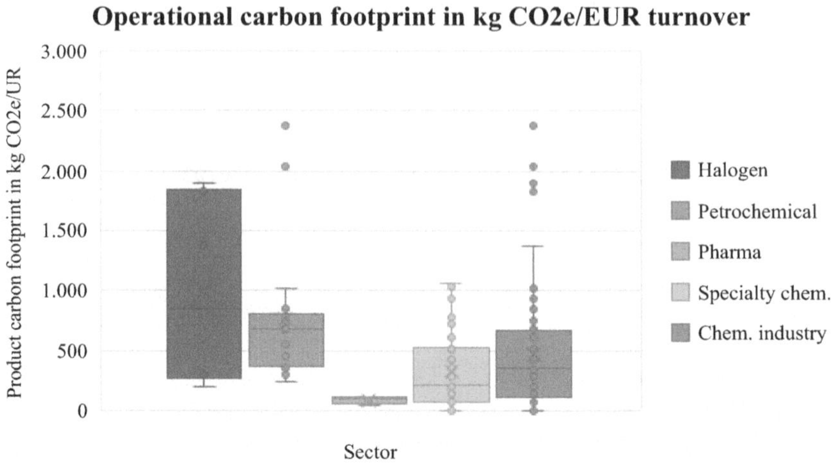


**Fig. 8.2** Operational carbon footprint in g CO2e / EUR by sector

A possible CO2 tax is likely to make products more expensive and to reduce margins. The halogen sector with the highest carbon footprint from products has the greatest pressure to implement strategies to reduce emissions. The pharmaceutical sector has the lowest carbon footprint for products with the lowest margin pressure (Fig. 8.3).

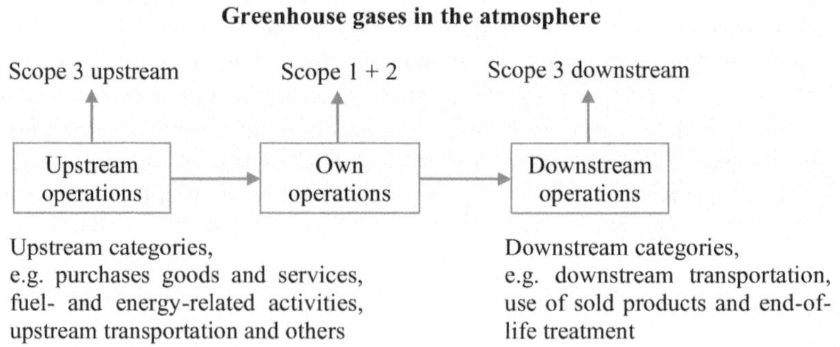


**Fig. 8.3** Scope 1, 2 and 3 emissions along the supply chain

The figure shows the relationship of Scope 1 + 2 emissions from own operations and Scope 3 emissions from the supply chain. Scope 1 are emissions from processes, heat and energy generation or process emissions of greenhouse gases from the company's own operations and Scope 2 are emissions from purchased energy (Fig. 8.4).

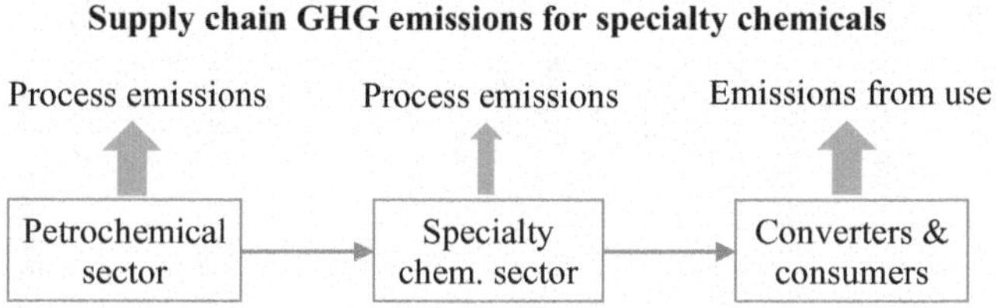


**Fig. 8.4** Supply chain GHG emissions for specialty chemicals

Scope 3 emissions are linked to the supply chain from upstream operations or downstream use, leakage or disposal of materials. Scope 1 + 2 from the company's own operations are under the direct control of the company and are accessible. Scope 1 + 2 emissions are transferred by suppliers into upstream Scope 3 for downstream users. Scope 3 emissions are beyond the direct control of companies. Data collection of these emission categories is complex and requires cooperation between suppliers and customers for exchange. The following bar chart shows the ratio of Scope 1, 2 and 3 emissions of selected companies with public emissions data (Fig. 8.5).

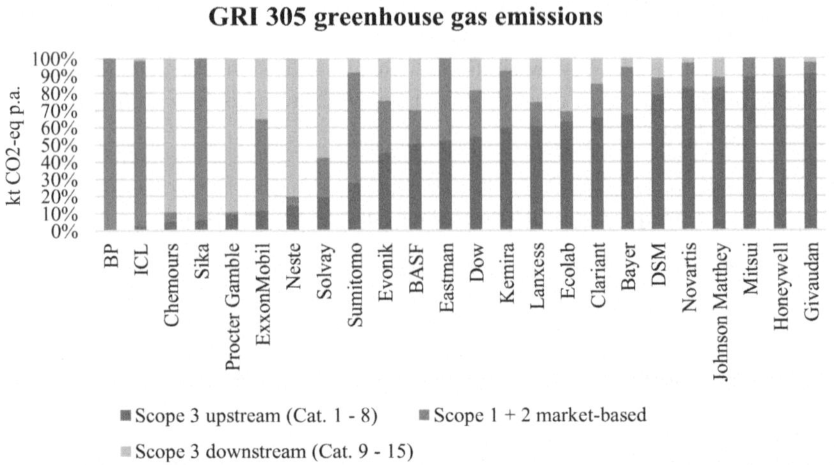


**Fig. 8.5** Scope 1, 2 and 3 emissions ratios of selected CEFIC corporate members

Examples of companies with high Scope 1 + 2 emissions are petrochemical companies with high energy requirements for refining petrochemicals, flaring and exploring petroleum. Examples of high Scope 3 downstream emissions are energy products from petrochemical companies with high emissions from the use of sold products, fluorinated gases with high emissions from disposal and consumer goods sold in applications where large emissions are released. The manufacturers of specialty chemicals are predominantly on the right-hand side of the bar chart and buy Scope 3 emissions from upstream operations. The bar chart reflects the technological regime shaped by MNCs with large refineries that produce intermediates and monomers for downstream specialty chemical manufacturers. Large Scope 1 + 2 emissions from companies' own operations require a switch to renewable energies or abatement technologies in order to reduce emissions from discharge into the atmosphere. Large Scope 3 emissions from upstream manufacturers show the need for strategies to switch raw materials to alternatives with a lower carbon footprint.

### 8.1.3 Corporates' Mission Statements

The following section collets mission statement for Scope 3 emission reduction which is linked to the supply chain and the use of renewable raw materials with lower carbon footprints than fossil feedstocks. No company from the halogen sector has published mission statements for Scope 3 reduction strategies. From the petrochemical sector, Sabic plans to establish Scope 3 emissions targets and remarks that *"there is currently no consensus on priority categories to address. That is why we are working with the SBTi advisory group to understand how other companies are defining Scope 3 and what is most relevant to SABIC"* (Sabic, 2021b). Total plans *"to achieve carbon neutrality (net zero emission) worldwide for indirect GHG emissions related to the use by customers of energy products sold for end use in 2050 or sooner (Scope 3)."* The company commits that *"this 30% reduction target is extended to all the Scopes 1, 2, 3 emissions in Europe"* and has a *"10%/year TOTAL's biofuels sales growth target by 2030"* (Total, 2021b). From the pharmaceutical sector, Merck reports that *"by 2040, we intend to achieve net zero carbon operations along our entire value chain. This target covers our Scope 1, 2 and 3 greenhouse gas emissions,"* based on fuel- and energy-related emissions, waste generated in operations and business travel. (Merck, 2021). *"Novartis has a goal to be carbon neutral across the entire value chain (Scopes 1, 2 and 3) by 2030, and to be plastic and water neutral by 2030"* (Novartis, 2021). From specialty chemical sector, Clariant announces *"the $CO_2$ reduction by 14 % for Scope 3 as a new target"* by 2030. *"Clariant is launching solutions to improve the $CO_2$ footprint of its customers (handprint), such as the sunliquid® investment."* The Sunliquid process uses second generation biomass as a renewable feedstock for bioethanol production and contributes to sustainability transition. *"Clariant supports this shift by promoting innovation in biofuels, bio-based chemicals, and feedstock"* (Clariant, 2021). *"Dow aspires to be carbon neutral (Scope 1 + 2 + 3 plus product benefits)"*. Actions to address Scope 3 emissions include *"improving our sustainability-focused supplier interaction,"* and the company identified measures like *"transportation optimization, …collaborating with suppliers, customers and logistics service providers (LSPs) to redesign new circular supply chains that reuse or recycle packaging, or incorporate post-consumer recycled (PCR) material"* (Dow, 2021b). These are a few examples of relevance for Scope 3 emission reduction. Mission statements prove a positive attitude of the leading firms toward use of renewable raw materials and confirm previous findings for attitude.

### 8.1.4 Corporates' Reduction Targets

GHG emission reduction targets and CDP scores from publications are listed in the electronic supplementary material (ESM) table 8, and are used to calculate the GHG emission scenario. 60 companies of corporate members publish Scope 1 + 2 emission reduction targets, 38 companies publish target years for net zero Scope 1 + 2 emissions. Only 12 companies publish Scope 3 emission reduction targets and 4 companies commit to achieving net zero Scope 3 emissions by 2050 (Fig. 8.6).

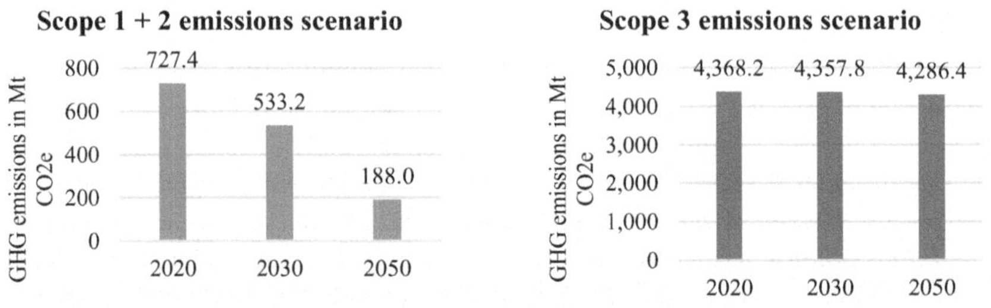


**Fig. 8.6** GHG emissions scenarios based on commitments as of August 2021

60 corporate members of the CEFIC group jointly intend to reduce the greenhouse gas emissions of Scope 1 + 2 by 27% by 2030 and by 71% by 2050, based on the available data and the greenhouse gas emission scenario in the electronic supplementary material (ESM) table 9. The forecast savings for Scope 1 + 2 by 2050 amount to 539,4 Mt CO2e of 727,4 Mt CO2e. The forecast Scope 3 savings by 2050 amount to 80,4 Mt CO2e of 4.368 Mt CO2e, which is less than 2% of total. The industry is less obliged to reduce Scope 3 emissions and the availability of Scope 1 + 2 emissions data and targets show a high level of commitment to reducing emissions operational GHG emissions. The majority of companies has not published any Scope 3 emission reduction targets or commitment yet, but companies report to gather information and drive strategy building.

### 8.1.5 Categorization by Scope 1 + 2 Reduction Targets

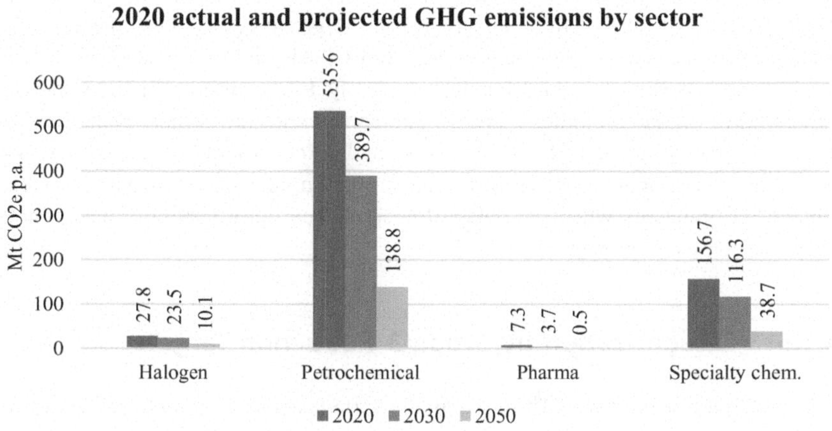


**Fig. 8.7** Scope 1 + 2 GHG emissions scenario by sector

The corporate members of the CEFIC group are sorted according to their absolute and relative reduction targets for Scope 1 and Scope 2 emissions, the year of net carbon neutrality and the CDP values. Corporate members of CEFIC group have all together reduction targets of 195,6 Mt CO2e by 2030. The 10 largest emitters have reduction targets of 137,3 Mt CO2e by 2030 or 70% of the group's savings according to the analysis listed in the electronic supplementary material (ESM) table 10. The 10 companies with highest absolute reduction targets plan 141,6 Mt CO2e savings by 2030 or 72% of the group's savings according to the analysis listed in the electronic supplementary material (ESM) table 11. The highest absolute emission reduction targets come from the petrochemical sector. 7 companies in the top 10 with the highest operational emissions also have the highest absolute greenhouse gas savings target in the industry, led by Sabic, Chevron, Versalis, ExxonMobil, Total, Shell and BP. The 10 companies with highest relative reduction targets plan 61,3 Mt CO2e savings by 2030 or 31% of the group's savings according to the analysis listed in the electronic supplementary material (ESM) table 12. The highest relative emission reduction targets come from the pharmaceutical and specialty chemicals sector, led by Archroma, Altana, Novartis and Procter & Gamble with the highest Scope 1 and Scope 2 reduction targets of 100% before 2030, followed by and Givaudan with 70% before 2030. The 20 companies with a highest CDP score A and A− together plan to save 58,8 Mt CO2e by 2030 or 30% of the total savings of the group according to the analysis listed in the electronic supplementary material (ESM) table 13. The group meets the highest reporting standard but has relatively low emissions savings targets compared to the large emitters. The 10 companies with the earliest plans for net carbon neutrality plan 9,5 Mt CO2e savings by 2030 or 5% of the group's savings according to the analysis listed in the electronic supplementary material (ESM) table 14. Companies with early plans for caron neutrality generally have small GHG emissions (Fig. 8.7).

### 8.1.6 Categorization by Scope 3 Reduction Targets

Corporate members of the CEFIC group are sorted according to Scope 3 emission reduction targets. Only 12 companies have numerical goals and the following table lists the 12 leading companies with Scope 3 emissions reduction targets (Table 8.4).

**Table 8.4** Scope 1, 2 and 3 emission reduction targets as of 2021

| Company | Segment | CDP Score | Scope 1+2 Mt CO2e | Scope 1+2 neutral | Scope 3 Mt CO2e | Scope 3 before 2050 |
|---|---|---|---|---|---|---|
| Arkema | Specialty chem. | A- | 3,4 | 2050 | 11,2 | -19% |
| Bayer | Pharma | A | 3,8 | 2050 | 8,9 | -12% |
| Clariant | Specialty chem. | B | 0,8 | n. a. | 3,3 | -14% |
| Dow | Specialty chem. | B | 34,8 | 2050 | 69,3 | -100% |
| DSM | Specialty chem. | A | 1,2 | 2050 | 12,0 | -28% |
| Evonik | Specialty chem. | A- | 5,4 | n. a. | 17,7 | -15% |
| Givaudan | Specialty chem. | A | 0,1 | 2040 | 1,9 | -100% |
| ICL | Specialty chem. | A- | 3,2 | 2050 | 0,1 | -45% |
| Johnson Matthey | Specialty chem. | B | 0,4 | 2040 | 3,1 | -20% |
| Merck | Pharma | B | 2,0 | 2040 | 0,3 | -100% |
| Novartis | Pharma | A- | 0,8 | 2030 | 0,0 | -100% |
| Total | Petrochemical | A- | 39,0 | 2050 | n. a. | -30% |

4 companies commit to net zero emissions of Scope 1, 2 and 3 by 2050. The majority of companies are more in a state of data collection, understanding and strategy development. Mission statements and sustainability strategies announce, that companies are in the data collecting stage before committing to Scope 3 emissions reduction targets. Scope 3 reduction targets and Scope 1 + 2 reduction targets are correlated, the Pearson correlation coefficient has a value of 0,42.

### 8.1.7 Categorization by Adopter Group

The Dutch court ruling from May 26, 2021 orders Royal Dutch Shell to cut carbon emissions by 45% by 2030 and the reduction obligation comes across as a benchmark for climate targets (McFarlane, 2021). Corporate members of the CEFIC group are categorized in 4 groups according to their relative Scope 1 + 2 reduction targets before 2030 and the result is listed in the electronic supplementary material (ESM) table 15 (Fig. 8.8).

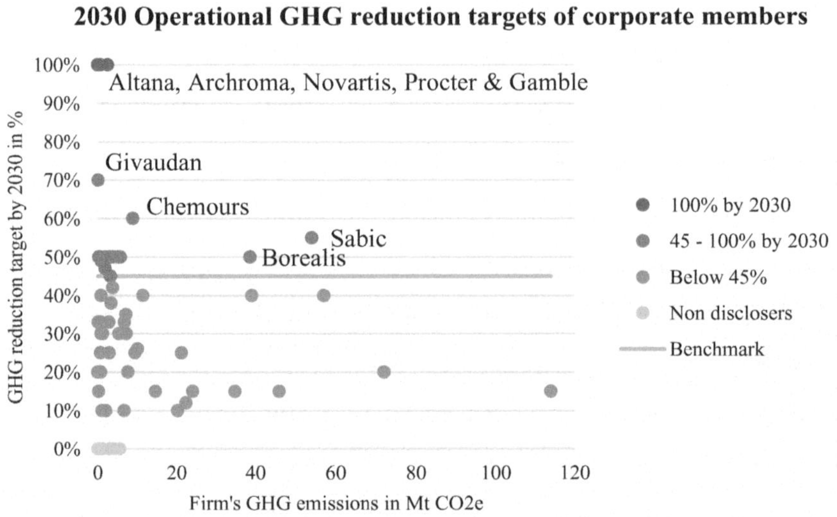


**Fig. 8.8** 2030 GHG reduction targets by adopter category vs benchmark

The categories are climate leaders for reduction targets of 100% before 2030, fast adopters for 45% – 100% reduction targets, majority for 10% to below 45% and no disclosures for companies without reduction targets. 4 climate leaders with 100% operational GHG reduction targets by 2030 lead the industry. Their contribution to the forecast GHG savings in the European chemical industry is only a small share of 3,6 Mt CO2e or 2% of the corporate members total savings. 16 fast adopters plan to reduce operational greenhouse gas emissions by 45 to 100% before 2030 and together contribute 67,0 Mt CO2e or 34% of the corporate members total savings. The majority of the 40 companies have plans to reduce greenhouse gas emissions below 45% by 2030 and contribute 126,7 million t CO2e to the forecast savings of the European chemical industry. 12 companies have not reported any savings targets or even announced that they will increase their greenhouse gas emissions. The group, representing 15% of CEFIC corporate members also has incomplete emissions data. Total projected operational GHG savings based on the available numbers are 194,2 Mt CO2e before 2030 (Fig. 8.9).

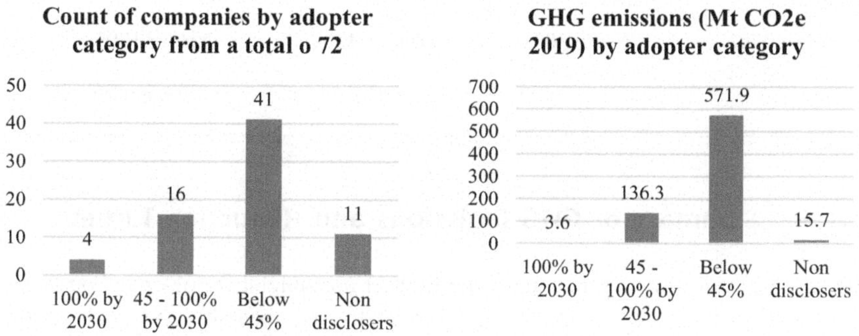


**Fig. 8.9** Greenhouse gas reduction targets by adopter category

### 8.1.8 Categorization by Industry Sector

Corporate members of the CEFIC group are sorted by sector and the results are found in the electronic supplementary material (ESM) table 16. Each sector is led by a group of leading companies with above-average emission reduction targets and earlier years to achieve net carbon neutrality for Scope 1 + 2 emissions. The highest Scope 1 and Scope 2 GHG reduction targets for 2030 are reported by companies in the specialty chemicals and pharmaceuticals sector. 4 companies have committed to achieving net carbon neutrality for Scope 1 and Scope 2 greenhouse gas emissions before 2030: Archroma, Altana, Novartis and Procter & Gamble, followed by Givaudan with Scope 1 and Scope 2 reduction targets of 70% by 2030. Companies with high Scope 1 and Scope 2 emission reduction targets generally gain higher CDP scores of A and A− level. Leading companies with higher than 45% Scope 1 and Scope 2 reduction targets by 2030 are Chemours, Albemarle and Orbia in the halogen sector, and Sabic, Borealis and Neste in the petrochemical sector (Table 8.5).

**Table 8.5** 2030 operational GHG reduction targets of sector leaders

| **2030 operational GHG reduction targets of sector leaders** | | | |
|---|---|---|---|
| **Halogen** | **Petrochemical** | **Pharma** | **Specialty chem.** |
| Chemours 60% | Sabic 55% | Novartis 100% | Altana 100% |
| Albemarle 49% | Borealis 50% | Merck 50% | Archroma 100% |
| Orbia 47% | Neste 50% | Bayer 42% | Procter 100% |
| | | | Givaudan 70% |

### 8.1.9 Summary of GHG Emissions and Reduction Targets

The petrochemical companies have the highest absolute share of greenhouse gas emissions in the sector with 74 %, followed by the specialty chemicals sector with 21 %. The contributions of the halogen sector at 4% and the pharmaceutical sector at 1% are small. The halogen sector has the largest product-related carbon footprint, followed by the petrochemical sector. The specialty chemicals sector is a downstream user of petrochemical intermediates and monomers and contributes a smaller share to the product carbon footprint in the supply chain. However, the oil-dependency of the industry passes on the product carbon footprint of upstream producers to downstream user and is thus made responsible for its raw material choice. The pharmaceutical sector has the smallest product carbon footprint. The keyword density reflects the attention paid to mitigation strategies and the use of renewable technologies in each sector. A group of 4 climate leaders intend to achieve carbon neutrality before 2030 but have only a small share of GHG emissions and emissions reduction targets in the sector. A group of 16 companies that are rapidly adopting emission reduction technologies plan to reduce GHG emissions by more than 45% by 2030. The group accounts for 19% of the industry's GHG emissions and plans to achieve 34% of the industry's reduction targets by 2030. The adopter group pays above-average attention to the use of renewable energy and recycling concepts (Fig. 8.10).

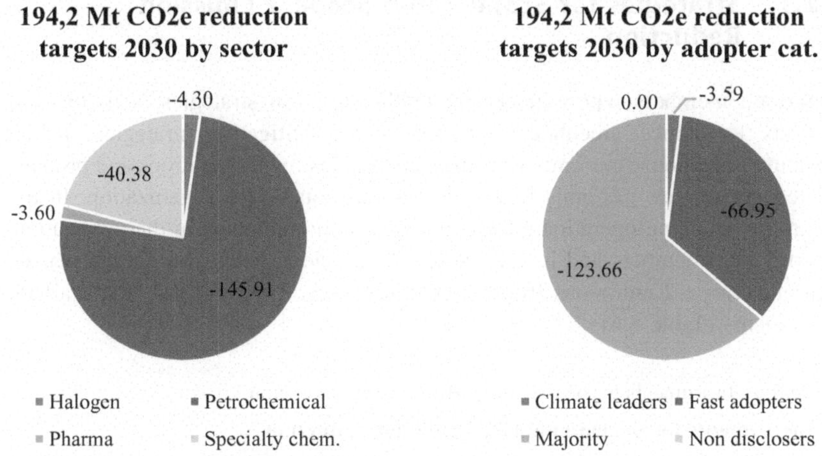


**Fig. 8.10** GHG reduction targets by industry sector and adopter category

The majority of the 40 companies plan GHG savings of less than 45% by 2030. The group is responsible for 57% of the industry's GHG emissions and intends to achieve the largest share of the industry's savings targets by 2030 at 64%. Most petrochemical and specialty chemical companies are in this group, which places above-average emphasis on efficiency improvements, use of bio-based feedstocks, and CCU technologies. A small group of 12 companies disclose little GHG emissions data, have no reduction targets, and have low participation in industry initiatives, low commitment to sustainable development goals, or low keyword density for mitigation strategies. It is likely that companies in this category can only be motivated to make GHG reductions through government restrictions and CO2 taxation.

## 8.2 Corporates' Emission Reduction Strategies

Mitigating climate change requires a variety of measures, ranging from operational to product-related reductions in greenhouse gas emissions. The instruments are analyzed in current company publications and described in the following sections. The strategies are organizational plans for emission reduction and indicators of intentions regarding climate protection measures.

### 8.2.1 Strategies for Scope 1 and Scope 2 Emission Reduction

Corporate members report in current publications on strategies, activities and projects to reduce greenhouse gas emissions. Mitigation strategies include reducing greenhouse gas emissions from companies' own operations and product-related greenhouse gas emissions from sources outside the organization. Instruments for reducing operational GHG emissions are published in the publications of corporate members and include Scope 1 emissions from own energy generation and Scope 2 emissions from purchased energy. The table lists the available instruments (Table 8.6).

**Table 8.6** Instruments for operational GHG emission reduction

| **Instruments for operational GHG emission reduction** |
|---|
| 1. Efficiency programs<br>• Reduce energy intensity<br>• Installation of abatement technologies to reduce CO2, methane, nitrous oxide and fluorinated gas emissions from chemical operations<br>2. Phase-down of production<br>3. Use of renewable energy for operations<br>• Own energy generation from wind, solar, hydropower, biomass or geothermal<br>• Sourcing of renewable energies for heat and electricity<br>• Use of renewable electricity for electrolysis or other chemical processes<br>4. Compensation schemes<br>• Virtual power purchase agreement and emissions trading<br>• CO2e offset programs, e.g. forests' conservation and afforestation |

The examples do not claim to be exhaustive and document the commitment of corporate members in operational GHG reduction activities and plans. Altana "*implemented projects to improve energy efficiency at various sites*" (Altana, 2021a). Novartis intends to reduce "*demand for energy by improving energy efficiency: Novartis held in 2019 to identify energy reduction opportunities across our sites have generated more than 300 projects*" (Novartis, 2020). Phase-down plans are reported by halogen sectors. "*3M made the decision to phase-out PFOS and PFOA. We chose to stop production ahead of any regulatory requirement*" (3M, 2021b). Chemours reports its "*commitment to support the phasedown of hydrofluorocarbons (HFCs) through the Kigali Amendment to the Montreal Protocol and US legislation*" (Chemours, 2020). Use of renewable energy is reported by the climate leaders. "*Some Altana sites already generate their own energy from renewable sources*" and "*Altana plans to reduce its CO2 impact in production and energy procurement to zero worldwide by 2025*" (Altana, 2021a). Procter & Gamble was "*able to reduce energy use per unit of production by 19%.*" "*P&G has achieved the 2020 goal to utilize 30% renewable energy.*" (Procter & Gamble, 2021b). Examples for credit transfer and compensation schemes are give by the petrochemical industry. Neste recognized emissions that cannot be removed in production by 2035. "*To reach carbon neutral production, we will prepare and implement credible compensation methods together with our partners*" (Neste, 2021) Shell invests in ecosystems and reports "*840,000 trees to be planted on 700 hectares of wildfire-devastated land, together with the Tŝilhqot'in National Government*" in Canada (Shell, 2021c).

### 8.2.2 Strategies for Scope 3 Emissions Reduction

Product related GHG emissions are categorized Scope 3 emissions and occur from sources outside the organization. Instruments for reduction of product GHG emissions are reported in corporate members publications and listed in the following table (Table 8.7).

**Table 8.7** Instruments for product GHG emission reduction

**Instruments for product GHG emission reduction**

1. Use of biobased raw materials
   - Use of plant derived feedstocks
   - Use of feedstocks from enzymes, algae and 3. generation biomass
2. Use of plastic waste
   - Mechanical and chemical plastic recycling
3. Carbon capture and utilization technologies
   - Use CO2 as starting molecule and green hydrogen for synthesis

Annual sustainability reports cover 80+ examples of bio-based raw material use, 50+ examples of plastic waste use, and 18 considerations of carbon capture and utilization. Examples of the use of bio-based raw materials are reported by the petrochemical industry. "*Neste is the world's largest producer of renewable diesel and sustainable aviation fuel*" (Neste, 2021). Also Sabic reports to produce monomers from biomass. "*In 2021, together with UPM Biofuels, Sabic produced renewable ethylene using tall oil feedstock.*" (Sabic, 2021). Plastic recycling is identified as alternative feedstock fand replacement of petroleum. Sabic reports reuse of plastic waste for chemical synthesis. "*Certified circular products are made from difficult-to-recycle used plastics produced through chemical recycling*" (Sabic, 2021b). Total "*is firmly committed to developing plastics recycling in order to address the issue of end-of-life of plastics and aims to produce 30% of its polymers from recycled materials by 2030*" (Total, 2021b). Novel carbon capture and utilization technologies are reported by large specialty chemical companies. BASF reports new process of methane pyrolysis. "*Methane pyrolysis requires around 80% less electricity than the alternative method of producing hydrogen using water electrolysis*" (BASF, 2021a). Persorp in a project, started in January 2019, "*has developed a concept to produce methanol from a large variety of recovered end-of-life streams and hydrogen from electrolysis in a combined Carbon Capture & Utilization (CCU) and gasification process*" (Perstorp, 2021). The examples are not exhaustive but document the engagement of corporate members of the CEFIC group in product GHG emission reduction activities and indications for intentions to use renewable raw materials.

### 8.2.3 Use of Biobased Feedstocks

New product developments and projects for use of biobased raw materials are reported by the petrochemical, pharmaceutical and specialty chemical industry. The petrochemical sector proposes biobased feedstocks as replacement for petroleum for refining of fuels and chemical intermediates. Sabic announces that "*certified renewable products consist of resins and chemicals made from tall oil, a bio-based renewable feedstock of a wood-based residue from pulping processes that are not in competition with the human food chain*" (Sabic, 2021b). Borealis reports that in September 2020, "*we launched the Bornewables™ portfolio of premium polyolefins. These products are based on renewable feedstocks that are 100% derived from waste and residue streams*" (Borealis, 2021). "*Neste is the world's largest producer of renewable diesel and sustainable aviation fuel*" and processes about 3,2 million tons of renewable products annually. Neste's renewable diesel enables "*its customers to reduce greenhouse gas (GHG) emissions by up to 90% compared to fossil diesel over the life cycle*" as a drop-in solution. The renewable carbon share at Neste is already about 8%, leading the petrochemical sector (Neste, 2021). Also, Cepsa and Repsol report raw material purchases from renewable sources. Raw materials from renewable sources account for about 2% at Cepsa and about 1% at Repsol (Cepsa, 2021; Repsol, 2021). The pharmaceutical sector proposes the use of biobased feedstocks primarily for plastic packaging. For Bayer, "*the share of renewable raw materials in Bayer's procurement portfolio plays a subordinated role in the Bayer Group. These materials are primarily used when it makes technical, economic and ecological sense to do so*" (Bayer, 2021c). Novartis reports that "*all our biologics development projects already use BioPET-A, a plant derived polyethylene terephthalate made from 30% renewable raw material*" (Novartis, 2021b). The specialty chemicals sector reports the highest renewable carbon share in the industry, lead by Seppic. Seppic uses 55% of raw materials derived from plants. Climate goal leader Altana reports a renewable carbon share of about 5% (Table 8.8).

**Table 8.8** Use of renewable raw materials by the specialty chemicals sector

| |
|---|
| "*55% of the raw materials Seppic uses are derived from plants*" (Seppic, 2021). |
| "*19% of organic raw materials are from renewable sources*" (Nouryon, 2021). |
| "R*enewable & secondary raw materials 15,2% on spend in 2020*" (DSM, 2021). |
| "*In 2020, renewables accounted for around 8,5% of raw materials*" (Evonik, 2021) |
| "*About 19 % were derived from natural raw materials such as bentonite; and 7 % were made of renewable raw materials*" (Clariant, 2021b) |
| "*A total of 571 kt of raw materials was needed of which 386,5 kt were fossil raw materials, 21,1 kt renewable materials*" (Altana, 2021). |

Several niche innovations in the embryonic stage are reported, as well es existent biobased feedstocks from oil plants. "*Evonik uses dextrose and saccharose for the fermentation of amino acids*" and "*palm oil, palm kernel oil and their derivatives to produce ingredients for the cosmetics, detergents and cleaning agents' industry*" (Evonik, 2021). DSM reports the launch of bio-based high-molecular-weight polyethylene "*Dyneema®, which is based on renewable ethylene derived from bio-based feedstock (residue of the wood pulping process)*". The company claims "*for at least 60% of Dyneema® fiber feedstock to be bio-based by 2030. Bio-based Dyneema® enables the transition from a fossil resource to a renewable resource and reduces carbon footprint*" (DSM, 2021). Clariant reports a long list of new sustainable product launches with the "*»Vita«-labeled bio-additives... based on renewable rice bran wax – a non-food competing by-product from the production of edible rice bran oil.*" Additional additives are "*...based on certified renewable ethylene and propylene from biomass feedstock such as non-food-competing residue oils*" (Clariant, 2021b). Clariant reports the ongoing construction of second-generation biofuels plant in Podari, Romania, where the company has set up a supply chain "*with almost 300 farmers, ensuring stable and reliable straw supply for the operational phase of the plant.*" Additionally, "*all feedstock is certified according to the International Sustainability & Carbon Certification (ISCC) system, which indicates that feedstock is from renewable source*" (Clariant, 2021b).

The investment project demonstrates how 2nd generation biomass is planned to contribute to GHG emission reduction (Fig. 8.11).

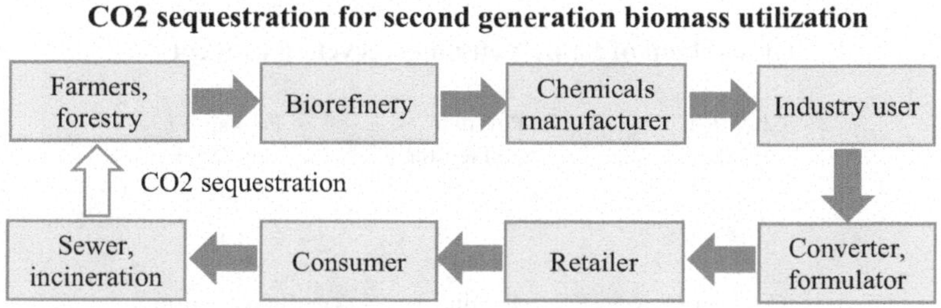


**Fig. 8.11** CO2 sequestration for second generation biomass utilization

The examples of sustainable product and process innovations reflect the efforts of industry to make biobased intermediates and specialty chemicals available. Increased use of renewable carbon reduces GHG emission and product carbon footprints. Petrochemical companies strive to make intermediates based on renewable feedstocks available and specialty chemicals companies attempt to meet customers' expectations with the supply of biobased substitutes in the known quality. The transformation towards carbon neutrality attempts to use existing supply and value chains and to make renewable feedstocks compatible with existing technological regimes.

### 8.2.4 Use of Plastic Waste

The use of plastic recycling for packaging materials and mechanical recycling as the main technology are reported across all industries. Chemours reports "*48% of the company's products sold in recyclable packaging*" (Chemours, 2020). Ombia reports, that "*in 2020, we completed a major expansion of our recycling capacity, reaching an annual 12,000 tons per year*" (Ombia, 2021b). Novartis plans to be "*plastic neutral by 2030: 60% reduction in single-use plastics in the workplace in 2020 vs. 2016 baseline*" (Novartis, 2021b). Procter & Gamble states, that "*our goal is to have 100% recyclable or reusable packaging by 2030*" (Procter & Gamble, 2021b). Petrochemical companies engage in chemical recycling and develop circular value chains to reuse and recycle plastic waste for chemical synthesis.

Recycling concepts require a high level of cooperation, as Sabic's case of packaging from chemical recycling and closing the loop or a circular use of plastics materials shows (Fig. 8.12).

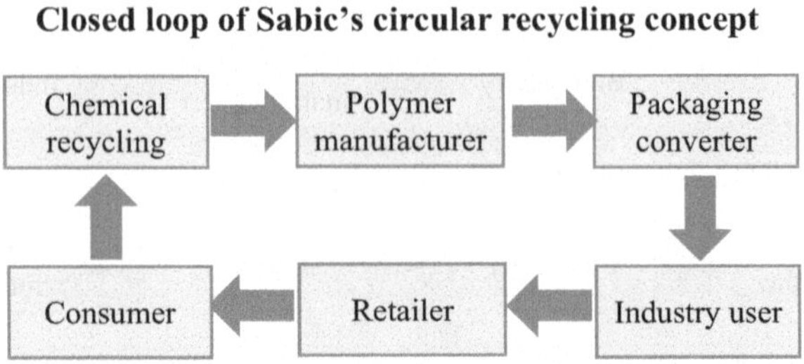


**Fig. 8.12** Closed loop of Sabic's circular recycling concept (Sabic, 2021)

Sabic cooperates with "*Tesco, that collects post-consumer flexible packaging that customers deposit in 10 U.K. retail stores. Plastic Energy then converts that waste into pyrolysis oil, which SABIC uses as feedstock to produce certified circular polymers. Sealed Air uses these polymer pallets to produce film for Bradbury Cheese products, which are then sold to Tesco*" (Sabic, 2021). "*TOTAL is firmly committed to developing plastics recycling in order to address the issue of end-of-life of plastics and aims to produce 30% of its polymers from recycled materials by 2030*" (Total, 2021b). Shell reports to "*use plastic waste as feedstock at our chemical plants*" (Shell, 2021). BP reports to "*scale up co-processing of biogenic feedstocks at our refineries*" and plans to "*grow our co-processing volume by 2025, together with the further development of waste and circular feedstock supply and processing capabilities*" (BP, 2021). LyondellBasell has "*established an ambition to produce and market two million metric tons of recycled and renewable-based polymers annually by 2030*" (LyondellBasell, 2021b) and Repsol has chemical recycling targets for "*recycled polyolefins 10% by 2025 and 20% by 2030*" (Repsol, 2021). The petrochemical industry uses existing refineries to process petroleum-based raw materials together with biomass and plastic waste. Bio-based raw materials and plastic recyclates are processed in the existing value chains of industry, which reduces complexity and increases the compatibility of the new raw materials. Challenges arise from closing the cycle for the circulation of the carbon flow. The circular supply chain includes 5 focus groups from polymer producers, packaging manufacturers, industrial users of packaging materials, retailers and consumers, and the circular economy requires end-users to learn new consumer behavior. The specialty chemicals industry is also rethinking the linear economy. The input materials for recycling concepts range from carbon containing sources to "*inorganic materials such as scrap iron, ferrous sulphate and spent pickling liquor bath. Industrial by-products are mainly from smelters, as well as steel and metal manufacturing*" (Kemira, 2021). Covestro intends "*to create more value and increase our carbon productivity by using fewer carbon-based fossil resources.*" The company claims that "*the goal is clear: We will be fully circular,*" and plans to develop chemical recycling processes as "*an important tool for Covestro in gradually replacing the use of fossil-based materials*" (Covestro, 2021). BASF aims "*to process 250,000 metric tons of recycled and waste-based raw materials in our production plants annually from 2025, replacing fossil raw materials*" and to reduce carbon footprint by "*using the mass balance approach, electricity from renewable sources and the ChemCycling™ method, a pyrolysis technology which turns plastic waste into a secondary raw material called pyrolysis oil.*" The company plans "*by 2030, we want to double our sales of solutions for the circular economy to €17 billion*" (BASF, 2021b). Carbon recovery from plastic waste and other carbon containing waste materials is in the focus as renewable feedstock for carbon demand of the chemical industry. Petrochemical companies, polymer manufacturers and backward-integrated specialty chemical companies are developing the pyrolysis processes. The industry is in the demonstration plant stage, and co-processing and mass balance approaches are cited as being best compatible with existing technological systems.

### 8.2.5 Use of CO2 as Starting Molecule

Carbon capture and utilization is reported by 18 corporate members in annual publications. Orbia targets at "*exploring carbon capture opportunities*" (Orbia, 2021) and "*Sabic joined the hydrogen council as a new steering member expanding the coalition of CEOs committed to accelerating to the transition to clean energy*" (Sabic, 2021b). Carbon capture for net zero carbon neutrality requires green hydrogen and investment activities in the novel technology are reported. Neste is "*investing in developing Power-to-X solutions*" and BP started a "*renewable hydrogen partnership with Ørsted at Lingen refinery, Germany*" (BP, 2021). Projects are also reported by the specialty chemicals sector. "*Evonik and Siemens Energy AG, Munich (Germany) took their Rheticus test facility into service.*" The facility "*uses carbon dioxide and water to produce chemicals. The innovative technology for artificial photosynthesis being tested in this facility should contribute to the success of the energy transition.*" (Evonik, 2021b). Eastman is "*exploring technologies like green hydrogen, CCUS (carbon capture, use, and sequestration)*" (Eastman, 2021). Nouryon participates "*in Carbon2Chem, a project focused on making methanol from CO2 and other off gases from steel production*" (Nouryon, 2021). Petrochemical and large specialty chemical companies explore carbon capture and utilization. Sources of pure CO2 come from steelworks and companies cooperate with partners from the electronics industry. The niche innovation is in the embryonic phase and investments in demonstration plants for the development of process engineering are made.

### 8.2.6 Drivers and Barriers in Publications

Company publications are studied for the five predictors that have been identified in case study research as innovation specific predictors for adoption of renewable raw materials, availability, costs, CO2 savings, compatibility and transparency of the supply chain. Neste confirms cost as predictor and "*evaluated that some of the critical low-carbon technologies are costly in the current situation, and a significantly higher price for emissions, even exceeding 100 EUR/tCO2e, will be needed to support global climate ambitions*" (Neste, 2021). Chevron confirms that renewable feedstocks require a price on carbon to compensate for higher costs, a price on carbon to "*be the primary policy to reduce emissions, be economywide to apply to all sectors, spur innovation.*" The company also points at the short supply of renewable feedstocks and focuses on "*(2) increasing renewables and offsets in support of our business, and (3) investing in low-carbon technologies to enable commercial solutions*" (Chevron, 2021b). Short supply of recyclates are reported as barrier for Borealis and the company sees a need for "*increasing amount of quality waste streams become available for recycling operations. Higher waste collection rates and further improvements to the efficiency of waste sorting are prerequisites to advancing the Group's recycling agenda*" (Borealis, 2021). For ExxonMobil, "*uncertainty associated with the emission estimates*" ... and "*availability of sufficient data, the quality of those data and methodology used for measurement and estimation*" are drivers for adoption (ExxonMobil, 2021). Another prove for CO2 savings as driver is provided by Neste. The supplier of renewable diesel ensures "*that the renewable raw materials that we use to produce renewable fuels always provide the required greenhouse gas emissions savings (in 2020 at least 50% reduction as per EU RED) over the fuels' life cycle*" (Neste, 2021) (Table 8.9).

**Table 8.9** Innovation-specific predictors from document analysis

| Innovation-specific predictors from document analysis |
|---|
| • Availability of renewable materials |
| • CO2 savings data |
| • Cost position |
| • Compatibility with existing technological regimes |
| • Transparency of the supply chain |

Another predictor from case study research is compatibility of the renewable feedstock with existing technological regimes. Borealis reports an example for incompatibility as barrier for adoption. "*For example, flexible packaging often uses multiple layers of different materials to protect and preserve the packaged goods, which due, to their incompatibility during the recycling process, makes separating and recycling those plastic layers extremely difficult*" (Borealis, 2021). Procter & Gamble reports barriers due to incompatibility "*in countries that do not have well-developed markets for renewable electricity*" (Procter & Gamble, 2021b). Finally, certification schemes are proposed as drivers to improve transparency of the supply chains. Neste reports that "*building industry-wide acceptance for the approach could significantly improve the overall transparency of palm oil supply chains*" (Neste, 2021). And Sabic cooperates with partners along the supply chain and is "*engaging more deeply with our suppliers to improve traceability and transparency*" (Sabic, 2021b). The examples provide further evidence for the five innovation-specific predictors identified in previous case study research. Cost position, availability of renewable feedstocks, CO2 savings data, compatibility with existing technological regimes and transparency of the supply chain are predictors for adoption of renewable raw materials. The examples also provide evidence for intentions of corporate members of the CEFIC group to use renewable raw materials with the aim to reduce product related GHG emissions.

## 8.3 Sector Specific Emission Reduction Strategies

Findings from the document analysis identify industry-specific strategies for companies to reduce greenhouse gas emissions. Petrochemical companies are upstream manufacturers that supply fuels, intermediates and process chemicals to downstream users in the specialty chemicals sector. Upstream producers have the potential to reduce greenhouse gas emissions with innovative product offerings based on biomass, plastic recycling and carbon capture technology. The demand for product-related GHG emission reductions offers a window of opportunity for innovations and new types of raw materials.

### 8.3.1 Keyword Density Analysis

Keyword density analysis is used as a tool to determine the relevance of mitigation strategies for each of the sectors, halogen, petrochemical, pharmaceutical and specialty chemicals. From 69 available annual, sustainability or integrated reports, five strategies are categorized according to topics and keywords are counted. Keywords are only counted if they relate to greenhouse gas reduction strategies and the results of the search are listed in the electronic supplementary material (ESM) table 17 (Fig. 8.13).

24% of the keywords relate to "efficiency" programs and installations to reduce energy intensity and incorporate abatement technologies. 24% of keywords relate to "renewable" energy, heat and electricity for operations. 24% of keywords relate to "recycling" and use of plastic waste for mechanical and chemical recycling. 27% of keywords relate to "biobased" raw materials, and 1% of keywords relate to "CCU" and the use of CO2 as starting molecule. Use of biobased raw materials receive above-average attention in the chemical industry, efficiency improvements in operations, renewable energy, circular technologies receive about equal attention in all chemical industry reports. Carbon capture and utilization has a small share. Keyword density by sector provides sector-specific attention to mitigation strategies. Keyword density is the number of keywords per report per 100 pages. The petrochemical sector has the highest keyword density of mitigation strategies, followed by the halogen sector. The specialty chemicals sector has a below-average keyword density and pharmaceutical sector has the lowest keyword density of mitigation strategies. The relevance of sustainability technologies is the ratio of the sector's keyword density compared to the chemical industry average (Fig. 8.14).

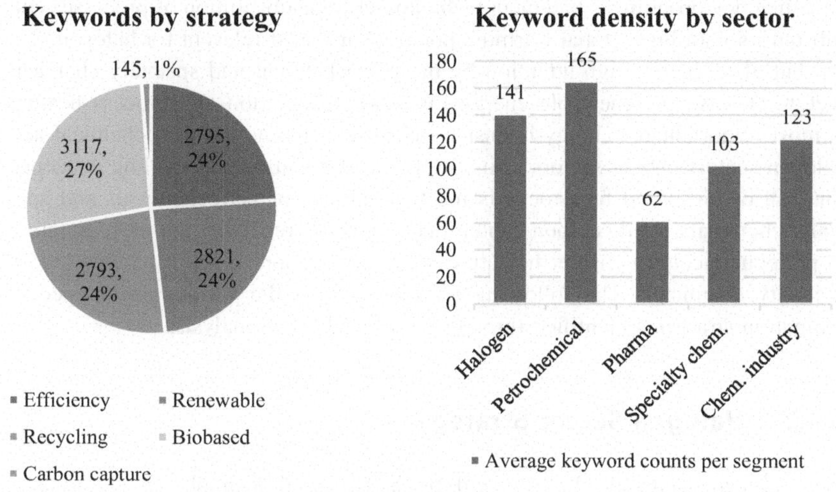


**Fig. 8.13** Keyword counts per mitigation strategy and sector

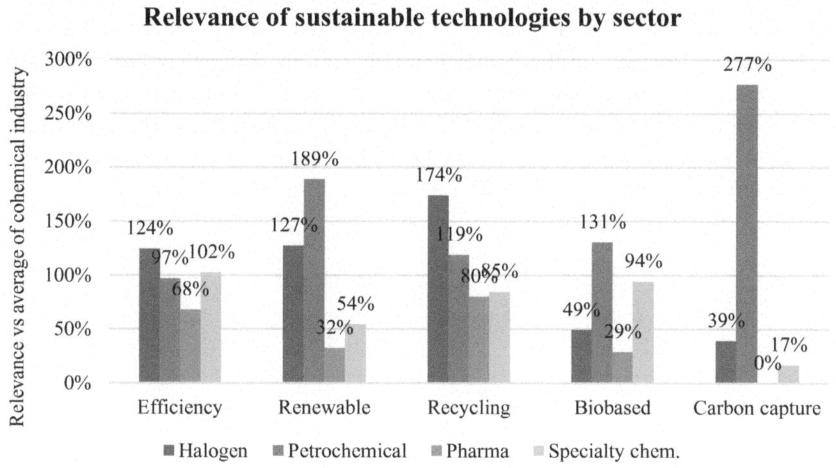


**Fig. 8.14** Relevance of sustainable technologies by sector

Efficiency programs, abatement technologies and substitution of processes and substances with high global warming potential are most relevant for halogen sector, but also receive high attention by the petrochemical and specialty chemical sector. The use of renewable energy for power generation and process heating is most important for energy-intensive industries such as the petrochemical and halogen sectors. These sectors also pay the most attention to recycling concepts. The use of bio-based feedstocks is most important for petrochemicals and specialty chemicals, while carbon capture technology is receiving the most attention in petrochemicals to ensure the future supply of carbon to downstream users in specialty chemicals. The following sections present the various sector-specific mitigation strategies identified through keyword density analysis.

### 8.3.2 Halogen Sector Strategy

The halogen sector is characterized by halogenated technologies, fluorinated products and chlorinated polymers. The sector has the highest average operational product carbon footprint of 1 kg CO2e/EUR sales. It contributes 4% of operational GHG emissions, and aggregate GHG reduction targets are −15% by 2030 and −64% by 2050. The relevance of sustainability innovations is determined by the keyword density in the company's publications. Efficiency programs, the use of renewable energy and recycling concepts are given more attention in the halogen sector than in the average of CEFIC company members. The use of bio-based raw materials and the capture and carbon capture and utilization are given less attention than the average of CEFIC corporate members (Fig. 8.15).

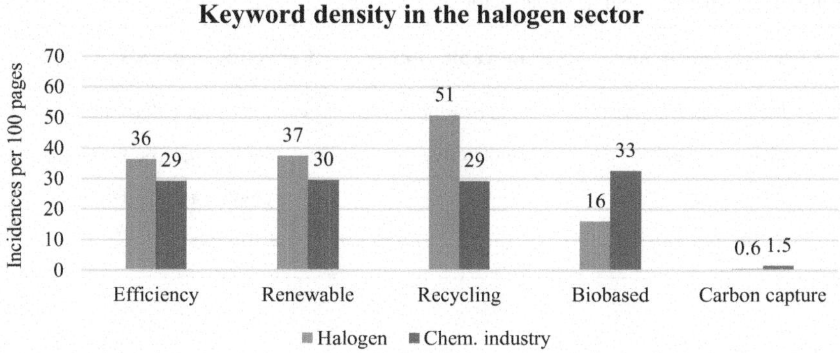


**Fig. 8.15** Keyword density in the halogen sector

Chemours, a fluorinated products manufacturer reports efficiency programs to reduce fluorinated organic compound (FOC) process emissions into the air. Abatement installations are planned to contribute toward the reductions. The companies' goal is to "*reduce FOC air process emissions by ambitious 99% or greater*" (Chemours, 2020). The focus is on efficiency programs, abatement technologies and the use of renewable energy and recycling concepts. "*The renewables as percent of total electricity use is 5%*" and 2019 targets are "*48% products sold in recyclable packaging*" (Chemours, 2020). Orbia's business comprises fluorinated solutions and halogenated polymers. The company announces targets for "*increasing our proportion of renewable electricity at our sites*" and "*exploring carbon capture opportunities.*" The key strategies are "*optimizing operational processes to drive incremental energy efficiencies in manufacturing*" and "*increasing our use of recycled raw materials.*" The company is "*engaging in material recovery operations, for example, refrigerant recovery through our Koura brand and recycling end-of-life drip lines by Netafim*" (Orbia, 2021) (Table 8.10).

**Table 8.10** Themes from halogen sector

| Efficiency programs | Renewable energy | Recycling concepts |
|---|---|---|
| • Incremental energy efficiency gains<br>• Abatement technologies | • Use of renewable electricity | • Use of recycled plastics<br>• Refrigerant recovery and recycling end-of-life drip lines |

### 8.3.3 Petrochemical Sector Strategy

The petrochemical sector has the largest share of GHG emissions in the chemical industry at 74% and the second highest average operational carbon footprint of 0,8 kg CO2e/EUR of sales. The sector needs to achieve the largest absolute reduction targets. The overall GHG emission reduction targets are −27% by 2030 and −70% by 2050 (Fig. 8.16).

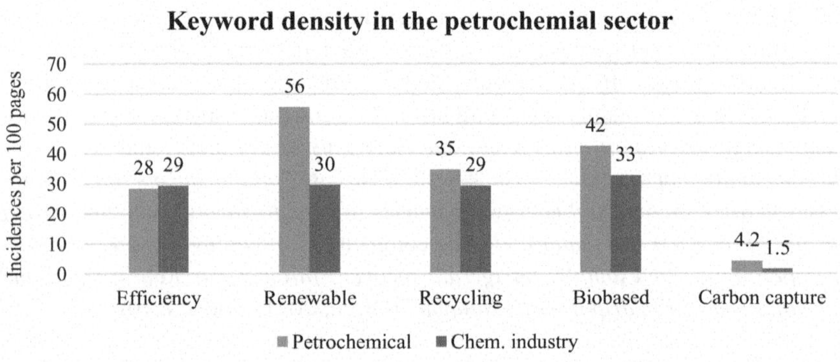


**Fig. 8.16** Keyword density in the petrochemical sector

Relevance of sustainability innovation is determined by keyword density. The use of renewable energies, recycling concepts, the use of bio-based raw materials and carbon capture and utilization receive more attention in the petrochemical industry than from the average of CEFIC corporate members, while efficiency programs receive similar amount of attention. The sector is led by Sabic, Borealis, Neste and Versalis with the highest GHG reduction targets of over 50%. Sabic announces the highest absolute emission reduction targets of 29,7 Mt CO2e by 2030 and plans to achieve climate goals through a variety of measures. Efficiency programs reduce energy demand and the expansion into the use of renewable energies is in alignment "*with Saudi Arabia's vision for the country to be 50% powered by renewable energy by 2030*" (Sabic, 2021b). Sabic is starting to use renewable raw materials to replace petroleum, namely recycled plastics and biomass, and the examples show the momentum of progress. Mechanical recycling uses recycled post-consumer materials for reuse in consumer electronics and accessories. Chemical recycling is used for waste plastics that are difficult to recycle. In this process, plastic waste is broken down into building blocks that can then be used to make polymers comparable to virgin materials. Applications include nonwovens and grocery bags. Resins and chemicals are made from tall oil, a bio-based renewable feedstock made from wood-based residues from pulping processes that does not compete with the human food chain. "*Together with UPM Biofuels, SABIC produced renewable ethylene using tall oil feedstock.*" Other developments include biobased intermediates for DSM fibers and renewable, bio-based polypropylene (Sabic, 2021b). Neste produces renewable diesel and aviation fuel as a drop-in replacement for fossil fuels to reduce greenhouse gas (GHG) emissions. The company claims to be "*the world's largest producer of renewable diesel and sustainable aviation fuel. Neste's share of the world's total renewable diesel production capacity is approximately 40%*" (Neste, 2021). The 2020 annual report announces efficiency programs to reduce GHG emissions and that "*nearly 30% of the electricity used at Neste's production sites in Finland will be renewable wind power in 2022*" (Neste, 2021). Finally, Neste participates in a development collaboration to research carbon capture, storage and utilization, and the production of renewable hydrogen through electrolysis (Neste, 2021). Borealis begins to purchase renewable energy and the use of renewable raw materials. "*Long-term purchase power agreements for renewable energy supply*" are signed. The company starts buying "*polymer additives which are produced using renewable feedstock, such as palm oil or rapeseed oil*," and manufacturing polyolefins based on renewable feedstock. Borealis focuses on "*plastics circularity by increasing the volume of recycled plastics solutions to 350,000 t/y by 2025 and ensuring that by 2025, 100% of consumer products made with Borealis polyolefins should be recyclable, reusable, or made using renewable content*" (Borealis, 2020). Eni, the principal of Versalis, "l*aunched initiatives focusing on the forest's protection, conservation and sustainable management*" by means of compensation schemes. In 2020, "*production from renewables increased more than fivefold vs. 2019*" (Eni,

2021). Versalis is "*is committed in developing mechanical, physical and chemical recycling technologies for plastics and rubber*". The company focuses on "*efficiency of resources throughout their life cycle and the recyclability of goods,*" and "*joined Circular Plastics Alliance (CPA) and pledges for plastic recycling to actively contribute to the ambitious European target*" (Versalis, 2021b). Other petrochemical companies with high greenhouse gas emission reduction targets include Chevron, ExxonMobil and Total. The companies are committed to mitigation strategies at various levels. Chevron reports state-level renewable power targets of 8,5% to 60% in the U.S. and sees opportunities through regulations in the UK and EU to achieve a 14% renewable fuels target by 2030 (Chevron, 2020b) (Table 8.11).

**Table 8.11** Themes from petrochemical sector

| Biobased feedstocks | Plastic recycling | Carbon Capture |
|---|---|---|
| • Tall oil, a bio-based renewable feedstock<br>• Biogas utilization<br>• Bioethanol fuel<br>• Biomass conversion to bio-jet fuel, biodiesel<br>• Bio-naphtha for use in biopolymer production<br>• biobased intermediates, ethylene, polypropylene | • Mechanical recycling<br>• Chemical recycling for breaking down to building blocks<br>• Ensuring recyclability of finished products | • Energy-rich bio-oils from $CO_2$ and sunlight with strains of algae<br>**Energy management**<br>• Compensation schemes<br>• Efficiency programs |

ExxonMobil is aiming for renewables to account for about 50% of global electricity supplies by 2040. The company reports to double the yield of biodiesel from a variety of cellulosic sugar and to purchase renewable diesel. Carbon capture and biofuels are being developed with partners, and a project to produce energy-rich bio-oil from $CO_2$ and sunlight with strains of algae is underway (ExxonMobil, 2021b). Total reports to install capacity in solar, wind, biogas and hydroelectricity, and seeks to "*enable its industrial, residential and power-generating customers to capture, store and reuse their CO2 emissions*". Solar and offshore wind projects are announced to increase the group's renewable energy capacity. Total expands renewable diesel and petrochemical bio-feedstocks in its biorefinery, explores projects to convert biomass into bio-jet fuel for aviation and bio-naphtha for use in biopolymer production.

### 8.3.4 Pharmaceutical Sector Strategy

The pharmaceutical sector is characterized by a low average operational carbon footprint of 0,09 kg CO2e/EUR turnover. The sector contributes only 1% of operational GHG emissions of the corporate members of the CEFIC group. Aggregated GHG reduction targets are −50% by 2030 and −94% by 2050. The keyword density in the companies' publications shows that mitigation strategies in general receive less attention in the annual reports compared with the average of the CEFIC corporate members. Efficiency programs and plastic recycling concepts receive relatively more attention in the sector than other mitigation strategies (Fig. 8.17).

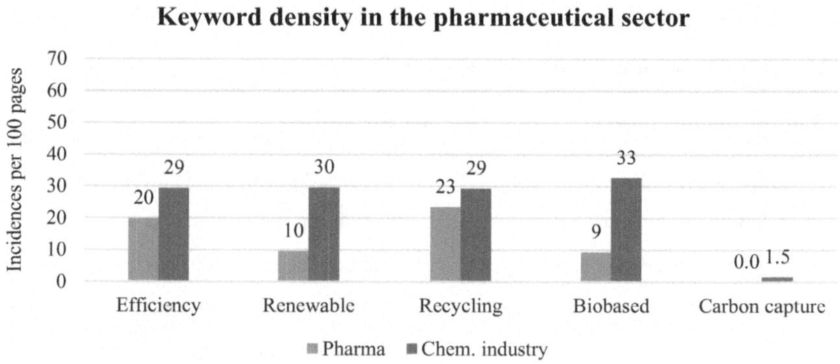


**Fig. 8.17** Keyword density in the pharmaceutical sector

The sector is represented by Novartis and Merck. With the climate goal to be carbon neutral in own operations by 2025, Novartis held workshops "*in 2019 to identify energy reduction opportunities*" and plans to compensate electricity purchases. "*All energy used in our US facilities is compensated with renewable energy credits generated through a virtual power purchase agreement (VPPA).*" In 2020, the company signed "*VPPAs with three developers for wind and solar energy projects to address the company's carbon footprint across its European operations.*" The transition "*makes Novartis the first pharmaceutical company set to achieve 100% renewable electricity in its European operations through VPPAs*". In contribution ti circular economy, the company is on track to "*eliminate polyvinyl chloride (PVC) in all secondary and tertiary packaging*" and plans "*to eliminate PVC before the end of 2021*". More environmentally friendly alternatives to PVC are evaluated and "*Bio-PET-A, a plantderived polyethylene terephthalate made from 30% renewable raw material and 70% oil-based raw material*" is already used. Merck is active in the healthcare, life science and materials business sectors. In 2020, Merck's "*emissions reduction efforts focused on purchasing electricity generated from renewable energy sources.*" The company aims "*to cover 80% of our electricity consumption with renewables by 2030*" (Merck, 2021b). The company develops bio-based solvents that are made from non-food, cellulosic resources and the life science business sector applies the "*Design for Sustainability (DfS) program for environmentally sound Life Science products.*" The design tool aims "*to reduce any adverse impact of our products on health and the environment.*" The company's sustainable packaging strategy is based on four goals: Reduce the amount of packaging, achieve zero deforestation, improve the sustainability of plastics and maximizing recycling (Merck, 2021b) (Table 8.12).

**Table 8.12** Themes from pharmaceutical sector

| Energy management | Plastic reuse |
|---|---|
| • Energy use reduction programs<br>• Credit compensation schemes through virtual power purchase agreements | • Biobased plastics and carton-based packaging materials<br>• Reduce the amount of packaging<br>• Achieve zero deforestation<br>• Improve sustainability of plastics<br>• Maximizing recycling |

### 8.3.5 Specialty Chemicals Sector Strategy

The specialty chemicals sector has the second highest absolute GHG emissions and an average operational carbon footprint of 0,4 kg CO2e / EUR sales. The sector contributes 21% of operational GHG emissions to the corporate members of the CEFIC group. The overall GHG reduction targets are −26% by 2030 and −75% by 2050. Climate leaders in the sector are Archroma, Altana and Procter & Gamble with 100% operational GHG reduction targets by 2030, followed by Givaudan, Lanxess, Evonik, Covestro and Ecolab (Fig. 8.18).

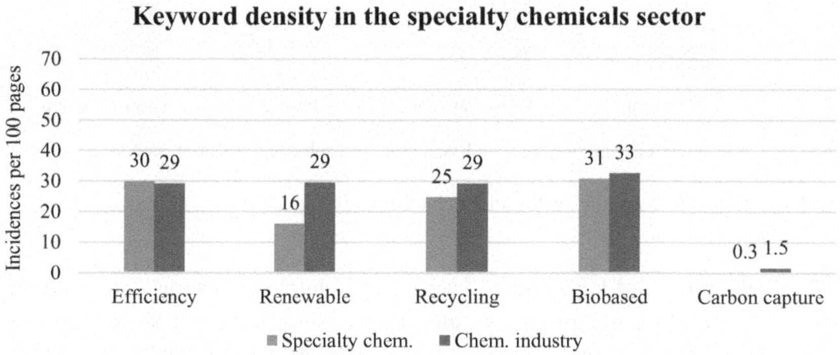


**Fig. 8.18** Keyword density in the specialty chemicals sector

Analysis of the keyword density in the companies' publications show that efficiency programs, recycling concepts and use of biobased raw materials are given similar attention in the specialty chemicals sector compared with the average of the CEFIC corporate members. Less attention is paid to the use of renewable energies and to carbon capture and utilization (Fig. 8.19).

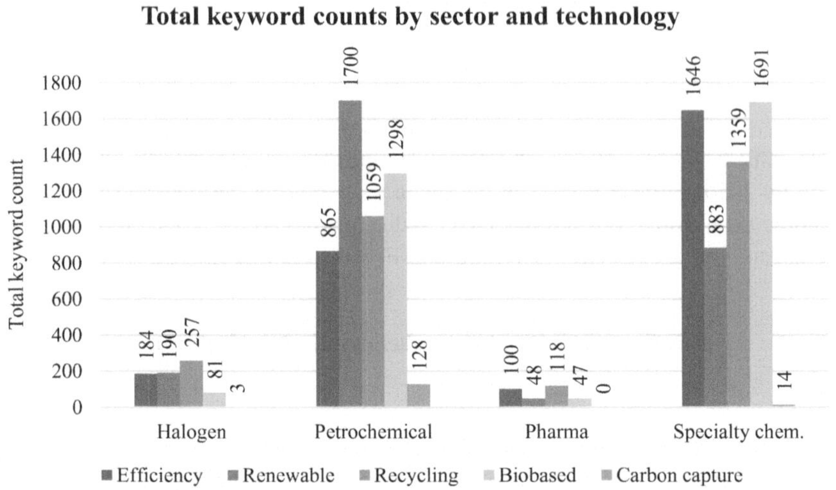


**Fig. 8.19** Keyword count by sector and technology

The total number of keywords by sector and technology illustrates the predominant focus on efficiency programs, plastics recycling and the use of bio-based feedstocks in the specialty chemicals sector. Climate leaders and fast adopters first aim to reduce their Scope 1 and Scope 2 emissions by renewable energy purchases for own operations. Additionally, the focus is on Scope 3 emissions and the use of renewable raw materials with lower carbon footprints than fossil materials. The specialty chemicals manufacturer Archroma plans to reduce energy intensity and to "*achieve carbon neutrality for Scope 1 and Scope 2 emissions in 2023*" by offsetting programs (Archroma, 2021). Altana applies several instruments apart from efficiency projects. "*Altana sites already generate their own energy from renewable sources*" and the company "*plans to reduce its CO2 impact in production and energy procurement to zero worldwide by 2025.*" A sustainable portfolio is launched and includes "*products based on recycled raw materials of fossil origin and bio-based materials in the form of plant-based resins.*" 5% of carbon flow is sourced from renewable feedstocks (Altana, 2021a). Procter & Gamble is a consumer goods manufacturer and was "*able to reduce energy use per unit of production by 19%.*" "*P&G has achieved the 2020 goal to utilize 30% renewable energy.*" The company is "*now purchasing 100% renewable electricity for all our operations in the U.S., Canada and Europe...*" and plans to "*purchase 100% renewable electricity globally, cut GHG emissions in half at P&G*

*sites and be carbon neutral for the decade.*" Palm oil is used as renewable vegetable oil. In a collaboration with Cargill, Procter & Gamble converts lactic acid into bio-based acrylic acid "*to deliver greener alternatives in the personal care space.*" The company creates technologies "*to substitute top petroleum-derived raw materials (resins, cleaning agents and acrylates) with renewable materials*" and works to "*incorporate 50% renewable or recycled materials by 2025*" in packaging materials. The goal is "*to have 100% recyclable or reusable packaging by 2030*" (Procter & Gamble, 2021b). Givaudan is a fine chemical manufacturer of flavors, nutrition ingredients and fragrance with plans to be net-carbon neutral before 2040. The company has 81% renewable electricity in use and moves "*from fossil fuels towards sources such as solar, wind, geothermal and biofuels*" and plans to "*cut the emissions of operations by 70% and our supply chain emissions by 20% before 2030.*" Givaudan focuses on efficiency gains from applying the 12 green chemistry rules and on the use of biobased raw materials. 100% naturally derived fragrances from renewable carbon are developed. "*Givaudan employs green chemistry methods for efficient carbon use, meaning that all carbon atoms in the starting molecule ends up in the final product, resulting in zero waste and thus limiting carbon emissions*" (Givaudan, 2021). Lanxess plans to be climate neutral by 2040 and its research focuses on resource efficiency, biobased raw materials and recycling concepts. "*Lanxess is working with partners to develop an innovative recycling concept*" together with Fraunhofer Institute. The aim is to separate polystyrene foam from construction waste and flame retardants that are now considered pollutants (Lanxess, 2021a) (Table 8.13).

**Table 8.13** Themes from specialty chemicals sector

| Energy management | Biobased feedstocks | Recycling concepts |
|---|---|---|
| • Reduces energy intensity<br>• Resource efficiency programs<br>• Purchase 100% renewable electricity<br>• energy management system<br><br>**Carbon capture technology**<br><br>• Photosynthesis to produce specialty chemicals from CO2 with the aid of bacteria & algae | • Plant-based feedstocks, e.g. dextrose, saccharose, palm oil, palm kernel oil<br>• Biobased intermediates and monomers<br>• Final products made from biobased materials<br>• Green chemistry methods for efficient carbon use | • Products based on recycled raw materials of fossil origin<br>• 100% recyclable or reusable packaging<br>• Closed loop systems<br>• Incorporate renewable or recycled materials in final materials<br>• Separation of construction polymers from hazardous additives<br>• Avoid downcycling of recyclates by choice of additives |

Evonik plans to optimize "*energy consumption in the Evonik group by digital energy management system*" and collects and implements ideas to avoid Scope 3 emissions. Production emissions of suppliers are reduced by "*sourcing raw materials produced from biomass or waste streams,*" and "*the results of our talks with suppliers are documented and the CO2 avoided by specific projects with suppliers is calculated*". "*In 2020, the proportion of renewable raw materials increased to 8,5% of production inputs,*" from 7,9% in 2019 (Evonik, 2021b). Evonik uses biobased feedstocks, like dextrose and saccharose for the fermentation of amino acids and palm oil, palm kernel oil and their derivatives to produce ingredients for the cosmetics, detergents and cleaning agents' industry. Evonik "*has a strong focus on re-useable packaging material*" and various recycling technologies. "*For example, Evonik has developed chemical recycling processes to break down PET packaging into the original monomers. In mechanical recycling of plastics and tires, our additives help make processes more efficient and avoid downcycling of the recyclates.*" "*Evonik is involved in several research projects focused on using CO2 as a starting product*" and cooperates with Siemens Energy for "*artificial photosynthesis to produce specialty chemicals from CO2, water and green electricity with the aid of bacteria.*" The technology platform is used in another research alliance with Beiersdorf to produce personal care products using CO2 (Evonik, 2021b). Covestro expects to reduce GHG emissions "*by 50% from the 2005 benchmark by the year 2025*". Energy is purchased "*with a significantly lower carbon footprint*" and "*existing energy- and resource-intensive plants*" are optimized. The specialty chemicals manufacturer plans "*increasing use of renewable energy and establish new recycling technologies,*" with the final goal of "*a closed loop system in the company.*" "*Focus on the circular economy, sustainability is now even more strongly rooted in the center of our activities*" says Markus Steilemann, the company's chief executive officer and VCI vice-president (Covestro, 2021a). 25 R&D projects are running, progress is made in polyurethane recycling, where chemical recycling processes reclaim the chemical precursors from used materials. Additionally, renewable intermediates are sourced like "*renewable phenol from our partners Borealis and Neste*" (Covestro, 2021a). Another specialty chemicals company is Ecolab, a solution provider for hygiene, infection prevention and water solutions. The company has a "*commitment to reduce absolute Scope 1 and Scope 2 GHG emissions by 50% by 2030 from a 2018 base year.*" Total renewable electricity use in 2020 was 67,6%, advancing towards "*the 2030 goal by reducing carbon emissions by 31% from a 2018 baseline*" (Ecolab, 2021b). The company is "*working with suppliers representing 70% of Scope 3 emissions to set similarly ambitious carbon targets by 2024*". The percentage of recycled packaging material in 2020 is 15,9% and "*Ecolab is committed to implementing circular economy principles, including increasing reuse and recycling*" (Ecolab, 2021b). Analysis of sector specific-reduction strategies provides further evidence for the five innovation-specific predictors identified in previous case study research and for intentions of corporate members of the CEFIC group to use renewable raw materials.

## 8.4 Organizational Predictors in Reports

Proposed predictor variables from case study research for adoption of renewable raw materials are attitude towards the use (V1) and behavioral intention (V2). Document analysis examines company commitment, climate goals, and mission statements as indicators for attitude (V1) and product developments, projects, investments, and cooperation plans as indicators for intention to use (V2). Proposed predictor variable for intention to use from the testable model is the cost position of renewable resources. Cost is a characteristic attribute of the innovation and type of renewable raw materials (V3). Proposed company-specific predictor variables from the testable model are the company's actual use of renewable raw materials (V4), the company's sustainability strategy (V5), management advocacy (V6), cooperation skills (V7), implementation of industry standards for renewable raw materials (V8), and expectation of government regulations for renewable raw materials (V9). The variables are now examined through document analysis. Recent publications from corporate members of the CEFIC group are used as secondary source for exploring company-specific adoption predictors, for hypothesis testing and triangulation with results from expert interview.

### 8.4.1 Industry's Attitude Towards Renewable Raw Materials

Corporate members of the CEFIC group together have combined targets to reduce operational GHG emissions by 27% by 2030 and 71% by 2050. Climate leaders as well as fast adopters and majority companies participate in voluntary initiatives and commit to GHG emission reduction in mission statements and quantitative reduction targets. The mission statements of leading companies across all chemical industry sectors commit to reducing GHG emissions, and the use of renewable raw materials is cited as an important tool. Analysis of the keyword density of corporate publications proves that companies have a positive attitude toward the use of bio-based raw materials, recycling concepts, and carbon capture and utilization, and hypothesis H1 is confirmed by the document analysis.

### 8.4.2 Industry's Intention to Use Renewable Raw Materials

Indicators for the intention to use renewable raw materials are companies' numerical Scope 3 greenhouse gas emissions reduction targets and reported actions to reduce product-related greenhouse gas emissions through projects, investments, and collaborations to use renewable raw materials. Innovations based on use of renewable raw materials – biomass, plastic waste recycling and CO2 as molecule for chemical synthesis in carbon capture technologies – are reported in annual reports and recent publications. New sustainable product launches, investment projects and collaborations with partners provide examples of current activities and demonstrate the intention to use renewable raw materials. Intention to use renewable raw materials is positively correlated with attitudes toward the use of renewable raw materials among corporate members of the CEFIC industry association representing the European chemical industry. Hypothesis H2 is confirmed by the document analysis.

### 8.4.3 Industry's Barriers to Adopt Renewable Raw Materials

Barriers for adoption of renewable resources are reported in corporates' publications. Increased costs from switching to renewable energy and raw materials, and availability is thematized. BASF reports, that "*as well as its availability, the price of green power is also a critical success factor. High prices are already hindering the more widespread adoption of green power today and impact the economic feasibility of future, new production processes*" (BASF, 2021b). Eastman mentions increased "*operational costs associated with a move from fossil-derived fuels and feedstocks to more renewable sources of energy and materials*" (Eastman, 2021b) (Table 8.14).

**Table 8.14** Industry's barriers for adoption

| **Industry's barriers for adoption** |
|---|
| • Increased costs from switching to renewable energy and raw materials |
| • Availability or renewable energy and raw materials |
| • Missing infrastructure |
| • Lack of competitiveness |
| • Technological research needs |

Neste has "*evaluated that some of the critical low-carbon technologies are costly in the current situation, and a significantly higher price for emissions, even exceeding 100 EUR/tCO2e, will be needed to support global climate ambitions*" (Neste, 2021). Lack of competitiveness is also thematized by Total and "*the Group is also studying the potential for developing a cost-effective phototrophic process for producing biofuels through bioengineering of microalgae and microalgae cultivation methods*" (Total, 2021b). ExxonMobil addresses the "*dual challenge of reducing the risks of climate change at the lowest societal cost, while balancing increased demand for affordable energy*" (ExxonMobil, 2021). Also, Ineos cooperates with "*academic and industry partners because it may provide a large scale, flexible, cost-effective way of reusing difficult-to-recycle mixed waste streams*" (Ineos, 2021b). Other barriers are missing infrastructure and lack of competitiveness. BASF proposes green electricity as energy source refunds for "*potential CO2 avoided by electrical heating concepts for steam crackers up to 90%*" (BASF, 2021a). Procter & Gamble reports obstacles to "*bring renewable electricity to sites in Asia and South America, including countries that do not have well-developed markets for renewable electricity. We are partnering with WWF and the Renewable Energy Buyers Alliance to tackle these challenges*" Procter & Gamble, 2021b). Neste reports that "*Neste's sustainable aviation fuel annual capacity is currently 100,000 tons. With the Singapore refinery expansion on the way, and with possible additional investment in the Rotterdam refinery, Neste will have the capacity to produce some 1.5 million tons of SAF annually by 2023*" (Neste, 2021b). Cost positions and raw material prices are thematizes in corporates' publications together with efforts to increase availability of insufficient supply of renewable fuels and raw materials. Hypothesis H3, that the intention to use renewable raw materials has stalled due to their lower financial attractiveness compared to fossil-based products, is confirmed by the available data.

### 8.4.4 Industry's Actual Use of Renewable Raw Materials

From the climate leader category, Altana sources 5% of carbon flow from renewable feedstocks and Procter & Gamble reports to use palm oil as feedstock (Altana, 2021a; Procter & Gamble, 2021b). Companies from the fast adopter category, majority and non-disclosure category also report existing use of renewable raw materials. Borealis aims at reducing GHG emissions by 50% and is categorized as fast adopters. "*Borealis buys polymer additives which are produced using renewable feedstock, such as palm oil or rapeseed oil*" (Borealis, 2020). Neste was a pure petrochemical refinery and started the first biodiesel production plant with a capacity of 170.000 tons per year in 2007 when "*Neste Oil's board of directors approved a strategy to aimed at making the company the world's leading producer of second-generation renewable diesel fuel*" (Green Car Congress, 2006). The company followed the strategy, shifts the portfolio to renewable fuels and sells existing assets in fossil fuels. "*Neste sold its 49.99% shares in Nynas AB, a Swedish manufacturer and marketer of naphthenic specialty oils and bitumen products*" (Neste, 2021). Examples for companies that are categorized in the majority adapter category are Bayer, DSM and Nouryon, having GHG emission reduction targets of below 45%. For Bayer, with a GHG reduction target of 42% by 2030, "*the share of renewable raw materials in Bayer's procurement portfolio plays a subordinated role in the Bayer Group*" (Bayer, 2021) (Table 8.15).

**Table 8.15** Actual use of renewable feedstock as percentage of total input materials

| Company | Segment | CDP Score | Emissions Mt CO2e | Scope 3 Goal 2030 | Actual use |
|---|---|---|---|---|---|
| Altana | Specialty chem | n. a. | 0,1 | n. a. | 5% |
| Arkema | Specialty chem | A- | 3,4 | -19% | 10% |
| BASF | Specialty chem | A- | 21,3 | n. a. | 4% |
| Cepsa | Petrochem | A- | 5,6 | n. a. | 2% |
| Clariant | Specialty chem | B | 0,8 | -14% | 7% |
| DSM | Specialty chem | A | 1,2 | -28% | 15% |
| Evonik | Specialty chem | A- | 5,4 | -15% | 9% |
| Kemira | Specialty chem | B | 0,9 | n. a. | 2% |
| Neste | Petrochem | A- | 2,9 | n. a. | 8% |
| Nouryon | Specialty chem | n. a. | 2,9 | n. a. | 19% |
| Repsol | Petrochem | A- | 22,4 | n. a. | 1% |
| Seppic | Specialty chem | A- | 0,007 | n. a. | 55% |

Renewable raw materials account for 15,2% on spend in 2020 at DSM. The company's climate goals are "*30% GHG structural improvement by 2030 vs 2016*"

(DSM, 2021) and at Nouryon, "*19% of organic raw materials are from renewable sources*". The company aims to reduce carbon footprint by 25% between 2020 and 2025 (Nouryon, 2021). Disclosure of the actual use of renewable raw materials is not mandatory and only a few companies mainly from the group of climate leaders and fast adopters disclose data. The largest share of renewable raw materials of the input materials has Seppic with 55%. The company has relatively small greenhouse gas emissions. Specialty chemicals manufacturers like Altana, Arkema, BASF, Clariant, DSM, Evonik and Nouryon report shares of renewable raw materials between 4 and 19%. Petrochemical companies like Cepsa, Neste and Repsol report shares of renewable raw materials between 1 and 8%. Companies without reported existing use of renewable raw materials like petrochemical manufacturers Sabic, ExxonMobil, Total and Borealis have higher GHG reduction target than several companies with the exiting use of renewable raw materials. The petrochemical sector has the highest keyword density of mitigation strategies than any other sector and has the highest absolute reduction targets. The petrochemical industry pays more attention to the use of renewable energy, recycling concepts, bio-based feedstocks, and carbon capture and utilization technologies than the average CEFIC corporate members. No sufficient data is available to conclude upon a linking logic between high existing use of renewable raw materials and intention to extend the use of renewable raw materials. Hypothesis H4, that companies already using renewable raw materials are more likely to intend and to expand the use of renewable raw materials, is not confirmed by the document analysis. Generalization of the thesis is not supported and hypothesis H4 is not confirmed.

### 8.4.5 Industry's CSR Strategies

Companies disclose their strategies to the market and employees and publish their sustainability values and corporate social responsibility mission statement. 70 of CEFIC's 72 member companies publish sustainability mission statements. Climate action and GHG reduction targets correlate positively with CDP ratings, UN SDG commitments, and prior years of carbon neutrality. Reducing GHG emissions requires Scope 1, Scope 2, and Scope 3 emission reduction measures, all of which may require the use of renewable energy and renewable resources. Intention to use renewable energy correlates with operational GHG emission reduction targets. The group of climate leaders, Altana, Archroma, Novartis, and Procter & Gamble have Scope 1 and Scope 2 reduction targets of 100%, followed by Givaudan at 70% (Fig. 8.20).

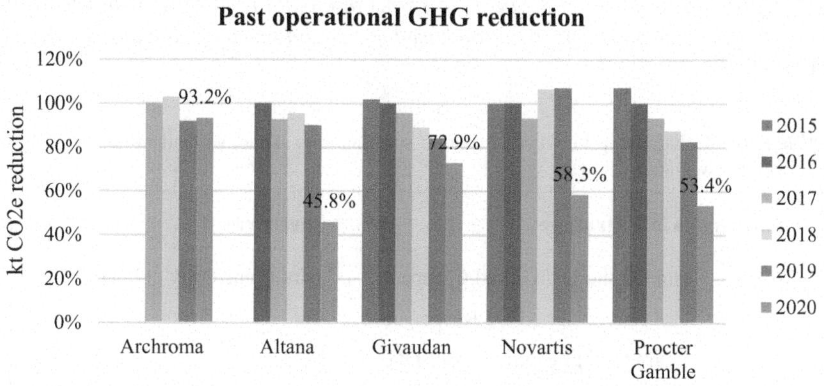


**Fig. 8.20** Past operational GHG emission reduction of leading companies

The efforts are also reflected in their achievements to date. Altana reduced operational emissions by 46% compared to 2016, Procter & Gamble by 53%, Novatis by 58% and Givaudan by 27%. Past achievements prove that companies are delivering on their promises. Archroma has reduced its absolute GHG emissions by only 7% but plans to be the first company in the CEFIC member group to achieve net-zero neutrality by 2023. Only 12 companies have Scope 3 reduction targets. Missing availability of Scope 3 emission data is stalling strategy setting. Examples are given by Altana and Procter & Gamble. Altana reports, that "*for the "raw materials" category, data is currently being obtained and a concept for further action developed*" (Altana (2021c). Procter & Gamble sees that "*the use phase of our products, especially those that use hot water during consumer use, is our single greatest opportunity for Scope 3 emissions.*" The company focusses on updating data and use of life cycle assessments for its portfolio (Procter & Gamble, 2021b). Examples with a relationship between CSR strategy and the use of renewable raw materials are the following. "*Novartis has a goal to be carbon neutral across the entire value chain (Scopes 1, 2 and 3) by 2030.*" The company plans to use "*BioPET-A, a plant derived polyethylene terephthalate made from 30% renewable raw material and 70% oil-based raw material. We also now use a fully carton-based packaging design instead of PVC*" (Novartis, 2021). Givaudan plans to "*become climate positive between 2040 and 2050*" for entire emissions, including Scope 3 emissions. The company is "*committed to reducing absolute direct and indirect (Scope 1 and 2) emissions by 70% by 2030 compared to 2015 levels and aims to reduce indirect (Scope 3) emissions by 20% over the same period.*" Givaudan is "*targeting a decrease in Scope 3 emissions through a joint effort with suppliers to reduce the carbon footprint of purchased goods and services*" (Givaudan, 2021) (Table 8.16).

**Table 8.16** Relationship between corporate sustainability strategies and intentions to use renewable raw materials

| Company | CSR Strategy | Measures |
|---|---|---|
| Altana | joined the UN Global Compact Initiative, signed the Responsible Care Global Charter, UN SDGs | data is currently collected |
| DSM | Climate & energy commitments, aligned to UN SDG 13, Scope 3 -28% by 2030 | suppliers are asked to take measures and investments |
| Dow | Aligned to UN SDG 13 | supplier interaction |
| Evonik | focus on UN SDGs, Scope 3 targets -15% by 2035 | using biomass or waste streams |
| Givaudan | Climate positive (scope 1, 2, 3) before 2050, Scope 3 -20% by 2030, -50% by 2040 | joint effort with suppliers to reduce the carbon footprint of purchased goods and service |
| Neste | committed to the UN Global Compact, wants to support customers with GHG targets | Switching from fossil diesel to renewable diesel results in up to 90% lower GHG emissions |
| Procter & Gamble | SBTi milestone setting, sustainability guidelines | updating data, life cycle assessments, supplier summits |
| Sabic | Reduce GHG intensity, carbon management, aligned to SBTi | Biofuels from biomass, chemical plastic recycling |

DSM reports "*a Scope 3 intensity reduction of 28% by 2030 versus baseline 2016 toward our net zero emissions by 2050 commitment.*" The main scope 3 categories are purchased goods and end-of-life treatment. DSM cooperates with the "*main scope-3-contributing suppliers,*" that take reduction measures and make "*investments to further reduce their emissions in 2021*" (DSM, 2021). Dow Chemicals reports "*total Scope 3 emissions for 2020 were 69,3 million metric tons. The largest category of our Scope 3 emissions remains purchased goods and services.*" The company is in the data collecting stage and started to address Scope 3 emissions by "*improving our sustainability-focused supplier interaction, with continuous emphasis on data quality and traceability*" (Dow, 2021b). Evonik plans to reduce "*absolute scope 3 emissions from the upstream value chain – principally from the "raw material backpack" – by 15% by 2035 (reference base 2020).*" Scope 3 emission reduction measures are implemented by "*sourcing raw materials, produced using biomass or waste streams, and reducing production emissions by our suppliers through process improvements and the use of renewable energy*" (Evonik, 2021b). Neste's mission is to "*support our customers with their carbon neutrality targets*" and offers that "*switching from 100% fossil diesel to 100% Neste MY Renewable Diesel™ results in up to 90% lower greenhouse gas emissions*" (Neste, 2021). The examples demonstrate the relationship between companies' sustainability strategies, efforts to collect data and the use of renewable raw materials. Companies with sustainability values and corporate social responsibility have the intention to use renewable raw materials, and hypothesis H5 of the study is confirmed by the document analysis.

### 8.4.6 Industry's Management Advocacy

Companies' management uses annual reports and publications to communicate strategy statements, targets and activities on climate action. Indicators for management advocacy are goal setting, investments in support of transition, remuneration schemes and decisions to use of renewable raw materials. Evidence for target setting is provided by Procter & Gamble, justifying business targets by ethics & corporate responsibility. The "*2020 commitment, that our global operations will be carbon neutral for the decade*", is set as a Science Based Targets initiative-approved 2-degree solution (Procter & Gamble, 2021b). Kemira announces to collect "*benchmarking data on our peers, customers and Science-Based Targets initiative methodologies*" (Kemira, 2021), "*Momentive is developing energy reduction and GHG reduction targets and will discuss… those targets in future reports*" (Momentive, 2020). A remuneration scheme for senior management is reported for Orbia, where a "*new ESG compensation modifier introduced to senior management compensation, applicable from 2021*" (Orbia, 2021) (Table 8.17).

**Table 8.17** Themes for companies' management advocacy

| Targets & strategy | Resource allocation | Portfolio strategy |
|---|---|---|
| • Communication of commitments, strategy and targets<br>• Remuneration schemes | • Funding innovation<br>• Investing in assets<br>• Cooperation, licensing, JVs<br>• Hiring new people | • Product portfolio to support customers to reduce GHG emissions |

Another management tool is resource allocation in support of climate targets. Procter & Gable invests in packaging innovation with the goal that "*100% of our packaging will be recyclable or reusable. We will reduce global use of virgin petroleum plastic in our packaging by 50%*" and in collaboration with Cargill to develop bio-based acrylic acid for use in superabsorbent polymers for hygiene products and thickeners in household paints. "*P&G has granted Cargill an exclusive license that allows Cargill to further develop and commercialize this technology.*" In 2019, LyondellBasell spent approximately 20% of the R&D budget "*to invest in the development of innovative lower-carbon products and technologies*" (LyondellBasell, 2021b). Sabic announces "*innovation projects in development that will contribute to our LT goals*" (Sabic, 2021b). Total centralized "*3,300 employees with technical skills and expertise, tasked with focusing on innovation and fast-growing new energies*" (Total, 2021) and BASF develops fundamentally new technologies "*in the Carbon Management R&D Program,*" and reports that "*BASF, SABIC and Linde have signed a joint agreement to develop and demonstrate solutions for electrically heated steam cracker furnaces*" (BASF, 2021b). Examples for product offerings to support customers to reduce GHG emissions are the following. Particularly refineries and petrochemical companies work on new product portfolios to reduce downstream users' carbon footprints. Neste developed renewable diesel that enables "*its customers to reduce greenhouse gas (GHG) emissions by up to 90%* compared to fossil diesel over the life cycle. As a drop-in solution*" (Neste, 2021). Repsol "*is focusing on the promotion of projects of advanced biofuels (based on non-food raw materials) with a strong* *technological content and high reduction of the carbon footprint*" (Repsol, 2021). And ExxonMobil "*signed an agreement with Global Clean Energy Holdings to purchase 2.5 million barrels of renewable diesel per year for five years, starting in 2022*" (ExxonMobil, 2021). Companies with a supportive management towards the use of renewable raw materials have the intention to use renewable feedstocks and hypothesis H6 of the case study is confirmed by document analysis.

### 8.4.7 Industry's Cooperation Activities

Corporate members of the CEFIC industry association report on sectoral and regional partnerships, collaboration with customers, suppliers and companies with complementary technologies, and cooperation with universities and research institutes. Examples of sectoral and regional partnerships and industry initiatives include the following. 3M cooperates in with Clean Air Asia initiative and announces that "*3M will collaborate with the international non-governmental organization on science-based air quality solutions for New Delhi, India, and Metro Manila, Philippines*" (3M, 2021b). "*Chevron is a founding partner of The Environmental Partnership*" and advances "*hydrogen opportunities through strategic partnerships*" (Chevron, 2021). Repsol collaborates "*with international bodies (OECD, UN, EU, etc.), governments and NGOs*" (Repsol, 2021b). Merck fosters an innovation ecosystem. "*This ecosystem includes a presence in Darmstadt (Germany), in Guangzhou and in Shanghai (both China) as well as in Silicon Valley (California, USA) with internal and outreach programs*" (Merck, 2021b) (Table 8.18).

**Table 8.18** Themes for companies' stakeholder engagement

| **Sectoral and regional partnerships** |
|---|
| • International bodies (OECD, UN, EU) |
| • Governments and NGOs |
| • Industry initiatives |
| • Innovation ecosystems |

On the customers' side, Wacker sees "*growing demand for specialty silanes … made using renewable raw materials*" (Wacker, 2021a) and Ineos reports, that "*our customers are looking to us for sustainable offerings for their applications*" (Ineos, 2021b). Sabic collaborates with "*Tesco, that collects post-consumer flexible packaging that customers deposit in 10 U.K. retail stores. Plastic Energy then converts that waste into pyrolysis oil, which SABIC uses as feedstock to produce certified circular polymers. Sealed Air uses these polymer pallets to produce film for Bradbury Cheese products, which are then sold to Tesco*" (Sabic, 2021b). The collaboration of Sabic with 4 partners Tesco, Plastic Energy, Sealed Air and Bradbury Cheese closes the loop for a recycling system with customer agreements to collect used plastic materials. Also, Neste reports a cooperation with "*Covestro to promote renewable raw materials in plastics production*" and a "*joint project to make hard-to-recycle plastic packaging recyclable*" with Unilever and RT. (Neste, 2021). And Bayer launched the Bayer Carbon Initiative "*to attain our target of a 30% reduction in greenhouse gas emissions from farming by 2030*". The smallholders initiative encourages to apply farming methods that enables greenhouse gas emissions to be lowered. "*700 farmers in Brazil and the United States are participating in the program during the 2020/2021 growing season*" (Bayer, 2021). Customer cooperation is seen as necessary for recycling concepts, closed-loop initiatives and to reclaim plastic waste as feedstock (Table 8.19).

**Table 8.19** Themes for companies' cooperation along the value chain

| Cooperation with customers | Cooperation with suppliers |
|---|---|
| • Growing demand from customers<br>• Closed-loop recycling system and claim of waste materials from customers<br>• Smallholder programs | • Suppler workshops and agreements for climate goals<br>• Sourcing of novel feedstocks |

Cooperation along the value chain also takes place with suppliers. "*Borealis' strategic cooperation with Neste*" and an agreement of "*Borealis supplying Covestro*" (Borealis, 2021). Clariant reports a partnership "*with Ineratec, a specialist in the production of sustainable fuels and chemicals*" and has successfully set up its supply chain in Romania. "*A feedstock team established long-term contracts with almost 300 farmers,*" using straw for its new second generation bioethanol plant (Clariant, 2021b). Ecolab works "*with suppliers representing 70% of Scope 3 emissions to set similarly ambitious carbon targets by 2024*" (Ecolab, 2021b). "*P&G*

*teams attended our first-ever Supplier Citizenship Summit at our Cincinnati global headquarters in October 2019*" (Procter & Gamble, 2021b) and Johnson Matthey announced a partnership "*Stena Recycling Group on technologies to recycle and reuse the scarce metals from used electric vehicle batteries In new battery materials*" (Johnson Matthey, 2021). Sumitomo Chemical calls on major suppliers to set GHG emission reduction targets and "*held a briefing session for about 30 major suppliers of ours in Japan to present our initiatives toward achieving our SBTs, and to ask our suppliers to set their own GHG emission reduction targets*" (Sumitomo Chemical, 2021b). Cooperation with suppliers is seen as useful to set GHG emission reduction targets for existing input materials and to source novel feedstocks to reach climate goals. Corporate members of the CEFIC industry association report cooperation with universities and external R&D institutions. Total partners "*with university chairs, such as the Climate Economics Chair at Paris-Dauphine University, the climate change research program of Massachusetts Institute of Technology (MIT), and Toulouse School of Economics*" (Total, 2021). BASF reports "*8 Academic Research Alliances with around 250 universities and research institutes.*" and collaborates on "*electrochemical energy storage with the Karlsruhe Institute of Technology (KIT) at the Battery and Electrochemistry Laboratory (BELLA), joint Catalysis Research Laboratory (CaRLa) on researching homogeneous catalysis in cooperation with the University of Heidelberg using CO2 as a chemical feedstock*" (BASF, 2021a). Lanxess is "*considering the possibility of a cooperation with the Karlsruhe Institute of Technology (KIT) in the field of thermochemical recycling*" for the development of an innovative recycling concept (Lanxess, 2021a). Use of biomass, plastic recycling and carbon capture technology requires to generate new knowledge and to explore new catalysts and process technology together with universities and external R&D institutions (Table 8.20).

**Table 8.20** Themes for companies' academic partnerships

| Universities and research institutes |
|---|
| • Research in new catalysts and process technology |
| • Cooperation with universities and external R&D institutions |

Finally, acquisitions and joint ventures are reported as management instrument to cooperate and to source new knowledge. Evonik reports the acquisition of Wilshire Technologies Inc., Princeton (NJ) with a "*business model centers on the development of products based on renewable, animal-free sources*" (Evonik, 2021b). Huntsman announces the acquisition of two companies, Demilec and Icynene-Lapolla. Both companies "*provide bio-preferred, renewable and recyclable products that reduce energy consumption*" (Huntsman, 2021). Companies with cooperation and joined development activities to use renewable raw materials, either with customers, suppliers, complementary businesses or external research have the intention to use renewable feedstocks and hypothesis H7 is confirmed.

### 8.4.8 Industry's Application of Industry Standards

Companies' endorsement of global, regional and sectoral norms is common, and the chemical industry adopts new sustainability standards as general practice. 61 companies refer to the UN Sustainable Development Goals (SDGs) in their mission and strategy statements, 60 companies publish their GHG emissions according to the GRI standard, and 53 companies participate in the voluntary Carbon Disclosure Program, signaling availability and awareness of climate action. The following table lists the firms of the climate leader category and their past references to the UN Sustainable Development Goals (SDGs), application of the GRI standards and participation in the Carbon Disclosure Program (Table 8.21).

**Table 8.21** Adoption of industry standards by climate goal leaders

| Company | Reference to UN SDG | Application of GRI standards | Participation in CDP |
|---|---|---|---|
| Altana | since 2019 | since 2016 | n. a. |
| Archroma | since 2018 | since 2018 | n. a. |
| Givaudan | since 2017 | before 2016 | before 2016 |
| Novartis | before 2016 | before 2016 | before 2016 |
| Procter & Gamble | since 2016 | before 2016 | before 2016 |

Further application of industry standards is described in recent publications. "*3M joined the Ellen MacArthur Foundation Circular Economy 100 (CE100) Network*" in 2019 (3M, 2021b). Also, Bayer reports to be a member of the nonprofit organization and BASF "*is a member of the Ellen MacArthur Foundation's New Plastics Economy initiative*" since 2017 (BASF, 2021a; Bayer, 2021c). Arkema achieved Bronze Award in the DJSI World and DJSI Europe Sustainability Yearbook 2021 and reports "*to Ecovadis and part of the 1% top rated companies in the sector since 2014 Sustainability Performance*" (Arkema, 2021). ISCC PLUS certification is a certification scheme to evaluate origin and supply chains for sustainable materials. Borealis "*received the ISCC PLUS certification issued by the International Sustainability and Carbon Certification (ISCC) organisation*" (Borealis, 2021). Also "*Eastman's ISCC PLUS certification confirms that all materials and processes are being appropriately tracked and accounted for within an established mass balance accounting standard*" (Eastman, 2021) (Table 8.22).

Other companies reporting ISCC PLUS certifications for renewable materials and processes are Lanxess, LyondellBasell, Perstorp, Repsol, Sabic and Total. BASF reports alternative certification scheme REDcert (BASF, 2021c). Together for Sustainability (TfS) is an industry standard for sustainable supply chains, evaluating and improving the sustainability performance of suppliers. "*In 2018 ICL joined Together for Sustainability (TfS), a sustainable procurement initiative of the global chemical industry*" (ICL, 2021). Kraton achieved "*the EcoVadis' Gold rating and joining Together for Sustainability (TfS) in early 2020*" (Kraton, 2021). The TfS initiative has a total number of 29 members in 2020 and partners with EcoVadis (Together for Sustainability, 2021). EcoVadis is a provider of a sustainability management platform that helps customers invite their trading partners to be rated and to manage trading partners' performance (EcoVadis, 2021). The following citations provide examples for the industry's involvement in voluntary initiatives. "*Röhm received the EcoVadis Silver medal*" (Röhm, 2021b). Seppic has received Ecovadis grade Gold standard and CDP climate A score. The company reports that "*the RSPO Mass Balance (MB) certification rate of our palm derivative (palm equivalent) purchases has increased significantly since 2015. In 2019, 70.5% of our palm derivative inputs were MB certified*" (Seppic, 2021). Finally, Sumitomo Chemical Group is "*certified by the Science Based Targets (SBT) initiative for our targets for the reduction of greenhouse gas (GHG) emissions, becoming the first diversified chemical company to receive this certification*" (Sumitomo Chemicals, 2021c). Also, Solvay is "*committed to the Science Based Targets initiative (SBTi) in 2020 and is preparing to submit targets for validation*" (Solvay, 2021). And Bayer calculates "*reduction target for Scope 3 emissions in line with SBTi*" (Bayer,

**Table 8.22** Industry initiatives and certification schemes

| **10 industry initiatives, rating programs and certification schemes** | |
|---|---|
| Carbon Disclosure Program (CDP) | Global sustainability rating agency |
| DJSI World and DJSI Europe Sustainability Yearbook | Global sustainability rating agency |
| EcoVadis | Global sustainability rating agency |
| Ellen MacArthur Foundation Circular Economy 100 | Industry initiative |
| GRI standard | Reporting standard |
| ISCC PLUS certification | Supply chain certification scheme |
| REDcert certification | Supply chain certification scheme |
| RSPO Mass Balance (MB) certification | Supply chain certification scheme |
| Science Based Targets initiative (SBTi) | Fee-based target validation service |
| Together for Sustainability (TfS) | Industry initiative |
| UN Sustainable development goals | Public pledges |

2021c). Companies conduct data collection and analysis as part of reporting standards and initiatives, and rating agencies help formulate company goals. Chemical companies with knowledge of existing and required standards for renewable raw materials have the intention to use them, and hypothesis H8 is confirmed by the document analysis.

### 8.4.9 Industry's Expectation of Government Regulations

Companies comment on existing and future government regulations in recent publications to justify their strategies and activities. Driving factors for GHG action is an "*increasing demands for disclosure of information*" and "*increased demand for products and technologies contributing to the mitigation of climate change*" (Sumitomo Chemical, 2021). The Russian petrochemical company Sibur reports, that "*a tightening of EU climate regulations for imported goods and the introduction of a tax on GHG emissions in Russia*" would push up prices across the entire supply chain (Sibur, 2020). Kemira sees the trend for "*growing environmental awareness, climate change mitigation, tightening environmental regulation,*" and for a "*focus on bio-based materials*" (Kemira, 2020a). UK's Johnson Matthey expects "*additional national greenhouse gas regulations*" (Johnson Matthey, 2021) and Sabic is "*proactively building a new climate change strategy that feeds into and aligns with overarching Government goals. ... In our home country we are working with Saudia Arabian Ministry of Energy and Saudi Energy Efficiency Center to meet national regulations*" (Sabic, 2021b). In particular, petrochemical companies are announcing that they expect more government regulations. ExxonMobil expects "*current and pending greenhouse gas regulations or policies may also increase our compliance costs*" (ExxonMobil, 2021), and Chevron expects "*carbon-pricing regulations, ... low-carbon fuel standards and methane regulations*" (Chevron, 2021). Neste's "*investments need a predictable business environment and policies that en-courage innovation*" (Neste, 2021). Ineos sees uncertainties about future regulations and states, that "*we cannot yet predict the form any such additional regulation will take in the chemical industry itself in various jurisdictions ... or, consequently, to estimate any costs that we may be required to incur.*" Possible regulations are cap-and-trade programs, technology mandates, emissions taxes or other regulatory mechanisms. Ineos plans to closely monitor the situation (Ineos, 2021). In regions with less uncertainties about future regulations, specialty chemicals companies set their strategy towards the use or renewable energies and feedstocks. Albemarle states, that "*in Amsterdam, where EU regulations demand 49% reduction of GHG-emissions by 2030, we have an active technology program to realize such reductions*" (Albemarle, 2020) and Clariant "*foresees increasing pressure from regulators and a heightened focus among investors, and is thus allocating increased resources to the topic and ramping up efforts to reduce CO2 emissions*" (Clariant, 2021b) (Table 8.23).

One barrier to the adoption of renewable raw materials is uncertainty about future emissions taxes and regulations. Policymakers must encourage innovation and create a predictable business environment. Companies that expect government regulations to promote renewable feedstocks intend to use them, and hypothesis H9 is confirmed by the document analysis.

**Table 8.23** Themes concerning companies' expectations

| **Themes concerning companies' expectations and Government regulations** |
|---|
| • Increasing pressure from regulators expected<br>• Uncertainty about regulation instruments<br>  ○ Cap-and-trade programs<br>  ○ Technology mandates<br>  ○ Emissions taxes<br>• Cooperation and information exchange with Governments and offices |

### 8.4.10 Summary of Organizational Predictors from Document Analysis

Finally, content analysis of latest sustainability reports of corporate members of the CEFIC group confirm the findings of the case study research and interview analysis. Document analysis provides even stronger evidence of the link between intention to use renewable raw materials and expected government regulations, as reports are direct communication tools used by management to address the public and employees (Table 8.24).

**Table 8.24** Organizational predictors from document analysis

| **Organization predictors derived from the document analysis** |
|---|
| • CSR strategy<br>• Management advocacy<br>• Cooperation skills<br>• Implementation of industry standards<br>• Government regulations |

# Discussion 9

The discussion begins with a summary of the results from the case study research and document analysis for this dissertation. The state of decarbonization of the chemical industry is recalled and innovation types and findings on chemical companies' responses to climate action, company-specific and innovation-specific predictors for adoption of mitigation technologies are discussed. In the second and third part of the chapter, results from this research are linked with multi-level perspective of socio-technical transition theory and technology innovation systems approach. Implications for practitioners and an outlook for further research close the chapter.

## 9.1 Summary of Results

The dissertation examines industrial strategies on how to achieve a reduction in greenhouse gas emissions and predictors for technologies that replace and best meet the need for net zero carbon neutrality. The literature suggests efficiency measures, the use of renewable energies and three alternative technology categories of renewable raw materials for chemical synthesis: Biomass, plastic recycling and carbon capture and utilization with CO2 as starting molecule. Frames of the business case are the European chemical industry with exposure to EU legislation and case study research was chosen as research method. Results from the content analysis of expert interviews and the document analysis of company publications are triangulated. Companies are at different stages

**Supplementary Information** The online version contains supplementary material available at https://doi.org/10.1007/978-3-658-45389-3_9.



H. H. E. Ahrens, *The Ecological Modernization of the Chemical Industry*, https://doi.org/10.1007/978-3-658-45389-3_9

in the implementation of reduction strategies and use sector-specific instruments (Bataille et al., 2018; Gross, 2021). The dissertation identifies the state of transition and patterns for introduction of renewable raw materials (Renning, 2000). The results suggest five innovation-specific predictors and five organization-specific predictors for low-carbon reorientation of the chemical industry (Geels, 2019).

### 9.1.1 Industry's State of Decarbonization

The published greenhouse gas emissions of the European chemical industry amounted to 128 Mt CO2e in 2018 (CEFIC, 2021a). The aggregated Scope 1 and Scope 2 emissions of the 72 corporate members of the CEFIC group in 2020 amounted to 727,4 Mt CO2e. Emission values from own research are based on a bottom-up approach and include global emissions from companies and the petrochemical sector. Excluding the petrochemicals sector leaves the corporate members of the CEFIC group with 191,8 Mt CO2e of global emissions. Another reason for difference in emission values are different calculation methods. Own research considers published, global emissions of the MNCs outside Europe, while CEFIC also takes into account the emissions of members of the CEFIC group with turnover below 1.000 MEUR. Both different sectoral and geographical boundaries for calculation may explain the deviation of numbers. According to CEFIC, CO2 emissions represent 91% of total GHG emissions, followed by nitrous oxide, representing 5,1% of total. Fluorinated gas emissions represent 3,0% and methane 1,2% of total GHG emissions of the European chemical industry in 2018 (CEFIC, 2021a). CO2 emissions come mainly from energy generation (55%) and from releases from large-scale chemical processes such as the production of ammonia, petrochemicals, carbon black and monomer components, with CO2 being produced from side reactions (Boulamanti & Moya, 2017). The chemical industry has developed strategies to reduce greenhouse gas emissions and several mitigation technologies are proposed to reduce them (Van Bylen, 2019). The focus is on the efficient use of energy and heat, upgrading existing operating units with newer devices to best-practice technology, abatement technologies to avoid formation or release, electrification of processes and the use of renewable energies for energy generation. Phasedown is an option for greenhouse gases with high global warning potential, high radiation and ozone depletion properties. Finally, increase in plastic recycling, biomass-based resources to avoid steam cracking and carbon capture and utilization complete the toolkit to achieve carbon neutrality in the European chemical industry (Fischedick et al., 2014; Carus et al., 2021).

### 9.1.2 Niche Innovations and Uncertainty

The chemical industry, along with the cement and steel industries, is reported as hard-to-decarbonize (Bataille et al., 2018; Gross, 2021). The reasons for lock-out effects for ecological innovations are the single-technology architecture based on petroleum raw materials and it is forced to leave the technological path of petroleum-based chemistry in a global socio-technical configuration with the transition to carbon neutrality (Bauer & Fuenfschilling, 2019). MNCs with high investments in existing infrastructure and economies of scale effects strengthen the continued use of fossil resources. Additional economic barriers arise from the ecological externalities of greenhouse gases that are not priced (Palley, 2017). Inferior cost position and lack of competitiveness of environmental innovations are cited in the literature as a stumbling block for change. Government regulations are instruments to mandate the use of alternative materials and to support, regulate or restrict the manufacture and marketing of chemicals (Hoff, 2012; Horbach, Rammer, & Rennings 2012). Uncertainties for industry arise from future policies and regulations for greenhouse gases and renewable resources. Additional uncertainties arise from the availability of raw materials, the technological progress of the three technologies biomass conversion, chemical plastics recycling and technologies for carbon capture and utilization as well as their cost positions. The risks for companies arise from the lack of resilience strategies amid these uncertainties (Fath, Dean & Katzmaier, 2015). In addition, at the landscape level, several separate technological and societal developments occur simultaneously and require transition management (Geels, 2011; Grin, Rotmans & Schot, 2010). Overlapping landscape trends are globalization, digitization, the change from a linear to a circular economy to supply scarce resources and climate protection. At least four separate developments offer a rare opportunity for niche innovations and represent risks for the collapse of existing technological paradigms. The prevailing question is: How much carbon is available to the chemical industry in a decarbonized world? On the one hand, incumbent agents can get confused by the uncertainty. On the other hand, there are opportunities for newcomers for quick exploration of niche innovations, testing and prototyping in the reorganization phase of the transition (Holling, Gunderson & Peterson, 2002). The chemical industry's transition to sustainability offers many opportunities but requires careful attention from policymakers and regulators to avoid victimization in moving to a low carbon economy (Sovacool, 2021). Essential windows of opportunity for the chemical industry are based on technological innovations, demand from users and consumers and institutions. Politics can initiate changes in a sectoral system (Lee & Malerba, 2017). Essential structural elements of the technological innovation system are actors influencing the institutional set-up and networks with functional patterns for knowledge creation, market formation and legitimization (Bergek, Jacobsson, Carlsson, Lindmark & Rickne, 2008). The global regime of the chemical industry is embedded in regional markets with supplies of intermediate products for chemical synthesis from local steam crackers. Regional sustainability initiatives in the direction of bio-based and circular economy contradict the global institutional regime and follow special niche sectors of the socio-technical configuration (Bauer & Fuenfschilling, 2019). Strategic niche management is proposed to expand technological capabilities in niches such as carbon capture and utilization (CCU), biomass processing, biotechnological processes, circular supply chain models and application of the 12 green principles targeting sustainable chemical processes. Standardization efforts are seen as the main driver for adoption and tailored policies to support the transition (Börner, Bröring & Laibach, 2019; Falcone & Hiete, 2019). The main obstacle to the transition is the limited availability of biomass. An extensive substitution of 15–25% of fossil fuels with biomass is expected to have a significant impact on production, demand and infrastructure (Wydra et al., 2021).

### 9.1.3 Agent-based Research Methodology

The dissertation provides insights into how the chemical industry deals with lock-in effects with regard to a necessary ecological modernization towards carbon neutrality (Loorbach & Wijsman, 2013, Vertesy, 2017). It identifies attributes of environmental innovations and which types are adopted for the transition to carbon neutrality and identifies market pull effects for the renewability or technical benefit of environmental innovations (Bröring, Golembiewski & Sick, 2015; Garcia, Wigger, & Hermann, 2019; Hoff, 2012). Second, the dissertation contributes insights into the attitudes and intentions of chemical companies towards the use of renewable raw materials as a substitute for fossil raw materials (Bröring, Golembiewski & Sick, 2015). Amid the high level of uncertainty caused by future technological developments, policies and regulations, a qualitative research design is chosen to capture the exploratory elements of the research for the adoption of renewable raw materials. The main study is an embedded case study of business cases in the European chemical industry and data collection is done through expert interviews with innovators familiar with the specialty chemical industry. Case study research provides the tools to analyze environmental innovations in complex and uncertain environments, and company specific characteristics (McDermott & O'Connor, 2002). Agent-based models are predictive tools for the adoption and actual use of innovations and the theoretical framework of reasoned action theory, planned behavior theory and the technological acceptance model is applied to the case study (Ajzen, 1991; Davis, 1985). A testable model based on reasoned action theory examines the impact of external factors defined by the characteristics of the corporate and industry environment. The reasoned action framework for the study is adapted for innovations to achieve carbon neutrality in chemical companies and uses the attitude towards use and behavioral intention as mediator variables to predict the actual use of renewable raw materials (Fishbein & Ajzen, 2010). Risks of social desirability response bias is mitigated by a semi-structured interview procedure with identical interview guidelines for each interviewee. The approach attempts to reduce under or over-reporting of certain behaviors. However, interview candidates with a lesser motivation to adopt Greenhouse gas emission may have declines the participation upfront. The same applied to candidates with a management that rejects the adoption of environmental innovations (Latkin, Edwards, Davey-Rothwell & Tobin, 2017). The secondary technique of document analysis of annual reports and publications by corporate members of the CEFIC group is trying to balance for social desirability response bias and erroneous study conclusions. Also, these documents are not neutral and may have been written in an attempt to promote corporate identity and social responsibility with the aim of self-enhancement and value creation in the financial community. Social desirability response can not be completely disregarded as a potential confounder for announcements and promises of a favorable environmental behavior (Vesely & Klöckner, 2020). But commitment, efforts and goals to reduce GHG emissions are challenged by customers and the public which increases the ambitions to deliver and reliability of data. Engagement in industry initiatives is also rated and made transparent by independent sustainability agencies. Respondents with a positive attitude may give biased responses but are expected to be a more knowledgeable source for organizational and innovation-specific predictors for adoption of renewable raw materials.

### 9.1.4 Organizational Engagement

14 industry experts from the chemical industry were interviewed in case study research between September 2020 and April 2021. Interview guidelines with in-depth questions are based on 9 hypotheses derived from the testable model. The model conceptualizes intention to use renewable raw materials as a function of attitude towards their use. The semantic orientation of meaning units in interview narratives is a measure of the attitude of experts (Fishbein & Ajzen, 2010). Respondents name motivators for a positive attitude such as market competition, customer needs and demands, opportunities from their own operational performance, strategic positioning, reputation and corporate identity as well as ecological and social responsibility towards scarcity of resources (Horbach, Rammer & Rennings, 2012). The drivers act as a justification for a positive attitude towards the use of renewable raw materials as feedstocks.

#### 9.1.4.1 Summary on Attitude Towards use of Renewable Raw Materials

Interview respondents report searching for information and experimentation with renewable raw materials. Their positive attitude is motivated by market forces, technological opportunities, company's environmental and social responsibility and personal conviction (Table 9.1).

The document analysis for the triangulation leads to the same result: Mission statements confirm a positive attitude towards the use of renewable raw materials and confirm previous findings from case study research about attitudes. 61 out of 72 corporate members of the CEFIC group refer in their strategy to the UN sustainability goals, 60 companies publish greenhouse gas emissions and savings targets according to GRI standards. 53 companies take part in the voluntary Carbon Disclosure Program. 39 companies or 54% are recognized for the active management of greenhouse gas emissions and receive high A and B scores in the Carbon Disclosure Program. 60 of 72 company members jointly intend to reduce Scope 1 and Scope 2 greenhouse gas emissions by 27% by 2030 and by 71% by 2050, based on the company publications available in August 2021.

**Table 9.1** Triangulation of attitude as predictor for intention to use

| Triangulation of attitude as predictor for intention to use | |
|---|---|
| **Interview results** | **Results from document analysis** |
| Justifications for positive attitude | Companies' climate goals |
| • Market competition<br>• Customer needs and demands<br>• Opportunities from own operational capabilities<br>• Strategically positioning<br>• Reputation and corporate identity<br>• Environmental and social responsibility<br>• Personal conviction | • Commitments<br>• Mission statements<br>• GHG emission reduction targets<br>• Companies' participation in sustainability industry initiatives<br>• Companies' data collection efforts<br>• Companies' strategy building processes |

#### 9.1.4.2 Summary on Intention to use of Renewable Raw Materials

Another central result of the interview analysis is the intention to use renewable raw materials (Table 9.2).

All respondents in the case study intend to use renewable raw materials for chemical syntheses or preparations. Industry experts report that they are engaged in activities in the field of renewable raw materials, such as planning innovations, testing renewable raw materials and prototyping end products. Finished products made from renewable raw materials are available for sampling from own innovations or are marketed by the competition. Piloting and implementation of reduction strategies are also confirmed by document analysis. The keyword density analysis is used as a quantitative method for weighting mitigation strategies for GHG reduction. The use of bio-based raw materials received the greatest attention with 27% of the keywords. Efficiency increases in operation and recycling technologies for renewable energies receive roughly the same attention with 24% of the keywords in all reports from the chemical industry. The carbon capture and utilization has a small share of 1%. New sustainable product launches, investment projects and collaborations with partners are examples of

**Table 9.2** Triangulation of intention to use renewable raw materials

| Triangulation of intention to use renewable raw materials | |
|---|---|
| **Interview results** | **Results from document analysis** |
| Activities leading to a choice to adopt renewable raw materials | |
| • Planning activities<br>• Testing renewable raw materials<br>• Upscaling of final products<br>• Sampling prototypes<br>• Commercialization | • Implementation of mitigation strategies<br>• New sustainable product launches<br>• Investment projects<br>• Cooperation with partners to reduce product-related GHG emissions |

current activities and demonstrate the intention to use renewable raw materials. Both the case study research and the document analysis show a positive attitude and intention to use renewable raw materials.

### 9.1.5 Organizational Determinants

Organizational predictors of the intention to use renewable raw materials are five determinants at the organizational, group and individual innovator level. The corporate sustainability strategy, management advocacy, the cooperation skills, the knowledge of industry standards for renewable raw materials and the expectations of government regulations for renewable raw materials are confirmed by case studies and document analyzes. The existing use of renewable raw materials has not been confirmed as a predictor of the intention to use renewable energies with the goal of CO2 neutrality. The adoption predictors for a low-carbon reorientation of companies at the individual, group, organizational and environmental level are summarized below and categorized by the organization requirements for innovations after Mumford & Hunter (2005) (Table 9.3).

**Table 9.3** Organizational predictors for innovation

| Organization predictors for renewable feedstocks in this dissertation |
|---|
| Cooperation activities |
| Management advocacy |
| Corporate sustainability strategy |
| Industry standardization |
| Government regulations |

#### 9.1.5.1 Actual use

Actual usage is tested as a driver, but not consistently confirmed by case study research and document analysis as a predictor of intention to use. The respondents report that companies without existing use of renewable raw materials have similar intentions to use renewable raw materials as companies with existing use. Companies with high GHG reduction targets, such as petrochemical companies with no existing use, have higher greenhouse gas reduction targets than companies with the discontinued use of renewable raw materials. The petrochemical sector has the highest absolute greenhouse gas reduction targets, and the keyword density of abatement strategies is higher than in any other sector. The hypothesis is not confirmed by either case study research or document analysis. The other determinants of successful environmental innovation at the organizational, group and individual level is confirmed by research (Mumford & Hunter, 2005).

#### 9.1.5.2 Corporate Sustainability Strategy

The respondents refer to the sustainability strategies of the companies as well as to the ecological and social responsibility for their ecological innovation activities. Marketing and product development strategies for the use of renewable raw materials are drivers for the intention to use renewable raw materials, while a lack of information is an obstacle. The document analysis of company publications showed that 70 companies out of 72 corporate members of the CEFIC Group publish sustainability guidelines, 60 companies publish greenhouse gas savings targets that demonstrate the intention to reduce greenhouse gas emissions. Climate leaders are planning climate neutrality before 2030, and the CEFIC group jointly intends to reduce Scope 1 + 2 greenhouse gas emissions by 27% by 2030 and by 71% by 2050.

#### 9.1.5.3 Management Advocacy

Respondents from business cases report on leadership focus, implementation of corporate strategies, new jobs, project support, investments in assets and acquisitions to support the supply of renewable raw materials. Supportive management is confirmed by case study research as a predictor of environmental innovation. The document analysis finds supporting management instruments for GHG reduction such as remuneration models, funding of R&D projects, hiring new employees with sustainability tasks and portfolio repositioning. Both case study research and document analysis confirm that management advocacy is a predictor of the intention to use renewable raw materials.

#### 9.1.5.4 Cooperation Skills

Respondents from the case study research report on cooperation activities with customers, suppliers, universities and research institutes as well as standardization bodies with the aim of using renewable raw materials. In the content analysis of interview narratives, actors were identified as essential structural elements and networks with functional models for generating knowledge (Bergek, Jacobsson, Carlsson, Lindmark & Rickne, 2008). Cooperation and joint development activities, be it with customers, suppliers, associations and external research institutes and universities, are indicated by the respondents. Company publications also report on industry and regional partnerships, cooperation with customers, suppliers and companies with complementary technologies as well as cooperation with universities and research institutes with the aim of using renewable raw materials. Results from case study research and document analysis confirms cooperation activities as a predictor of the intention to use renewable raw materials. Members of the social system—the technological innovation system (TIS)—are one of the four elements for the diffusion of innovations after Rogers (2003) and the flow of information is enabled by the cooperation of actors.

#### 9.1.5.5 Implementation of Industry Standards

The respondents to the case study research report that the use of renewable raw materials requires new standards and evaluation methods. Transparency of supply chains and the availability of standards are named as drivers for the intention to use renewable raw materials. Traceability and proof of origin of materials is standardized through supply chain certificates and the 14 C radiocarbon method is used as an analysis method for the biogenic carbon content. Complexity of sustainability goals, e.g. origin of the material, competition with food and feed, effects on biodiversity and biodegradability are obstacles to the intended use. The need for additional standards and evaluation methods for e.g. biodiversity, CO2 footprint calculations and other criteria of the life cycle assessment are reported by the industry experts. In their climate activities, companies refer to industry initiatives, norms, standards and certification systems to enable data-driven decision-making. The GRI standard is a reporting standard for comparability. The Carbon Disclosure Program (CDP), the Ellen MacArthur Foundation, EcoVadis, the Science Based Targets Initiative (SBTi) and Together for Sustainability (TfS) support companies in formulating data collection methods and setting goals. Certification programs such as ISCC PLUS, REDcert2 and RSPO Mass Balance (MB) certification are important tools for gaining customer confidence. Decision making involving CCU technologies is currently hampered due to lack of a consistent basis for life cycle assessments. A lack of uniform life cycle assessments, calculation methods for GHG emissions and balancing conflicts between land use and land use change, use of bio-based raw materials, GHG emission reduction and biodegradability are mentioned as barriers and increase the uncertainty in business decision-making (Müller et al., 2018; Tanzer & Ramírez, 2019).

#### 9.1.5.6 Alignment with Governmental Regulations

Case study research respondents report expectations of tightening EU climate rules but have uncertainties about the timeframe and type of policy. CO2 taxes, import duties and regulatory subsidies are perceived as drivers for the use of renewable raw materials. The uncertainty about future regulations interferes with the intention to use renewable raw materials. Not all respondents expect state regulations despite their intention to use them. A group of experts are skeptical about future regulations in support of renewable raw materials and refer to market pull effects in their decision making. The hypothesis that the intention to use renewable raw materials correlates with expected government regulations is not confirmed by all respondents in case study research. On the other hand, CEFIC group corporations report expectations for tightening of EU climate regulations, additional national greenhouse gas regulations and introduction of a tax on GHG emissions. Petrochemical companies in particular expect more government regulation, rising compliance costs and increasing pressure from regulators. Companies also report uncertainties about future regulations, but the majority of companies expect cap-and-trade programs, technology mandates, emission taxes, active technology programs to implement such reductions or other regulatory mechanisms in the EU. Companies plan to monitor the situation closely. Barriers to the introduction of renewable raw materials are uncertainties. Policies need to encourage innovation and create a predictable business environment. The proposition that companies expecting Governmental regulations have the intention for use renewable raw materials is confirmed by document analysis.

### 9.1.6 Innovation-Specific Determinants

Five characteristics for innovations from innovation theory after Rogers (2003) are relative advantage, complexity, compatibility with existing technology, trialability and observability. The relative advantage of renewable raw materials in reducing greenhouse gas emissions is determined by the greenhouse gas saving effect and the reduced carbon footprint of the material. In addition, the relative advantage is determined by the cost position compared to a next best alternative. The suggested first and second predictors are costs and potential CO2 savings based on findings from case study research. It was found that renewable raw materials are in shot supply, and availability is a third predictor of adoption. The fourth and fifth predictors are similar to the characteristics for innovations from innovation diffusion model (Rogers, 2003). The compatibility with existing technological regimes as well as the transparency of the supply chains and the origin of the material are given as additional predictors (Table 9.4).

**Table 9.4** Five innovation-specific predictors for renewable feedstocks

| Five innovation-specific predictors for adoption of renewable feedstocks in this dissertation |
|---|
| Cost of raw materials |
| CO2 saving potential |
| Availability |
| Compatibility |
| Transparency |

Case study research and document analyzes confirm inferior cost position and the lack of competitiveness of renewable raw materials as major stumbling blocks for their introduction. Further evidence is provided from the document analysis.

Barriers to accepting renewable raw materials are higher prices and limited availability (Hoff, 2012; Horbach, Rammer, & Rennings 2012). Companies report on activities to increase capacity, get involved in recycling concepts and invest in projects, pilot plants and joint ventures. Chemical recycling and technologies for using CO2 as a starting molecule are still in the exploration phase. Additional restrictions result from the short supply of renewable energies and the greatest uncertainty for the transition to carbon neutrality is how much carbon is available for the chemical industry in a decarbonized world. Respondents are concerned about the incompatibility with other sustainable development goals, such as competition with food and feed and the loss of biodiversity. Certification schemes are proposed to increase the transparency of the supply chain. Mass balanced approaches and segregated approaches are implemented by companies as accounting models (Mol & Oosterveer, 2015). However, experts also report a lack of standardization of management practices, a lack of guidelines for life cycle assessments and CO2 savings evaluations. CO2 savings data are not yet available and a lack of standards for data collection reduces market efficiency and the flow of information on sustainability criteria (Mujica, 2019; Paton, 2000). Decision making involving CCU technologies is currently hampered due to lack of a consistent basis for life cycle assessments. Methodological guidelines have been developed but there is inconsistent practice, different views of the double role of CO2 as emission and feedstock and insufficient comparability of studies (Müller et al., 2018). Inconsistencies in accounting practice in negative emission technologies comes from lack of clear consensus on the use of different system boundaries and evaluation of e.g. CO2 capture, sequestration or indirect land use change for biobased feedstocks. There is currently limited agreement on what negative emissions are and transparency is needed for the interpretation and reporting guidelines (Tanzer & Ramírez, 2019).

## 9.2 Conceptualizing Low-Carbon Reorientation

In addition to the findings on predictor variables for transition, the dissertation examines the theoretical framework of innovation studies and sustainability transition sciences. Multi-level perspective of socio-technical systems provides a framework for understanding of technological transitions and governance for transition management (Geels, 2001; Geels & Schot, 2007). The analysis of the technological innovation system identifies complementary technologies within industry sectors with positive interactions and competing constellations (Markard & Hoffmann, 2016).

### 9.2.1 Alternative Technologies

The European Green Deal communicated three overlapping sustainability goals that affect the chemical industry. Three alternative technologies that are compatible with these goals are proposed as a substitute for fossil raw materials: Biomass, plastic recycling and CO2 as starting molecule (Table 9.5).

**Table 9.5** Multiple policy goals and alternative renewable feedstock response

| Sustainability goals | Alternative renewable feedstocks |
|---|---|
| • Climate action (UN SDG 13) | • Biobased feedstocks |
| • Circular economy (UN SDG 12) | • Plastic recycling |
| • Toxic-free environment, biodiversity (UN SDG 15) | • Electricity based processes and CO2 as starting molecule |

Contributions to the circular economy help to ensure sustainable consumption and production patterns. Research results of actor-related patterns provide the evidence for transition theory (Geels, 2005b). The road to carbon neutrality is part of a broader agenda to combat climate change, and a pollution-free environment promotes the sustainable use of terrestrial ecosystems. Further goals are sustainable forest management and biodiversity, jointly defining the European framework for the chemical industry (European Commission, 2019; UN, 2015a). Landscape pressure from a combination of goals for sustainable development is driving the advancement of a technology mix. Respondents in the case study report on the use of renewable raw materials such as cellulose, plastic recycling, polylactic acid biopolymers and bio-based intermediates. The existing use of bio-based raw materials ranges from 5% to 55% for selected specialty chemical companies that source bio-based raw materials and oleochemicals for chemical synthesis. Neste reports refining of sustainable aviation fuels and a share of 8% renewable carbon of the total output, leading the petrochemical companies. Clariant is investing in a bio-refinery to use crop residues for secondary bioethanol. These efforts document the expanded use of biomass for bio-based drop-ins (Carus, Dammer, Puente, Raschka & Arendt, 2017). Efforts to improve mechanical and chemical recycling processes for reusing plastics as raw materials are also reported. Sabic is working with partners to close the loop of a recycling concept and uses plastic waste as raw material to produce certified circular polymers. BASF,

Covestro and petrochemical companies such as Borealis are developing pyrolysis processes for chemical recycling as sustainable raw materials. The third pillar for achieving carbon neutrality is based on the use of CO2 as starting molecule and new electricity-based processes. Case study research and document analysis in annual sustainability reports find little evidence of carbon capture and utilization efforts. The technology receives the least amount of attention in corporate publications. However, the technology is needed to close the cap for a carbon neutral chemical industry (Carus, Kähler, Porc & vom Berg, 2021). Electricity-based processes are to replace conventional processes with no CO2 emissions in the years 2035 to 2050 and the greatest CO2 savings will not be recorded until the 2040 s according to a report of the German chemical industry association (VCI, 2019). The fastest contribution to GHG saving is expected from the use of renewable electricity. for wind and solar energy generation and electrolysis of hydrogen. Green hydrogen is available as raw material for ammonia, fertilizers and the use in refineries to partially decarbonize the production of fossil fuels or for other downstream processes (Scheuermann, 2021; Wieser, 2021). Complementary components in a technological innovation system accelerate the emergence of new technologies, and a model is developed as analysis framework of complementarities after Markard & Hoffmann (2016). The model helps to visualize complementing components but identifies also competing configurations (Markard & Hoffmann, 2016). Focal technologies are presented in the following figure (Fig. 9.1).

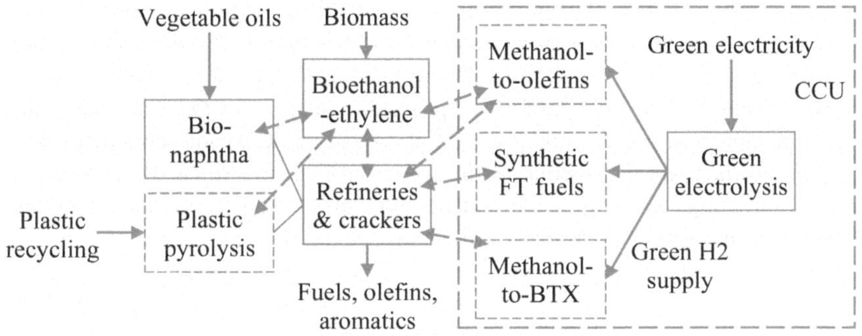


**Fig. 9.1** Complementarities for renewable feedstock technologies

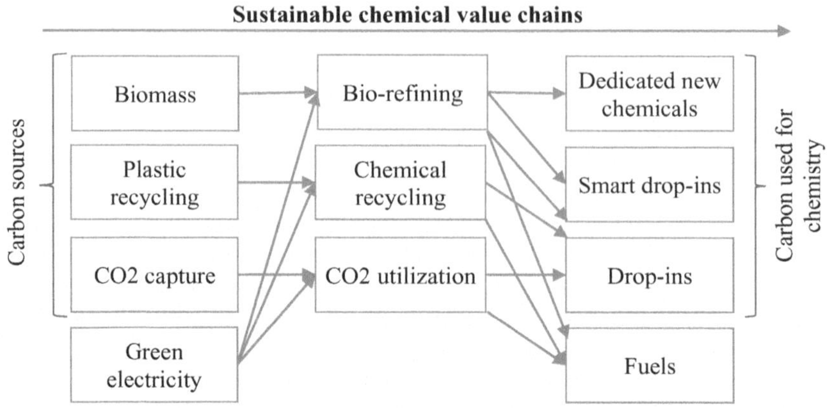


**Fig. 9.2** Visualization of sustainable chemical value chains

Dashed boxes indicate that the technology is in the demonstration stage. Solid lines and arrows indicate complementary technologies while dashed arrows indicate competing technologies. Petrochemical companies use refining and catalytic cracking that is complementary to bio-naphtha and plastic pyrolysis. The output materials are fuels, olefins and aromatics and compete with a similar range of output materials from carbon capture and utilization technology. Commercially available and thus more advanced is ethylene from bioethanol, and biofuels and olefins from bio-naphtha. Given the limited availability of biomass and recycling rates, major challenge in a decarbonized world is providing sufficient carbon for chemistry from carbon capture and utilization technologies. An embryonic innovation is the power-to-liquid (PtL) process, which uses CO2 from the atmosphere or industrial sources and converts hydrogen and CO2 into chemicals with methanol as the main intermediate (Kätelhön, Meys, Deutz, Suh & Bardow, 2019; Zitscher, Neuling, Habersetzer & Kaltschmitt, 2020). The technological regime change requires sufficient supply of green electricity and new sources for carbon demand of the industry on the input side of the sustainable chemical value chains. The creation of new infrastructure and the development of skills will likely have longer lead times. On the output side of the sustainable value chains, the technologies are competing with one another and may cause disruptive shifts in the marketplace (Kemp, 2003). The following figure attempts to visualize sustainable chemical value chains. Green electricity is needed for chemical processing and heat with an additional demand from CO2 utilization. The value chain employs three different feedstocks, biomass for processing in bio-refineries, plastic waste for chemical recycling and CO2 as starting molecule for synthesis. Th resulting intermediates are either used as drop-ins for existing chemicals or fuels, or as dedicated drop-ins with new properties. Bio-refining has the additional potential to offer dedicated new chemicals without existing equivalents (Fig. 9.2).

### 9.2.2 Possible Transition Pathway

In the absence of landscape pressure, the continued increase of efficiency and phasing-out of coal and greenhouse gases with higher global warming potential further reduces emissions, following the reproduction process of technological trajectories (Geels & Schot, 2007). The European Green Deal announced on December 11, 2019 has changed the landscape and put the industry under pressure. Regulatory governance is likely to encourage "endogenous renewal" of the chemical industry. Niche innovations for substitution of fossil feedstocks are new supply chains depend on biomass, plastic waste and CO2 as the starting molecule, but have not yet been developed. A transformation pathway (P1) is likely under these circumstances or, if the existing use of biomass and plastics recycling could be expanded as available, a reconfiguration path (P4) will emerge. If regulators are too quick or too aggressive to promote a "purposive transition," the pressures can have a destabilizing effect for industry sector. Under strong pressure from regulators, de- and re-alignment is possible, with multiple niche innovations being developed simultaneously and competing with each other until one niche innovation displaces the other. The de- and realignment path (P2) is a scenario that threatens established companies and enables new market participants to set the direction with a dominant design (Geels & Schot, 2007; Smith, Stirling & Berkhout, 2004) (Fig. 9.3).

Respondents from the case study and findings from document analysis provide hints, that the emerging technologies are in the stages of experimentation, piloting and small-scale demonstration plants. Several new technologies are reported and offered at the developmental stage to grow into the new regime (Loorbach, Frantzeskaki & Avelino, 2017). Biomass and mechanical plastics recycling are more advanced than chemical recycling, electricity-based processes and the use of CO2 as a starting molecule. These radical innovations are already partly developed, and regulatory pressure offers an opportunity for technological substitution (P3). However, the respondents cite higher prices than fossil materials and short supply as barriers to use. The prices for every type of renewable raw material are too high, availability is scarce and there is a lack of data on CO2 emissions

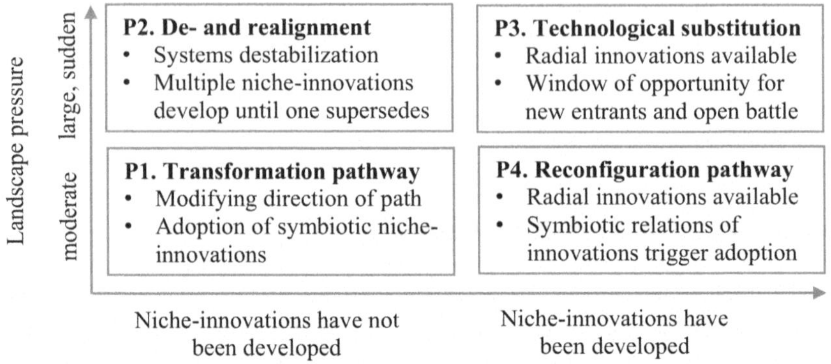


**Fig. 9.3** Sociotechnical transition pathways after Geels & Schot (2007)

savings. Chemical plastics recycling and CO2 as starting molecules are described as emerging technologies and are not available on an industrial scale. Biomass also competes with food and feed supplies and may conflict with biodiversity and sustainable land use. In the event of regulatory pressure and a CO2 tax on fossil fuels, the availability of biomass will remain limited as a sustainable source for carbon of the chemical industry (Wydra et al., 2021). Along with the short supply of alternative technologies and moderate pressure from regulatory authorities, a transformation pathway (P1) to climate neutrality is likely for the European chemical industry. There is a risk that new entrants from emerging markets could shift niche innovations to areas with cheaper energy and raw material supplies. Standardization of intermediates and bulk chemicals could make renewable technologies footloose to move outside the EU, unless the production is embedded in grown territorial contexts (Binz & Truffer, 2017). Analysis of annual sustainability reports identifies the development of CCU technology mainly at petrochemical companies and backward integrated specialty chemical companies. This gives the hint, that incumbent firms develop the new niche technology and prepare for the co-evolution of technologies and response scenarios to climate change (Hoogstraaten, Frenken & Boon, 2020). Due to the different stages of the development, a diffusion of the technologies will likely occur at different rates for each sector (Fig. 9.4).

The analysis of the available data from corporate publications suggests that greenhouse gas emission savings from operations will commence with solar and wind technologies and increased use of biomass, leading to a first S-shaped reduction of the industry's GHG emissions. A second S-shaped GHG reduction curve

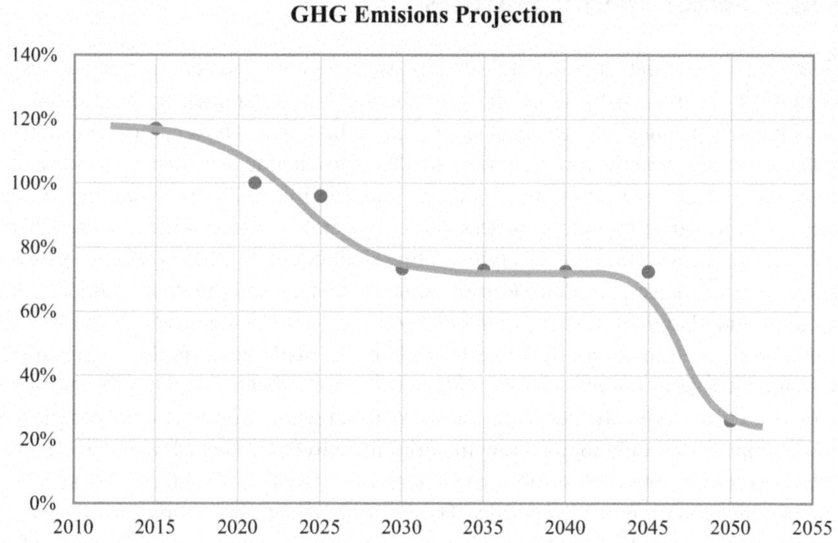


**Fig. 9.4** Scope 1 and Scope 2 greenhouse gas emission reduction projection based on company publications

will follow by advancements in chemical plastic recycling and carbon capture and utilization technologies after 2040. As a result, innovations are likely to diffuse into the chemical industry in two overlapping s-curves. First, renewable energies from wind power and solar are adopted together with the extended use of biomass. In a second wave, chemical recycling and carbon capture and utilization technology will be adopted in an attempt to fill the gap for carbon demand. However, commitments of the industry are not enough for a full decarbonization and Government regulations are needed to convince companies that have not yet committed to climate action. Last to change are the difficult to change sectors of the chemical industry. Government policies though trigger the change in sustainability transitions and are the major force to overcome lock-out effects and the missing competitiveness of renewable raw materials. Policymakers must encourage innovation and need to create a predictable business environment for investments in environmental innovations (Sovacool, Noel & Orsato, 2017).

### 9.2.3 Sector Specific Practices

Global regimes in the chemical industry focus on regional clusters of steam crackers that use fossil feedstocks as platform chemicals to manufacture intermediates for polymers, plastics and specialty chemicals. The transition to carbon neutrality aims to use sustainable raw materials in the petrochemical refineries towards a bio-based and circular economy (Bauer & Fuenfschilling, 2019). Examples from case study research include coprocessing of vegetable oils or biowaste together with petroleum for cracking of alpha-olefins (Hilbers et al., 2015). Plastic pyrolysis is proposed as a similar drop-in solution and as intermediate product for cracking and chemical synthesis (Jha & Kannan, 2021; Wang et al., 2021). On a minor level, the transition offers specialty chemical manufacturers the opportunity to replace existing supply chains with new bio-based intermediates. Examples from the case study are polylactic acid as a substitute for fossil polyethylene terephthalate or bioethanol as a raw material for ethylene. These bio-based chemicals are replacements for similar substances from fossil raw materials or special new chemicals with novel properties. They offer new entrants a window of opportunity for a substitution pathway (Carus, Dammer, Puente, Raschka & Arendt, 2017). One result of the case study is the customer preference for segregated bio-based consumer specialties. Consumers have a positive relationship with terms such as "green", "natural", "eco" and "bio" and are willing to pay a higher price for segregated bio-based consumer specialties such as household and personal care products with verifiable biogenic carbon content. The motivation for the preference is probably not GHG savings, but health and wellbeing associated with the use of biogenic ingredients. According to the results from case study research, customer preferences favor segregated supply chains over mass balanced supply chains and segregated biobased raw materials over coprocessing and recycling concepts with respect to consumer specialties. Businesses should focus on technological advancement with a heavy reliance on government policies. Five common organization predictors and five common innovation-specific predictors have been identified in this dissertation. Findings from case study research and document analysis complement each other, and examples from annual sustainability reports document the engagement of CEFIC corporate members in activities and plans to reduce greenhouse gas emissions (Table 9.6).

Results of the research also disclose differences in technology focus and sector-specific strategies. 24% of the keywords in the CEFIC group's annual sustainability reports relate to renewable energy for operations, 24% of the keywords relate to the recycling of plastic waste and 27% of the keywords relate to the use of bio-based raw materials. Only 1% of the keywords relate to carbon capture

**Table 9.6** Common decarbonization strategies for chemical companies

| Common decarbonization strategies for chemical companies |
|---|
| • Focus on technological advancement<br>• Strong path dependency on Government policies<br>• Business model adaptation under consideration of organizational and innovation-specific predictors |

and the use of CO2 as a starting molecule. The relationship underpins the early stages of CCU technologies in the industry. Sector-specific practices are discussed below (Table 9.7).

**Table 9.7** Preferred sustainable technologies by sector

| Sector | Halogen | Petrochemical | Pharma | Specialty chem. |
|---|---|---|---|---|
| Efficiency programs | + | + | | + |
| Renewable energy | + | + | + | |
| Recycling concepts | + | + | + | |
| Biobased feedstocks | | + | | + |
| CCU | | + | | |

The most relevant strategy for the halogen sector are efficiency programs, the use of renewable energies and recycling concepts. The petrochemical sector is focused on all technologies to reduce emissions, including considerations for the use of carbon capture technology and CO2 as starting molecules. The pharmaceutical sector has the lowest carbon footprint in the chemical industry, minimal need for action and below average attention to emission reduction technologies. The sector considers compensation schemes to reach climate neutrality, along with renewable electricity and plastic packaging recycling. The specialty chemicals sector pays above-average attention to efficiency programs and the use of bio-based raw materials for chemical synthesis (Table 9.8).

The halogen sector with the highest average operational product carbon footprint of 1 kg CO2e / EUR turnover is characterized by industry-specific emissions from energy-intensive processes and fluorinated gases with a high global warming potential. Efficiency programs, retrofit installations, abatement technologies and phase down strategies aim to reduce Scope 1 air process emissions of fluorinated organic compounds. The replacement of fluorinated gases with the highest GWP with less harmful substances, refrigerant recovery and end-of-life collection are intended to support customers and reduce downstream Scope 3 emissions of fluorinated gases. Another important source of the halogen sector is the high energy demand of the sector. Using electricity from renewable sources aims to reduce Scope 1 and Scope 2 emissions, and chlor-alkali electrolysis using renewable

**Table 9.8** Summary of sector specific strategies

| **Halogen sector** |
|---|
| • High energy intensity<br>• Sector specific emission reduction strategies for fluorinated gases and renewable energies<br>• Climate leaders switch energy supply to reach net-zero<br>• Scope 1 and 2 GHG reduction strategies with renewable energies<br>• Scope 3 GHG reduction with renewable raw materials |

electricity produces green caustic soda and hydrogen, as reported in case study research (Table 9.9).

**Table 9.9** Summary of sector specific strategies

| **Petrochemical sector** |
|---|
| • Highest absolute GHG emissions<br>• Technology mix to secure carbon supply<br>• Scope 1 and 2 GHG reduction strategies with renewable energies, biomass, plastic recycling, CCU |

With 74%, the petrochemical industry has the greatest burden of GHG emissions in the chemical industry. The aggregated targets for reducing greenhouse gases are −27% by 2030 and −70% by 2050. The sector focuses on a technology mix to secure carbon supplies and to reduce Scope 1 and Scope 2 greenhouse gas emissions. Petroleum-based raw materials are being replaced by biomass, plastic recycling and technologies for carbon capture and utilization. The use of renewable energies, recycling concepts, the use of bio-based raw materials and carbon capture and utilization are given greater consideration in the petrochemical industry than the average for the CEFIC corporate group, while efficiency programs are given a similar amount of attention as the average. Companies in the sector purchase new bio-based raw materials such as tall oil and biogas. Biomass is converted into bio-jet fuel, biodiesel and bioethanol fuel. Bio-naphtha is provided for use in biopolymer production and for bio-based intermediates such as ethylene and propylene. The circular economy involves various methods of reusing and recycling plastic waste. Material recycling is being expanded and cooperation with partners along the value chain opens up the potential for recovering plastic waste from consumer markets. Chemical recycling for breaking down plastics to building blocks is developed and finished products are designed to ensure recyclability. Finally, embryonic carbon capture experiments with energy-rich bio-oils from $CO_2$ and sunlight with strains of algae or manufacturing of methanol from CO2 and green hydrogen is reported (Table 9.10).

**Table 9.10** Summary of sector specific strategies

| |
|---|
| **Pharmaceutical & specialty chemicals sector** |
| • Climate leaders switch energy supply to reach net-zero before 2030 |
| • Scope 1 and 2 GHG reduction strategies with renewable energies |
| • Scope 3 GHG reduction with renewable raw materials |

The pharmaceutical sector has the lowest average operational carbon footprint of below 0,1 kg CO2e / EUR turnover and contributes only 1% of operational GHG emissions. Aggregated GHG emission reduction targets are -50% by 2030 and -94% by 2050. Compared to the average of the corporate members of the CEFIC group, reduction strategies are given less attention in the annual reports. Energy management, compensation systems and the reuse of plastic are mentioned most frequently in reports as important mitigation strategies. The specialty chemicals sector contributes 21% to operational GHG emissions from the chemical industry, and the aggregated greenhouse gas reduction targets from operations are -26% by 2030 and -75% by 2050. Climate leaders and early adopters from the sector are first to reduce their Scope 1 and Scope 2 emissions by purchasing renewable energy for their own operations. Efficiency programs, recycling concepts and the use of bio-based raw materials are given similar attention in specialty chemicals as the average for the companies in the CEFIC group. The technology toolbox includes the use of bio-based raw materials and recycling concepts. Plant-based feedstocks, e.g. dextrose, sucrose, palm oil, palm kernel oil, bio-based intermediates and monomers are sources and end products are made from bio-based materials. 12 green chemistry rules for efficient carbon use is employed for design driven innovations. Recycling concepts are based on recycled raw materials of fossil origin and the industry-wide focus is on 100% recyclable or reusable packaging. Companies that manufacture plastics and polymers try closed loops and incorporate renewable or recycled materials into the end materials. The downcycling of recyclates is avoided through the choice of additives and existing construction waste is separated from hazardous compounds to reclaim the neat polymer for reuse.

## 9.3 Implications for Practitioners and Research

Multi-level perspective of the socio-technical transition and transition management studies of technological system are both examining governance of sustainability transitions with actors and industry networks. However, political decision-makers, society and managers in companies have different perspectives on transitions. Regulators in socio-institutional transition need to develop ideal innovation policies for governance and to avoid adverse events during the low-carbon transformation (Boon & Edler, 2018; Geels, Pflugger & Rogge, 2020). Companies at the micro level are looking for appropriate assessments of opportunities and responses to threats for their business models (Bergek, Jacobsson, Carlsson, Lindmark & Rickne, 2008). The following section discusses suggestions for businesses and summarizes the implications of this dissertation for practitioners in the industry. Finally, an outlook for further research of the academic community is given.

### 9.3.1 Transition Management for Business

Five organizational and five innovation-specific predictors were identified as the main determinants for chemical companies to adopt renewable raw materials. Applying the five organizational predictors from this study provides a toolbox to prepare for transition to carbon neutrality and the adoption of renewable raw materials as replacement of fossil feedstocks. The company's corporate sustainability strategy, management advocacy, collaborative skills, adoption of industry standards and following government regulations are suggested from this study as the main 5 elements of corporate management toolbox in sustainability transition. Company leadership should foster engagement of employees and apply performance management tools with respect to the changes in the sectoral system and towards sustainability transition. Corporate sustainability strategy should consider GHG emission reduction targets of greater than 45% by 2030 as compared to 2019 levels (The Hague District Court, 2021). Management advocacy and cooperation skills with partners are levers to enhance the innovation process and efficiency. The implementation of industry standards and monitoring of Government regulations are further prerequisite to innovation adoption. Results from case study research and document analysis emphasize corporate sustainability strategy, a supportive management for an ambidextrous innovation culture and cooperation skills as essential. Knowledge flows are vital elements for environmental innovations and enable co-creation, cooperation and open innovation projects (Horbach, 2020). The landscape pressure from users and consumers, public policies and novel niche-innovations initiate the changes in the sectoral system and create a window of opportunity for co-evolution of several new technologies to reach carbon neutrality (Lee & Malerba, 2017). The opportunities come from renewable energies and novel feedstocks for chemistry. Alternative raw materials for fossil feedstocks are biomass, plastic recyclates, green hydrogen and CO2 as starting molecule. Biomass and plastic recycling currently receive the greatest attention by companies, but availability is limited. Projections see the need for carbon capture and utilization to fill the gap for carbon demand of the chemical industry in a decarbonized world (Carus, Kähler, Porc & vom Berg, 2021). This study identifies the development of CCU technology at petrochemical companies and backward integrated specialty chemical companies. Companies prepare for the co-evolution of the novel technologies and develop appropriate response scenarios (Hoogstraaten, Frenken & Boon, 2020) (Table 9.11).

Applying the five innovation-specific predictors from this research—availability of the renewable feedstock, price, CO2 savings, compatibility with existing regimes and transparency of the supply chain—provides a framework for assessing novel technologies. Any capability that increases availability, reduces costs and GHG emissions and improves compatibility and transparency of origin of materials enhances the adoption. Adoption is supported by compatibility with existing use paradigms, production processes, consumer expectations, reduced environmental impact, health and safety requirements and need to be complementary to existing fossil-based products. Compatibility with existing infrastructure including supply networks and refineries is seen as a driver and coprocessing of renewable feedstocks and mass balancing of different types of renewable raw materials—biomass, plastic recyclates and intermediated from carbon capture and utilization—facilitates the adoption. Segregation of different feedstocks adds to the complexity although consumer niche markets may favor pure traceable

**Table 9.11** Organization and innovation-specific predictors for chemical transition management

| Organizational predictors for chemical transition management | Innovation-specific predictors for chemical transition management |
|---|---|
| Cooperation activities | Low cost of raw materials |
| Management advocacy | High CO2 saving potential |
| Corporate sustainability strategy | Sufficiently availability |
| Industry standardization | Compatible with technological regimes |
| Government regulations | Transparency of origin of material |

biobased chemicals. Greater compatibility overcomes lock-out effects and avoids financial difficulties for companies in the sustainable transition (Sovacool, Noel & Orsato, 2017). Another key finding from this research is the value of transparency for adoption of renewable raw materials. Users and consumers require verification of sustainability claims on origin of material and CO2 savings and third-party certification schemes aim to increase transparency of the supply chains and credibility of the chain of custody (International Organization for Standardization, 2019). Independent auditing bodies and certification agencies enhance the reliability along the chain of custody, particularly for mass balanced supply chains where sustainable and non-sustainable feedstocks are processed at the same time, at least at the beginning. Certification schemes also try to provide definitions of what is green and sustainable depending on carbon footprint, water footprint, impact on biodiversity and contribution to circular economy and are backed by NGOs to prepare for a healthy consumer life, toxic-free environment and waste-free economy (Mol & Oosterveer, 2015; ISCC, 2018). Mass balancing is the preferred technology for majority of industries because it provides the greatest contribution to the circular economy and is compatible with existing processes and products, raw material categories and different types of renewable feedstocks. The five predictors serve as selection criteria for technical variants and support product design (Yap & Truffer, 2019). Technological monitoring focuses on creating knowledge and capability building for adjacent and emerging technologies that complement, compete and interact with one another in the innovation system (Bergek et al., 2015). Government policies are the major triggers of change in sustainability transitions. The critical time-to-market for niche innovations is the time between entry into force of new regulations and their date of applicability. The European Green Deal, announced on Dec 11, 2019, can be seen as the beginning of transition to promote alternative technologies. Now, the industry needs to prepare for enactment of individual sector and technology specific directives. Monitoring the policies is essential to adjust business models and to develop novel technologies early enough. The time of application can be seen as the time-to-take-off from which the diffusion process of the novel technology becomes self-sustaining in view of Everett M. Rogers' diffusion model (2003).

### 9.3.2 Sector Specific Implications

This dissertation collects also sector specific differences for transition management. Transition management of the companies is embedded in the environment of the organization and is influenced by market forces of the economic context, and sector specific regulatory policies (Wirth, Markard, Truffer & Rohracher, 2013). The halogen sector has specific product related challenges linked to emission reduction strategies for fluorinated gases and high energy demands. Petrochemical business models are petroleum dependent. The industry explores new synthesis routes and feedstocks for carbon supply of the chemical industry. The emergence of new sources of carbon for chemistry opens up a window of opportunities for new entrants and the study of complementarities and competing technologies provides a tool to anticipate future market shifts (Table 9.12).

**Table 9.12** Technology mix to reach carbon neutrality by the chemical industry

| Scope 1 and 2 emission reduction | Scope 3 emission reduction |
|---|---|
| • Efficiency programs to reduce energy intensity<br>• Use of renewable energy<br>• Phase-down of production<br>• Compensation schemes | • Use of feedstocks made from biobased raw materials, recyclates and CO2 as starting molecule<br>• Green hydrogen for synthesis<br>• Application of recycling concepts |

Specialty chemical companies are downstream users of feedstocks supplied by the petrochemical industry. They need to prepare for new supply chains, higher price levels of feedstocks and changes in availability and a new competitive situation. Instruments to reduce Scope 1 and Scope 2 emissions for specialty chemical companies are efficiency programs and use of renewable energy for operations. Installations of retrofits and abatement technologies reduce emissions from processes. Chemical companies need to prepare for phasedowns of chemicals with very high global warming potential. Instruments to reduce Scope 3 emissions for specialty chemicals companies are the use of renewable raw materials from biomass, plastic recyclates, green hydrogen and CO2 as starting molecule.

### 9.3.3 Outlook for Further Research

This qualitative research explored a set of 10 predictor variables for adoption of environmental innovations to reduce GHG emissions. The five organizational predictors for chemical transition management are management advocacy, corporate sustainability strategy, cooperation activities, adaption of industry standards and timely implementation of Government regulations. The five innovation-specific predictors are availability, cost and CO2 saving potential of renewable raw materials, compatibility with existing technological regimes and transparency of supply chains. Further research may focus on quantitative methods to confirm the linking logic of chemical transition management predictors and the adoption of renewable raw materials to reach carbon neutrality. Econometric analyses with structural equation modelling can use surveys of European chemical companies with structured questionnaires containing company- and innovation specific questions on the proposed predictors of this dissertation and performance indicators on e. g. raw material use, GHG emissions and emissions reduction, production volume, sales and innovation and investment activities. Surveys can have several different research subjects, e. g. longitudinal case studies that analyze interactions in an industry sector between innovations and regulations, industry standardization, customer expectations and supply chain certifications. Continued research can enable companies and regulators to more efficiently manage the transition to sustainability and mitigate the risk of unproductive use of resources. Another quantitative research approach for structural equation modeling is the analysis of innovation diffusion using patent data and a set of established patent indicators reflecting the 10 predictors of this research. The quantitative approach can also collect data through face-to-face interviews with managers of chemical companies or from regional or sectoral focus groups of the European chemical industry to develop structural equation models. And quantitative research can apply the theory of planned behavior to gather empirical evidence through interviews with industry respondents using a validated 5- or 7-point Likert scale from a sufficiently large sample size. The data can be used for statistical analysis to confirm and identify the rigor of each of the proposed predictors of this dissertation. Next to the continued research on predictors for adoption of renewable raw materials, the dissertation identified further subjects for business research (Table 9.13).

**Table 9.13** Further questions for research

| **Business questions for further research** | |
|---|---|
| 1. | How much carbon supply is available for chemistry in a decarbonized world? |
| 2. | What are the superseding technologies of carbon supply for chemistry? |
| 3. | What is green and sustainable carbon supply for chemistry? |
| 4. | What life cycle assessments and carbon footprint calculation will be accepted? |
| 5. | How will National Governments and the EU promote the transition? |

Future corporate research needs to gather information on how much carbon supply and from what sources will be available for chemistry in a decarbonized world. Availability, demand and supply will have a determining effect for price levels and interdisciplinary research on biomass availability, recycling concepts, sources and technologies for the collection of concentrated CO2 is required to predict the carbon supply for fossil fuel replacement. Second, future corporate research must monitor the further development of the superseding technologies. Availability of renewable carbon in the form of intermediate products is related to technological advances in chemical plastics recycling, the availability of second and third generation biomass for biochemical processes, and carbon capture and utilization technologies. Renewable energy sources, green hydrogen and concentrated CO2 play key roles, and market shifts will depend on the availability and costs of renewable alternatives. Third, corporate research needs to identify science-based targets for chemistry that consider all environmental and social impact categories. It is not clear today what is green and sustainable and how to reconcile conflicting sustainable development goals. GHG reduction can conflict with biodiversity, biodegradability, competition from biomass for food, feed, fuel and chemicals, water use, land use and land use change, and responsible use of other finite resources such as lithium, rare metals and phosphorus. In order to avoid a further lock-in effect, a balance between different sustainability goals is required. Fourth, more research is needed on life cycle assessment and carbon footprint calculation methods accepted by industry, governments and environmental organizations. The dissertation confirmed existing inconsistencies in application methods that delay the availability of product carbon footprint data. Practitioners apply different boundaries for emission factors and do not have a common understanding for assessing biogenic carbon uptake by biomass. The different assessments are already described in the scientific literature and were confirmed by this research. Finally, qualitative research is proposed to continuously collect information from various sources including academic papers, policy documents, industry journals, expert interviews and statistical databases. Corporate leadership must closely monitor and follow the political discourse and the elaboration of policies, laws and regulations at national, European and global levels. Corporate research needs regulatory oversight of the activities and policy changes of the European Commission, the European Parliament and the European Chemicals Agency. Central to the European chemical industry is the European Commission's policy agenda and national carbon pricing as the main policy tool to incentivize reduction.

# Corporate Publications for Document Analysis

3M (2021a). *2020 Annual report.* St. Paul, MN: 3M Corporate Headquarter.
3M (2021b). *2020 Sustainability report, improving every life.* St. Paul, MN: 3M Corporate Headquarter.
AGC Group (2020). *Sustainability data book 2020 For the year ended December 31, 2019. August 2020.* Tokyo, JAPAN: AGC Inc.
Albemarle (2020). *2021 Sustainability report. Release 21.08.2020.* Charlotte, N.C.: Albemarle Corporation.
Albemarle (2021). *2020 Sustainability report. Release 03.06.2021.* Charlotte, N.C.: Albemarle Corporation.
Allnex (2021). *Environmental, social and governance report 2021.* Frankfurt The Squaire, Germany: Allnex Group Corporate Center.
Altana (2016). *Annual report 2015.* Wesel, Germany: Altana AG.
Altana (2017). *Annual and sustainability report 2016.* Wesel, Germany: Altana AG.
Altana (2018). *Corporate report 2017.* Wesel, Germany: Altana AG.
Altana (2019). *Corporate report 2018.* Wesel, Germany: Altana AG.
Altana (2020). *Corporate report 2019.* Wesel, Germany: Altana AG.
Altana (2021a). *Corporate report 2020.* Wesel, Germany: Altana AG.
Altana (2021b). *Facts and figures on sustainability 2020.* Wesel, Germany: Altana AG.
Altana (2021c). *Altana to be CO2-neutral by 2025.* Retrieved from https://www.altana.com/sustainability/climate-neutrality/facts-and-figures.html
Archroma (2018). *Sustainability report financial year 2017.* Reinach, Switzerland: Archroma Management LLC.
Archroma (2020a). *Sustainability report financial year 2018.* Reinach, Switzerland: Archroma Management LLC.
Archroma (2020b). *Sustainability report FY2019.* Reinach, Switzerland: Archroma Management LLC.
Archroma (2021). *Sustainability report fiscal year 2020.* Reinach, Switzerland: Archroma Management LLC.
Arkema (2021). Universal registration document including the annual financial report 2020. Colombes, France: Arkema – Société Anonyme.
Ashland (2020). *2019 GRI Index.* Wilmington, Del: Ashland Global Holdings Inc.
Ashland (2021). *Annual report fiscal 2020.* Wilmington, Del: Ashland Global Holdings Inc.



H. H. E. Ahrens, *The Ecological Modernization of the Chemical Industry*,
https://doi.org/10.1007/978-3-658-45389-3

Atotech (2021a). *Environmental and resource performance.* Retrieved from https://www.atotech.com/sustainability/environmental-and-resource-performance/#:~:text=Our%20objective,environmental%20performance%20and%20resource%20efficiency

Atotech (2021b). Form 20-F. *Annual report pursuant to section 13 or 15(d) of the securities exchange act of 1934 for the fiscal year ended December 31, 2020.* Retrieved from https://www.sec.gov/edgar/searchedgar/mutualsearch.html

BASF (2021a). *BASF Report 2020 Economic, environmental and social performance. Published on February 26, 2021.* Ludwigshafen, Germany: BASF AG.

BASF (2021b). *Our carbon management. Published April 2021.* Ludwigshafen, Germany: BASF AG.

Bayer (2021a). *Annual report 2020.* Leverkusen, Germany: Bayer AG.

Bayer (2021b) *Bayer AG – Climate change 2020.* Leverkusen, Germany: Bayer AG.

Bayer (2021c) *Sustainability report 2020.* Leverkusen, Germany: Bayer AG.

Borealis (2021). Combined annual report 2020. Vienna, Austria: Borealis AG.

BP (2021). *bp sustainability report 2020.* London, UK: bp p.l.c.

Celanese (2020) Sustainability metrics 2019. Irving TX: Celanese Corp.

Celanese (2021). *Form 10-K. Annual report pursuant to section 13 or 15(d) of the securities exchange act of 1934 for the fiscal year ended December 31, 2020.* Retrieved from https://www.sec.gov/edgar/searchedgar/mutualsearch.html

Cepsa (2021). *2020 Integrated management report.* Madrid, Spain: Compañía Española de Petróleos S.A.

Chemours (2021a). *Chemours Co / The 2020 annual report.* Wilmington, Delaware: The Chemours Company.

Chemours (2021b). *Chemours Co / The climate change 2020.* Wilmington, Delaware: The Chemours Company.

Chemours (2020). *2019 Chemours corporate responsibility commitment index report.* Wilmington, Delaware: The Chemours Company.

Chevron (2021). *2020 corporate sustainability report.* San Ramon, CA: Chevron Corporation.

Clariant (2021a). GRI report 2020. Muttenz, Switzerland: Clariant International Ltd.

Clariant (2021b). *Integrated report 2020.* Muttenz, Switzerland: Clariant International Ltd.

Covestro (2021a). *Annual report 2020.* Leverkusen, Germany: Covestro AG.

Covestro (2021b). *Sustainability @ Covestro March 2021.* Leverkusen, Germany: Covestro AG.

Croda (2021a). *Annual report and accounts 2020.* Goole, UK: Croda International Plc.

Croda (2021b). *Sustainability report 2020.* Goole, UK: Croda International Plc.

Dow (2021a). *Annual report 2020.* Midland, MI: Dow Inc.

Dow (2021b). *2020 environmental, social and governance report.* Midland, MI: Dow Inc.

DSM (2021). *Royal DSM integrated annual report 2020.* Heerlen, Netherlands: Royal DSM N.V.

Dupont (2021a). *Form 10-K. Annual report pursuant to section 13 or 15(d) of the securities exchange act of 1934 for the fiscal year ended December 31, 2020.* Retrieved from https://www.sec.gov/edgar/searchedgar/mutualsearch.html

Dupont (2021b). *Thriving together 2021 GRI index.* Wilmington, Delaware: DuPont de Nemours, Inc.

Eastman (2021a). *Enhancing the quality of life in a material way. Annual report 2020.* Kingsport, Tennessee: Eastman Chemical Company.
Eastman (2021b). *2020 Sustainability report.* Kingsport, Tennessee: Eastman Chemical Company.
Ecolab (2021a). *2020 Annual report.* St. Paul, MN: Ecolab USA Inc.
Ecolab (2021b). *2020 Corporate sustainability report.* St. Paul, MN: Ecolab USA Inc.
Eni (2021). *Annual Report 2020.* Rome, Italy: Eni SpA.
Eurochem (2021). *2020 Annual report and accounts.* Zug, Switzerland: EuroChem Group AG.
Evonik (2021a). *Financial report 2020.* Essen, Germany: Evonik Industries AG.
Evonik (2021b). *Sustainability report 2020.* Essen, Germany: Evonik Industries AG.
ExxonMobil (2021a). *2020 Annual report.* Irving, Texas: Exxon Mobil Corporation.
ExxonMobil (2021b). *Sustainability report highlights 2019.* Irving, Texas: Exxon Mobil Corporation.
Givaudan (2016). *Sustainability report 2015.* Vernier, Switzerland: Givaudan AG.
Givaudan (2017). *Sustainability report 2016.* Vernier, Switzerland: Givaudan AG.
Givaudan (2018). *Sustainability report 2017.* Vernier, Switzerland: Givaudan AG.
Givaudan (2019). *2018 Sustainability progress review.* Vernier, Switzerland: Givaudan AG.
Givaudan (2020). *2019 Integrated annual report.* Vernier, Switzerland: Givaudan AG.
Givaudan (2021). *Annual integrated report 2020.* Vernier, Switzerland: Givaudan AG.
Hexion (2021a). *2020 Sustainability report.* Columbus, OH: Hexion Inc.
Hexion (2021b). *Form 10-K. Annual report pursuant to section 13 or 15(d) of the securities exchange act of 1934 for the fiscal year ended December 31, 2020.* Columbus, OH: Hexion Inc.
Honeywell (2021a). *2020 Annual report.* Charlotte, NC: Honeywell International Inc.
Honeywell (2021b). *Corporate citizenship report 2020.* Charlotte, NC: Honeywell International Inc.
Honeywell (2021c). *Honeywell international Inc. CDP climate change questionnaire 2020.* Charlotte, NC: Honeywell International Inc.
Huntsman (2019). *Huntsman Corporation CDP climate change questionnaire 2019 Wednesday, July 3, 2019.* The Woodlands, Texas: Huntsman Corporation.
Huntsman (2021a). *2020 Annual report.* The Woodlands, Texas: Huntsman Corporation.
Huntsman (2021b). *2020 Sustainability report.* The Woodlands, Texas: Huntsman Corporation.
ICL (2019). *ICL CDP climate change questionnaire 2019 Tuesday, August 27, 2019.* Tel Aviv, Israel: ICL Group Ltd.
ICL (2021a). *Form 10-K. Annual report pursuant to section 13 or 15(d) of the securities exchange act of 1934 for the fiscal year ended December 31, 2020.* Tel Aviv, Israel: ICL Group Ltd.
ICL (2021b). *Sustainability strategy.* Retrieved from https://icl-group-sustainability.com/reports/goals-performance/
Ineos (2021). *2020 Sustainability report.* London, UK: Ineos Group Holdings S.A.
Inospec (2020). *2019 Responsible business report.* Englewood, CO: Inospec Inc.
Inospec (2021). *Form 10-K. Annual report pursuant to section 13 or 15(d) of the securities exchange act of 1934 for the fiscal year ended December 31, 2020.* Englewood, CO: Inospec Inc.

Johnson Matthey (2020). *Johnson Matthey CDP climate change questionnaire 2020 Wednesday, August 26, 2020.* London, UK: Johnson Matthey Plc.
Johnson Matthey (2021). *2021 Annual report and accounts.* London, UK: Johnson Matthey Plc.
Kemira (2021a). *Annual review 2020.* Helsinki, Finland: Kemira Oyj.
Kemira (2021b). *Kemira annual review 2020 Annex: GRI-report.* Helsinki, Finland: Kemira Oyj.
Kraton (2020). *2019 Corporate sustainability report.* Houston, TX: Kraton Corp.
Kraton (2021). *Form 10-K. Annual report pursuant to section 13 or 15(d) of the securities exchange act of 1934 for the fiscal year ended December 31, 2020.* Houston, TX: Kraton Corp.
Lanxess (2021a). *2020 Annual report.* Cologne Germany: Lanxess AG.
Lanxess (2021b). *Lanxess AG – climate change 2020.* Cologne Germany: Lanxess AG.
Lubrizol (2021a). *2020 Company report.* Wickliffe, OH: Lubrizol Corp.
Lubrizol (2021b). *Global sustainability scorecard data.* Retrieved from https://www.lubrizol.com/Sustainability/Resources/Scorecard
Lyondellbasell (2021a). *2020 Sustainability report.* Rotterdam, Netherlands: Lyondellbasell Industries N.V.
Lyondellbasell (2021b). *Form 10-K. Annual report pursuant to section 13 or 15(d) of the securities exchange act of 1934 for the fiscal year ended December 31, 2020.* Rotterdam, Netherlands: Lyondellbasell Industries N.V.
Mapei (2021a). *2019 Consolidated financial statements.* Milan, Italy: Mapei SpA.
Mapei (2021b). *Summary of the 2019 sustainability report.* Milan, Italy: Mapei SpA.
Merck (2021a). *Annual report 2020.* Darmstadt, Germany: Merck KGaA.
Merck (2021b). *Sustainability report 2020.* Darmstadt, Germany: Merck KGaA.
Mitsubishi (2021a). *Integrated report 2020.* Tokyo, Japan: Mitsubishi Chemical Corp.
Mitsubishi (2021b). *Sustainability report 2020.* Tokyo, Japan: Mitsubishi Chemical Corp.
Mitsui Chemicals (2020a). *Integrated report 2020.* Tokyo, Japan: Mitsu & Co., Ltd.
Mitsui Chemicals (2020b). *Sustainability report 2020. Environmental Performance Data. p. 49–53.* Tokyo, Japan: Mitsu & Co., Ltd.
Mol (2021a). *Mol group integrated annual report 2020.* Budapest, Hungary: MOL Hungarian oil and gas public limited company.
Momentive (2020). *2019 Momentive Sustainability Report.* Waterford, New York: Momentive Performance Materials Inc.
Neste (2016). *Neste in 2015.* Espoo, Finland: Neste Oyj.
Neste (2017). *Annual Report 2016.* Espoo, Finland: Neste Oyj.
Neste (2018). *Annual Report 2017.* Espoo, Finland: Neste Oyj.
Neste (2019). *Annual Report 2018.* Espoo, Finland: Neste Oyj.
Neste (2020). *Annual report 2019.* Espoo, Finland: Neste Oyj.
Neste (2021). *Annual report 2020.* Espoo, Finland: Neste Oyj.
Nouryon (2021). *Sustainability report 2020.* Amsterdam, Netherlands: Nouryon Chemicals B.V.
Novartis (2016). *Corporate responsibility performance report 2015.* Basel, Switzerland: Novartis AG.
Novartis (2017). *Corporate responsibility performance report 2016.* Basel, Switzerland: Novartis AG.

Novartis (2018). *Corporate responsibility performance report 2017.* Basel, Switzerland: Novartis AG.
Novartis (2019). *Novartis in society 2018.* Basel, Switzerland: Novartis AG.
Novartis (2020). *Novartis in society ESG Report 2019.* Basel, Switzerland: Novartis AG.
Novartis (2021a). *Annual report 2020.* Basel, Switzerland: Novartis International AG.
Novartis (2021b). *Novartis in society ESG Report 2020.* Basel, Switzerland: Novartis AG.
Olin (2021a). *Form 10-K. Annual report pursuant to section 13 or 15(d) of the securities exchange act of 1934 for the fiscal year ended December 31, 2020.* Clayton, MO: Olin Corporation.
Olin (2021b). *2020 Inaugural sustainability report.* Clayton, MO: Olin Corporation.
OQ Chemicals (2020). *sustainability report 2019.* Monheim, Germany: OQ Chemicals GmbH.
OQ Chemicals (2021). *OQ Chemicals Holding Zwei GmbH, Monheim am Rhein. Jahresabschluss zum Geschäftsjahr vom 01.01.2019 bis zum 31.12.2019.* Retrieved from https://www.bundesanzeiger.de/pub/de/suchergebnis?8
Orbia (2021). *Orbia sustainability report 2020.* Mexico City, Mexico: Orbia Advance Corporation.
Perstorp (2021). *Annual and sustainability report 2020.* Malmö, Sweden: Perstorp Holding AB.
Procter & Gamble (2016). *2015 Sustainability report.* Cincinnati, OH: Procter & Gamble Company.
Procter & Gamble (2017). *P&G 2016 citizenship report.* Cincinnati, OH: Procter & Gamble Company.
Procter & Gamble (2018). *P&G 2017 citizenship report.* Cincinnati, OH: Procter & Gamble Company.
Procter & Gamble (2019). *P&G 2018 citizenship report.* Cincinnati, OH: Procter & Gamble Company.
Procter & Gamble (2020). *P&G 2019 citizenship report.* Cincinnati, OH: Procter & Gamble Company.
Procter & Gamble (2021a). *2020 Annual report.* Cincinnati, OH: Procter & Gamble Company.
Procter & Gamble (2021b). *P&G 2020 citizenship report.* Cincinnati, OH: Procter & Gamble Company.
Repsol (2021a). *Annual financial report 2020.* Madrid, Spain: Repsol, S.A.
Repsol (2021b). *Integrated Management Report 2020.* Madrid, Spain: Repsol, S.A.
Röhm (2021a). *Röhm Group 2020 Non-Financial Declaration.* Darmstadt, Germany: Röhm GmbH.
Röhm (2021b). *Track2030 The Röhm sustainability program.* Retrieved form https://www.roehm.com/en/reducing-the-carbon-footprint
Sabic (2021a). *Thriving with resilience annual report 2020.* Riyadh, Saudi Arabia: Saudi Basic Industries Corporation.
Sabic (2021b). *Thriving responsibility sustainability report 2020.* Riyadh, Saudi Arabia: Saudi Basic Industries Corporation.
Seppic (2020). *Caring.* La Garenne Colombes Cedex, France: Seppic S.A.
Shell (2021a). *Annual report and accounts 2020.* The Hague, The Netherlands: Royal Dutch Shell Plc.

Shell (2021b). *CDP climate change 2020 information request – Royal Dutch Shell plc.* The Hague, The Netherlands: Royal Dutch Shell Plc.
Shell (2021c). *Sustainability report 2020.* The Hague, The Netherlands: Royal Dutch Shell Plc.
Sibur (2019). *2025 Sustainability strategy.* Moscow, Russia: PJSC Sibur Holding.
Sibur (2020). *Sustainability report 2019.* Moscow, Russia: PJSC Sibur Holding.
Sika (2021). *Sika business year 2020.* Baar, Switzerland: Sika AG.
Sika (2021). *Sika GRI report 2020.* Baar, Switzerland: Sika AG.
Socar (2020). *Annual sustainable development report 2019.* Baku, Azerbaijan; State Oil Company of Azerbaijan Republic.
Solenis (2021). *Solenis sustainability report 2020.* Wilmington, Delaware: Solenis LLC.
Solvay (2021). *Solvay 2020 annual report.* Brussels, Belgium: Solvay S.A.
Sumitomo Chemical (2021a). *Consolidated Annual Results FY2020 (Year ended March 31, 2021).* Tokyo, Japan: Sumitomo Corporation.
Sumitomo Chemical (2021b). *Integrated Report 2020.* Tokyo, Japan: Sumitomo Corporation.
Sumitomo Chemical (2021c). *Sustainability data book 2020.* Tokyo, Japan: Sumitomo Chemical Company, Limited.
Teva (2021). *2020 Environmental, social and governance progress report.* Tel Aviv-Yafo, Israel: Teva Pharmaceutical Industries Ltd.
Total (2021a). *Getting to net zero September 2020.* Courbevoie, France: Total S.A.
Total (2021b). *Universal registration document 2020.* Courbevoie, France: Total S.A.
Tronox (2020). *2019 Sustainability report.* Grimsby, UK: Tronox Holdings Plc.
Tronox (2021). *2020 Annual report.* Grimsby, UK: Tronox Holdings Plc.
Venator (2021a). *2020 Annual report.* Stockton-On-Tees, UK: Venator Materials Plc.
Venator (2021b). *2020 Sustainability report.* Stockton-On-Tees, UK: Venator Materials Plc.
Versalis (2021a). *Annual report 2019.* Rome, Italy: Versalis SpA.
Versalis (2021b). *Sustainability highlights 2020.* Rome, Italy: Versalis SpA.
Wacker (2021a). *Annual report 2020.* Munich, Germany: Wacker Chemie AG.
Wacker (2021b). *Global compact progress report 2020.* Munich, Germany: Wacker Chemie AG.

# Bibliography

Ahrens, H. (2021, January 24) *Reflexivity in action WS19/20, pilot study.* San Gwann, Malta: Triagon Academy Ltd.
Aiken, M. (2019). An updated evaluation of Google Translate accuracy. *Studies in Linguistics and Literature 3*(3), 253–260.
Ajzen, I. (1985). From intentions to actions: A theory of planned behavior. In Kuhl, J. & Beckmann, J. (Eds.), *Action control, from cognition to behavior.* Berlin, Germany: Springer Verlag.
Ajzen, I. (1991). The theory of planned behavior. *Organizational Behavior and Human Decision Processes 50*(2), 179–211.

Ajzen, I. (2011). The theory of planned behaviour: reactions and reflections. *Psychology and Health, 26*(9), 1113–1127.

Ajzen, I. (2012). The theory of planned behavior. In Lange, A., Kruglanski W. & Higgins E. T. (Eds.), *Handbook of theories of social psychology, vol. 1* (pp. 438–459). London, UK: Sage.

Ajzen, I. & Fishbein, M. (2005), The influence of attitudes on behavior. In D. Albarracín, B. T. Johnson, M. P. Zanna (Ed.), *The handbook of attitudes* (pp. 173–223). Mahwah, NJ: Lawrence Erlbaum Associates.

Alajamy, M., Al-Mamari, S., Martins, J.T., Nunes, J.M.B. & Zhou, L. (2010). Contextual sensitivity in grounded theory: the role of pilot studies. *The Electronic Journal of Business Research Methods 8*(2), 73–84.

Almutairi, A. F., Gardner, G. E. & McCarthy, A. (2014). Practical guidance for the use of a pattern-matching technique in case-study research: A case presentation. *Nursing and Health Sciences 16*(2), 239–244.

Alos-Simo, L., Verdu-Jover, A. J. &Gomez-Gras, J.-M. (2020). The dynamic process of ambidexterity in eco-innovation. *Sustainability 2020*(12), 2023. https://doi.org/10.3390/su12052023

Alvares de Souza Soares, P. (2020, January 22). Nachhaltigkeit – Chemiekonzerne verkaufen sich am besten. *Manager Magazin.* Retrieved from https://www.manager-magazin.de/unternehmen/artikel/nachhaltigkeit-studie-hering-schuppener-zu-dax-konzernkommunikation-a-1304195.html

Amara, N., Landry, R., Becheikh, N. & Ouimet, M. (2004, June 14–16). *Radical innovations in traditional manufacturing industries.* Paper presented on the DRUID Summer Conference 2004 on industrial dynamics, innovation and development, Helsingør, Denmark. Retrieved from https://www.researchgate.net/publication/228789585

American Chemical Society (2019), *Public policy statement climate change* (2019–2022). Retrieved from https://www.acs.org/content/dam/acsorg/policy/publicpolicies/sustainability/globalclimatechange/climate-change.pdf

Anastas, P. T. & Kirchhoff, M. M. (2002). Origins, current status, and future challenges of green chemistry. *Accounts of Chemical Research 35*(9), 686–694.

Anastassiadis, S. G. (2016). Carbon sources for biomass, food, fossils, biofuels and biotechnology – review article. *World Journal of Biology and Biotechnology, 1*(1), 1–32.

Appunn, K. (2021, July 7). *German government and industry agree vision for greening chemicals industry.* Retrieved from https://www.cleanenergywire.org/news/german-government-and-industry-agree-vision-greening-chemicals-industry

Armstrong, J. S. & Green, K. C. (2012). Effects of corporate social responsibility and irresponsibility policies. *MPRA paper no. 43007*, posted 04 December 2012 17:19 UTC. Retrieved from https://mpra.ub.uni-muenchen.de/43007/1/MPRA_paper_43007.pdf

Arpan, L., Chen, C.-F. & Xu, X. (2017). Between the technology acceptance model and sustainable energy technology acceptance model: Investigating smart meter acceptance in the United States. *Energy Research & Social Science 25*, 93–104.

Antonak, R. F. & Livneh, H. (1995). Direct and indirect methods to measure attitudes toward persons with disabilities, with an exegesis of the error-choice test method. *Rehabilitation Psychology 40*(1), 3–24.

Australian Government (2018). *Australia's HFC phase-down. Department of the Environment and Energy, 2018.* https://www.environment.gov.au/system/files/resources/e36dd736-b747-47ee-9e7f-10b12e016549/files/hfc-phase-down-factsheet.pdf

Arrasvuori, J., Liang, L. & Kuusisto, K. (2014, November 14–17). *Management of confidential business information and trade secrets: Findings of an international survey.* Proceedings of the 11th International Conference on Innovation and Management (ICIM 2014), Vaasa, Finland. Retrieved from https://www.researchgate.net/publication/300088044

B2B International (2021). *What is the value proposition canvas? Talk to the research experts.* Retrieved from https://www.b2binternational.com/research/methods/faq/what-is-the-value-proposition-canvas/

Bataille, C., Åhman, M., Neuhoff, K., Nilsson, L. J., Fischedick, M. Lechtenböhmer, S., … Rahbar, S. (2018). A review of technology and policy deep decarbonization pathway options. *Journal of Cleaner Production 187*(2018), 960–973. https://doi.org/10.1016/j.jclepro.2018.03.107

Bailey, J. (2008). First steps in qualitative data analysis: Transcribing. *Family Practice 25*(2), 127–131.

Barringer, B. R., & Ireland, R. D. (2010). *Entrepreneurship* (3rd ed.). Upper Saddle River, N.J.: Pearson Education.

Bass, F. M. (1969). A new product growth for model consumer durables. *Management Science 15*(5), 215–227.

Battisti, G. & Stoneman, P. (1998). The diffusion of unleaded petrol: An Anglo-Italian comparison. *Labour* 12(2), 255–278.

Bauer, F. & Fuenfschilling, L. (2019). Local initiatives and global regimes – multi-scalar transition dynamics in the chemical industry. *Journal of Cleaner Production 216*(2019), 172–183.

Bazzanella, M. & Ausfelder, F. (2017). *Low carbon energy and feedstock for the European chemical industry.* Frankfurt am Main, Germany: DECHEMA e.V.

Belin, J., Horbach, J. & Oltra, V. (2011). Determinants and specificities of eco-innovations – An econometric analysis for the French and German industry based on the Community innovation survey. *Cahiers du GREThA no. 2011–17.* Pessac, France: Université Montesquieu Bordeaux IV.

Bengtsson, M. (2016). How to plan and perform a qualitative study using content analysis. *Nursing Plus Open 2*(2016), 8–14.

Bergek, A., Berggren, C. Magnusson, T. & Hobday, M. (2013). Technological discontinuities and the challenge for incumbent firms: Destruction, disruption or creative accumulation? *Research Policy 42*(6-7), 1210–1224.

Bergek, A. & Berggren, C. (2014). The impact of environmental policy instruments on innovation: A review of energy and automotive industry studies. *Ecological Economics 106*(2014), 112–123.

Bergek, A., Hekkert, M. & Jacobsson, S. (2008). Chapter 4. Functions in innovation systems: A framework for analysing energy dynamics and identifying goals for system-building activities by entrepreneurs and policymakers. In Foxon, T., Köhler, J. & Oughton, C. (Eds.). *Innovation do a low carbon economy: Economic, institutional and management approaches.* Northampton, MA, USA: Edward Elgar.

Bergek, A., Hekkert, M., Jacobsson, S., Markard, J., Sanden, B. & Truffer, B. (2015). Technological innovation systems in contexts: Conceptualizing structures and interaction dynamics. *Environmental Innovation and Societal Transitions 16*(2015), 51–64.

Bergek, A., Jacobsson, S., Carlsson, B., Lindmark, S. & Rickne, A. (2008). Analyzing the functional dynamics of technological innovation systems: A scheme of analysis. *Research Policy 37*(2008), 407–429.

Berkhout G. (2020). *Computer models not ready for policy making. There is no climate emergency.* Retrieved from https://www.newswire.ca/news-releases/no-climate-emergency-says-nasa-award-winning-climate-scientist-climate-activists-undermine-your-freedoms-says-investigative-journalist-845177826.html

Bhartia, U. S. (2020). *We believe in green.* Retrieved from http://www.indiaglycols.com/aboutus/note_from_the_chairman.htm

Billen, P., Maes, B., Larrain, M. & Braet, J. (2020). Replacing SF6 in electrical gas-insulated switchgear: Technological alternatives and potential life cycle greenhouse gas savings in an EU-28 perspective. *Energies 13*(2020), 1807. https://doi.org/10.3390/en13071807

Binz, C., Gosens, J., Hansen, T. & Hansen, U. E. (2017). Toward technology-sensitive catching-up policies: Insights from renewable energy in China. *World Development 96*(2017), 418–437.

Binz, C. & Hipp, A. (2020). Firm survival in complex value chains and global innovation systems: Evidence from solar photovoltaics. *Research Policy 49*(2020), 103876.

Binz, C. & Truffer, B. (2017). Global innovation systems – a conceptual framework for innovation dynamics in transnational contexts. *Research Policy 46*(2017), 1284–1298.

Bioplastics News (2018 May 07). *BioAmber is bankrupt* [Bloc Post]. Retrieved from https://bioplasticsnews.com/2018/05/07/bioamber-is-bankrupt/

Bissinger, K., Brandi, C., Cabrera de Leicht, S., Fiorini, M., Schleifer, P., Fernandez de Cordova, S., Ahmed, N. (2020). *Linking voluntary standards to sustainable development goals.* Geneva, Switzerland: International Trade Centre.

Biswas, A. (2016). A study of consumers' willingness to pay for green products. *Journal of Advanced Management Science 4*(3), 211–215.

Blaauw, R., van Haveren, J., Scott E. L & Bos, H. L, (2008). *Biomass for the Dutch chemical industry. Opportunities for agriculture.* Wageningen, The Netherlands: Wageningen University, Agrotechnology and Food Sciences Group.

BMU (2018). *GreenTech made in Germany 2018.* Berlin, Germany: Federal Ministry for the Environment, Nature Conservation and Nuclear Safety (BMU).

Bokhove, C. & Downey, C. (2018). Automated generation of 'good enough' transcripts as a first step to transcription of audio-recorded data. *Methodological Innovations May-August* (2018), 1–14. https://doi.org/10.1177/2059799118790743

Börner, J., Bröring, S. & Laibach, N. (2019). Exploring the future of the bioeconomy: An expert-based scoping study examining key enabling technology fields with potential to foster the transition toward a bio-based economy. *Technology in Society 58*(2019), 101118.

Bolderston, A. (2012). Conducting a research interview. *Journal of Medical Imaging and Radiation Sciences 43*(2012), 66–76.

Bond Jr., C. F., Krosnick, J. A., Ostrom, T. M. & Sedikides, C. (1994). Attitude scales. How we measure the unmeasurable. In Shavitt, S. & Brook, T. C. (Eds.), *Persuasion: Psychological insights and perspectives.* Boston, MA: Allyn and Bacon.

Boon, W. & Edler, J. (2018). Demand, challenges, and innovation. Making sense of new trends in innovation policy. *Science and Public Policy, Oxford University Press 45*(4), 435–447.

Boons, F. & Lüdeke-Freund, F. (2013). Business models for sustainable innovation: State-of-the-art and steps towards a research agenda. *Journal of Cleaner Production 45*(2013), 9–19.

Boulamanti, A. & Moya, J. A. (2017). *Energy efficiency and GHG emissions: Prospective scenarios for the chemical and petrochemical industry*. EUR 28471 EN. https://doi.org/10.2760/20486

Bowen, G. A. (2009). Document analysis as a qualitative research method. *Qualitative Research Journal 9*(2), 27–40. https://doi.org/10.3316/QRJ0902027

Bray, D. & von Storch, H. (2016). *The Bray and von Storch 5th international survey of climate scientists 2015/2016*. Geesthacht, Germany: Helmholtz-Zentrum Geesthacht, Zentrum für Material- und Küstenforschung GmbH

Briganti, S. (2019). How to drive a culture of innovation. Leadership excellence. *Harvard Business Review 2*(2019), 32–35.

Broekhoff, D., Gillenwater, M., Colbert-Sangree, T. & Cage, P. (2019). *Securing Climate benefit: A guide to using carbon offsets* [Brochure]. (November 13, 2019). Retrieved from http://www.offsetguide.org/wp-content/uploads/2020/03/Carbon-Offset-Guide_3122020.pdf

Bröring, S., Golembiewski, B. & Sick, N. (2015). The emerging research landscape on bioeconomy: What has been done so far and what is essential from a technology and innovation management perspective? *Innovative Food Science and Emerging Technologies 29*(2015), 308–317.

Brudermüller, M. (2020). *How to build a more climate-friendly chemical industry: World Economic Forum Annual Meeting, 21.01.2020*. Retrieved from https://www.weforum.org/agenda/2020/01/how-to-build-a-more-climate-friendly-chemical-industry/

Brulle, R. (2018, June 19). 30 years ago global warming became front-page news – and both Republicans and Democrats took it seriously. *The Conversation*. Retrieved from https://www.nationalgeographic.com/magazine/article/embark-essay-climate-change-pollution-revkin

Bundesanzeiger (2014). *Energiepark Süptitz GmbH Dreiheide OT Süptitz. Jahresabschluss zum Geschäftsjahr vom 01.01.2012 bis zum 31.12.2012 Lagebericht*. Retrieved from https://www.bundesanzeiger.de/ebanzwww/wexsservlet?session.sessionid=b449a07d1f2f126b5fce3bcae21ffb47&page.navid=detailsearchdetailtodetailsearchdetailprint&fts_search_list.destHistoryId=12851&fts_search_list.selected=4316b2ca4c32f774

Bundesanzeiger (2019). *Energiepark Abwicklungs GmbH (vormals: Energiepark Süptitz GmbH), Dreiheide OT Süptitz. Jahresabschluss zum Geschäftsjahr vom 01.01.2013 bis zum 29.04.2013*. Retrieved from https://www.bundesanzeiger.de/ebanzwww/wexsservlet?session.sessionid=b449a07d1f2f126b5fce3bcae21ffb47&page.navid=detailsearchdetailtodetailsearchdetailprint&fts_search_list.destHistoryId=12851&fts_search_list.selected=de3149081f4453a9

Bunsom, T., Keyuravong, S. & Vidhayasai, T. (2015). Investigating the use of Google Translate in "terms and conditions" in an airline's official website: Errors and implications. *The PASAA Journal 49*(January – June 2015), 137–169.

Busch, T. & Judick, L. (2021). Climate change – that is not real! A comparative analysis of climate-sceptic thinktanks in the USA and Germany. *Climatic Change, 164*(2021), 1–18. https://doi.org/10.1007/s10584-021-02962-z

Cadle J., Paul D. & Turner, P. (2014). *Business analysis techniques. 99 essential tools for success.* Swindon, UK: BCS The Chartered Institute for IT.

Cainelli, G., d'Amato, A. & Mazzanti, M. (2020). Resource efficient eco-innovations for a circular economy: Evidence from EU. *Research Policy 49*(2020), 103827.

Cainelli, G., de Marchi, V. & Grandinetti, R. (2015). Does the development of environmental innovation require different resources? Evidence from Spanish manufacturing firms. *Journal of Cleaner Production 94*(2015), 211–220.

Cacioppo J. T. & Petty R. E. (1986). The elaboration likelihood model of persuasion. In Berkowitz, L. (Ed.), *Advances in experimental social psychology, vol. 19* (1st ed., pp. 123–205). Amsterdam, Netherlands: Academic Press, Elsevier.

Carus, M., Dammer, L., Dietrich, F., Krause, L., Raschka, A., Ruiz, P. & Skoczinski, P. (2020). *Chemical recycling – status, trends, and challenges,* (November 2020). Hürth, Germany: Nova-Institute GmbH, Chemiepark Knapsack, Industriestraße 300, 50354 Hürth. Retrieved from www.bio-based.eu/reports

Carus, M., Dammer, L., Puente, A., Raschka, A. & Arendt, O. (2017). *Bio-based drop-in, smart drop-in and dedicated chemicals.* Retrieved from https://www.roadtobio.eu/uploads/news/2017_October/RoadToBio_Drop-in_paper.pdf

Carus, M., Kähler, F., Porc, O. & vom Berg, C. (2021). *Turning off the tap for fossil carbon. Future prospects for a global chemical and derived material sector based on renewable carbon.* (April 2021). Hürth, Germany: Nova-Institute GmbH, Chemiepark Knapsack, Industriestraße 300, 50354 Hürth. Retrieved from https://renewable-carbon.eu/publications/product/turning-off-the-tap-for-fossil-carbon-future-prospects-for-a-global-chemical-and-derived-material-sector-based-on-renewable-carbon/

CDP (2019). *Scoring methodology.* Retrieved from https://www.cdp.net/en/cities/cities-scores/scoring-methodology

CDP (2021). *Transparency to the transformation: A chain reaction. CDP global supply chain report 2020* [Brochure]. New York, NY: CDP North America, Inc.

CEFIC (2013). *European chemistry for growth. Unlocking a competitive, low carbon and energy efficient future* (April 2013). Brussels, Belgium: Cefic aisbl.

CEFIC (2019). *Statues. Update 1 January 2019.* Brussels, Belgium: European Chemical Industry Council - Cefic aisbl. Retrieved from https://cefic.org/app/uploads/2019/01/Cefic_Statutes.pdf

CEFIC (2020). *The European chemical industry: Facts and figures 2021. A vital part of Europe's future, January 2020* [Presentation]. Brussels, Belgium: The European Chemical Industry Council, AISBL. Retrieved from https://cefic.org/a-pillar-of-the-european-economy/facts-and-figures-of-the-european-chemical-industry/

CEFIC (2021a). *The European chemical industry: A vital part of Europe's future. Facts & figures 2021.* Brussels, Belgium: European Chemical Industry Council - Cefic aisbl.

CEFIC (2021b). *Methane emissions in the chemical industry. CEFIC Paper March 2021.* Brussels, Belgium: European Chemical Industry Council - Cefic aisbl. Retrieved from https://cefic.org/app/uploads/2021/03/Methane-emissions-in-the-chemical-industry-March-2021.pdf

CEFIC (2021c). *List of Cefic sector groups. Published February 2021.* Brussels, Belgium: European Chemical Industry Council - Cefic aisbl. Retrieved from https://cefic.org/app/uploads/2021/02/List-of-Cefic-Sector-groups-February-2021.pdf

CEFIC (2021d). *Organization. Industry sectors and Cefic sector groups.* Brussels, Belgium: European Chemical Industry Council - Cefic aisbl. Retrieved from https://cefic.org/about-us/organization/cefic-sector-groups/

CEFIC (2021e). *List of corporate members (ACOM). January 2021.* Brussels, Belgium: European Chemical Industry Council - Cefic aisbl. Retrieved from https://cefic.org/app/uploads/2021/01/ACOM-Public-Website-January-2021.pdf

Centi, G., Iaquaniello, G. & Perathoner, S. (2019). Chemical engineering role in the use of renewable energy and alternative carbon sources in chemical production. *BMC Chemical Engineering, 1*(5), 1–16. https://doi.org/10.1186/s42480-019-0006-8

Chan, H. K., Dai, J., Lim, M. K. & Yee, R. W. Y. (2016). The moderating effect of environmental dynamism on green product innovation and performance. *International Journal of Production Economics 181*(2016), 384–391.

Cheng, C. C. J., Yang, C.-L. & Sheu, C. (2014). The link between eco-innovation and business performance: A Taiwanese industry context. *Journal of Cleaner Production 64*(2014), 81–90.

Chesbrough, H. (2003). *Open innovation, the new imperative for creating and profiting from technology.* Boston, MA: Harvard Business School Press.

Chesbrough, H., Gassmann, O. & Enkel, E. (2010). The future of open innovation. *R&D Management 40*(3), 213–221.

Chesbrough, H., Salter, A., Vanhaverbeke, W., & Westa, J. (2014). Open innovation: The next decade. *Research Policy 43*(2014), 805–811.

Christensen, C. M. (1992). Exploring the limits of the technology S-curve. Part I: Component technologies. *Production and Operations Management 1*(4), 334–357.

Christensen, C. M. (1997). *The innovator's dilemma. When new technologies cause great firms to fail.* Boston, MA: Harvard Business School Press.

Christensen, C. M. & Overdorf, M. (2000). Meeting the challenge. *Harvard Business Review 78*(2), 66–76.

Christoff, P. (2013). Climate discourse complexes, National climate regimes and Australian climate policy. *Australian Journal of Politics and History 59*(3), 349–367.

Coast, J., Al-Janabi, H., Sutton, E. J., Horrocks, S. A., Vosper, A.; Swancutt, D. R. & Flynn, T. N. (2012). Using qualitative methods for attribute development for discrete choice experiments: Issues and recommendations. *Health Economics 21*(2012), 730–741.

Collantes, G. & Sperling, D. (2008). The origin of California's zero emission vehicle mandate. *Transportation Research Part A 42*(2008), 1302–1313.

Cook, J., Oreskes, N., Doran, P. T., Anderegg, W.R.L, Verheggen, B., Maibach, E. W., … Rice. K. (2016). Consensus on consensus: a synthesis of consensus estimates on human-caused global warming. *Environ. Res. Lett., 11*(2016), 048002.

Cook, P. & Stevenson, S. (2010). Automatically identifying changes in the semantic orientation of words. In Calzolari, N., Choukri, K., Maegaard, B., Mariani, J., Odijk, J., Piperidis, S., Rosner, M. & Tapias, D. (Eds.), *Proceedings of the seventh international conference on language resources and evaluation (LREC'10)* (pp. 28–34). Valletta, Malta: European Language Resources Association (ELRA).

Cooper, R. G. (1990). Stage-Gate Systems: A new tool for managing new products. *Business Horizons 33*(3), 44–54.

*Council Directive 73/404/EEC of 22 November 1973 on the approximation of the laws of the member states relating to detergents.* Brussels, Belgium: Official Journal of the European Communities

*Council Directive 79/117/EEC of 21 December 1978 prohibiting the placing on the market and use of plant protection products containing certain active substances.* Brussels, Belgium: Official Journal of the European Communities

Creswell, J. W. (2015). *Educational research. Planning, conducting, and evaluating quantitative and qualitative research (5th ed.).* Upper Saddle River, New Jersey: Pearson Education, Inc.

Damanpour, F. (1991). Organizational Innovation: A meta-analysis of effects of determinants and moderators. *Academy of Management Journal 34*(3), 555–590.

Damanpour, F. & Schneider, M. (2006). Phases of the adoption of innovation in organizations: effects of environment, organization and top managers. *British Journal of Management 17*(2006), 215–236.

Davidson, P. M. & Halcomb, E. J. (2006). Is verbatim transcription of interview data always necessary? *Applied Nursing Research 19*(2006), 38–42.

Davis, F.D. (1985). *A Technology Acceptance Model for empirically testing new end-user information systems* (Doctoral dissertation). Massachusetts Institute of Technology, Cambridge, MA.

Davis, F.D. (1989). Perceived usefulness, perceived ease of use and user acceptance of information technology. *MIS Quarterly/September 1989*, 319–340.

De Graaff, M. (2015). *Electrification of chemical industry. An opportunity for chemical and electricity sector.* Delft, The Netherlands: TNO Sustainable Chemical Industry.

Delmas, M. A., Nairn-Birch, N. & Balzarova, M. (2013). Choosing the right eco-label for your product. *MIT Sloan Management Review SUMMER 2013, 54*(4), 10–11.

Deloitte (2017). *Chemistry 4.0 Growth through innovation in a transforming world* (September 2017). Retrieved from https://www.vci.de/vci/downloads-vci/publikation/vci-deloitte-study-chemistry-4-dot-0-short-version.pdf

Depoers, F., Jeanjean, T. & Jérôme, T. (2016). Voluntary disclosure of greenhouse gas emissions: Contrasting the carbon disclosure project and corporate reports. *Journal of Business Ethics 134*(2016), 445–461.

DG Communication (2019). *2019 Parlementer – focus on climate change.* Retrieved from https://www.europarl.europa.eu/resources/library/media/20191129RES67708/20191129RES67708.pdf

Dilling, L. & Moser, S. C. (2004). Making climate hot. *Environment, 12*(46), 32–46.

DIN, (2020). *About standard. A brief introduction to standards.* DIN Deutsches Institut für Normung e. V. Retrieved from https://www.din.de/en/about-standards/a-brief-introduction-to-standards

*Directive (EU) 2018/2001 of the European Parliament and the Council of 11 December 2018 on the promotion of the use of energy from renewable sources.* Brussel, Belgium: Official Journal of the European Union.

*Directive (EU) 2019/904 of the European Parliament and the Council of 5 June 2019 on the reduction of the impact of certain plastic products on the environment.* Brussel, Belgium: Official Journal of the European Union.

Dosi, G. (1982). Technological paradigms and technological trajectories. *Research Policy 11*(3), 147–162.

Dundon, E. (2002). *The seeds of innovation.* New York, NY: Amacom.

Eckholm, B. & Rockström, J. (2019). Digital technology can cut global emissions by 15 Percent. *World economic forum annual meeting 22—25 January 2019.* Retrieved from https://www.weforum.org/agenda/2019/01/why-digitalization-is-the-key-to-exponential-climate-action/

EEG (2000). *Gesetz für den Vorrang Erneuerbarer Energien (Erneuerbare-Energien-Gesetz – EEG) sowie zur Änderung des Energiewirtschaftsgesetzes und des Mineralölsteuergesetzes vom 29. März 2000.* Retrieved from https://www.bgbl.de/xaver/bgbl/start.xav?start=%2F%2F*%5B%40attr_id%3D%27bgbl100s0305.pdf%27%5D#__bgbl__%2F%2F*%5B%40attr_id%3D%27bgbl100s0305.pdf%27%5D__1628584946647

Eisenstadt, S. N. (1966). *Modernization, protest and change.* Eaglewood Cliffs, N.J.: Prentice-Hall.

Elgin, B. (2020, December 9). These trees are not what they seem. *Bloomberg Green.* Retrieved from https://www.bloomberg.com/features/2020-nature-conservancy-carbon-offsets-trees/

Elkington, J. (1998). Partnerships from cannibals with forks: The triple bottom line of 21st century business. *Environmental Quality Management* (1998 Autumn), 37–51.

Elkington, J. (2018, June 25). *25 Years ago I coined the phrase "triple bottom line." Here's why it's time to rethink it.* Harvard Busines Review. Retrieved from https://hbr.org/2018/06/25-years-ago-i-coined-the-phrase-triple-bottom-line-heres-why-im-giving-up-on-it

Energias Market Research (2019, March 06). *Global bio-based feedstock market to witness a CAGR of 3.11% during 2018–2024.* Retrieved from https://www.globenewswire.com/news-release/2019/03/06/1748711/0/en/Global-Bio-based-Feedstock-Market-to-witness-a-CAGR-of-3-11-during-2018-2024.html

Enzensberger, N., Wietschel, M. & Rentz, O. (2002). Policy instruments fostering wind energy projects a multi-perspective evaluation approach. *Energy Policy 30*(2002), 793–801.

Erhard, J., Kubis, C., Krebs, J.-M. & Liedke, A. (2019). *Discussion paper. Overcoming barriers for corporate Scope 3 action in supply chain.* Berlin, Germany: WWF Germany, Reinhardtsraße 18, 10117 Berlin.

Erikson, C. (2004). Can green consumerism replace environmental regulation? – A differentiated-products example. *Resource and Energy Economics 2004*(26), 281–293.

Erlingsson, C. & Brysiewicz, P. (2017). A hands-on guide to doing content analysis. *African Journal of Emergency Medicine 7*(2017), 93–99.

*Erneuerbare-Energien-Gesetz – EEG (2000). Gesetz für den Vorrang erneuerbarer Energien sowie zur Änderung des Energiewirtschaftsgesetzes und des Mineralölsteuergesetzes vom 29. März 2000.* Bonn, Germany: Bundesgesetzblatt Jahrgang 2000 Teil I Nr. 13, ausgegeben zu Bonn 31. März 2000

European Commission (2019). *Communication from the Commission to the European Parliament, the European Council, the European Economic and Social Committee and the Committee of the Regions – The European Green Deal, 11.12.2019.* Brussels, Belgium: European Commission.

European Commission (2020). *Report from the Commission assessing the availability of alternatives to fluorinated greenhouse gases in switchgear and related equipment, including medium-voltage secondary switchgear. Document C(2020) 6635 final dd. 30.9.2020.* Brussels, Belgium: European Commission

European Commission (2021, July 14). *Proposal for a Regulation of the European Parliament and the Council on the deployment of alternative fuels infrastructure, and repealing Directive 2014/94/EU of the European Parliament and of the Council. COM(2021) 559 final.* Brussels, Belgium: European Commission.

European Commission (2021a). *Causes of climate change.* Retrieved from https://ec.europa.eu/clima/change/causes_en

European Commission (2021b). *Renewable energy targets* (17.08.2021). Retrieved from https://ec.europa.eu/energy/topics/renewable-energy/directive-targets-and-rules/renewable-energy-targets_en

European Communities (2008). *Eurostat NACE Rev. 2 – Statistical classification of economic activities in the European Community.* Luxembourg, Luxembourg: Eurostat. Retrieved from https://ec.europa.eu/eurostat/documents/3859598/5902521/KS-RA-07-015-EN.PDF

*European Directive 2009/28/EC of the European Parliament and the Council on the promotion of the use of energy from renewable sources and amending and subsequently repealing Directives 2001/77/EC and 2003/30/EC of 23 April 2009.* Brussel, Belgium: Official Journal of the European Union.

European Environment Agency (2020). *Annual European Union greenhouse gas inventory 1990–2018 and inventory report 2020* (27 May 2020). Brussels, Belgium: European Commission. Retrieved from https://www.eea.europa.eu/publications/european-union-greenhouse-gas-inventory-2020

EEA (2021). *Trends in atmospheric concentrations of CO2 (ppm).* Copenhagen, Denmark: European Environmental Agency. Retrieved from https://www.eea.europa.eu/data-and-maps/daviz/atmospheric-concentration-of-carbon-dioxide-5#tab-chart_5_filters=%7B%22rowFilters%22%3A%7B%7D%3B%22columnFilters%22%3A%7B%22pre_config_polutant%22%3A%5B%22CH4%20(ppb)%22%5D%7D%7D

EPA (2021a). *Global greenhouse gas emissions data* (July 27, 2021). Retrieved from https://www.epa.gov/ghgemissions/overview-greenhouse-gases

EPA (2021b). *Overview of greenhouse gases* (July 27, 2021). Retrieved from https://www.epa.gov/ghgemissions/overview-greenhouse-gases

Falcone, P. M. & Hiete, M. (2019). Exploring green and sustainable chemistry in the context of sustainability transition: The role of visions and policy. *Current Opinion in Green and Sustainable Chemistry 19*(2019), 66–75.

Fang, W.-T., Ng, E., Wang, C.-M. & Hsu, M.-L. (2017). Normative beliefs, attitudes, and social norms: People reduce waste as an index of social relationships when spending leisure time. *Sustainability 9*(2017), 1696. https://doi.org/10.3390/su9101696

Farla, J., Markard, J., Raven, R. & Coenen, L. (2012). Sustainability transitions in the making: A closer look at actors, strategies and resources. *Technological Forecasting & Social Change 79*(2012), 991–998.

Fath, B. D., Dean, C. A. & Katzmair, H. (2015). Navigating the adaptive cycle: An approach to managing the resilience of social systems. *Ecology and Society 20*(2), 24. https://doi.org/10.5751/ES-07467-200224

Fawzy, S., Osman, A., Doran, J. & Rooney, D. W. (2020). Strategies for mitigation of climate change: A review. *Environmental Chemistry Letters 18*(2020), 2069–2094. https://doi.org/10.1007/s10311-020-01059-w

Fischedick, M., Roy, J., Abdel-Aziz, A., Acquaye, A., Allwood, J. M., Ceron, J-P., … Tanaka, K. (2014). Chapter 10. Industry. In Edenhofer, O., Pichs-Madruga, R., Sokona, Y., Farahani, E., Kadner, S., Seyboth, K., … Minx, J. C. (Eds.), *Climate change 2014: Mitigation of climate change. Contribution of working group III to the fifth assessment report of the Intergovernmental Panel on Climate Change* (pp. 739–810). Cambridge, United Kingdom and New York, NY, USA: Cambridge University Press.

Fischer, A. R. H. (2017). Perception, attitudes, intentions, decisions and actual behavior. In Emilien, G., Lüdicke. F. & Weitkunat, R. (Eds.). *Consumer perception of product risks and benefits* (pp. 303–318). Cham, Switzerland: Springer International Publishing AG.

Fishbein, M. & Ajzen, I. (1975). *Belief, attitude, intention and behaviour: An introduction to theory and research.* Reading, MA: Addison-Wesley.

Fishbein, M. & Ajzen, I. (2010). *Predicting and changing behavior – the reasoned action approach.* New York, NY: Psychology Press, Taylor & Francis Group.

Flatworld Solutions Pvt. Ltd. (2020). *Importance of proofreading in translation and transcription business.* Retrieved from https://www.flatworldsolutions.com/translation/articles/importance-of-proofreading-in-translation.php

Fobbe, L. (2020). Analysing organisational collaboration practices for sustainability. *Sustainability 2020*(12), 2466. https://doi.org/10.3390/su12062466

Form 8-K (2018, May 4). *Current report, Bioamber Inc.* Washington, DC: United States Securities and Exchange Commission. Retrieve from https://www.sec.gov/Archives/edgar/data/1534287/000119312518156001/d582086d8k.htm

Fradette, L., Lefebvre, S. & Carley, J. (2017). Demonstration results of enzyme-accelerated CO2 capture. *Energy Procedia 114*(2017), 1100–1109.

Frank, M.W. (1998). Schumpeter on entrepreneurs and innovation: A reappraisal. *Journal of the History of Economic Thought*, *20*(4), 505–515.

Frantzeskaki, N. & Loorbach, D. (2010). Towards governing infrasystem transitions. Reinforcing lock-in or facilitating change? *Technological Forecasting & Social Change 77*(2010), 1292–1301.

Freeman, C. (1995). The 'national system of innovation' in historical perspective. *Cambridge Journal of Economics 19*(1995), 5–24.

Freeman, C. & Soete, L. (1994). *The economics of industrial innovation* (3rd ed.). Oxon, United Kingdom: Routledge.

Freeman, C. & Soete, L. (2009). Developing science, technology and innovation indicators: What we can learn from the past. *Research Policy 38*(2009), 583–589.

Friedlingstein, P., O'Sullivan, M., Jones, M. W., Andrew, R. M., Hauck, J., Olsen, A., … Zaehle, S. (2020). Global carbon budget 2020. *Earth Syst. Sci. Data, 12*(2020), 3269–3340. https://doi.org/10.5194/essd-12-3269-2020

García-Granero, E. M., Piedra-Munoz. L. & Galdeano-Gomez, E. (2018). Eco-innovation measurement: A review of firm performance indicators. *Journal of Cleaner Production 191*(2018), 304–317.

Garside, M. (2021). *Chemical industry greenhouse gas emissions in the EU 1990–2018. Published Jan 8, 2021.* Retrieved from https://www.statista.com/statistics/536106/european-union-chemical-industry-greenhouse-gas-emissions/

Geels, F. W. (2002). Technological transitions as evolutionary reconfiguration processes: A multi-level perspective and a case-study. *Research Policy 31*(2002), 1257–1274
Geels, F. W. (2005a). Co-evolution of technology and society: The transition in water supply and personal hygiene in the Netherlands (1850–1930) – a case study in multi-level perspective. *Technology in Society 27*(2005), 363–397.
Geels, F. W. (2005b). The dynamics of transitions in socio-technical systems: A multi-level analysis of the transition pathway from horse-drawn carriages to automobiles (1860–1930). *Technology Analysis & Strategic Management 17*(4), 445–476.
Geels, F. W. (2006). Co-evolutionary and multi-level dynamics in transitions: The transformation of aviation systems and the shift from propeller to turbojet (1930–1970). *Technovation 26*(2006), 999–1016.
Geels, F. W. (2011). The multi-level perspective on sustainability transitions: Responses to seven criticisms. *Environmental Innovation and Societal Transitions 1*(2011), 24–40.
Geels, F. W. (2014). Regime resistance against low-carbon transitions: introducing politics and power into the multi-level perspective. *Theory, Culture & Society 31*(5), 21–40.
Geels, F. W. (2018). Disruption and low-carbon system transformation: Progress and new challenges in socio-technical transitions research and the multi-level perspective. *Energy Research & Social Science 37*(2018), 224–231.
Geels, F. W. (2019). Socio-technical transitions to sustainability: A review of criticisms and elaborations of the multi-level perspective. *Current Opinion in Environmental Sustainability 39*(2019), 187–201.
Geels, F. W., Kern, F., Fuchs, G., Hinderer, N., Kungl, G., Mylana,J., Neukirch, M. & Wassermann, S. (2016). The enactment of socio-technical transition pathways: A reformulated typology and a comparative multi-level analysis of the German and UK low-carbon electricity transitions (1990–2014). *Research Policy 45* (2016), 896–913.
Geels, F. W., Pfluger, B. & Rogge, K. S. (2020). Transformative policy mixes in socio-technical scenarios: The case of the low-carbon transition of the German electricity system (2010–2050). *Technological Forecasting & Social Change 151* (2020), 119259.
Geels, F. W. & Schot, J. (2007). Typology of sociotechnical transition pathways. *Research Policy 36*(2007), 399–417.
Geels, F. W., Sovacool, B. J., Schwanen, T. & Sorrell, S. (2017). Sociotechnical transitions for deep decarbonization. *Science 357*(6357), 1242–1244. https://doi.org/10.1126/science.aao3760
Ghisetti, C. & Rennings, K. (2014). Environmental innovations and profitability: How does it pay to be green? An empirical analysis on the German innovation survey. *Journal of Cleaner Production 75*(2014), 106–117.
Gibbs, D. (1988). Ecological Modernisation: a basis for regional development? In *partnership and leadership: Building alliances for a sustainable future*. Proceedings of the 7th international conference of the greening of industry network, Rome 15–18 November 1998. Rome, Italy.
Gil, B., Szczepanowska, A. & Rosiek, S. (2021). New HFC/HFO blends as refrigerants for the vapor-compression refrigeration system (VCRS). *Energies, 14*(2021), 946. https://doi.org/10.3390/en14040946
Gleim, M. R., Smith, J. S., Andrews, D. & Cronin, J. J. (2017). Against the green: A multi-method examination of the barriers to green consumption. *Journal of Retailing 89*(2013), 1, 44–61.

Global Voices Ltd (2020). *What is the difference between editing and proofreading in translation.* Retrieved from https://www.globalvoices.co.uk/translation-services/proofreading/difference-between-editing-and-proofreading-in-translation/

Govindarajan, V. & Kopalle, P. K. (2006). Disruptiveness of innovations: Measurement and an assessment of reliability and validity. *Strategic Management Journal 27*(2006), 189–199.

Graneheim, U. H. & Lundman, B. (2004). Qualitative content analysis in nursing research: Concepts, procedures and measures to achieve trustworthiness. *Nurse Education Today 24*(2004), 105–112.

Greenhouse Gas Protocol (2017). *Emission factors from cross sector tools March 2017. Table 1. CO2 emission factors by fuel – GHG protocol.* Washington, DC: WRI World Resources Institute. Retrieved from https://ghgprotocol.org/life-cycle-databases

Greenhouse Gas Protocol (2021). *Global warming potential values.* Retrieved from https://www.ghgprotocol.org/sites/default/files/ghgp/Global-Warming-Potential-Values%20%28Feb%2016%202016%29_1.pdf

Greenpeace. (2021, June 29). *We're living in a golden age of greenwash* [Blog post]. Retrieved from https://www.greenpeace.org.uk/news/golden-age-of-greenwash/

*GRI 305: Emissions 2016.* (2018). Amsterdam, The Netherlands: Global Reporting Initiative GRI, PO Box 10039, 1001 EA Amsterdam, The Netherlands.

Grenier, L. (2018). *How to analyze open-ended questions in 5 steps* [Blog post]. Retrieved from https://www.hotjar.com/blog/analyze-open-ended-questions/

Grin, J., Rotmans, J & Schot, J. (2010). *Transitions to sustainable developments.* New York, NY: Routledge Inc.

Gross, S. (2021). *The challenge of decarbonizing heavy industry.* Washington, DC: The Brookings Institution.

Gunderson, L. H. & Holling, C. S. (Eds.). (2002). Chapter 2 Resilience and adaptive cycles. In *Panarchy, understanding transformations in human and natural systems.* Washington, DC: Island Press.

Gunderson, L. H., Holling, C. S. & Peterson, G. D. (2002). Chapter 3 Sustainability and panarchies. In Gunderson, L. H. & Holling, C. S. (Eds.), *Panarchy, understanding transformations in human and natural systems.* Washington, DC: Island Press.

Hagger, M. S. (2019). The reasoned action approach and the theories of reasoned action and planned behavior. In Dunn, D. S. (Ed.), *Oxford bibliographies in psychology.* New York, NY: Oxford University Press. https://doi.org/10.1093/OBO/9780199828340-0240

Hahn, T. & Scheermesser, M. (2006). Approaches to corporate sustainability among German companies. *Corp. Soc. Responsib. Environ. Mgmt. 13*(3), 150–165.

Hannula, I., Kaisalo, N. & Simell, P. (2020). Preparation of synthesis gas from CO2 for Fischer-Tropsch synthesis – comparison of alternative process configurations. *Journal of Carbon Research 6*(2020), 55. https://doi.org/10.3390/c6030055

Hekkert, M. P., Suurs, R. A. A., Negro, S. O., Kuhlmann, S. & Smits, R. E. H. M. (2007). Functions of innovation systems: A new approach for analysing technological change. *Technological Forecasting & Social Change 74*(2007), 413–432.

Hellsmark, H., Mossberg, J., Söderholm, P. & Frishammar, J. (2016). Innovation system strengths and weaknesses in progressing sustainable technology: The case of Swedish biorefinery development. *Journal of Cleaner Production 131*(2016), 702–715.

Hemmelskamp, J. (1996). Environmental policy instruments and their effects on innovation. *ZEW Discussion Papers 96*(22) 1–27. Mannheim, Germany: Zentrum für Europäische Wirtschaftsforschung (ZEW).

Hilbers, T. J., Sprakel, L. M. J., van den Enk, L. B. J., Zaalberg, B., van den Berg, H. & van der Ham, L. G. J. (2015). Green diesel from hydrotreated vegetable oil process design study. *Chem. Eng. Technol., 38*(4), 651–657.

Hill, C. W. & Rothaermel, F. T. (2003). The performance of incumbent firms in the face of radical technological innovation. *Academy of Management Review 28*(2), 257–274.

Hirsch, R.D., Peters, M.P., & Shepherd, D.A. (2010). *Entrepreneurship* ($8^{th}$ ed.). New York, NY: McGraw-Hill/Irwin.

Hoff, P. H. (2012). *Greentech innovation and diffusion, Doctoral Thesis.* St. Gallen, Switzerland: University of St. Gallen.

Hojnik, J., Ruzzier, M. & Konecnik Ruzzier, M. (2019). Transition towards sustainability: Adoption of eco-products among consumers. *Sustainability 11*(2019), 4308. https://doi.org/10.3390/su11164308

Holt, A. (2010). Using the telephone for narrative interviewing: A research note. *Qualitative Research 10*(1), 113–121.

Hoogstraaten, M. J., Frenken, K. & Boon, W.P.C. (2020). The study of institutional entrepreneurship and its implications for transition studies. *Environmental Innovation and Societal Transitions 36*(2020), 114–136.

Hoppmann, J. (2018). The role of interfirm knowledge spillovers for innovation in mass-produced environmental technologies: Evidence from the solar photovoltaic industry. *Organization & Environment, 31*(1), 3–24.

Horbach, J. (2016). Empirical determinants of eco-innovation in European countries using the community innovation survey. *Environmental Innovation and Societal Transitions 19*(2016), 1–14.

Horbach, J. (2020, December). The importance of regional spill-over effects for eco-innovations in German start-ups. *SEEDS Working Paper 16*(2020), 1–17.

Horbach, J. & Rennings, K. (2013). Environmental innovation and employment dynamics in different technology fields e an analysis based on the German community innovation survey 2009. *Journal of Cleaner Production 57*(2013), 158–165.

Horbach, J., Rammer, C. & Rennings, K. (2012). Determinants of eco-innovations by type of environmental impact – The role of regulatory push/pull, technology push and market pull. *Ecological Economics 78*(2012), 112–122.

Huber, J. (2000). Towards industrial ecology: Sustainable development as a concept of ecological modernization. *Journal of Environmental Policy and Planning 2*(4), 269–285.

Huizingh, E. K. R. E. (2011). Open innovation: state of the art and future perspectives. *Technovation 31*(2011), 2–9.

Huffcutt, A. I. & Culbertson, S. S. (2011). Interviews. In S. Zedeck (Ed.), *APA handbooks in psychology. APA handbook of industrial and organizational psychology, vol. 2. Selecting and developing members for the organization* (pp. 185–203). Washington, DC: American Psychological Association. https://doi.org/10.1037/12170-006

Inger, M., Moszowski, B., Ruszak, M., Rajewski, J. & Wilk, M. (2020). Two-stage catalytic abatement of N2O emission in nitric acid plants. *Catalysts, 10*(2020), 987. https://doi.org/10.3390/catal10090987

International Association of Oil & Cas Producer (2021). *Our members. Upstream member* (14.08.2021). Brussels, Belgium: International Association of Oil & Cas Producer. Retrieved from https://www.iogp.org/members/

IPCC (2021a), *History.* Retrieved from https://archive.ipcc.ch/organization/organization_history.shtml

IPCC (2021b): Summary for policymakers. In Masson-Delmotte, V., Zhai, P., Pirani, A., Connors, S. L., Péan, C., Berger, S., … Zhou, B. (Eds.), *Climate change 2021: The physical science basis. Contribution of working group I to the sixth assessment report of the Intergovernmental Panel on Climate Change* (pp. 1–41). Cambridge, United Kingdom: Cambridge University Press.

IPCC (2021c), *The Intergovernmental Panel on Climate Change.* Retrieved from https://www.ipcc.ch/

ISCC (2018). *ISCC 203, Traceability and chain of custody Version 3.1.* Cologne, Germany: ISCC System GmbH.

Jansen, J. J. P., Van Den Bosch, F. A. J. & Volberda, H. K. (2006, November). Exploratory innovation, exploitative innovation, and performance: Effects of organizational antecedents and environmental moderators. *Management Science 52*(11), 1661–1674.

Jensen, F., Schäfer, D. & Stephan, A. (2019). Financial constraints of firms with environmental innovation. *Vierteljahrshefte zur Wirtschaftsforschung 88*(3), 43–65. https://doi.org/10.3790/vjh.88.3.43

Jansson, J., Nielsson, J., Nordlund, A. & Westin, K. (2020). Goal framing as a tool for changing people's car travel behavior in Sweden. *Sustainability 12*(2020), 3695. https://doi.org/10.3390/su12093695.

Jha, K. K. & Kannan, T. T. M. (2021). Recycling of plastic waste into fuel by pyrolysis – a review. *Materials Today: Proceedings, 37*(2021), 3718–3720.

Jørgensen, R. B. & Moen, Ø. (2015). Eco labelling from the consumer perspective: A case study of indoor paint products. *Journal of Research for Consumer 2015*(7), 1–7. Retrieved from http://www.jrconsumers.com/Consumer_Articles/issue_27/

Jylhä, K. M. (2017). Denial versus reality of climate change. In Della Sala, D. A. & Goldstein, M. I. (Eds.), *Encyclopedia of the Anthropocene.* Amsterdam, Netherlands: Elsevier.

Kätelhön, A., Meys, R., Deutz, S., Suh, S. & Bardow, A. (2019). Climate change mitigation potential of carbon capture and utilization in the chemical industry. *Proceedings of the National Academy of Sciences Jun 2019, 116*(23), 11187–11194. Retrieved from https://www.pnas.org/content/pnas/116/23/11187.full.pdf

Karakaya, E., Hidalgo, A. &Nuur, C. (2014). Diffusion of eco-innovations: A review. *Renewable and Sustainable Energy Reviews 33*(2014), 392–399.

Karakaya, E. & Nevzorova, T. (2020). Explaining the drivers of technological innovation systems: The case of biogas technologies in mature markets. *Journal of Cleaner Production 259*(2020), 120819.

Keim, W. & Röper, M. (2010). *Change in the raw materials base.* Frankfurt a. M., Germany: Gesellschaft Deutscher Chemiker e.V. (GDCh) (German Chemical Society).

Kemp, R. (2003). Technology and the transition to environmental sustainability: The problem of technological regime shifts. *Futures 26*(10), 1023–1046.

Kemp, R. (2008). *Measuring eco-innovation. Research brief 1.* Maastricht, The Netherlands: United Nations University – Maastricht Economic and social Research and training center on Innovation and Technology.

Kezar, A. (2000). The importance of pilot studies: Beginning the hermeneutic circle. *Research in Higher Education 41*(3), 385–400.
Kiefer, C. P., Del Río González, P. & Carrillo-Hermosilla, J. (2019). Drivers and barriers of eco-innovation types for sustainable transitions: A quantitative perspective. *Business Strategy and the Environment 28*(1), 155–172. https://doi.org/10.1002/bse.2246
Knappich, F., Schlummer, M., Eggert, K., Wolff, F. & Agulla, K. (2017). Light at the end of the tunnel. *Kunststoffe International, 6–7*(2017), 51–54.
Koh, S. C. L., et al. (2013). Decarbonising product supply chains: Design and development of an integrated evidence-based decision support system – the supply chain environmental analysis tool (SCEnAT). *International Journal of Production Research 51*(7), 2092–2109.
Kotler, P., Wong, V., Saunders, J. & Armstrong, G. (2005). *Principles of marketing* (4th European ed.). Harlow, United Kingdom: Pearson Education.
Krikke, H., le Blanc, I. & van de Velde, S. (2004). Product modularity and the design of closed-loop supply chains. *California Management Review 46*(2), 23–39.
Krosnick, J. A., Judd, C. M. & Wittenbrink, B. (2005). The measurement of attitudes. In Albarracin, D., Johnson, B. T. & Zanna M. P. (Eds.), *The handbook of attitudes* (pp. 21–76). Mahwah, NJ: Lawrence Erlbaum Associates Publishers.
Kruglanski, A. W., Baldner, C., Chernikova, C., Destro, C. L. & Pierro, A. (2018). A new perspective on the attitude-behavior relation: The essential function of goals. *Polish Psychological Bulletin 49*(1), 31–39.
Kvale S. (1996). *Interviews: an introduction to qualitative research interviewing*. Thousand Oaks, CA: Sage Publications.
Lagarde, C. (2021, June 29). *Financing a green and digital recovery. Speech by Christine Lagarde, President of the ECB, at the Brussels economic forum 2021*. Frankfurt am Main, Germany: European Central Bank. Retrieved from https://www.ecb.europa.eu/press/key/date/2021/html/ecb.sp210629~e6458f8392.en.html
Larsen, M.D. (2002). The psychology of survey response [Review of the book Tourangeau, R., Rops, L.J. & Rasinski, K. (2000). The psychology of survey response. Cambridge, UK: Cambridge University Press]. *Journal of the American Statistical Association 97*(457), 358–359.
Latkin, C. A., Edwards, C., Davey-Rothwell, M. A. & Tobin, K. E. (2017). The relationship between social desirability bias and self-reports of health, substance use, and social network factors among urban substance users in Baltimore, Maryland. *Addictive Behaviors 73*(2017), 133–136. https://doi.org/10.1016/j.addbeh.2017.05.005
Lee, K. (2005). Making a technological catch-up: Barriers and opportunities. *Asian Journal of Technology Innovation 13*(2), 97–131.
Lee, K. & Malerba, F. (2017). Catch-up cycles and changes in industrial leadership: Windows of opportunity and responses of firms and countries in the evolution of sectoral systems. *Research Policy 46*(2017), 338–351.
Lee, R. A. & Lavoie, J.-M. (2013). From first- to third-generation biofuels: Challenges of producing a commodity from a biomass of increasing complexity. *Animal Frontiers, 3*(2), 6–11.
Lee, Y.-M. & Hu, J.-L. (2018). Integrated approaches for business sustainability: The perspective of corporate social responsibility. *Sustainability 2018*(10), 2318.

Leibowicz, B. D. (2016, November 13). Technology-push, demand-pull, and strategic R&D Investment. *INFORMS annual meeting Nashville, TN*. Retrieved from http://sites.utexas.edu/leibowicz/files/2017/02/INFORMS_16.pdf

Leone, L., Perugini, M. & Ercolania, E. P. (1999). Comparison of three models of attitude-behavior relationships in the studying behavior domain. *European Journal of Social Psychology 29*(1999), 161–189.

Leonidou, L. C., Christodoulides, P., Kyrgidou, L. P. & Palihawadana, D. (2017). Internal drivers and performance consequences of small firm green business strategy: The moderating role of external forces. *J Bus Ethics 140*(2017), 585–606.

Li, G., Zhao, M., Xu, F., Yang, B., Li, X., Meng, X., Teng, L., Sun, F, & Li, Y. (2020). Synthesis and biological application of polylactic acid. *Molecules 25*(2020), 5023. https://doi.org/10.3390/molecules25215023

Liao, Z., Xu, C.-k.,Cheng, H. & Dong, J. (2018). What drives environmental innovation? A content analysis of listed companies in China. *Journal of Cleaner Production 198*(2018), 1567–1573.

Liebold, R. & Trinczek, R. (2009). Experteninterview. In Stefan Kühl, S., Strodtholz, P. & Taffertshofer, A. (Eds.), *Handbuch Methoden der Organisationsforschung, Quantitative und Qualitative Methoden* (pp. 32–56). Wiesbaden, Germany: VS Verlag für Sozialwissenschaften / GWV Fachverlage GmbH.

Loorbach D. (2010). Transition management for sustainable development: A prescriptive, complexity-based governance framework. *Governance 23*(2010), 161–183.

Loorbach, D. & Frantzeskaki, N. (2010). Towards governing infrasystem transitions Reinforcing lock-in or facilitating change? *Technological Forecasting & Social Change 77*(2010),1292–1301.

Loorbach, D. & Rotmans, J. (2010). The practice of transition management: Examples and lessons from four distinct cases. *Futures 42*(2010), 237–246.

Loorbach, D. & Wijsman, K. (2013). Business transition management: exploring a new role for business. *Journal of Cleaner Production 45*(2013), 20–28.

Lucas, J. W. (2003). Theory testing, generalization, and the problem of external validity. *Sociological theory 21*(2), 236–253.

Lundvall, B.-Å., (2005, June 27–29). *National innovation systems – analytical concepts and development tool.* Paper presented on the DRUID Tenth Anniversary Summer Conference 2005 on Dynamics of industry and innovation: organizations, networks and systems. Copenhagen, Denmark. Retrieved from http://citeseerx.ist.psu.edu/viewdoc/download?doi=10.1.1.112.4793&rep=rep1&type=pdf

Lundvall, B.-Å., (2005, September 23–26). *The origins of the national innovation system concept and its usefulness in the era of the globalizing economy.* Paper presented at the 13th Globelics Conference 2015 in Havana September 23–26. Havana, Cuba. Retrieved from http://t1.daumcdn.net/brunch/service/user/4oiQ/file/iPYO0ksgxdk6x9XIUW4cVHlgvuU.pdf

Madrid-Guijarro, A., Garcia, D. & Van Auken, H. (2009). Barriers to innovation among Spanish manufacturing SMEs. *Journal of Small Business Management 47*(4), 465–488.

Mahajan, V., Muller, E. & Bass, F. M. (1990). New product diffusion models in marketing: A review and for research. *Journal of Marketing B4*(1990, January), 1–26.

Markard, J. (2020). The life cycle of technological innovation systems. *Technological Forecasting & Social Change 153*(2020), 119407.

Markard, J., Geels, F. W. & Raven, R. (2020). Challenges in the acceleration of sustainability transitions. *Environmental Research Letters 15*(2020), 081001.

Markard, J. & Hoffmann, V. H. (2016). Analysis of complementarities: Framework and examples from the energy transition. *Technological Forecasting & Social Change 111*(2016), 63–75.

Markard, J., Suter, M. & Ingold, K. (2016). Socio-technical transitions and policy change – advocacy coalitions in Swiss energy policy. *Environmental Innovation and Societal Transitions 18*(2016), 215–237.

McClelland, E. (2001). *Measurement issues and validity tests for using attitude indicators in contingent valuation research.* Working paper #01–01 (November 2001). Washington, DC: U.S. Environmental Protection Agency. Retrieved from https://www.epa.gov/sites/production/files/2014-12/documents/measurement_issues_and_validity_tests_for_using_attitude.pdf

McDermott, C. M. & O'Connor, G. C. (2002). Managing radical innovation: An overview of emergent strategy issues. *The Journal of Product Innovation Management 19*(2002), 424–438.

McFarlane, S. (2021, May 26). Shell ordered by Dutch court to cut carbon emissions. *The Wall street Journal.* Retrieved from https://www.wsj.com/articles/shell-ordered-by-dutch-court-to-cut-carbon-emissions-11622038961

Meadows, D. H., Meadows, D. L., William, J. R. & Behrens W. W. III (1972). *The limits to growth. A report of the Club of Rome's project on the predicament of mankind.* New York, New York: Universe Books.

Mezirow, J. (1990). How critical reflection triggers transformative learning. In Mezirow J. & Associates, *Fostering critical reflection in adulthood.* Hoboken, New Jersey: Jossey Bass.

Mirow, C., Hoelzle, K. & Gemuenden, H. G. (2017). The ambidextrous organization in practice: Barriers to innovation within research and development [Proceeding]. (Published Online 30 November 2017). *Academy of Management Annual Meeting Proceeding.* Retrieve from https://journals.aom.org/doi/pdf/10.5465/ambpp.2008.33717691

Mol, A. P. J. (2002) Ecological modernization and the global economy. *Global Environmental Politics 2*(2), 92–115.

Mol, A. P. J. & Oosterveer, P. (2015). Certification of markets, markets of certificates: Tracing sustainability in global agro-food value chains. *Sustainability 2015*(7), 12258–12278.

Mol, A. P. J. & Spaargaren, G. (1992). Sociology, environment, and modernity: Ecological modernization as a theory of social change. *Society and Natural Resources 5*(1992), 323–344.

Mol, A. P. J. & Spaargaren, G. (2000). Ecological modernization theory in debate: A review. *Ecological Modernisation Around the World Perspectives and Critical Debates 9*(1), 17–49.

Mol, A. P. J., Spaargaren, G. & Sonnenfeld, D. A. (2009). Ecological modernization theory: Where do we stand? In Bemmann, M., Metzger, B. & von Detten, R. (Eds). *Ökologische Modernisierung. Zur Geschichte und Gegenwart eines Konzepts in Umweltpolitik und Sozialwissenschaften* (pp. 35–66). Frankfurt, Germany: Campus Verlag.

Mood, S. H., Golfeshan, A. H., Tabatabaei, M., Jouzani, H. J., Najafi, G. H., Golami, M. & Ardjmand, M. (2013). Lignocellulosic biomass to bioethanol, a comprehensive review with a focus on pretreatment. *Renewable and Sustainable Energy Reviews, 27*(2013), 77–93.

Moore, G. C. & Benbasat, I. (1991). Development of an instrument to measure perceptions of adopting an information technology innovation. *Information Systems Research, 2*(3), 192–222.

Müller, L. J., Kätelhön, A., Bachmann, M., Zimmermann, A., Sternberg, A. & Bardow, A. (2018). A Guideline for life cycle assessment of carbon capture and utilization. *Frontiers in Energy Research 8*(2018), 15. https://doi.org/10.3389/fenrg.2020.00015

Mujica, S. (2019). Why international standards are so badly needed. *ISOfocus Your gateway to international standards September-October 2019*(136) 2–3.

Mumford, M. D. (2000). Managing creative people, strategies and tactics for innovation. *Human Resource Management Review 10*(3), 313–351.

Mumford, M. D., & Hunter, S. T. (2005). Innovation in organizations: A multi-level perspective on creativity. In Dansereau, F. & Yammarino, F. J. (Eds.), *Research in multi-level issues, vol. 4* (pp. 11–73). Oxford, UK: Elsevier.

NASA (2021a). *The causes of climate change.* Retrieved from https://climate.nasa.gov/causes/

NASA (2021b). *Scientific consensus: Earth's climate is warming.* Retrieved from https://climate.nasa.gov/scientific-consensus/

NASA (2021c). *What is the greenhouse effect?* Retrieved from https://climate.nasa.gov/faq/19/what-is-the-greenhouse-effect/

National Research Council (1999). *Industrial environmental performance metrics: Challenges and opportunities.* Washington, DC: The National Academies Press. https://doi.org/10.17226/9458.

Nelson, R. R. (1995). Co-evolution of industry structure, technology and supporting institutions, and the making of comparative advantage. *International Journal of the Economics of Business 2*(2), 171–184.

Nelson R. R. & Winter, S. G. (1982) *An evolutionary theory of economic change.* Cambridge, MA: The Belknap Press of Harvard University Press.

Nidumolu, R., Prahalad, c. K. & Rangaswami M. R. (2009). Why sustainability is now the key driver of innovation. *Harvard Business Review* (September 2009). Retrieve from https://hbr.org/2009/09/why-sustainability-is-now-the-key-driver-of-innovation

Niederman, F., Ferratt, T. W. & Trauth, E. M. (2016). On the co-evolution of information technology and information systems personnel. *The Data Base for Advances in Information Systems 47*(1), 29–50.

Nishitani, K. & Itoh, M. (2016). Product innovation in response to environmental standards and competitive advantage: A hedonic analysis of refrigerators in the Japanese retail market. *Journal of Cleaner Production 113*(2016), 873–883.

OECD (2005). *Oslo manual. The measurement of scientific and technological activities* (3rd ed.). Paris, France: OECD Publications.

OECD (2009). *Eco-innovation in industry: Enabling green growth.* Retrieved from https://www.oecd.org/sti/ind/44424374.pdf.

Oehmig, C. (2015). When analysts turn into boxers: aA introduction to pre-sales requirements engineering. *Complex systems informatics and modeling quarterly 3*(2015), 1–14.

Ostadi, M., Paso, K. G., Rodriguez-Fabia, S., Øi, L. E., Manenti, F. & Hillestad, M. (2020). Process integration of green hydrogen: Decarbonization of chemical industries. *Energies 13*(2020), 4859. https://doi.org/10.3390/en13184859

Osterwalder, A., Pigneur, Y., Bernarda, G., Smith A., & Papadakos, P. (2014). *Value proposition design.* Hoboken, New Jersey: John Wiley & Sons, Inc.

Otto, I. M., Donges, J. F., Cremades, R. Bhowmik, A., Hewitt, R. J., Lucht, W. … Schellnhuber, H. J. (2020). Social tipping dynamics for stabilizing Earth's climate by 2050. *Proceeding of the National Academy of Science of the United States of America 117*(5), 2354–2365. Retrieved from www.pnas.org/cgi/doi/https://doi.org/10.1073/pnas.1900577117

Paton, B. (2000). Voluntary environmental initiatives and sustainable industry. *Bus. Strat. Env. 9*(2000), 328–338.

Perez, C. & Soete, L. (1988). Catching-up in technology: Entry barriers and windows of opportunity. In Dosi, G., Freeman, C., Nelson, R., Silverberg, G. & Soete, L. (Eds.), *Technical change and economic* (pp. 459–478). London, UK: Pinter Publishers.

Peukert, J., & Sahr, K. (2010). Sustainability in the chemical and pharmaceutical industry – results of a benchmark analysis. *Journal of Business Chemistry 7*(2) 97–106.

Pinget, A., Bocquet, R. & Mothe, C. (2015). Barriers to environmental innovation in SMEs: Empirical evidence from French firms. *M@n@gement 18*(2), 132–155.

Popper, K. (2002). *The Logic of Scientific discovery.* New York, NY: Routledge Classics.

Porter, M. E. & van der Linde, C. (1995). Toward a new conception of the environment-competitiveness relationship. *Journal of Economic Perspectives 9*(4), 97–118.

Ragaert, K., Delva, L. & van Geem, K. (2017). Mechanical and chemical recycling of solid plastic waste. *Waste Management, 69*(2017), 24–58.

Raven, R. & Smith, A. (2012). What is protective space? Reconsidering niches in transitions to sustainability. *Research Policy 41*(2012), 1025–1036.

The Hague District Court (2021, May 26). *The Hague District Court has ordered Royal Dutch Shell (RDS) to reduce the CO2 emissions of the Shell group by net 45% in 2030, compared to 2019 levels, through the Shell group's corporate policy.* Den Haag, The Netherlands: Rechtbank. Retrieved from https://uitspraken.rechtspraak.nl/inziendocument?id=ECLI:NL:RBDHA:2021:5339

*Regulation (EU) No 517/2014 of the European Parliament and of the Council of 16 April 2014 on fluorinated greenhouse gases and repealing Regulation (EC) No 842/2006.* Brussel, Belgium: Official Journal of the European Union.

*Regulation (EC) No 1005/2009 of the European Parliament and of the Council of 16 September 2009 on substances that deplete the ozone layer.* Brussel, Belgium: Official Journal of the European Union.

Rehfeld, K.-M., Rennings, K. & Ziegler, A. (2007). Integrated product policy and environmental product innovations: An empirical analysis. *Ecological Economics 61*(2007), 91–100.

Rennings, K. (2000). Redefining innovation – eco-innovation research and the contribution from ecological economics. *Ecological Economics 32*(2000), 319–332.

Revelle, R. & Suess, H. E. (1957). Carbon dioxide exchange between atmosphere and ocean and the question of an increase of atmospheric CO2, during the past decades. *Tellus 9*(1957), 18–27.

Rincon, L. (2018). *Guide for transcribing audio records.* Retrieved from https://www.researchgate.net/publication/333059442_Guide_for_transcribing_audio_records

Rip, A., & Kemp, R. (1998). Technological change. In Rayner, S. & Malone, E. L. (Eds.), *Human choice and climate change: Volume II, resources and technology* (pp. 327–399). Columbus, OH: Battelle Press.

RobecoSAM (2017). *Measuring intangibles. Corporate sustainability assessment methodology* [Brochure]. Zürich, Switzerland: RobecoSAM AG.

Rocklage, M. D. & Fazio, R. H. (2015). The evaluative lexicon: Adjective use as a means of assessing and distinguishing attitude valence, extremity, and emotionality. *Journal of Experimental Social Psychology 56*(2015), 214–227.

Rogers, E. M. (2002). Diffusion of preventive innovations. *Addictive Behaviors 27*(2002), 989–993.

Rogers, E. M. (2003). *Diffusion of innovations* ($5^{th}$ ed.). New York, NY: Free Press.

Saunders, M., Lewis, P. & Thornhill, A. (2012). *Research methods for business students* (6th ed.). Harlow, England: Pearson Education Ltd.

Sonnack, M., Thomke, S. & von Hippel, E. (1999). Creating breakthroughs at 3M. *Harvard Business Review* (September-October), 47–57.

Rosental, M., Fröhlich, T. & Liebich, A. (2020). Life cycle assessment of carbon capture and utilization for production of large volume organic chemicals. *Frontiers in Climate 2*(2020), 586199. https://doi.org/10.3389/fclim.2020.586199

Rothermel, J. (2020, October 29). *The chemical industry – seeking and offering solutions for a CO2-netral future* [Presentation]. Frankfurt a. M., Germany: Verband der chemischen Industrie e.V. Retrieved from https://www.umsicht.fraunhofer.de/content/dam/umsicht/de/dokumente/vortraege/2020/carbon2chem/Rothermel-Chemical-Industry.pdf

RSPO (2017). *RSPO supply chain certification systems* [Brochure]. Kuala Lumpur, Malaysia: Roundtable on Sustainable Palm Oil.

Rylan, A., Ryley, T. & Thring, R. (2018). The influence of knowledge and persuasion on the decision to adopt or reject alternative fuel vehicles. *Sustainability 10*(2018), 2997. https://doi.org/10.3390/su10092997

Santiago-Advisors (2019, September 26). *Expectations of customer industries for chemical industry.* Retrieved from https://www.santiago-advisors.com/en/news/expectations-of-customer-industries-for-the-chemical-industry/

Schein, E. H. (2004). *Organizational culture and leadership* ($3^{rd}$ ed.). San Francisco, CA: John Wiley & Sons, Inc.

Scheuermann, A. (2021, June 08). *200-MW-Projekt in den Niederlanden. Shell beauftragt Worley mit dem Bau einer Wasserstoff-Elektrolyse.* Retrieved from https://www.chemietechnik.de/anlagenbau/shell-beauftragt-worley-mit-dem-bau-einer-wasserstoff-elektrolyse-338.html#:~:text=in%20den%20Niederlanden-,Shell%20beauftragt%20Worley%20mit%20dem%20Bau%20einer%20Wasserstoff%2DElektrolyse,Maasvlakte%20II%20bei%20Rotterdam%20entstehen

Schill, S. R. (2015). *Croda to manufacture surfactant from ethanol, opening new market.* Retrieved from http://ethanolproducer.com/articles/12058/croda-to-manufacture-surfactant-from-ethanol-opening-new-market

Schiller, M. A. (1998). Technology success and failure in winner-take-all markets: The impact of learning orientation, timing, and network externalities. *Academy of Management Journal 45*(2), 387–398.

Smith, A., Stirling, A. & Berkhout, F. (2005). The governance of sustainable socio-technical transitions. *Research Policy 34*(2005), 1491–1510.

Schneidewind, U. & Augenstein, K. (2012). Analyzing a transition to a sustainability-oriented science system in Germany. *Environmental Innovation and Societal Transitions 3*(2012), 16–28.

Schwartz, S. H. (1994). Are there universal aspects in the structure and contents of human values? *Journal of Social Issues 50*(4), 19–45.

Schwarz, N. & Ernst, A. (2009). Agent-based modeling of the diffusion of environmental innovations – an empirical approach. *Technological Forecasting & Social Change 76*(2009), 497–511.

Seeley, J., Bernays, S., Kabunga, E., Mbonye, M., Mugisha, J. O., Rutakumwa, R. & Tumwekwase, G. (2020). Conducting in-depth interviews with and without voice recorders: a comparative analysis. *Qualitative Research 20*(5), 565–581.

Servatius, H.-G. (2012). Wandel zu einem nachhaltigen Energiesystem mit neuen Geschäftsmodellen. In Servatius, H.-G., Schneidewind, U. & Rohlfing, U. (Eds.), *Smart Energy* (pp. 1–44). Berlin, Heidelberg, Germany: Springer-Verlag.

Shaviv, N. (2015). *How might climate be influenced by cosmic rays?* Retrieved from https://www.ias.edu/ideas/2015/shaviv-milky-way

Slavtchev, V. & Fritsch, M. (2005). The role of regional knowledge sources for innovation: An empirical assessment. *Freiberger Arbeitspapiere 2005*(15). Freiberg, Germany: Technische Universität Bergakademie Freiberg, Fakultät für Wirtschaftswissenschaften.

Shogren, R., Wood, D., Orts, W. & Glenn, G. (2019). Plant-based materials and transitioning to a circular economy. *Sustainable Production and Consumption, 19*(2019), 194–215.

Sinkovics, N. (2018). Chapter 28. Pattern matching in qualitative analysis. In Cassell, C, Cunliffe, A. & Grandy, G., *The SAGE handbook of qualitative business and management research methods* (pp. 468–484). Thousand Oaks, US: Sage Publisher.

Slaper, T. F. & Hall, T. J. (2011). The triple bottom line: What is it and how does it work? *Indiana Business Review 86*(1), 1–8. Retrieved from https://www.ibrc.indiana.edu/ibr/2011/spring/article2.html

Söllner, F. (2002). Die Selbstverpflichtung als umweltpolitisches Instrument. *Wirtschaftsdienst 8*(2002), 478–485.

Souto, J. E. & Rodriguez, A. (2015). The problems of environmentally involved firms: Innovation obstacles and essential issues in the achievement of environmental innovation. *Journal of Cleaner Production 101*(2015), 49–58.

Sovacool, B. K. (2021). Who are the victims of low-carbon transitions? towards a political ecology of climate change mitigation. *Energy Research & Social Science 73*(2021), 101916.

Sovacool, B. K., Noela, L. & Orsato, R. J. (2017). Stretching, embeddedness, and scripts in a sociotechnical transition: Explaining the failure of electric mobility at better place (2007–2013). *Technological Forecasting & Social Change 123*(2017), 24–34.

Spaargaren, G. (2003). Sustainable consumption: A theoretical and environmental policy perspective. *Society and Natural Resources, 16*(2003), 687–701.

Stern, P. C. (2000). Toward a coherent theory of environmentally significant behavior. *Journal of Social Issues 56*(3), 407–424.

Stocker, T.F., Qin, D., Plattner, G.-K., Alexander, V. L., Allen, S. K., Bindoff, N. L., … Xie, S.-P. (2013). Technical Summary. In Stocker, T.F., Qin, D., Plattner, G.-K., Tignor, M., Allen, S.K., Boschung, J., …Midgley, P. M. (Eds.), *Climate change 2013: The physical science basis. Contribution of working group I to the fifth assessment report of the Intergovernmental Panel on Climate Change* (pp. 33–115). Cambridge, United Kingdom and New York, NY, USA: Cambridge University Press.

*Sustainable development goals* [Brochure]. (2015). Retrieved from https://www.undp.org/content/dam/undp/library/corporate/brochure/SDGs_Booklet_Web_En.pdf

Taboada, M., Anthony, C. & Voll, K. (2006). Methods for creating semantic orientation dictionaries. In *Proceedings of fifth international conference on language resources and evaluation (LREC 2006)* (pp. 427–432). Genoa, Italy.

Taboada, M., Brooke, J., Tofiloski, M., Voll, K. & Stede, M. (2011). Lexicon-based methods for sentiment analysis. *Computational Linguistics 37*(2), 267–307.

Tanzer, S. E. & Ramírez, A. (2019). When are negative emissions negative emissions? *Energy & Environmental Science 12*(2019), 1210–1218.

Teddlie, C. & Tashakkori, A. (2009). *Foundations of mixed methods research.* Thousand Oaks, CA: SAGE Publications, Inc.

Tillmann, U. & Peter, F. (2021, September 14). Wege in die Klimaneutralität. *Chemanager,* p. 1.

The Royal Society (2020). *Climate change, evidence & causes.* London, United Kingdom: The Royal Society.

Thomas, B. (2017, April 20). *Beginner transcriber guide and quick tips* [Blog post]. Retrieved from https://scribie.com/blog/2017/04/beginner-transcriber-guide-and-quick-tips/

Thomond, P., & Lettice, F. (2002). *Disruptive innovation explored.* Proceeding on 9th IPSE international conference on concurrent engineering: research and applications, 27–31 July 2002. Cranfield, United Kingdom.

Tiseo, I. (2021). *Global historical C02 emissions 1758–2020. Published 05.01.2021.* Retrieved from https://www.statista.com/statistics/264699/worldwide-co2-emissions/

Tiseo, I. (2021). *Greenhouse gas emissions in the EU-27 1990–2019, by sector. Published June 3, 2021.* Retrieved from https://www.statista.com/statistics/1171183/ghg-emissions-sector-european-union-eu/

Together for Sustainability (2021). *Chemical supply chains for a better world* [Brochure]. Brussels, Belgium: tfs-initiative.com

Tornatzky, L. G. & Klein, K. J. (1982). Innovation characteristic and innovation adoption-implementation: A meta-analysis of findings. *IEEE Transactions on Engineering Management, 29*(1) 28–43.

Tourangeau, R. (2000). Remembering what happened: Memory errors and survey reports. In Stone, A. A., Turkkan, J. S., Bachrach, C. A., Jobe, J. B., Kurtzman, H. S., & Cain, V. S. (Eds.). *The science of self-report: Implications for research and practice* (pp. 29–47). New Jersey, United States: Lawrence Erlbaum Associates Publishers.

Tourangeau, R., Rips, L. J. & Rasinski, K. (2000). *The psychology of survey response.* Cambridge, UK: Cambridge University Press.

Trochim, W. M. K. (1989). Outcome pattern matching. *Evaluation and Program Planning 12*(1989), 355–366.

Umweltbundesamt (2011). *Avoiding fluorinated greenhouse gases. Prospects for phasing out.* Dessau-Roßlau, Germany: Federal Environment Agency (Umweltbundesamt). Retrieved from https://www.umweltbundesamt.de/publikationen/avoiding-fluorinated-greenhouse-gases

Umweltbundesamt (2019, January 31). *Nitrous oxide and methane.* Dessau-Roßlau, Germany: Federal Environment Agency (Umweltbundesamt). Retrieved from https://www.umweltbundesamt.de/en/topics/soil-agriculture/ecological-impact-of-farming/nitrous-oxide-methane

Umweltbundeamt (2021). *Carbon offsetting.* Retrieved from https://8billiontrees.com/carbon-offsets-credits/best-programs-providers-companies-2021/

UN (1992). *United Nations framework convention on climate change.* New York, NY: United Nations. Retrieved from https://unfccc.int/files/essential_background/background_publications_htmlpdf/application/pdf/conveng.pdf

UN (1997). *UN conference of the parties, United Nations framework convention on climate change, December 1997, Kyoto, Japan.* Retrieved from http://www.un-documents.net/kyoto.htm

UN (2015a). *Transforming our world: The 2030 agenda for sustainable development. Resolution 70/1 adopted by the General Assembly on 25 September 2015.* Retrieved from https://www.un.org/ga/search/view_doc.asp?symbol=A/RES/70/1&Lang=E

UN (2015b). *Adoption of the Paris agreement, Framework convention on climate change, 12 December 2015, FCCC/CP/2015/L.9/Rev.1.* New York, NY: United Nations. Retrieved from https://unfccc.int/resource/docs/2015/cop21/eng/l09r01.pdf

UN (2015c). *Framework convention on climate change Paris Agreement.* Retrieved from https://unfccc.int/sites/default/files/english_paris_agreement.pdf

UN (2016). *Amendment to the Montreal protocol on substances that deplete the ozone layer: Kigali, 15 October 2016.* New York, NY: United Nations.

UN (2020). *Sustainable development goals. Guidelines for use of the SDG logos.* Retrieved from https://www.un.org/sustainabledevelopment/wp-content/uploads/2019/01/SDG_Guidelines_AUG_2019_Final.pdf

U.S. Energy Information Administration (2021). *Renewable energy explained* (May 20, 2021). Retrieved from https://www.eia.gov/energyexplained/renewable-sources/

Vachon, S. & Klassen, R. D. (2008). Environmental management and manufacturing performance: The role of collaboration in the supply chain. *Int. J. Production Economics 111*(2008), 299–315.

Van Bylen, H. (2019). *Ausführungen von Herrn Hans Van Bylen, Präsident des Verbandes der Chemischen Industrie (VCI), am 3. Dezember 2019 auf der Jahrespressekonferenz in Frankfurt.* Frankfurt a.M., Germany: Verband der chemischen Industrie e.V.

Vandepitte, S. (2017). Translation product quality: A conceptual analysis. In Svoboda, T., Biel, Ł. & Łoboda, K. (Eds.), *Quality aspects in institutional translation, vol. 8* (pp. 15–29). Berlin, Germany: Language Science Press.

Van Kranenburg, K., Schols, E., Gelevert, H., de Kler, R., van Delft, Y. & Weeda, M. (2016). *Empowering the chemical industry: Opportunities for electrification* (May 2016). Delft, The Netherlands: TNO Sustainable Chemical Industry. Retrieved from https://www.tno.nl/media/7514/voltachem_electrification_whitepaper_2016.pdf

VCI (2019). *Working towards a greenhouse gas neutral chemical industry in Germany.* Frankfurt, Germany: Verband der Chemischen Industrie e. V. (VCI).

Venkatesh, V., & Davis, F. D. (2000). Theoretical extension of the technology acceptance model: Four longitudinal field studies. *Management Science, 46*(2), 186–204.

Verones, F. et al., 2017). LCIA framework and cross-cutting issues guidance within the UNEPSETAC life cycle initiative. *Journal of Cleaner Production 161*(2017), 957–967.

Vertesy, D. (2017). Preconditions, windows of opportunity and innovation strategies: Successive leadership changes in the regional jet industry. *Research Policy 46*(2017), 388–403.

Vesely, S. & Klöckner, C. A. (2020). Social Desirability in Environmental Psychology Research: Three Meta-Analyses. *Frontiers in Psychology 11*(2020), 1395. https://doi.org/10.3389/fpsyg.2020.01395

Von Hippel, E. (1986). Lead users: A source of novel product concepts. *Management Science 32*(7), 791–805.

Wang, S., Kim, H., Lee, D., Lee, Y.-R., Won, Y., Hwang, B. W., …Lee, K. H. (2021). Drop-in fuel production with plastic waste pyrolysis oil over catalytic separation, *Fuel 305*(2021), 121440.

Washington, H. (2011). *Climate change denial. Heads in the sand*. London, United Kingdom: Routledge.

West, M. A. (1999). *Innovation und Kreativität.* Weinheim, Germany: Beltz Verlag.

Weichhold, M. (2019). Pretest. In Baur, N. & Blasius, J. (Eds.), *Handbuch Methoden der empirischen Sozialforschung* (pp. 349–357). Wiesbaden, Germany: Springer Fachmedien Wiesbaden GmbH.

Wieser, S. (2021, Apr. 09). *CO2-neutrale Industrie. Top 10: Das sind die größten Wasserstoff-Projekte.* Retrieved from https://www.produktion.de/co2-neutrale-industrie/top-10-das-sind-die-groessten-wasserstoff-projekte-103.html

Williams, M. (2009). Translation quality assessment. *Mutatis mutandis 2*(1), 3–23.

Winiwarter, W., Höglund-Isaksson, L., Klimont, Z., Schöpp, W. & Amann, M. (2018). Technical opportunities to reduce global anthropogenic emissions of nitrous oxide. *Environmental Research Letters 13*(2018) 014011. https://doi.org/10.1088/1748-9326/aa9ec9

Wirth, S., Markard, J., Truffer, B. & Rohracher, H. (2013). Informal institutions matter: professional culture and the development of biogas technology. *Environmental Innovation and Societal Transitions 8*(2013), 20–41.

Woodman, R. W., Sawyer, J. E. & Griffin, R. G. (1993). Toward a theory of organizational creativity. *The Academy of Management Review 18*(2), 293–321.

Wydra, S., Hüsing, B., Köhler, J., Schwarz, A., Schirrmeister, E. & Voglhuber-Slavinsky, A. (2021). Transition to the bioeconomy – analysis and scenarios for selected niches. *Journal of Cleaner Production 294*(2021), 126092.

Xu, L., Xiong, J. & Li, Q. (2018). Towards industry upgrading: A study of catching up strategies of Chinese sectors. *Journal of Eastern European and Central Asian Research5*(1), 1–19.

Yap, X.-S. & Truffer, B. (2019). Shaping selection environments for industrial catch-up and sustainability transitions: A systemic perspective on endogenizing windows of opportunity. *Research Policy 48*(2019), 1030–1047.

Yin R. K. (2003). Case study research, design and methods (3rd ed.). In Bickman, L. & Rog, D. J. (Eds.), *Applied social research methods series, vol 5.* London, UK: Sage Publications Inc.

Yin, R. K. (2018). *Case study research and application: Design and methods* (6th ed.). Thousand Oaks, CA: SAGE Publications.

Yoon, B., Lee, J. H. & Byun, R. (2018). Does ESG performance enhance firm value? Evidence from Korea. *Sustainability 10*(2018), 3635. https://doi.org/10.3390/su10103635

Yukl, G. (2010). *Leadership in organization* (7th ed.). Upper Saddle River, New Jersey: Prentice Hall Pearson Education.

Zeng, Y., Dong, P. Shi, Y, Wang, L. & Li, Y. (2020). Analyzing the co-evolution of green technology diffusion and consumers' pro-environmental attitudes: An agent-based model. *Journal of Cleaner Production 256*(2020), 120384.

Zhang, Q., Loh, L. & Wu, W. (2020). How do environmental, social and governance initiatives affect innovative performance for corporate sustainability? *Sustainability 12*(2020), 3380. https://doi.org/10.3390/su12083380

Zhang, D., Sogn-Grundvåg, G., Asche, F. & Young, J. A. (2018) Eco-labeling and retailer pricing strategies: The U.K. haddock market. *Sustainability 2018*(10), 1522. https://doi.org/10.3390/su10051522

Zhang, H., Shi, Y., Liu, J. & Wu, X. (2021). How do technology strategies affect the catch-up progress of high-tech latecomers? Evidence from two Chinese research-institute-transformed telecommunications firms. *Journal of Business Research 122*(2021), 805–821.

Zhao, Z., Chong, K., Jiang, J., Wilson, K., Zhanga, X. & Wang, F. (2018). Low-carbon roadmap of chemical production: A case study of ethylene in China. *Renewable and Sustainable Energy Reviews, 97*(2018), 580–591.

Zikmund, W. G., Babin, B. J., Carr, J. C. & Griffin, M. (2013). *Business research methods* (9th int. ed.). Hampshire, United Kingdom: South-Western Cengage Learning.

Zitscher, T., Neuling, U., Habersetzer, A. & Kaltschmitt, M. (2020). Analysis of the German industry to determine the resource potential of CO2 emissions for PtX. *Resources 9*(2020), 149. Retrieved from https://www.mdpi.com/2079-9276/9/12/149

**SPRINGER NATURE**

# GPSR Compliance

*The European Union's (EU) General Product Safety Regulation (GPSR) is a set of rules that requires consumer products to be safe and our obligations to ensure this.*

*If you have any concerns about our products, you can contact us on ProductSafety@springernature.com*

In case Publisher is established outside the EU, the EU authorized representative is:

Springer Nature Customer Service Center GmbH
Europaplatz 3
69115 Heidelberg, Germany

The manufacturer's authorised representative in the EU is Springer Nature Customer Service Centre GmbH, Europaplatz 3, 69115 Heidelberg, Germany. If you have any concerns regarding our products, please contact ProductSafety@springernature.com

Printed and bound by CPI Group (UK) Ltd, Croydon, CR0 4YY

01/10/2026

02225834-0004